Moral Sentiments and Material Interests

Economic Learning and Social Evolution
General Editor
Ken Binmore, Director of the Economic Learning and Social
Evolution Centre, University College London

Moral Sentiments and Material Interests

The Foundations of Cooperation in Economic Life

edited by
Herbert Gintis, Samuel Bowles, Robert Boyd, and Ernst Fehr

The MIT Press
Cambridge, Massachusetts
London, England

MIT Press books may be purchased at special quantity discounts for business or sales promotional use. For information, please e-mail special_sales@mitpress.mit.edu or write to Special Sales Department, The MIT Press, 55 Hayward Street, Cambridge, MA 02142.

This book was set in Palatino on 3B2 by Asco Typesetters, Hong Kong, and was printed and bound in the United States of America.

Library of Congress Cataloging-in-Publication Data

Moral sentiments and material interests : the foundations of cooperation in economic life / edited by Herbert Gintis ... [et al.].
    p.   cm. — (Economic learning and social evolution ; 6)
Includes bibliographical references and index.
ISBN 978-0-262-07252-6(hc.:alk. paper)—978-0-262-57237-8(pb.:alk.paper)
1. Cooperation. 2. Game theory. 3. Economics—Sociological aspects. I. Gintis, Herbert. II. MIT Press series on economic learning and social evolution ; v. 6.
HD2961.M657 2004
330′.01′5193—dc22   2004055175

10 9 8 7 6 5 4 3

To Adele Simmons who, as President of the John D. and Catherine T. MacArthur Foundation, had the vision and courage to support unconventional transdisciplinary research in the behavioral sciences.

Contents

Series Foreword

The MIT Press series on Economic Learning and Social Evolution reflects the continuing interest in the dynamics of human interaction. This issue has provided a broad community of economists, psychologists, biologists, anthropologists, mathematicians, philosophers, and others with such a strong sense of common purpose that traditional interdisciplinary boundaries have melted away. We reject the outmoded notion that what happens away from equilibrium can safely be ignored, but think it no longer adequate to speak in vague terms of bounded rationality and spontaneous order. We believe the time has come to put some beef on the table.

The books in the series so far are:

• *Evolutionary Games and Equilibrium Selection*, by Larry Samuelson (1997). Traditional economic models have only one equilibrium and therefore fail to come to grips with social norms whose function is to select an equilibrium when there are multiple alternatives. This book studies how such norms may evolve.

• *The Theory of Learning in Games*, by Drew Fudenberg and David Levine (1998). John Von Neumann introduced "fictitious play" as a way of finding equilibria in zero-sum games. In this book, the idea is reinterpreted as a learning procedure and developed for use in general games.

• *Just Playing*, by Ken Binmore (1998). This book applies evolutionary game theory to moral philosophy. How and why do we make fairness judgments?

• *Social Dynamics*, edited by Steve Durlauf and Peyton Young (2001). The essays in this collection provide an overview of the field of social dynamics, in which some of the creators of the field discuss a variety of approaches, including theoretical model-building, empirical studies, statistical analyses, and philosophical reflections.

• *Evolutionary Dynamics and Extensive Form Games*, by Ross Cressman (2003). How is evolution affected by the timing structure of games? Does it generate backward induction? The answers show that orthodox thinking needs much revision in some contexts.

Authors who share the ethos represented by these books, or who wish to extend it in empirical, experimental, or other directions, are cordially invited to submit outlines of their proposed books for consideration. Within our terms of reference, we hope that a thousand flowers will bloom.

Preface

The behavioral sciences have traditionally offered two contrasting explanations of cooperation. One, favored by sociologists and anthropologists, considers the willingness to subordinate self-interest to the needs of the social group to be part of human nature. Another, favored by economists and biologists, treats cooperation as the result of the interaction of selfish agents maximizing their long-term individual material interests. *Moral Sentiments and Material Interests* argues that a significant fraction of people fit neither of these stereotypes. Rather, they are *conditional cooperators* and *altruistic punishers*. We show that a high level of cooperation can be attained when social groups have a sufficient fraction of such types, which we call *strong reciprocators*, and we draw implications of this phenomenon for political philosophy and social policy.

The research presented in this book was conceived in 1997, inspired by early empirical results of Ernst Fehr and his coworkers at the University of Zürich and the analytical models of cultural evolution pioneered by Robert Boyd and Peter Richerson. Behavioral scientists from several disciplines met at the University of Massachusetts in October 1998 to explore preliminary hypotheses. We then commissioned a series of papers from a number of authors and met again at the Santa Fe Institute in March 2001 to review and coordinate our results, which, suitably revised and updated, together with some newly commissioned papers, are presented in the chapters below.

This research is distinctive not only in its conclusions but in its methodology as well. First, we rely on data gathered in controlled laboratory and field environments to make assertions concerning human motivation. Second, we ignore the disciplinary boundaries that have thwarted attempts to develop generally valid analytical models of human behavior and combine insights from economics, anthropology, evolutionary and human biology, social psychology, and sociology. We bind these disciplines analytically by relying on a common lexicon of game theory and a consistent behavioral methodology.

We would like to thank those who participated in our research conferences but are not represented in this book. These include Leda Cosmides, Joshua Epstein, Steve Frank, Joel Guttman, Kevin McCabe, Arthur Robson, Robert Solow, Vernon Smith, and John Tooby. We benefitted from the generous financial support and moral encouragement of the John D. and Catherine T. MacArthur Foundation, which allowed us to form the Network on the Nature and Origins of Norms and Preferences, to run experiments, and to collect and analyze data from several countries across five continents. We extend special thanks to Ken Binmore, who contributed to our first meeting and encouraged us to place this volume in his MIT Press series, *Economic Learning and Social Evolution*, and to Elizabeth Murry, senior editor at The MIT Press, who brought this publication to its fruition. We extend a special expression of gratitude to Adele Simmons who, as president of the MacArthur Foundation, championed the idea of an interdisciplinary research project on human behavior and worked indefatigably to turn it into a reality.

I   Introduction

1

Moral Sentiments and Material Interests: Origins, Evidence, and Consequences

Herbert Gintis, Samuel Bowles, Robert Boyd, and Ernst Fehr

1.1 Introduction

Adam Smith's *The Wealth of Nations* advocates market competition as the key to prosperity. Among its virtues, he pointed out, is that competition works its wonders even if buyers and sellers are entirely self-interested, and indeed sometimes works better if they are. "It is not from the benevolence of the butcher, the brewer, or the baker that we expect our dinner," wrote Smith, "but from their regard to their own interest" (19). Smith is accordingly often portrayed as a proponent of *Homo economicus*—that selfish, materialistic creature that has traditionally inhabited the economic textbooks. This view overlooks Smith's second—and equally important—contribution, *The Theory of Moral Sentiments*, in which Smith promotes a far more complex picture of the human character.

"How selfish soever man may be supposed," Smith writes in *The Theory of Moral Sentiments*, "there are evidently some principles in his nature, which interest him in the fortunes of others, and render their happiness necessary to him, though he derives nothing from it, except the pleasure of seeing it." His book is a thorough scrutiny of human behavior with the goal of establishing that "sympathy" is a central emotion motivating our behavior towards others.

The ideas presented in this book are part of a continuous line of intellectual inheritance from Adam Smith and his friend and mentor David Hume, through Thomas Malthus, Charles Darwin, and Emile Durkheim, and more recently the biologists William Hamilton and Robert Trivers. But Smith's legacy also led in another direction, through David Ricardo, Francis Edgeworth, and Leon Walras, to contemporary neoclassical economics, that recognizes only self-interested behavior.

The twentieth century was an era in which economists and policy makers in the market economies paid heed only to the second Adam Smith, seeing social policy as the goal of improving social welfare by devising material incentives that induce agents who care only for their own personal welfare to contribute to the public good. In this paradigm, ethics plays no role in motivating human behavior. Albert Hirschman (1985, 10) underscores the weakness of this approach in dealing with crime and corruption:

Economists often propose to deal with unethical or antisocial behavior by raising the cost of that behavior rather than proclaiming standards and imposing prohibitions and sanctions.... [Yet, a] principal purpose of publicly proclaimed laws and regulations is to stigmatize antisocial behavior and thereby to influence citizens' values and behavior codes.

Hirschman argues against a venerable tradition in political philosophy. In 1754, five years before the appearance of Smith's *Theory of Moral Sentiments*, David Hume advised "that, in contriving any system of government ... every man ought to be supposed to be a knave and to have no other end, in all his actions, than his private interest" (1898 [1754]). However, if individuals are sometimes given to the honorable sentiments about which Smith wrote, prudence recommends an alternative dictum: *Effective policies are those that support socially valued outcomes not only by harnessing selfish motives to socially valued ends, but also by evoking, cultivating, and empowering public-spirited motives*. The research in this book supports this alternative dictum.

We have learned several things in carrying out the research described in this book. First, interdisciplinary research currently yields results that advance traditional intradisciplinary research goals. While the twentieth century was an era of increased disciplinary specialization, the twenty-first may well turn out to be an era of *transdisciplinary synthesis*. Its motto might be: *When different disciplines focus on the same object of knowledge, their models must be mutually reinforcing and consistent where they overlap.* Second, by combining economic theory (game theory in particular) with the experimental techniques of social psychology, economics, and other behavioral sciences, we can empirically test sophisticated models of human behavior in novel ways. The data derived from this unification of disciplinary methods allows us to deduce explicit principles of human behavior that cannot be unambiguously derived using more traditional sources of empirical data.

The power of this experimental approach is obvious: It allows deliberate experimental variation of parameters thought to affect behavior while holding other parameters constant. Using such techniques, experimental economists have been able to estimate the effects of prices and costs on altruistic behaviors, giving precise empirical content to a common intuition that the greater the cost of generosity to the giver and the less the benefit to the recipient, the less generous is the typical experimental subject (Andreoni and Miller 2002).[1] The resulting "supply function of generosity," and other estimates made possible by experiments, are important in underlining the point that other-regarding behaviors do not contradict the fundamental ideas of rationality. They also are valuable in providing interdisciplinary bridges allowing the analytical power of economic and biological models, where other-regarding behavior is a commonly used method, to be enriched by the empirical knowledge of the other social sciences, where it is not.

Because we make such extensive use of laboratory experiments in this book, a few caveats about the experimental method are in order. The most obvious shortcoming is that subjects may behave differently in laboratory and in "real world" settings (Loewenstein 1999). Well-designed experiments in physics, chemistry, or agronomy can exploit the fact that the behavior of entities under study—atoms, agents, soils, and the like—behave similarly whether inside or outside of a laboratory setting. (Murray Gell-Mann once quipped that physics would be a lot harder if particles could think). When subjects *can* think, so-called "experimenter effects" are common. The experimental situation, whether in the laboratory or in the field, is a highly unusual setting that is likely to affect behavioral responses. There is some evidence that experimental behaviors are indeed matched by behaviors in non-experimental settings (Henrich et al. 2001) and are far better predictors of behaviors such as trust than are widely used survey instruments (Glaeser et al. 2000). However, we do not yet have enough data on the behavioral validity of experiments to allay these concerns about experimenter effects with confidence. Thus, while extraordinarily valuable, the experimental approach is not a substitute for more conventional empirical methods, whether statistical, historical, ethnographic, or other. Rather, well-designed experiments may complement these methods. An example, combining behavioral experiments in the field, ethnographic accounts, and cross-cultural statistical hypotheses testing is Henrich et al. 2003.

This volume is part of a general movement toward transdisciplinary research based on the analysis of controlled experimental studies of human behavior, undertaken both in the laboratory and in the field—factories, schools, retirement homes, urban and rural communities, in advanced and in simple societies. Anthropologists have begun to use experimental games as a powerful data instrument in conceptualizing the specificity of various cultures and understanding social variability across cultures (Henrich et al. 2003). Social psychologists are increasingly implementing game-theoretic methods to frame and test hypotheses concerning social interaction, which has improved the quality and interpretability of their experimental data (Hertwig and Ortmann 2001). Political scientists have found similar techniques useful in modeling voter behavior (Frohlich and Oppenheimer 1990; Monroe 1991). Sociologists are finding that analytically modeling the social interactions they describe facilitates their acceptance by scholars in other behavioral sciences (Coleman 1990; Hechter and Kanazawa 1997).

But the disciplines that stand to gain the most from the type of research presented in this volume are economics and human biology. As we have seen, economic theory has traditionally posited that the basic structure of a market economy can be derived from principles that are obvious from casual examination. An example of one of these assumptions is that individuals are *self-regarding*.[2] Two implications of the standard model of self-regarding preferences are in strong conflict with both daily observed preferences and the laboratory and field experiments discussed later in this chapter. The first is the implication that agents care only about the *outcome* of an economic interaction and not about the *process* through which this outcome is attained (e.g., bargaining, coercion, chance, voluntary transfer). The second is the implication that agents care only about what they *personally gain and lose* through an interaction and not what other agents gain or lose (or the nature of these other agents' intentions). Until recently, with these assumptions in place, economic theory proceeded like mathematics rather than natural science; theorem after theorem concerning individual human behavior was proven, while empirical validation of such behavior was rarely deemed relevant and infrequently provided. Indeed, generations of economists learned that the accuracy of its predictions, not the plausibility of its axioms, justifies the neoclassical model of *Homo economicus* (Friedman 1953). Friedman's general position is doubtless defensible, since all tractable models simplify reality. However, we now know that predictions based on the model of the self-regarding actor often do not hold up under empirical scrutiny, rendering the model inapplicable in many contexts.

A similar situation has existed in human biology. Biologists have been lulled into complacency by the simplicity and apparent explanatory power of two theories: inclusive fitness and reciprocal altruism (Hamilton 1964; Williams 1966; Trivers 1971). Hamilton showed that we do not need amorphous notions of species-level altruism to explain cooperation between related individuals. If a behavior that costs an individual c produces a benefit b for another individual with degree of biological relatedness r (e.g., $r = 0.5$ for parent-child or brother, and $r = 0.25$ for grandparent-grandchild), then the behavior will spread if $r > c/b$. Hamilton's notion of inclusive fitness has been central to the modern, and highly successful, approach to explaining animal behavior (Alcock 1993). Trivers followed Hamilton in showing that even a selfish individual will come to the aid of an unrelated other, provided there is a sufficiently high probability the aid will be repaid in the future. He also was prescient in stressing the fitness-enhancing effects of such seemingly "irrational" emotions and behaviors as guilt, gratitude, moralistic aggression, and reparative altruism. Trivers' reciprocal altruism, which mirrors the economic analysis of exchange between self-interested agents in the absence of costless third-party enforcement (Axelrod and Hamilton 1981), has enjoyed only limited application to nonhuman species (Stephens, McLinn, and Stevens 2002), but became the basis for biological models of human behavior (Dawkins 1976; Wilson 1975).

These theories convinced a generation of researchers that, except for sacrifice on behalf of kin, what appears to be altruism (personal sacrifice on behalf of others) is really just long-run material self-interest. Ironically, human biology has settled in the same place as economic theory, although the disciplines began from very different starting points, and used contrasting logic. Richard Dawkins, for instance, struck a responsive chord among economists when, in *The Selfish Gene* (1989[1976], v.), he confidently asserted "We are survival machines—robot vehicles blindly programmed to preserve the selfish molecules known as genes.... This gene selfishness will usually give rise to selfishness in individual behavior." Reflecting the intellectual mood of the times, in his *The Biology of Moral Systems*, R. D. Alexander asserted, "Ethics, morality, human conduct, and the human psyche are to be understood only if societies are seen as collections of individuals seeking their own self-interest...." (1987, 3).

The experimental evidence supporting the ubiquity of non–self-regarding motives, however, casts doubt on both the economist's and the biologist's model of the self-regarding human actor. Many of these experiments examine a nexus of behaviors that we term *strong reciprocity*. Strong reciprocity is *a predisposition to cooperate with others, and to punish (at personal cost, if necessary) those who violate the norms of cooperation, even when it is implausible to expect that these costs will be recovered at a later date.*[3] Standard behavioral models of altruism in biology, political science, and economics (Trivers 1971; Taylor 1976; Axelrod and Hamilton 1981; Fudenberg and Maskin 1986) rely on repeated interactions that allow for the establishment of individual reputations and the punishment of norm violators. Strong reciprocity, on the other hand, remains effective even in non-repeated and anonymous situations.[4]

Strong reciprocity contributes not only to the analytical modeling of human behavior but also to the larger task of creating a cogent political philosophy for the twenty-first century. While the writings of the great political philosophers of the past are usually both penetrating and nuanced on the subject of human behavior, they have come to be interpreted simply as having either assumed that human beings are essentially self-regarding (e.g., Thomas Hobbes and John Locke) or, at least under the right social order, entirely altruistic (e.g., Jean Jacques Rousseau, Karl Marx). In fact, people are often neither self-regarding nor altruistic. Strong reciprocators are *conditional cooperators* (who behave altruistically as long as others are doing so as well) and *altruistic punishers* (who apply sanctions to those who behave unfairly according to the prevalent norms of cooperation).

Evolutionary theory suggests that if a mutant gene promotes self-sacrifice on behalf of others—when those helped are unrelated and therefore do not carry the mutant gene and when selection operates only on genes or individuals but not on higher order groups—that the mutant should die out. Moreover, in a population of individuals who sacrifice for others, if a mutant arises that does not so sacrifice, that mutant will spread to fixation at the expense of its altruistic counterparts. Any model that suggests otherwise must involve selection on a level above that of the individual. Working with such models is natural in several social science disciplines but has been generally avoided by a generation of biologists weaned on the classic critiques of group selection by Williams (1966), Dawkins (1976), Maynard Smith (1976), Crow and Kimura (1970), and others, together with the plausible alternatives offered by Hamilton (1964) and Trivers (1971).

But the evidence supporting strong reciprocity calls into question the ubiquity of these alternatives. Moreover, criticisms of group selection are much less compelling when applied to humans than to other animals. The criticisms are considerably weakened when (a) Altruistic punishment is the trait involved and the cost of punishment is relatively low, as is the case for *Homo sapiens*; and/or (b) Either pure cultural selection or gene-culture coevolution are at issue. Gene-culture coevolution (Lumsden and Wilson 1981; Durham 1991; Feldman and Zhivotovsky 1992; Gintis 2003a) occurs when cultural changes render certain genetic adaptations fitness-enhancing. For instance, increased communication in hominid groups increased the fitness value of controlled sound production, which favored the emergence of the modern human larynx and epiglottis. These physiological attributes permitted the flexible control of air flow and sound production, which in turn increased the value of language development. Similarly, culturally evolved norms can affect fitness if norm violators are punished by strong reciprocators. For instance, antisocial men are ostracized in small-scale societies, and women who violate social norms are unlikely to find or keep husbands.

In the case of cultural evolution, the cost of altruistic punishment is considerably less than the cost of unconditional altruism, as depicted in the classical critiques (see chapter 7). In the case of gene-culture coevolution, there may be either no within-group fitness cost to the altruistic trait (although there is a cost to each individual who displays this trait) or cultural uniformity may so dramatically reduce within-group behavioral variance that the classical group selection mechanism—exemplified, for instance, by Price's equation (Price 1970, 1972)—works strongly in favor of selecting the altruistic trait.[5]

Among these models of multilevel selection for altruism is pure genetic group selection (Sober and Wilson 1998), according to which the fitness costs of reciprocators is offset by the tendency for groups with a high fraction of reciprocators to outgrow groups with few reciprocators.[6] Other models involve cultural group selection (Gintis 2000; Henrich and Boyd 2001), according to which groups that transmit a culture of reciprocity outcompete societies that do not. Such a process is as modeled by Boyd, Gintis, Bowles, and Richerson in chapter 7 of this volume, as well as in Boyd et al. 2003. As the literature on the coevolution of genes and culture shows (Feldman, Cavalli-Sforza, and Peck 1985; Bowles, Choi, and Hopfensitz 2003; Gintis 2003a, 2003b), these two alternatives can both be present and mutually reinforcing. These explanations have in common the idea that altruism increases the fitness of members of groups that practice it by enhancing the degree of cooperation among members, allowing these groups to outcompete other groups that lack this behavioral trait. They differ in that some require *strong* group-level selection (in which the within-group fitness disadvantage of altruists is offset by the augmented average fitness of members of groups with a large fraction of altruists) whereas others require only *weak* group-level selection (in which the within-group fitness disadvantage of altruists is offset by some social mechanism that generates a high rate of production of altruists within the group itself). Weak group selection models such as Gintis (2003a, 2003b) and chapter 4, where supra-individual selection operates only as an equilibrium selection device, avoid the classic problems often associated with strong group selection models (Maynard Smith 1976; Williams 1966; Boorman and Levitt 1980).

This chapter presents an overview of *Moral Sentiments and Material Interests*. While the various chapters of this volume are addressed to readers independent of their particular disciplinary expertise, this chapter makes a special effort to be broadly accessible. We first summarize several types of empirical evidence supporting strong reciprocity as a schema for explaining important cases of altruism in humans. This material is presented in more detail by Ernst Fehr and Urs Fischbacher in chapter 5. In chapter 6, Armin Falk and Urs Fischbacher show explicitly how strong reciprocity can explain behavior in a variety of experimental settings. Although most of the evidence we report is based on behavioral experiments, the same behaviors are regularly observed in everyday life, for example in cooperation in the protection of local environmental public goods (as described by Elinor Ostrom in chapter 9), in wage setting by firms (as described by Truman Bewley in chapter 11), in political attitudes and voter behavior (as described by Fong, Bowles, and Gintis in chapter 10), and in tax compliance (Andreoni, Erard, and Feinstein 1998).

"The Origins of Reciprocity" later in this chapter reviews a variety of models that suggest why, under conditions plausibly characteristic of the early stages of human evolution, a small fraction of strong reciprocators could invade a population of self-regarding types, and a stable equilibrium with a positive fraction of strong reciprocators and a high level of cooperation could result.

While many chapters of this book are based on some variant of the notion of strong reciprocity, Joan Silk's overview of cooperation in primate species (chapter 2) makes it clear that there are important behavioral forms of cooperation that do not require this level of sophistication. Primates form alliances, share food, care for one another's infants, and give alarm calls—all of which most likely can be explained in terms of long-term self-interest and kin altruism. Such forms of cooperation are no less important in human society, of course, and strong reciprocity can be seen as a generalization of the mechanisms of kin altruism to nonrelatives. In chapter 3, Hillard Kaplan and Michael Gurven argue that human cooperation is an extension of the complex intrafamilial and interfamilial food sharing that is widespread in contemporary hunter-gatherer societies. Such sharing remains important even in modern market societies.

Moreover, in chapter 4, Eric Alden Smith and Rebecca Bliege Bird propose that many of the phenomena attributed to strong reciprocity can be explained in a costly signaling framework. Within this framework, individuals vary in some socially important quality, and higher-quality individuals pay lower marginal signaling costs and thus have a higher optimal level of signaling intensity, given that other members of their social group respond to such signals in mutually beneficial ways. Smith and Bliege Bird summarize an n-player game-theoretical signaling model developed by Gintis, Smith, and Bowles (2001) and discuss how it might be applied to phenomena such as provisioning feasts, collective military action, or punishing norm violators. There are several reasons why such signals might sometimes take the form of group-beneficial actions. Providing group benefits might be a more efficient form of broadcasting the signal than collectively neutral or harmful actions. Signal receivers might receive more private benefits from allying with those who signal in group-beneficial ways. Furthermore, once groups in a population vary in the degree to which signaling games produce group-beneficial outcomes, cultural (or even genetic) group selection might favor those signaling equilibria that make higher contributions to mean fitness.

We close this chapter by describing some applications of this material to social policy.

1.2 The Ultimatum Game

In the ultimatum game, under conditions of anonymity, two players are shown a sum of money (say $10). One of the players, called the *proposer*, is instructed to offer any number of dollars, from $1 to $10, to the second player, who is called the *responder*. The proposer can make only one offer. The responder, again under conditions of anonymity, can either accept or reject this offer. If the responder accepts the offer, the money is shared accordingly. If the responder rejects the offer, both players receive nothing.

Since the game is played only once and the players do not know each other's identity, a self-regarding responder will accept any positive amount of money. Knowing this, a self-regarding proposer will offer the minimum possible amount ($1), which will be accepted. However, when the ultimatum game is actually played, *only a minority of agents behave in a self-regarding manner.* In fact, as many replications of this experiment have documented, under varying conditions and with varying amounts of money, proposers routinely offer respondents very substantial amounts (fifty percent of the total generally being the modal offer), and respondents frequently reject offers below thirty percent (Camerer and Thaler 1995; Güth and Tietz 1990; Roth et al. 1991).

The ultimatum game has been played around the world, but mostly with university students. We find a great deal of individual variability. For instance, in all of the studies cited in the previous paragraph, a significant fraction of subjects (about a quarter, typically) behave in a self-regarding manner. Among student subjects, however, average performance is strikingly uniform from country to country.

Behavior in the ultimatum game thus conforms to the strong reciprocity model: "fair" behavior in the ultimatum game for college students is a fifty-fifty split. Responders reject offers less than forty percent as a form of altruistic punishment of the norm-violating proposer. Proposers offer fifty percent because they are altruistic cooperators, or forty percent because they fear rejection. To support this interpretation, we note that if the offer in an ultimatum game is generated by a computer rather than a human proposer (and if respondents know this), low offers are very rarely rejected (Blount 1995). This suggests that players are motivated by *reciprocity*, reacting to a violation of behavioral norms (Greenberg and Frisch 1972).

Moreover, in a variant of the game in which a responder rejection leads to the responder receiving nothing, but allowing the proposer to keep the share he suggested for himself, respondents never reject offers, and proposers make considerably smaller (but still positive) offers. As a final indication that strong reciprocity motives are operative in this game, after the game is over, when asked why they offer more than the lowest possible amount, proposers commonly say that they are afraid that respondents will consider low offers unfair and reject them. When respondents reject offers, they usually claim they want to punish unfair behavior.

1.3 Strong Reciprocity in the Labor Market

In Fehr, Gächter, and Kirchsteiger 1997, the experimenters divided a group of 141 subjects (college students who had agreed to participate in order to earn money) into a set of "employers" and a larger set of "employees." The rules of the game are as follows: If an employer hires an employee who provides effort e and receives wage w, his profit is $100e - w$. The wage must be between 1 and 100, and the effort between 0.1 and 1. The payoff to the employee is then $u = w - c(e)$, where $c(e)$ is the "cost of effort" function, which is increasing and convex (the marginal cost of effort rises with effort). All payoffs involve real money that the subjects are paid at the end of the experimental session.

The sequence of actions is as follows. The employer first offers a "contract" specifying a wage w and a desired amount of effort e^*. A contract is made with the first employee who agrees to these terms. An employer can make a contract (w, e^*) with at most one employee. The employee who agrees to these terms receives the wage w and supplies an effort level e, which *need not equal the contracted effort, e^**. In effect, there is no penalty if the employee does not keep his or her promise, so the employee can choose any effort level, e between .1 and 1 with impunity. Although subjects may play this game several times with different partners, each employer-employee interaction is a one-shot (non-repeated) event. Moreover, the identity of the interacting partners is never revealed.

If employees are self-regarding, they will choose the zero-cost effort level, $e = 0.1$, no matter what wage is offered them. Knowing this, employers will never pay more than the minimum necessary to get the employee to accept a contract, which is 1. The employee will accept this offer, and will set $e = 0.1$. Since $c(0.1) = 0$, the employee's payoff is $u = 1$. The employer's payoff is $(0.1 \times 100) - 1 = 9$.

In fact, however, a majority of agents failed to behave in a self-regarding manner in this experiment.[7] The average net payoff to employees was $u = 35$, and the more generous the employer's wage offer to the employee, the higher the effort the employee provided.

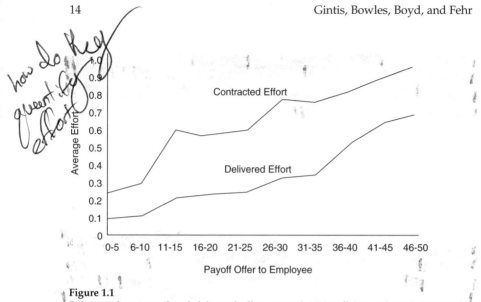

Figure 1.1
Relation of contracted and delivered effort to worker payoff (141 subjects). From Fehr, Gächter, and Kirchsteiger (1997).

In effect, employers presumed the strong reciprocity predispositions of the employees, making quite generous wage offers and receiving higher effort, as a means of increasing both their own and the employee's payoff, as depicted in figure 1.1. Similar results have been observed in Fehr, Kirchsteiger, and Riedl (1993, 1998).

Figure 1.1 also shows that although there is a considerable level of cooperation, there is still a significant gap between the amount of effort agreed upon and the amount actually delivered. This is because, first, only fifty to sixty percent of the subjects are reciprocators, and second, only twenty-six percent of the reciprocators delivered the level of effort they promised! We conclude that strong reciprocators are inclined to compromise their morality to some extent.

This evidence is compatible with the notion that the employers are purely self-regarding, since their beneficent behavior vis-à-vis their employees was effective in increasing employer profits. To see if employers are also strong reciprocators, the authors extended the game following the first round of experiments by allowing the employers to respond reciprocally to the *actual effort choices* of their workers. At a cost of 1, an employer could *increase* or *decrease* his employee's payoff by 2.5. If employers were self-regarding, they would of course do neither, since they would not interact with the same worker a second time. However, sixty-eight percent of the time employers punished employees that did not fulfill their contracts, and seventy percent of the time employers rewarded employees who overfulfilled their contracts. Indeed, employers rewarded forty-one percent of employees who *exactly* fulfilled their contracts. Moreover, employees *expected* this behavior on the part of their employers, as shown by the fact that their effort levels *increased significantly* when their bosses gained the power to punish and reward them. Underfulfilling contracts dropped from eighty-three to twenty-six percent of the exchanges, and overfulfilled contracts rose from three to thirty-eight percent of the total. Finally, allowing employers to reward and punish led to a forty-percent increase in the net payoffs to all subjects, even when the payoff reductions resulting from employer punishment of employees are taken into account.

We conclude from this study that the subjects who assume the role of employee conform to internalized standards of reciprocity, even when they are certain there are no material repercussions from behaving in a self-regarding manner. Moreover, subjects who assume the role of employer expect this behavior and are rewarded for acting accordingly. Finally, employers draw upon the internalized norm of rewarding good and punishing bad behavior when they are permitted to punish, and employees expect this behavior and adjust their own effort levels accordingly.

1.4   The Public Goods Game

The *public goods game* has been analyzed in a series of papers by the social psychologist Toshio Yamagishi (1986, 1988a, 1998b), by the political scientist Elinor Ostrom and her coworkers (Ostrom, Walker, and Gardner 1992), and by economists Ernst Fehr and his coworkers (Gächter and Fehr 1999; Fehr and Gächter 2000a, 2002). These researchers uniformly found that *groups exhibit a much higher rate of cooperation than can be expected assuming the standard model of the self-regarding actor,* and this is especially the case when subjects are given the option of incurring a cost to themselves in order to punish free-riders.

A typical public goods game has several rounds, say ten. The subjects are told the total number of rounds and all other aspects of the game and are paid their winnings in real money at the end of the session. In each round, each subject is grouped with several other subjects—say three others—under conditions of strict anonymity. Each subject is then given a certain number of "points," say twenty, redeemable at the end of the experimental session for real money. Each subject then places some fraction of his points in a "common account" and the remainder in the subject's own "private account."

The experimenter then tells the subjects how many points were contributed to the common account and adds to the private account of each subject some fraction of the total amount in the common account, say forty percent. So if a subject contributes his or her whole twenty points to the common account, each of the four group members will receive eight points at the end of the round. In effect, by putting her or his whole endowment into the common account, a player loses twelve points but the other three group members gain a total of twenty-four ($= 8 \times 3$) points. The players keep whatever is in their private accounts at the end of each round.

A self-regarding player will contribute nothing to the common account. However, only a fraction of subjects in fact conform to the self-interest model. Subjects begin by contributing on average about half of their endowments to the public account. The level of contributions decays over the course of the ten rounds, until in the final rounds most players are behaving in a self-regarding manner (Dawes and Thaler 1988; Ledyard 1995). In a metastudy of twelve public goods experiments, Fehr and Schmidt (1999) found that in the early rounds, average and median contribution levels ranged from forty to sixty percent of the endowment, but in the final period seventy-three percent of all individuals ($N = 1042$) contributed nothing, and many of the other players contributed close to zero. These results are not compatible with the selfish-actor model (which predicts zero contribution in all rounds), although they might be predicted by a reciprocal altruism model, since the chance to reciprocate declines as the end of the experiment approaches.

However this is not in fact the explanation of the moderate but deteriorating levels of cooperation in the public goods game. The subjects' own explanation of the decay of cooperation after the experiment is that cooperative subjects became angry with others who contributed less than themselves and retaliated against free-riding low contributors in the only way available to them—by lowering their own contributions (Andreoni 1995).

Experimental evidence supports this interpretation. When subjects are allowed to punish noncontributors, they do so at a cost to themselves (Orbell, Dawes, and Van de Kragt 1986; Sato 1987; Yamagishi 1988a, 1988b, 1992). For instance, in Ostrom, Walker, and Gardner

(1992), subjects interacted for twenty-five periods in a public goods game. By paying a "fee," subjects could impose costs on other subjects by "fining" them. Since fining costs the individual who uses it, and the benefits of increased compliance accrue to the group as a whole, assuming agents are self-regarding, no player ever pays the fee, no player is ever punished for defecting, and all players defect by contributing nothing to the common pool. However, the authors found a significant level of punishing behavior in this version of the public goods game.

These experiments allowed individuals to engage in strategic behavior, since costly punishment of defectors could increase cooperation in future periods, yielding a positive net return for the punisher. Fehr and Gächter (2000a) set up an experimental situation in which the possibility of strategic punishment was removed. They employed three different methods of assigning study subjects to groups of four individuals each. The groups played six- and ten-round public goods games with costly punishment allowed at the end of each round. There were sufficient subjects to run between ten and eighteen groups simultaneously. Under the *partner treatment*, the four subjects remained in the same group for all ten rounds. Under the *stranger treatment*, the subjects were randomly reassigned after each round. Finally, under the *perfect stranger treatment*, the subjects were randomly reassigned and assured that they would never meet the same subject more than once.

Fehr and Gächter (2000a) performed their experiment over ten rounds with punishment and then over ten rounds without punishment.[8] Their results are illustrated in figure 1.2. We see that when costly punishment is permitted, cooperation does not deteriorate, and in the partner game, despite strict anonymity, cooperation increases to almost full cooperation, even in the final round. When punishment is not permitted, however, the same subjects experience the deterioration of cooperation found in previous public goods games. The contrast in cooperation rates between the partner and the two stranger treatments is worth noting, because the strength of punishment is roughly the same across all treatments. This suggests that the credibility of the punishment threat is greater in the partner treatment because the punished subjects are certain that, once they have been punished in previous rounds, the punishing subjects remain in their group. The impact of strong reciprocity on cooperation is thus more strongly manifested when the group is the more coherent and permanent.

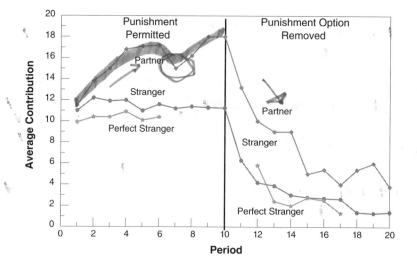

Figure 1.2
Average contributions over time in the partner, stranger, and perfect stranger treatments
when the punishment condition is played first. Adapted from Fehr and Gächter 2000a.

1.5   Intentions or Outcomes?

One key fact missing from the discussion of public goods games is a
specification of the relationship between contributing and punishing.
The strong reciprocity interpretation suggests that high contributors
will be high punishers and punishees will be below-average contributors. This prediction is borne out in Fehr and Gächter (2002), where
seventy-five percent of the punishment acts carried out by the 240 subjects were executed by above-average contributors, and the most important variable in predicting how much one player punished another
was the difference between the punisher's contribution and the punishee's contribution.

   Another key question in interpreting public goods games is: Do
reciprocators respond to fair or unfair *intentions* or do they respond
to fair or unfair *outcomes*? The model of strong reciprocity unambiguously favors intentions over outcomes. To answer this question, Falk,
Fehr, and Fischbacher (2002) ran two versions of the "moonlighting
game"—an intention treatment (I-treatment) where a player's intentions could be deduced from his action, and a no-intention treatment
(NI-treatment), where a player's intentions could not be deduced.
They provide clear and unambiguous evidence for the behavioral rele-

vance of intentions in the domain of both negatively and positively reciprocal behavior.

The moonlighting game consists of two stages. At the beginning of
the game, both players are endowed with twelve points. At the first
stage player A chooses an action a in $\{-6, -5, \ldots, 5, 6\}$. If A chooses
$a > 0$, he gives player B a tokens, while if he chooses $a < 0$, he takes
away $|a|$ tokens from B. In case $a \geq 0$, the experimenter triples a so that
B receives $3a$. After B observes a, he can choose an action b in
$\{-6, -5, \ldots 17, 18\}$. If $b \geq 0$, B gives the amount b to A. If $b < 0$, B loses
$|b|$, and A loses $|3b|$. Since A can give and take while B can reward or
sanction, this game allows for both positively and negatively reciprocal
behavior. Each subject plays the game only once.

If the Bs are self-regarding, they will all choose $b = 0$, neither
rewarding nor punishing their A partners, since the game is played
only once. Knowing this, if the As are self-regarding, they will all
choose $a = -6$, which maximizes their payoff. In the I-treatment, A
players are allowed to choose a, whereas in the NI-treatment, A's
choice is determined by a roll of a pair of dice. If the players are not
self-regarding and care only about the fairness of the outcomes and
not intentions, there will be no difference in the behavior of the B
players across the I- and the NI-treatments. Moreover, if the A players
believe their B partners care only about outcomes, their behavior will
not differ across the two treatments. If the B players care only about
the intentions of their A partners, they will never reward or punish in
the NI-treatment, but they will reward partners who choose high $a > 0$
and punish partners who choose $a < 0$.

The experimenters' main result was that the behavior of player B
in the I-treatment is substantially different from the behavior in the
NI-treatment, indicating that the attribution of fairness intentions is
behaviorally important. Indeed, As who gave to Bs were generally
rewarded by Bs in the I-treatment much more that in the NI-treatment
(significant at the 1 level), and As who took from Bs were generally
punished by Bs in the I-treatment much more than in the NI-treatment
(significant at the 1 level).

Turning to individual patterns of behavior, in the I-treatment, no
agent behaved purely selfishly (i.e., no agent set $b = 0$ independent of
a), whereas in the NI-treatment thirty behaved purely selfishly. Conversely, in the I-treatment seventy-six percent of subjects rewarded or
sanctioned their partner, whereas in the NI-treatment, only thirty-nine
percent of subjects rewarded or sanctioned. We conclude that most

agents are motivated by the intentionality of their partners, but a significant fraction care about the outcome, either exclusively or in addition to the intention of the partner.

1.6 Crowding Out

There are many circumstances in which people voluntarily engage in an activity, yet when monetary incentives are added in an attempt to increase the level of the activity, the level actually decreases. The reason for this phenomenon, which is called *crowding out*, is that the number of contributors responding to the monetary incentives is more than offset by the number of discouraged voluntary contributors. This phenomenon was first stressed by Titmuss (1970), noting that voluntary blood donation in Britain declined sharply when a policy of paying donors was instituted alongside the voluntary sector. More recently, Frey (1997a, 1997b, 1997c) has applied this idea to a variety of situations. In chapter 9 of this volume, Elinor Ostrom provides an extremely important example of crowding out. Ostrom reviews the extensive evidence that when the state regulates common property resources (such as scare water and depletable fish stocks) by using fines and subsidies to encourage conservation, the overuse of these resources may actually increase. This occurs because the voluntary, community-regulated, system of restraints breaks down in the face of relatively ineffective formal government sanctions.

In many cases, such crowding out can be explained in a parsimonious manner by strong reciprocity. Voluntary behavior is the result of what we have called the *predisposition to contribute to a cooperative endeavor*, contingent upon the cooperation of others. The monetary incentive to contribute destroys the cooperative nature of the task, and the threat of fining defectors may be perceived as being an unkind or hostile action (especially if the fine is imposed by agents who have an antagonistic relationship with group members). The crowding out of voluntary cooperation and altruistic punishment occur because the preconditions for the operation of strong reciprocity are removed when explicit material incentives are applied to the task.

This interpretation is supported by the laboratory experiment of Fehr and Gächter (2000b), who show that in an employer–employee setting (see Strong Reciprocity in the Labor Market) if an employer explicitly threatens to fine a worker for malfeasance, the worker's willingness to cooperate voluntarily is significantly reduced. Similarly,

Fehr and List (2002) report that chief executive officers respond in a less trustworthy manner if they face a fine compared to situations where they do not face a fine.

As a concrete example, consider Fehr and Rockenbach's (2002) experiment involving 238 subjects. Mutually anonymous subjects are paired, one subject having the role of *investor*, the other *responder*. They then play a *trust game* in which both subjects receive ten money units (MUs). The investor can transfer any portion of his endowment to the responder and must specify a *desired return* from the responder, which could be any amount less than or equal to what the responder receives as a result of tripling the investor's transfer. The responder, knowing both the amount sent and the amount the investor wants back, chooses an amount to send back to the investor (not necessarily the amount investor requested). The investor receives this amount (which is not tripled), and the game is over.

There were two experimental conditions—a *trust* condition with no additional rules and an *incentive* condition that adds one more rule: the investor has the option of precommitting to impose a fine of four MUs on the responder should the latter return less than the investor's desired return. At the time the investor chooses the transfer and the desired return, he also must specify whether to impose the fine condition. The responder then knows the transfer, the desired return, and whether the fine condition was imposed by the investor.

Since all the interactions in this game are anonymous and there is only one round, self-regarding respondents will return nothing in the trust condition and at most four MUs in the incentive condition. Thus, self-regarding investors who expect their partners to be self-regarding will send nothing to responders in the trust condition and will not ask for more than four MUs back in the incentive condition. Assuming a respondent will only avoid the fine if he can gain from doing so, the investor will transfer two MUs and ask for three MUs back, the responder will get six MUs and return three MUs to the investor. It follows that if all agents are self-regarding and all know that this is the case, investors will always choose to impose the fine condition and end up with eleven MUs, while the responders end up with thirteen MUs.

In contrast to this hypothesis, responders actually paid back substantial amounts of money under all conditions. In addition, responders' returns to investors were highest when the investor *refrained* from imposing the fine in the incentive condition and were lowest when the investor imposed the fine condition in the incentive condition. Returns were intermediate under the trust condition where fines could not be imposed.

The experimenters ascertained that the greater return when the fine was not imposed could not be explained either by investors in that situation transferring more to the responders or by investors requesting more modest returns from the respondents. But if we assume that imposing the fine condition is interpreted as a hostile act by the respondent, and hence not imposing this condition is interpreted as an act of kindness and trust, then strong reciprocity supplies a plausible reason why responders increase their compliance with investors' requests when the investors refrain from fining them. *feeling guilt when you hurt some-one's trust*

1.7 The Origins of Strong Reciprocity

Some behavioral scientists, including many sociologists and anthropologists, are quite comfortable with the notion that altruistic motivations are an important part of the human repertoire and explain their prevalence by cultural transmission. Support for a strong cultural element in the expression of both altruistic cooperation and punishment can be drawn from the wide variation in strength of both cooperation and punishment exhibited in our small-scale societies study (Henrich et al. [2001] and this chapter's discussion of the ultimatum game), and our ability to explain a significant fraction of the variation in behavior in terms of social variables (cooperation in production and degree of market integration). Even though altruists must bear a fitness cost for their behavior not shared by self-regarding types, in most cases this cost is not high—shunning, gossip, and ostracism, for instance (Bowles and Gintis 2004). Indeed, as long as the cultural system transmits altruistic values strongly enough to offset the fitness costs of altruism, society can support motivations that are not fitness-maximizing indefinitely (Boyd and Richerson 1985; Gintis 2003b). Moreover, societies with cultural systems that promote cooperation will outcompete those that do not, and individuals tend to copy the behaviors characteristic of successful groups. Together, these forces can explain the diffusion of group-beneficial cultural practices (Soltis, Boyd, and Richerson 1995; Boyd and Richerson 2002).

While culture is part of the explanation, it is possible that strong reciprocity, like kin altruism and reciprocal altruism, has a significant genetic component. Altruistic punishment, for instance, is not culturally transmitted in many societies where people regularly engage in it (Brown 1991). In the Judeo-Christian tradition, for example, charity and forgiveness ("turn the other cheek") are valued, while seeking revenge is denigrated. Indeed, willingness to punish transgressors is not seen as an admirable personal trait and, except in special circumstances, people are not subject to social opprobrium for failing to punish those who hurt them.

If this is the case, the altruistic behaviors documented and modeled in this book indicate that gene-culture coevolution has been operative for human beings. This is indeed what we believe to be the case, and in this section we describe some plausible coevolutionary models that could sustain strong reciprocity. It is thus likely that strong reciprocity is the product of gene-culture coevolution. It follows that group level-characteristics that enhance group selection pressures—such as relatively small group size, limited migration, or frequent intergroup conflicts—coevolved with cooperative behaviors. This being the case, we concluded that cooperation is based in part on the distinctive capacities of humans to construct institutional environments that limit within-group competition and reduce phenotypic variation within groups, thus heightening the relative importance of between-group competition and allowing individually-costly but ingroup-beneficial behaviors to coevolve within these supporting environments through a process of interdemic group selection.

The idea that the suppression of within-group competition may be a strong influence on evolutionary dynamics has been widely recognized in eusocial insects and other species. Boehm (1982) and Eibl-Eibesfeldt (1982) first applied this reasoning to human evolution, exploring the role of culturally transmitted practices that reduce phenotypic variation within groups. Examples of such practices are leveling institutions, such as monogamy and food sharing among nonkin (namely, those practices which reduce within-group differences in reproductive fitness or material well-being). By reducing within-group differences in individual success, such structures may have attenuated within-group genetic or cultural selection operating against individually-costly but group-beneficial practices, thus giving the groups adopting them advantages in intergroup contests. Group-level institutions are thus constructed environments capable of imparting distinctive direction and pace to the process of biological evolution and cultural change. Hence, the evolutionary success of social institutions that reduce phenotypic variation within groups may be explained by the fact that they retard selection pressures working against ingroup–beneficial individual traits and that high frequencies of bearers of these traits reduces the likelihood of group extinctions (Bowles, Choi, and Hopfensitz 2003).

In chapter 8, Rajiv Sethi and E. Somanathan provide an overview of evolutionary models of reciprocity conforming to the logic described in the previous paragraph and also present their own model of common property resource use. In their model, there are two types of individuals: *reciprocators* who choose extraction levels that are consistent with efficient and fair resource use, monitor other users, and punish those who over-extract relative to the norm; and *opportunists* who choose their extraction levels optimally in response to the presence or absence of reciprocators and do not punish. Since monitoring is costly, and opportunists comply with the norm only when it is in their interest to do so, reciprocators obtain lower payoffs than opportunists within all groups, regardless of composition. However, since the presence of reciprocators alters the behavior of opportunists in a manner that benefits all group members, a population of opportunists can be unstable under random (non-assortative) matching. More strikingly, even when a population of opportunists is stable, Sethi and Somanathan show that stable states in which a mix of reciprocators and opportunists is present can exist.

In chapter 7, Robert Boyd, Herbert Gintis, Samuel Bowles, and Peter J. Richerson explore a deep asymmetry between altruistic cooperation and altruistic punishment. They show that altruistic punishment allows cooperation in quite large groups because the payoff disadvantage of altruistic cooperators relative to defectors is independent of the frequency of defectors in the population, while the cost disadvantage of those engaged in altruistic punishment declines as defectors become rare. Thus, when altruistic punishers are common, selection pressures operating against them are weak. The fact that punishers experience only a small disadvantage when defectors are rare means that weak within-group evolutionary forces, such as conformist transmission, can stabilize punishment and allow cooperation to persist. Computer simulations show that selection among groups leads to the evolution of altruistic punishment when it could not maintain altruistic cooperation without such punishment.

The interested reader will find a number of related cultural and gene-culture coevolution models exhibiting the evolutionary stability of altruism in general, and strong reciprocity in particular, in recent papers (Gintis 2000; Bowles 2001; Henrich and Boyd 2001; and Gintis 2003a).

1.8 Strong Reciprocity: Altruistic Adaptation or Self-Interested Error?

There is an alternative to our treatment of altruistic cooperation and punishment that is widely offered in reaction to the evidence upon which our model of strong reciprocity is based. The following is our understanding of this argument, presented in its most defensible light.

Until about 10,000 years ago—before the advent of sedentary agriculture, markets, and urban living—humans were generally surrounded by kin and long-term community consociates. Humans were thus rarely called upon to deal with strangers or interact in one-shot situations. During the formative period in our evolutionary history, therefore, humans developed a cognitive and emotional system that reinforces cooperation among extended kin and others with whom one lives in close and frequent contact, but developed little facility for behaving differently when facing strangers in non-repeatable and/or anonymous settings. Experimental games therefore confront subjects with settings to which they have not evolved optimal responses. It follows that strong reciprocity is simply irrational and mistaken behavior. This accounts for the fact that the same behavior patterns and their emotional correlates govern subject behavior in both anonymous, one-shot encounters and when subjects' encounters with kin and long-term neighbors. In sum, strong reciprocity is an historically evolved form of enlightened self- and kin-interest that falsely appears altruistic when deployed in social situations for which it was not an adaptation.

From an operational standpoint, it matters little which of these views is correct, since human behavior is the same in either case. However, if altruism is actually misapplied self-interest, we might expect altruistic behavior to be driven out of existence by consistently self-regarding individuals in the long run. If these arguments are correct, it would likely lead to the collapse of the sophisticated forms of cooperation that have arisen in civilized societies. Moreover, the alternative suggests that agents can use their intellect to "learn" to behave selfishly when confronted with the results of their suboptimal behavior. The evidence, however, suggests that cooperation based on strong reciprocity can unravel when there is no means of punishing free-riders but that it does not unravel simply through repetition.

What is wrong with the alternative theory? First, it is probably not true that prehistoric humans lived in groups comprised solely of close kin and long-term neighbors. Periodic social crises in human prehistory, occurring at roughly thirty-year intervals on average, are probable, since population contractions were common (Boone and Kessler 1999) and population crashes occurred in foraging groups at a mean rate of perhaps once every thirty years (Keckler 1997). These and related archaeological facts suggest that foraging groups had relatively short lifespans.

If the conditions under which humans emerged are similar to the conditions of modern primates and/or contemporary hunter-gatherer societies, we can reinforce our argument by noting that there is a constant flow of individuals into and out of groups in such societies. Exogamy alone, according to which young males or females relocate to other groups to seek a mate, gives rise to considerable intergroup mixing and frequent encounters with strangers and other agents with whom one will not likely interact in the future. Contemporary foraging groups, who are probably not that different in migratory patterns from their prehistoric ancestors, are remarkably outbred compared to even the simplest farming societies, from which we can infer that dealing with strangers in short-term relationships was a common feature of our evolutionary history. Henry Harpending (email communication) has found in his studies of the Bushmen in the Kalahari that there were essentially random patterns of mating over hundreds of kilometers. See Fix (1999) for an overview and analysis of the relevant data on this issue.

Second, if prehistoric humans rarely interacted with strangers, then our emotional systems should not be finely tuned to degrees of familiarity—we should treat all individuals as neighbors. But we in fact are quite attuned to varying degrees of relatedness and propinquity. Most individuals care most about their children, next about their close relatives, next about their close neighbors, next about their conationals, and so on, with decreasing levels of altruistic sentiment as the bonds of association grow weaker. Even in experimental games, repetition and absence of anonymity dramatically increase the level of cooperation and punishment. There is thus considerable evidence that altruistic cooperation and punishment in one-shot and anonymous settings is the product of evolution and not simply errant behavior.

1.9 Strong Reciprocity and Cultural Evolution

Strong reciprocity is a *behavioral schema* that is compatible with a wide variety of cultural norms. Strong reciprocators are predisposed to cooperate in social dilemmas, but the particular social situations that will be recognized as appropriate for cooperation are culturally variable. Strong reciprocators punish group members who behave selfishly, but the norms of fairness and the nature of punishment are culturally variable.

In this section, we first present evidence that a wide variety of cultural forms are compatible with strong reciprocity. We then argue that the strong reciprocity schema is capable of stabilizing a set of cultural norms, whether or not these norms promote the fitness of group members. Finally, we suggest that the tendency for strong reciprocity to be attached to prosocial norms can be accounted for by intergroup competition, through which societies prevail over their competitors to the extent that their cultural systems are fitness enhancing.

1.9.1 Cultural Diversity

What are the limits of cultural variability, and how does strong reciprocity operate in distinct cultural settings? To expand the diversity of cultural and economic circumstances of experimental subjects, we undertook a large cross-cultural study of behavior in various games including the ultimatum game (Henrich et al. 2001; Henrich et al. 2003). Twelve experienced field researchers, working in twelve countries on four continents, recruited subjects from fifteen small-scale societies exhibiting a wide variety of economic and cultural conditions. These societies consisted of three foraging groups (the Hadza of East Africa, the Au and Gnau of Papua New Guinea, and the Lamalera of Indonesia), six slash-and-burn horticulturists and agropasturalists (the Aché, Machiguenga, Quichua, Tsimané, and Achuar of South America, and the Orma of East Africa), four nomadic herding groups (the Turguud, Mongols, and Kazakhs of Central Asia, and the Sangu of East Africa) and two sedentary, small-scale agricultural societies (the Mapuche of South America and Zimbabwean farmers in Africa).

We can summarize our results as follows. First, the canonical model of self-regarding behavior is not supported in *any* of the societies studied. In the ultimatum game, for example, in all societies either responders, proposers, or both behaved in a reciprocal manner. Second, there is considerably more behavioral variability across groups than

had been found in previous cross-cultural research. While mean ultimatum game offers in experiments with student subjects are typically
between forty-three and forty-eight percent, the mean offers from proposers in our sample ranged from twenty-six to fifty-eight percent.
While modal ultimatum game offers are consistently fifty percent
among university students, sample modes with the data range in this
study ranged from fifteen to fifty percent. Rejections were extremely
rare, in some groups (even in the presence of very low offers), while in
others, rejection rates were substantial, including frequent rejections of
hyper-fair offers (i.e., offers above fifty percent). By contrast, the Machiguenga have mean offer of twenty-six percent but no rejections. The
Aché and Tsimané distributions resemble inverted American distributions. The Orma and Huinca (non–Mapuche Chileans living among
the Mapuche) have modes near the center of the distribution, but
show secondary peaks at full cooperation.

Third, *differences between societies in "market integration" and "cooperation in production" explain a substantial portion (about fifty percent) of the
behavioral variation between groups.* The higher the degree of market
integration and the higher the payoffs to cooperation, the greater the
level of cooperation and sharing in experimental games. The societies
were rank-ordered in five categories—market integration (how often
do people buy and sell, or work for a wage?), cooperation in production (is production collective or individual?), plus anonymity (how
prevalent are anonymous roles and transactions?), privacy (how easily
can people keep their activities secret?), and complexity (how much
centralized decision-making occurs above the level of the household?).
Using statistical regression analysis, only the first two characteristics
were significant, and they together accounted for about fifty percent of
the variation among societies in mean ultimatum game offers. Fourth,
individual-level economic and demographic variables do not explain
behavior either within or across groups. Finally, the nature and degree
of cooperation and punishment in the experiments is generally consistent with economic patterns of everyday life in these societies.

The final point of this experiment is in some respects the most important for future research. In a number of cases, the parallels between
experimental game play and the structure of daily life were quite striking. Nor was this relationship lost on the subjects themselves. The
Orma immediately recognized that the public goods game was similar
to the *harambee*, a locally-initiated contribution that households make
when a community decides to construct a road or school. They dubbed

the experiment "the harambee game" and gave generously (mean fifty-eight percent with twenty-five percent full contributors).

Among the Au and Gnau, many proposers offered more than half the total amount and many of these hyper-fair offers were rejected! This reflects the Melanesian culture of status-seeking through gift giving. Making a large gift is a bid for social dominance in everyday life in these societies, and rejecting the gift is a rejection of being subordinate.

Among the whale-hunting Lamalera, sixty-three percent of the proposers in the ultimatum game divided the total amount equally, and most of those who did not offered more than fifty percent (the mean offer was fifty-seven percent). In real life, a large catch—always the product of cooperation among many individual whalers—is meticulously divided into predesignated proportions and carefully distributed among the members of the community.

Among the Aché, seventy-nine percent of proposers offered either forty or fifty percent, and sixteen percent offered more than fifty percent, with no rejected offers. In daily life, the Aché regularly share meat, which is distributed equally among all households irrespective of which hunter made the catch.

In contrast to the Aché, the Hadza made low offers and had high rejection rates in the ultimatum game. This reflects the tendency of these small-scale foragers to share meat but with a high level of conflict and frequent attempts of hunters to hide their catch from the group.

Both the Machiguenga and Tsimané made low ultimatum game offers, and there were virtually no rejections. These groups exhibit little cooperation, exchange, or sharing beyond the family unit. Ethnographically, both groups show little fear of social sanctions and care little about "public opinion."

The Mapuche's social relations are characterized by mutual suspicion, envy, and fear of being envied. This pattern is consistent with researchers' interviews with the Mapuche following the ultimatum game. Mapuche proposers rarely claimed that their offers were influenced by fairness but rather by a fear of rejection. Even proposers who made hyper-fair offers claimed that they feared the remote possibility of spiteful responders, who would be willing to reject even fifty-fifty offers.

1.9.2 Cultural Evolution

Suppose a group, in the name of promoting group harmony, has adopted the norm of peaceful adjudication of disputes. If the members are self-interested, no third party will intervene in a dispute between two members to thwart a violent interaction and punish its perpetrators. By contrast, a group with a sufficient fraction of reciprocators will intervene, allowing the norm to persist over time, even in the face of the indifference of the self-interested and the opposition of an appreciable fraction of troublemakers. Thus, strong reciprocity can stabilize prosocial norms that otherwise could not be sustained in the group.

Conversely, suppose in the name of preventing invidious distinctions, a group has adopted a work norm that discourages members from supplying effort above a certain approved level. Such a norm is, of course, fitness-reducing for the group's members. Indeed, if members are self-interested, some will violate the norm, and no others will intervene to protect it. The fitness-reducing norm will thus disappear. However, a small fraction of strong reciprocators who accept the norm and who punish its violators can stabilize the norm even when many would prefer to violate it.

Our point here is simple. For most of human history (until a few thousand years ago), there were no schools, churches, books, laws, or states. There was, therefore, no centralized institutional mechanism for enforcing norms that affect the members of a group as a whole. Strong reciprocity evolved because groups with strong reciprocators were capable of stabilizing prosocial norms that could not be supported using principles of long-term self-interest alone, because it is generally fitness-enhancing for an individual to punish only transgressions against the individual himself and then only if the time horizon is sufficiently lengthy to render a reputation for protecting one's interests. On the other hand, the same mechanisms that have the ability to enforce prosocial norms can almost as easily enforce fitness-neutral and antisocial norms (Edgerton 1992; Boyd and Richerson 1992; Richerson and Boyd 2003).

In this framework, prosocial norms evolve not because they have superior fitness within groups, but because groups with prosocial norms outcompete groups that are deficient in this respect. It is not surprising, for instance, that the "great religions" (Judaism, Christianity, Buddhism, Islam, Hinduism, and so forth) stress prosocial norms—such as helping one's neighbors, giving each his due, turning the other cheek, and the like.

There is considerable evidence for the operation of natural selection in cultural evolution (Richerson and Boyd 2003). For instance, religious practice differences entail fertility and survival differentials (Roof and

McKinney 1987), and the organization of human populations into units which engage in sustained, lethal combat with other groups leads to the survival of groups with prosocial organizational and participatory forms. Soltis, Boyd, and Richerson (1995) reviewed the ethnography of warfare in simple societies in highland New Guinea. The pattern of group extinction and new group formation in these cases conforms well to a cultural evolution model. The strength of cultural group selection in highland New Guinea was strong enough to cause the spread of a favorable new social institution among a metapopulation in about 1,000 years. Cases of group selection by demic expansion are quite well described, for example the spread of the southern Sudanese Nuer at the expense of the Dinka (Kelly 1985), the expansion of the Marind-anim at the expense of their neighbors by means of large, well-organized head-hunting raids at the expense of their neighbors, including the capture and incorporation of women and children (Knauft 1993), and the Hispanic conquest of Latin America (Foster 1960).

1.10 Applications to Social Policy

Economic policy has generally been based on a model of the self-regarding individual. It would be surprising if our model of strong reciprocity did not suggest significant revisions in standard economic policy reasoning, and indeed it does. This section includes several applications of the strong reciprocity model to social policy. In fact, only a relatively weak version of strong reciprocity enters into policy analysis. All that is required is that agents be conditional cooperators and altruistic punishers in public and repeated situations where reputations can be established—an assumption amply justified by the behavioral evidence. Specifically, it is unimportant for these analyses whether strong reciprocity is the product of purely cultural or gene-culture coevolutionary dynamics—whether this behavior is truly altruistic or includes some difficult-to-observe personal payoff (such as costly signaling, as suggested by Smith and Bliege Bird in chapter 4), or whether it is fundamentally adaptive or maladaptive.

Elinor Ostrom argues in chapter 9 that common pool resource management has often failed when based on the standard model of incentives, whereas a more balanced program of local community management and government regulation—often the former alone—can contribute to effective conservation and egalitarian distribution of common pool resources. This alternative policy framework flows naturally from the strong reciprocity model and depends on the presence of a fraction of strong reciprocators in the population for its effectiveness.

As Christina Fong, Samuel Bowles, and Herbert Gintis show in chapter 10, approaches to egalitarian income redistribution are also strengthened by the use of the strong reciprocity model. During the last few decades of the twentieth century in the United States, there emerged an unprecedented malaise concerning the system of egalitarian redistribution in public opinion. Many interpret this shift, which has led to important changes in the social welfare system, as a resurgence of self-interest on the part of the country's nonpoor and of racist attitudes on the part of the majority white citizenry. Fong, Bowles, and Gintis present a body of evidence that disputes this view and argue in favor of model of voter behavior based on strong reciprocity.

In chapter 11, Truman Bewley uses strong reciprocity to model unemployment in the macroeconomy of the United States. Bewley tackles one of the oldest, and most controversial, puzzles in economics: why nominal wages rarely fall (and real wages do not fall enough) when unemployment is high. He does so in a novel way, through interviews with over 300 businessmen, union leaders, job recruiters, and unemployment counselors in the northeastern United States during the early 1990s recession. Bewley concludes that employers resist pay cuts largely because the savings from lower wages are usually outweighed by the cost of reducing worker morale: pay cuts are seen by workers as an unfriendly and unfair act, and employees retaliate by working less hard and less in line with managements' goals. Bewley thus shows that even the most standard of economic problems, that of wage determination, cannot be understood outside the framework of an empirical and behavioral approach to individual behavior.

Nowhere has the standard model of the self-regarding actor had more influence than in legal theory and the politics of legislation. Beginning with the work of economist Ronald Coase (1960) and developed by the legal scholar Richard Posner (1973), "Law and Economics" has become a potent analytical framework for studying the effect of legislation on social welfare. While we do not doubt the value of this work, its abstraction from reciprocity and other non–self-regarding motives limits its general relevance. In chapter 12, Dan M. Kahan addresses the relevance of reciprocity to law and public policy. He suggests that individuals will often contribute voluntarily to collective goods so long as they believe that most others are willing to do the same. Promoting trust, in the form of reason to believe that fellow citizens are contributing their fair share, is thus a potential alternative to costly incentive schemes for solving societal collective action problems. Indeed, conspicuous penalties and subsidies, reciprocity theory implies, might sometimes aggravate rather than ameliorate collective action problems by giving citizens reason to doubt that other citizens are contributing voluntarily to societal collective goods. He illustrates these conclusions by analyzing several regulatory problems—including tax evasion, the location of toxic waste facilities, and the production of information and technology.

In the final chapter of this volume, Samuel Bowles and Herbert Gintis offer a larger and more synthetic vision of what a deeper appreciation of moral sentiments might imply for social structure and policy. They argue that the moral sentiments documented and analyzed in this book lead us to a new view of social communities and an understanding of why the two preeminently anonymous modern institutions—the market and the state—only incompletely addresses modern social problems.

If Bowles and Gintis are right in asserting that communities work well relative to markets and states where the tasks are qualitative and hard to capture in explicit contracts, and the conflicts of interest among the members are limited, it seems likely that extremely unequal societies will be competitively disadvantaged in the future because their structures of privilege and material reward limit the capacity of community governance to facilitate the qualitative interactions that underpin the modern economy. Political democracy, policies that limit the extent of social and economic inequality, and widespread civil liberties may thus not only be desirable in terms of political ethics, but may in fact be necessary to harness moral sentiments to future economic and social development around the world.

Notes

1. We say an action is *altruistic* when it confers benefits to other members of a group at a cost to the actor. Note that this definition says nothing about the intentions of the actor. Note also that an action can be altruistic yet increase the subjective utility of the actor. Indeed, any voluntary, intended act of altruism will have this property.

2. Since we care about behavior rather than its subjective correlates, throughout this chapter we use the term "self-regarding" rather than "self-interested." For instance, if one truly cares about others, it may be self-interested to sacrifice on their behalf, even though it is manifestly non–self-regarding to do so.

3. While the term "strong reciprocity" is new, the idea certainly is not, having been studied by Homans (1958), Gouldner (1960), Moore Jr. (1978), Frank (1988), and Hirshleifer and Rasmusen (1989), among others.

4. The adaptive significance of the human ability to detect cheaters was stressed by Cosmides and Tooby (1992) who, in contrast with our usage, consider this capacity as individually fitness-enhancing rather than altruistic. The precommitment to punish transgressors has been insightfully analyzed by Hirshleifer (1987) and Frank (1988).

5. Classical group selection involves the altruistic behavior having fitness costs as compared with behavior of non-altruistic group members, but these costs being more than offset by the higher fitness of groups with many altruists, as compared with groups in which altruism is rare or absent.

6. By *multilevel selection* (Keller 1999), we mean that selection operates at some level other than that of the gene or individual. For instance, the social organization of a beehive contributes to the fitness of individual bees, which leads to the growth of beehives.

7. The observed behavior was predicted by Akerlof (1982).

8. For additional experimental results and analysis, see Bowles and Gintis (2002) and Fehr and Gächter (2002).

References

Akerlof, George A. "Labor Contracts as Partial Gift Exchange," *Quarterly Journal of Economics* 97, 4 (November 1982): 543–569.

Alcock, John. *Animal Behavior: An Evolutionary Approach*. Sunderland, MA: Sinauer, 1993.

Alexander, Richard D. *The Biology of Moral Systems*. New York: Aldine, 1987.

Andreoni, James. "Cooperation in Public Goods Experiments: Kindness or Confusion," *American Economic Review* 85, 4 (1995): 891–904.

Andreoni, James, and John H. Miller. "Giving According to GARP: An Experimental Test of the Consistency of Preferences for Altruism," *Econometrica* 70, 2 (2002): 737–753.

Andreoni, James, Brian Erard, and Jonathan Feinstein. "Tax Compliance," *Journal of Economic Literature* 36, 2 (June 1998): 818–860.

Axelrod, Robert, and William D. Hamilton. "The Evolution of Cooperation," *Science* 211 (1981): 1390–1396.

Blount, Sally. "When Social Outcomes Aren't Fair: The Effect of Causal Attributions on Preferences," *Organizational Behavior & Human Decision Processes* 63, 2 (August 1995): 131–144.

Boehm, Christopher. "The Evolutionary Development of Morality as an Effect of Dominance Behavior and Conflict Interference," *Journal of Social and Biological Structures* 5 (1982): 413–421.

Boone, James L., and Karen L. Kessler. "More Status or More Children? Social Status, Fertility Reduction, and Long-Term Fitness," *Evolution & Human Behavior* 20, 4 (July 1999): 257–277.

Boorman, Scott A., and Paul Levitt. *The Genetics of Altruism*. New York: Academic Press, 1980.

Bowles, Samuel. "Individual Interactions, Group Conflicts, and the Evolution of Preferences," in Steven N. Durlauf and H. Peyton Young (eds.) *Social Dynamics*. Cambridge, MA: MIT Press, 2001, 155–190.

Bowles, Samuel, and Herbert Gintis. "Homo Reciprocans," *Nature* 415 (10 January 2002): 125–128.

———. "The Evolution of Strong Reciprocity: Cooperation in Heterogeneous Populations," *Theoretical Population Biology* 65 (2004): 17–28.

Bowles, Samuel, Jung-kyoo Choi, and Astrid Hopfensitz. "The Co-evolution of Individual Behaviors and Social Institutions," *Journal of Theoretical Biology* 223 (2003): 135–147.

Boyd, Robert, and Peter J. Richerson. *Culture and the Evolutionary Process*. Chicago: University of Chicago Press, 1985.

———. "Punishment Allows the Evolution of Cooperation (or Anything Else) in Sizeable Groups," *Ethology and Sociobiology* 113 (1992): 171–195.

———. "Group Beneficial Norms Can Spread Rapidly in a Cultural Population," *Journal of Theoretical Biology* 215 (2002): 287–296.

Bowles, Samuel, Herbert Gintis, Samuel Bowles, and Peter J. Richerson. "Evolution of Altruistic Punishment," *Proceedings of the National Academy of Sciences* 100, 6 (March 2003): 3531–3535.

Brown, Donald E. *Human Universals*. New York: McGraw-Hill, 1991.

Camerer, Colin, and Richard Thaler. "Ultimatums, Dictators, and Manners," *Journal of Economic Perspectives* 9, 2 (1995): 209–219.

Coase, Ronald H. "The Problem of Social Cost," *Journal of Law and Economics* 3 (October 1960): 1–44.

Coleman, James S. *Foundations of Social Theory*. Cambridge, MA: Belknap, 1990.

Cosmides, Leda, and John Tooby. "Cognitive Adaptations for Social Exchange," in Jerome H. Barkow, Leda Cosmides, and John Tooby (eds.) *The Adapted Mind: Evolutionary Psychology and the Generation of Culture*. New York: Oxford University Press, 1992, 163–228.

Crow, James F., and Motoo Kimura. *An Introduction to Population Genetic Theory*. New York: Harper & Row, 1970.

Dawes, Robyn M., and Richard Thaler. "Cooperation," *Journal of Economic Perspectives* 2 (1988): 187–197.

Dawkins, Richard. *The Selfish Gene*. Oxford: Oxford University Press, 1976.

———. *The Selfish Gene, 2nd Edition*. Oxford: Oxford University Press, 1989.

Durham, William H. *Coevolution: Genes, Culture, and Human Diversity*. Stanford: Stanford University Press, 1991.

Edgerton, Robert B. *Sick Societies: Challenging the Myth of Primitive Harmony*. New York: The Free Press, 1992.

Eibl-Eibesfeldt, I. "Warfare, Man's Indoctrinability and Group Selection," *Journal of Comparative Ethnology* 60, 3 (1982): 177–198.

Falk, Armin, Ernst Fehr, and Urs Fischbacher. "Testing Theories of Fairness and Reciprocity-Intentions Matter," 2002. University of Zürich.

Fehr, Ernst, and Bettina Rockenbach. "Detrimental Effects of Incentives on Human Altruism?" *Nature* 422 (March 2003): 137–140.

Fehr, Ernst, and J. List. "The Hidden Costs and Returns of Incentives: Trust and Trustworthiness among CEOs," 2002. Working Paper, Institute for Empirical Research, University of Zürich.

Fehr, Ernst, and Simon Gächter. "Cooperation and Punishment," *American Economic Review* 90, 4 (September 2000a): 980–994.

———. "Do Incentive Contracts Crowd Out Voluntary Cooperation?" 2000b. Working Paper No. 34, Institute for Empirical Research, University of Zürich.

———. "Altruistic Punishment in Humans," *Nature* 415 (10 January 2002): 137–140.

Fehr, Ernst, and Klaus M. Schmidt. "A Theory of Fairness, Competition, and Cooperation," *Quarterly Journal of Economics* 114 (August 1999): 817–868.

Fehr, Ernst, Simon Gächter, and Georg Kirchsteiger. "Reciprocity as a Contract Enforcement Device: Experimental Evidence," *Econometrica* 65, 4 (July 1997): 833–860.

Fehr, Ernst, Georg Kirchsteiger, and Arno Riedl. "Does Fairness Prevent Market Clearing?" *Quarterly Journal of Economics* 108, 2 (1993): 437–459.

———. "Gift Exchange and Reciprocity in Competitive Experimental Markets," *European Economic Review* 42, 1 (1998): 1–34.

Feldman, Marcus W., and Lev A. Zhivotovsky. "Gene-Culture Coevolution: Toward a General Theory of Vertical Transmission," *Proceedings of the National Academy of Sciences* 89 (December 1992): 11935–11938.

Feldman, Marcus W., Luca L. Cavalli-Sforza, and Joel R. Peck. "Gene-Culture Coevolution: Models for the Evolution of Altruism with Cultural Transmission," *Proceedings of the National Academy of Sciences* 82 (1985): 5814–5818.

Fix, Alan. *Migration and Colonization in Human Microevolution*. Cambridge: Cambridge University Press, 1999.

Foster, George M. *Culture and Conquest: America's Spanish Heritage*. New York: Wenner-Gren, 1960.

Frank, Robert H. *Passions Within Reason: The Strategic Role of the Emotions*. New York: Norton, 1988.

Frey, Bruno. "A Constitution for Knaves Crowds Out Civic Virtue," *Economic Journal* 107, 443 (July 1997): 1043–1053.

———. "The Cost of Price Incentives: An Empirical Analysis of Motivation Crowding Out," *American Economic Review* 87, 4 (September 1997): 746–755.

———. *Not Just for the Money: An Economic Theory of Personal Motivation*. Cheltenham, UK: Edward Elgar, 1997.

Friedman, Milton. *Essays in Positive Economics.* Chicago: University of Chicago Press, 1953.

Frohlich, Norman, and Joe Oppenheimer. "Choosing Justice in Experimental Democracies with Production," *American Political Science Review* 84, 2 (June 1990): 461–477.

Fudenberg, Drew, and Eric Maskin. "The Folk Theorem in Repeated Games with Discounting or with Incomplete Information," *Econometrica* 54, 3 (May 1986): 533–554.

Gächter, Simon, and Ernst Fehr. "Collective Action as a Social Exchange," *Journal of Economic Behavior and Organization* 39, 4 (July 1999): 341–369.

Gintis, Herbert. "Strong Reciprocity and Human Sociality," *Journal of Theoretical Biology* 206 (2000): 169–179.

———. "Solving the Puzzle of Human Prosociality," *Rationality and Society* 15, 2 (May 2003): 155–187.

———. "The Hitchhiker's Guide to Altruism: Genes, Culture, and the Internalization of Norms," *Journal of Theoretical Biology* 220, 4 (2003): 407–418.

Gintis, Herbert, Eric Alden Smith, and Samuel Bowles. "Costly Signaling and Cooperation," *Journal of Theoretical Biology* 213 (2001): 103–119.

Glaeser, Edward, David Laibson, Jose A. Scheinkman, and Christine L. Soutter. "Measuring Trust," *Quarterly Journal of Economics* 65 (2000): 622–846.

Gouldner, Alvin W. "The Norm of Reciprocity: A Preliminary Statement," *American Sociological Review* 25 (1960): 161–178.

Greenberg, M. S., and D. M. Frisch. "Effect of Intentionality on Willingness to Reciprocate a Favor," *Journal of Experimental Social Psychology* 8 (1972): 99–111.

Güth, Werner, and Reinhard Tietz. "Ultimatum Bargaining Behavior: A Survey and Comparison of Experimental Results," *Journal of Economic Psychology* 11 (1990): 417–449.

Hamilton, W. D. "The Genetical Evolution of Social Behavior," *Journal of Theoretical Biology* 37 (1964): 1–16, 17–52.

Hechter, Michael, and Satoshi Kanazawa. "Sociological Rational Choice," *Annual Review of Sociology* 23 (1997): 199–214.

Henrich, Joseph, and Robert Boyd. "Why People Punish Defectors: Weak Conformist Transmission Can Stabilize Costly Enforcement of Norms in Cooperative Dilemmas," *Journal of Theoretical Biology* 208 (2001): 79–89.

Henrich, Joe, Robert Boyd, Samuel Bowles, Colin Camerer, Ernst Fehr, and Herbert Gintis. *Foundations of Human Sociality: Ethnography and Experiments in Fifteen Small-scale Societies.* Oxford: Oxford University Press, 2004.

Henrich, Joe, Robert Boyd, Samuel Bowles, Colin Camerer, Ernst Fehr, Herbert Gintis, and Richard McElreath. "Cooperation, Reciprocity and Punishment in Fifteen Small-scale Societies," *American Economic Review* 91 (May 2001): 73–78.

Hertwig, Ralph, and Andreas Ortmann. "Experimental Practices in Economics: A Methodological Challenge for Psychologists?" *Behavioral and Brain Sciences* 24 (2001): 383–451.

Hirschman, Albert. "Against Parsimony," *Economic Philosophy* 1 (1985): 7–21.

Hirshleifer, David, and Eric Rasmusen. "Cooperation in a Repeated Prisoners' Dilemma with Ostracism," *Journal of Economic Behavior and Organization* 12 (1989): 87–106.

Hirshleifer, Jack. "Economics from a Biological Viewpoint," in Jay B. Barney and William G. Ouchi (eds.) *Organizational Economics*. San Francisco: Jossey-Bass, 1987, 319–371.

Homans, George C. "Social Behavior as Exchange," *American Journal of Sociology* 65, 6 (May 1958): 597–606.

Hume, David. *Essays: Moral, Political and Literary*. London: Longmans, Green, 1898(1754).

Keckler, C. N. W. "Catastrophic Mortality in Simulations of Forager Age-of-Death: Where Did all the Humans Go?" in R. Paine (ed.) *Integrating Archaeological Demography: Multidisciplinary Approaches to Prehistoric Populations*. Center for Archaeological Investigations, Occasional Papers No. 24, 205–228.

Keller, Laurent. *Levels of Selection in Evolution*. Princeton, NJ: Princeton University Press, 1999.

Kelly, Raymond C. *The Nuer Conquest: The Structure and Development of an Expansionist System*. Ann Arbor: University of Michigan Press, 1985.

Knauft, Bruce. "South Coast New Guinea Cultures: History, Comparison, Dialectic," *Cambridge Studies in Social and Cultural Anthropology* 89 (1993).

Ledyard, J. O. "Public Goods: A Survey of Experimental Research," in J. H. Kagel and A. E. Roth (eds.) *The Handbook of Experimental Economics*. Princeton, NJ: Princeton University Press, 1995, 111–194.

Loewenstein, George. "Experimental Economics from the Vantage Point of View of Behavioural Economics," *Economic Journal* 109, 453 (February 1999): F25–F34.

Lumsden, C. J., and E. O. Wilson. *Genes, Mind, and Culture: The Coevolutionary Process*. Cambridge, MA: Harvard University Press, 1981.

Maynard Smith, John. "Group Selection," *Quarterly Review of Biology* 51 (1976): 277–283.

Monroe, Kristen Renwick. *The Economic Approach to Politics*. Reading, MA: Addison Wesley, 1991.

Moore, Jr., Barrington. *Injustice: The Social Bases of Obedience and Revolt*. White Plains: M. E. Sharpe, 1978.

Orbell, John M., Robyn M. Dawes, and J. C. Van de Kragt. "Organizing Groups for Collective Action," *American Political Science Review* 80 (December 1986): 1171–1185.

Ostrom, Elinor, James Walker, and Roy Gardner. "Covenants with and without a Sword: Self-Governance Is Possible," *American Political Science Review* 86, 2 (June 1992): 404–417.

Posner, Richard. *Economic Analysis of Law*. New York: Little, Brown, 1973.

Price, G. R. "Selection and Covariance," *Nature* 227 (1970): 520–521.

———. "Extension of Covariance Selection Mathematics," *Annals of Human Genetics* 35 (1972): 485–490.

Richerson, Peter J., and Robert Boyd. *The Nature of Cultures*. Chicago: University of Chicago Press, 2003.

Roof, Wade Clark, and William McKinney. *American Mainline Religion: Its Changing Shape and Future*. New Brunswick, NJ: Rutgers University Press, 1987.

Roth, Alvin E., Vesna Prasnikar, Masahiro Okuno-Fujiwara, and Shmuel Zamir. "Bargaining and Market Behavior in Jerusalem, Ljubljana, Pittsburgh, and Tokyo: An Experimental Study," *American Economic Review* 81, 5 (December 1991): 1068–1095.

Sato, Kaori. "Distribution and the Cost of Maintaining Common Property Resources," *Journal of Experimental Social Psychology* 23 (January 1987): 19–31.

Smith, Adam. *The Theory of Moral Sentiments*. Indianapolis: Liberty Fund, 1982(1759).

Smith, Adam. *The Wealth of Nations*. New York: Prometheus Books, 1991(1776).

Sober, Elliot, and David Sloan Wilson. *Unto Others: The Evolution and Psychology of Unselfish Behavior*. Cambridge, MA: Harvard University Press, 1998.

Soltis, Joseph, Robert Boyd, and Peter J. Richerson. "Can Group-functional Behaviors Evolve by Cultural Group Selection: An Empirical Test," *Current Anthropology* 36, 3 (June 1995): 473–483.

Stephens, W., C. M. McLinn, and J. R. Stevens. "Discounting and Reciprocity in an Iterated Prisoner's Dilemma," *Science* 298 (13 December 2002): 2216–2218.

Taylor, Michael. *Anarchy and Cooperation*. London: John Wiley and Sons, 1976.

Titmuss, R. M. *The Give Relationship*. London: Allen and Unwin, 1970.

Trivers, R. L. "The Evolution of Reciprocal Altruism," *Quarterly Review of Biology* 46 (1971): 35–57.

Williams, G. C. *Adaptation and Natural Selection: A Critique of Some Current Evolutionary Thought*. Princeton, NJ: Princeton University Press, 1966.

Wilson, Edward O. *Sociobiology: The New Synthesis*. Cambridge, MA: Harvard University Press, 1975.

Yamagishi, Toshio. "The Provision of a Sanctioning System as a Public Good," *Journal of Personality and Social Psychology* 51 (1986): 110–116.

———. "The Provision of a Sanctioning System in the United States and Japan," *Social Psychology Quarterly* 51, 3 (1988a): 265–271.

———. "Seriousness of Social Dilemmas and the Provision of a Sanctioning System," *Social Psychology Quarterly* 51, 1 (1988b): 32–42.

———. "Group Size and the Provision of a Sanctioning System in a Social Dilemma," in W. B. G. Liebrand, David M. Messick, and H. A. M. Wilke (eds.) *Social Dilemmas: Theoretical Issues and Research Findings*. Oxford: Pergamon Press, 1992, 267–287.

II

The Behavioral Ecology of Cooperation

2   The Evolution of Cooperation in Primate Groups

Joan B. Silk

Primates do not donate to National Public Radio or give blood, but they do perform a variety of altruistic behaviors. That is, they act in ways that reduce their own fitness, but increase the fitness of their partners. For example, male chimpanzees form alliances and patrol the borders of their territories, sometimes launching lethal attacks on members of other communities (Goodall et al. 1979; Nishida, Hiraiwa-Hasegawa, and Takahata 1985; Boesch and Boesch-Achermann 2000; Watts and Mitani 2001); vervet monkeys give alarm calls when they detect predators (Struhsaker 1967; Seyfarth et al. 1980); captive cebus monkeys and chimpanzees allow others to share their food (de Waal 1997a, 1997b, 2000); macaque females defend juveniles from harassment by other group members (Chapais 1992); langurs and howlers spend considerable amounts of time carrying other females' infants (Paul 1999); and monkeys in a number of species spend ten to twenty percent of their waking hours removing dirt, debris, and ectoparasites from the hair and skin of other group members (Dunbar 1991).

Over the last twenty-five years, primatologists have collected large quantities of information about the distribution of these charitable activities. Evolutionary theory predicts that altruism will occur when benefits increase the actor's own inclusive fitness (Hamilton 1964) or when benefits are exchanged by reciprocating partners (Trivers 1971; Axelrod and Hamilton 1981). Thus, examinations of kinship and reciprocity have dominated efforts to account for the distribution of altruistic behavior among primates (Gouzoules and Gouzoules 1987; Dugatkin 1997; Silk 1987, 2002). Data that do not conform to predictions derived from these models have been discounted, denied, or simply ignored because they do not fit into our theoretical paradigms. However, empirical and theoretical work in experimental economics suggests that humans cooperate when standard evolutionary theory tells us that they should not. Efforts to develop systematic explanations of human behavior that explain these anomalies have generated new models of the motives that give rise to human cooperation, including strong reciprocity (Gintis 2000, this volume).

The goal of this chapter is to review what we know about the evolutionary forces that underlie cooperation in primate groups and to evaluate the possibility that the motives that give rise to strong reciprocity in humans also produce cooperation in primate groups. The literature provides very strong evidence that kin selection plays a fundamental role in the lives of nonhuman primates—shaping social organization, dispersal strategies, dominance hierarchies, and patterning of affiliative interactions. There is reasonably good evidence of reciprocity and interchange within nonhuman primate dyads, but very little systematic evidence of punishment. Experimental studies indicate that cooperation is contingent on the nature of previous interactions among partners, but the proximate mechanisms that generate these contingencies are largely unknown.

Analyses of the evolutionary mechanisms underlying cooperation in primates rely on assumptions about the relative magnitude and nature of the effects of these kinds of behaviors on individual fitness. In fact, it is virtually impossible to quantify the effects of a single behavioral act or social interaction on lifetime fitness. This problem is common to almost all studies of the adaptive function of social behavior in animals. We rely on what Grafen (1991) calls the "phenotypic gambit," the assumption that the short-term benefits that individuals derive from social interactions are ultimately translated into long-term differences in fitness. Animals who are regularly supported in agonistic confrontations, protected from harassment, or allowed to share access to desirable resources are expected to gain short-term benefits that are ultimately translated into fitness gains.

2.1 The Evolution of Altruism by Kin Selection

In general, natural selection favors the evolution of behaviors that increase an individual's relative fitness. Altruistic behaviors that reduce individual fitness contradict this logic. The theory of kin selection, developed by the late W. D. Hamilton, relies on the insight that relatives share some of their genetic material because they have a common ancestor (Hamilton 1964). If individuals behave altruistically toward their relatives, then they have some chance of conferring benefits upon individuals who carry copies of their own genes. The likelihood of this happening is based upon the genetic relationship between the actor and the recipient. Hamilton demonstrated that altruistic behaviors will be favored by selection when the costs of performing the behavior, c, are less than the benefits, b, discounted by the coefficient of relatedness between actor and recipient, r. The coefficient of relatedness is the average probability that two individuals acquire the same allele through descent from a common ancestor. This principle, which is generally called Hamilton's Rule, is stated as: $rb > c$.

Two basic insights can be derived from Hamilton's Rule. First, it is clear that when $r = 0$, this inequality cannot be satisfied. This means that unconditional altruism (via kin selection) will be restricted to kin ($r > 0$). Second, costly altruism will be limited to close kin, as the conditions for Hamilton's Rule become progressively more difficult to satisfy as costs rise. During the 1950s, the famous British evolutionary biologist, J. B. S. Haldane, is said to have worked through these simple calculations on the back of an envelope one evening in a pub and announced that he would give up his life to save two brothers or eight cousins.

Multi-level selection models (Wilson 1997) provide an alternative mathematical representation of the processes that underlie Hamilton's model of kin selection. In the inclusive fitness approach, fitness effects are accounted to the bodies in which the genes causing the effects are expressed, while in the multi-level selection approach, fitness effects are partitioned into within-group and between-group components (Reeve and Keller 1999). The two approaches are mathematically equivalent, but their heuristic value may vary in different circumstances.

2.2   Kin Recognition

The coefficient of relatedness, r, is the critical element for determining an adaptive course of action in social interactions that are influenced by kin selection (Hamilton 1987). In order to meet the conditions of Hamilton's Rule, animals must make sure that they limit altruistic behavior toward kin ($r > 0$). For species in which kin are clustered in discrete locations, such as burrows or nests, spatial location may provide sufficient information for kin discrimination (Blaustein, Bekoff, and Daniels 1987). For other animals, however, the problem is more complicated. Hamilton (1987) predicted that the ability to identify kin would be most fully developed in species that live in social groups—when there are opportunities for costly behaviors (such as egg dumping), and when passive, context-dependent mechanisms for distinguishing kin from nonkin are not likely to be effective.

Primates fit all three of these conditions. Most primates live in large and relatively stable social groups (Smuts et al. 1987). Even the most solitary primates, like orangutans and galagos, have regular interactions with familiar conspecifics (Bearder 1987; Galdikas 1988), and kinship may structure their communities (Wimmer, Tautz, and Kappeler 2002; Radespiel et al. 2003). Primates engage in a variety of fitness-reducing behaviors, including infanticide (van Schaik and Janson 2000); severe intragroup aggression (McGrew and McLuckie 1986); and intense feeding competition (Dittus 1979, 1988). Most primates live for extended periods of time in groups that include both relatives and nonrelatives, so context-driven mechanisms for distinguishing kin are likely to be of limited use. Thus, primates are expected to exhibit finely developed kin recognition abilities.

A number of different perceptual mechanisms underlie kin recognition in animal species. For example, sea squirts are able to recognize other sea squirts that carry the same allele on the hypervariable histocompatability locus (Pfennig and Sherman 1995). Some animals, including most mammals, are thought to learn who their relatives are during the course of development, drawing cues about kinship from patterns of association and interactions.

Close association early in life is generally thought to be the basis for kin recognition in primate groups (Bernstein 1991; Walters 1987). Nepotistic biases in association and interaction provide accurate and useful cues that monkeys use to identify their maternal relatives. An infant may learn who its relatives are by observing its mother's pattern of interaction and association with other group members. Similarly, a juvenile learns who its younger siblings are by watching its mother interact with her newborn infants.

Early association allows for recognition of maternal kin, but not paternal kin. Close associations between males and females are uncommon in most nonmonogamous primate species, limiting infants' abilities to learn who their fathers are. Other proxies for paternity are prone to error. For example, in multi-male species, male rank is often correlated with reproductive success, but the association is far from perfect. In some species that form one-male groups, such as patas and blue monkeys, incursions by nonresident males may occur during the mating season (Cords 1987). Even in pair-bonded species, like gibbons and callicebus monkeys, females sometimes mate with males from outside their groups (Mason 1966; Palombit 1994; Reichard 1995).

For species in which a single male monopolizes mating opportunities, age may be a good cue of paternal kinship (Altmann 1979). Among baboons in Amboseli, Kenya, high-ranking males monopolize access to females (Altmann et al. 1996) and agemates are therefore likely to be paternal half-siblings. Adult females interact at higher rates with agemates than others, generating significant differences in the rate of interactions between paternal half-siblings and unrelated females (Smith, Alberts, and Altmann 2003). Similar patterns characterize female rhesus macaques on Cayo Santiago (Widdig and Nürnberg 2001). In Amboseli, male baboons also recognize their own offspring. Adult males selectively support their own genetic offspring in agonistic encounters (Buchan et al. 2003). It is not clear what cues males use to identify their offspring. They may rely on their previous mating history, females' responses to males after they give birth, phenotypic cues, or some combination of these factors.

There is also tantalizing evidence that monkeys and apes may actually be able to recognize paternal kin based on phenotypic cues alone. In baboons and rhesus macaques, females distinguished *among* agemates, showing slight preferences for paternal half-siblings over nonkin (Smith, Alberts, and Altmann 2003; Widdig and Nürnberg 2001).

2.3   Social Organization Facilitates Kin Selection

The structure of social groups in many primate species facilitates the evolution of cooperation via kin selection (Silk 2002). Virtually all monkeys and apes live in stable social groups. Primate infants are completely dependent on their mothers (and sometimes their fathers) for support at birth, but become gradually more independent as they mature. Bonds between mothers and their offspring commonly continue beyond weaning, which marks the end of nutritional dependence. In some species, such as pair-bonded siamangs and owl monkeys, fathers are active participants in offspring care. In some species, such as marmosets and tamarins, older offspring act as "helpers at the nest" and their support enhances parental reproductive success (Garber 1997). Extended family ties are presumably the product of kin selection.

Dispersal patterns play an important role in the evolution of cooperation via kin selection. In all primate species, members of one or both sexes disperse from their natal groups (Pusey and Packer 1987). While natal dispersal presumably evolved to prevent inbreeding (Pusey and Wolf 1996), the *patterns* of dispersal may reflect selective pressures that favor kin-selected altruism (Wrangham 1980). In many primate species, members of only one sex (usually males) disperse, while members of the other sex remain in their natal group throughout their lives (Pusey and Packer 1987). When only one sex disperses, members of the nondispersing (philopatric) sex live among kin of varying degrees of relatedness. Thus, in baboon, macaque, and vervet groups, females grow up within a complex network of maternal and paternal kin: mother, grandmother, sisters, brothers, aunts, uncles, and cousins.

In these species, maternal kin spend much of their time in close proximity, and virtually all behaviors that are generally classified as altruistic, including grooming, food sharing, benign alloparenting, and alarm calling show matrilineal kin biases (reviewed by Bernstein 1991; Silk 1987; Gouzoules and Gouzoules 1987; Walters 1987; Silk 2002). We do not know whether the distribution of these behaviors fits predictions derived form Hamilton's Rule because the costs and benefits associated with these behaviors have not been measured. Nonetheless, the matrilineal bias in social behavior seems likely to be the product of kin selection.

More compelling evidence comes from studies of coalition formation—interactions in which one individual intervenes on behalf of another in an ongoing agonistic interaction. Monkeys who intervene in ongoing disputes put themselves at some risk, as monkeys are equipped with sharp teeth that they sometimes use to bite their opponents. Primates can be wounded in these disputes, sometimes seriously. Thus, coalitions provide "the clearest evidence of primates engaging in behavior that benefits another at some risk and/or cost to self" (Bernstein 1991).

Monkeys, particularly females, often intervene in ongoing disputes in support of their relatives. Females are significantly more likely to support kin than nonkin in aggressive disputes (Berman 1983a, 1983b, 1983c; Chapais 1983; Cheney 1983; Datta 1983a, 1983b; Kaplan 1977, 1978; Kurland 1977; Massey 1977; Silk 1982; Silk, Alberts, and Altmann 2004), particularly against higher ranking opponents (Chapais 1983, Chapais, Girard, and Primi 1991; Cheney 1983; Hunte and Horrocks 1987; Kurland 1977; Netto and van Hooff 1986; Pereira 1989; Silk 1982; Walters 1980; Watanabe 1979). Since allies run some risk of being threatened, chased, attacked, or injured when they intervene against higher-ranking monkeys, females are evidently willing to take greater risks on behalf of kin than on behalf of nonkin.

Support has both short-term and long-term consequences. In the short term, animals that obtain support are more likely to win disputes and less likely to become involved in escalated attacks. In the long term, support facilitates rank acquisition (see Chapais 1992 for a detailed analysis of this process). Infants are protected by their mothers and close female kin when they are threatened by other group members, particularly females that are of lower rank than their own mothers (Berman 1980; Datta 1983a; Cheney 1977; de Waal 1977; de Waal and Luttrell 1985; Horrocks and Hunte 1983; Johnson 1987; Lee 1983a, 1983b; Lee and Oliver 1979; Paul and Kuester 1987; Pereira 1989; Walters 1980). As they grow older, young juveniles obtain support when they challenge peers whose mothers are lower-ranking than their own mothers and when they challenge adults who are subordinate to their own mothers. Initially, juveniles can defeat older and larger juveniles only when their own mothers are nearby (Datta 1983a, 1983b; Horrocks and Hunte 1983; Walters 1980). Eventually, immatures are able to defeat all group members who are subordinate to their own mothers, even when their mothers are not in the vicinity. Since juveniles are able to defeat everyone that their own mothers can defeat (but not their mothers themselves), offspring acquire ranks just below their mothers.

The same process, repeated over generations and across families, generates matrilineal dominance hierarchies in which all members of the same matriline occupy contiguous ranks. Moreover, all members of a given matriline rank above or below all the members of other matrilines. Matrilineal dominance hierarchies have now been documented in at least seven species of macaques, baboons, and vervet monkeys (Chapais 1992). These dominance hierarchies are remarkably linear and stable over time, although the mechanisms that maintain this stability are not well understood (Silk, Alberts, and Altmann 2004). These arrangements have important fitness consequences for females: high-ranking females typically mature at earlier ages, give birth to healthier infants, and have shorter interbirth intervals than low-ranking females (reviewed by Silk 1987, 1993; Harcourt 1987).

Primates are discriminating nepotists. Thus, Japanese macaques and rhesus macaques treat distant kin much like nonkin (Kapsalis and Berman 1996a; Chapais et al. 1997). It is not clear whether monkeys do not recognize distant relatives as kin (Kapsalis and Berman 1996a) or if support for distant kin fails to meet the criteria for altruism specified by Hamilton's Rule.

Nepotism is also contingent on the circumstances. Among Japanese macaques, younger sisters commonly rise in rank over their older sisters. This process is sometimes contentious, and younger sisters "target" their older sisters for rank reversals. When females intervene in disputes involving their older sisters and subordinate nonkin, they are as likely to intervene against their sisters as they are to support them. In contrast, when females intervene in conflicts involving kin that are not targeted for rank reversals, females are much more likely to intervene on behalf of their relatives than their opponents (Chapais, Prud'homme, and Teijeiro 1994). Thus, females "apparently solve the conflict of interest between egotism and nepotism by maximizing their own rank among their kin on the one hand, and by maximizing the rank of their kin in relation to non-kin on the other" (Chapais 1995: 129).

When females disperse and males remain in their natal group, there are parallel opportunities for kin-selected altruism among males. Male philopatry is associated with strong male bonds among chimpanzees (Goodall 1986), muriquis (Strier 1992, 2000), spider monkeys (Symington 1990), Costa Rican squirrel monkeys (Boinski 1994), and in some populations of red colobus monkeys (Struhsaker 2000; but also see Starin 1994). For those interested in the evolutionary roots of human behavior, male bonding in chimpanzees is of particular interest. Male chimpanzees spend much of their time in the company of other males. They groom one another, hunt together, share meat, and collectively patrol the borders of their territories (Goodall 1986; Mitani, Merriwether, and Zhang 2000; Simpson 1973; Watts 2000; Wrangham and Smuts 1980). In some populations, pairs or trios jointly control access to receptive females and share matings (Watts 1998).

Primatologists have generally assumed that kin selection underlies male cooperation, but affiliative and cooperative behavior is not linked to matrilineal kinship in two Ugandan chimpanzee communities (Goldberg and Wrangham 1997; Mitani, Merriwether, and Zhang 2000). However, there is a strong tendency for males to form close ties to age-mates (Mitani et al. 2002). Thus, it seems possible that paternal kinship could underlie cooperative activity among chimpanzees.

When both sexes disperse, opportunities for kin selection to operate are more limited, but may still be important. Red howlers provide a particularly compelling example of this phenomenon. The number of females in red howler groups is confined within narrow limits—

groups with too few females are unable to defend their territories, while groups with too many females face competition for food and become more attractive targets for male takeovers, which leads to infanticide (Pope 2000b).

Therefore, when groups reach the optimal size, maturing females must disperse. Dispersal is very costly for females, particularly when local habitats are fully saturated. Some females never succeed in establishing new groups and those that do succeed begin to reproduce later than females who remain in their natal groups. The high costs of dispersal generate intense competition among females over recruitment opportunities for their daughters. Adult females actively harass maturing females in an effort to force them to emigrate. Females actively intervene on behalf of their daughters in these contests (Crockett 1984; Crockett and Pope 1993). In most cases, "only the daughters of a single presumably dominant adult female are successful at remaining to breed" (Pope 2000a).

Kin selection also shapes the life histories of male red howlers. Males gain access to breeding females in a variety of ways. When habitats are not crowded, they may join up with migrant females and help them establish new territories. But as habitats become more saturated, males can only gain access to breeding females by taking over established groups and evicting male residents. This is a risky strategy because males are often injured in takeover attempts (Crockett and Pope 1988). Moreover, males tend to remain in their natal groups longer, helping their fathers resist takeover attempts. Thus, when habitats are saturated, single males are at a distinct disadvantage in obtaining access to breeding females.

Competition among males generates powerful incentives for cooperation. Thus, single males form coalitions and cooperate in efforts to evict male residents from bisexual groups. After they have established residence, males collectively defend the group against incursions by extragroup males. However, cooperation involves clear fitness costs because only one male fathers infants within the group. Not surprisingly, coalitions that are made up of related males last on average 8.2 years, while coalitions among unrelated males last only 2.3 years (Pope 1990). Coalitions composed of kin are also less likely to experience the dominance changes that often lead to infanticide than are coalitions composed of unrelated males (Pope 1990).

In summary, there seems to be little doubt that kin selection plays an important role in the evolution of cooperation in primate groups. Our efforts to evaluate the *extent* of kin selection are limited by the difficulty of quantifying the effects of social behavior on fitness and our limited knowledge of paternal kinship.

2.4   Reciprocity in Primate Groups

Reciprocal altruism provides another vehicle for cooperation in primate groups (Axelrod and Hamilton 1981; Trivers 1971). Primates easily meet the necessary conditions for reciprocal altruism: they recognize their partners as individuals and have frequent opportunities to interact with group members. Moreover, they seem to be able to monitor and remember their partners' responses and adjust their subsequent behavior accordingly.

Although primates are prime candidates for reciprocal altruism, there is much less evidence of reciprocity than of kin selection (Seyfarth and Cheney 1988; Noë and Hammerstein 1995). This may be due to the fact that it is difficult to detect reciprocal altruism in nature (Seyfarth and Cheney 1988). We can tabulate the frequency and duration of services performed within dyads, but we cannot translate these values directly into fitness units and calculate the balance between benefits given and received. This is particularly complicated when exchanges involve different currencies or when reciprocity is delayed over time. Even if we find tight associations between altruism given and received among partners, it is possible that the association is causally linked to a third variable that we have not taken into account, such as kinship (Hemelrijk and Ek 1991). In naturalistic settings, it is often difficult to determine whether the delivery of benefits is contingent on reciprocity.

Much of what primatologists have written about reciprocity involves grooming. Grooming is an obvious candidate for reciprocal exchanges because it is common and involves complementary roles—I'll scratch your back if you scratch mine. Grooming is the most common form of social behavior among nonhuman primates, occupying up 20 percent of every day (Dunbar 1991). The functions of grooming are not fully understood. Grooming is thought to be beneficial to the recipient because ectoparasites—such as ticks, lice, and botflies—are removed and wounds are cleaned (Saunders 1988; Henzi and Barrett 1999). This suggests that grooming would be concentrated on regions of the body that animals cannot reach themselves, and this is often the case (Pérez and Veà 2000). However, grooming solicitations do not correspond perfectly to accessibility, and this suggests that other factors may also be

in play. Anyone observing monkeys grooming one another would suspect that grooming is intensely pleasurable—animals who are being
groomed seem to be utterly relaxed. In fact, grooming lowers heart
rates and raises levels of beta-endorphins (Aureli and Smucny 2000).
Grooming may also have social functions (Dunbar 1988, 1991), providing a means to reinforce social bonds and cultivate valuable social
relationships.

While grooming seems to be beneficial to recipients, those who
provide these services incur some costs. At the very least, the groomer
expends time and energy in servicing its partner. The groomer may
also become more vulnerable to attacks by predators or other group
members because vigilance is reduced during grooming (Cords 1995;
Maestripieri 1993).

If grooming is the product of reciprocal altruism, then grooming
(among nonkin) should be limited to reciprocating partners. Several
lines of evidence suggest that this may be the case. First grooming in
large groups is restricted to a relatively limited subset of potential partners. For example, female baboons in the Okavango Delta of Botswana
groomed on average only eight of the other eighteen adult females in
their group; and most females concentrated their grooming on an even
smaller number of females (Silk, Cheney, and Seyfarth 1999). In general, the extent of selectivity is related to the number of available partners. In small groups, females distribute their grooming evenly across
the group, but as groups grow larger, grooming is less evenly allocated
across potential partners (Silk, Cheney, and Seyfarth 1999). This may
reflect cognitive constraints on females' ability to keep track of large
numbers of relationships (Henzi and Barrett 1999) or ecological constraints that limit the amount of time that females can afford to spend
grooming (Dunbar 1991; Henzi, Lycett, and Weingrill 1997).

Is grooming reciprocated? A definitive answer to this question is
surprisingly elusive. Among male chimpanzees, there are positive correlations between the amount of grooming given and received, but
grooming is not evenly balanced within most dyads (Watts 2000).
There are also cases in which grooming is evenly balanced within
the majority of dyads. Thus, adult female baboons in the Okavango
Delta tended to groom each of their partners as often as their partners
groomed them (Silk, Cheney, and Seyfarth 1999). Similarly, in white-
faced capuchins, grooming is evenly balanced within the majority of
dyads (Manson et al. 1999). In some cases, grooming roles are alter-
nated within bouts (Barrett et al. 1999; Muroyama 1991), but others in

which grooming tends to be reciprocated over longer time periods (Manson et al. 2004).

There are many groups in which grooming is unbalanced within dyads, and disparities in grooming given and received are sometimes linked to dominance rank. In some groups, high-ranking partners receive more grooming than they give each of their partners (Chapais 1983; Fairbanks 1980; Seyfarth 1980; Silk 1982; Sambrook, Whiten, and Strum 1995; Stammbach 1978; Watts 2000; Manson et al. 2004), in other groups high-ranking partners give more grooming than they receive in return (Altmann, Myles, and Combes 1998; O'Brien 1993; Di Bitetti 1997; Linn et al. 1995; Parr et al. 1997). Most primatologists assume that these imbalances exist because grooming is exchanged for other commodities such as coalitionary support (Seyfarth 1977), food (de Waal 1997a), tolerance (Silk 1982; Fairbanks 1980), access to attractive infants (Muroyama 1994; Henzi 2001), or maintaining group cohesion (Altmann, Myles, and Combes 1998).

Seyfarth (1977) was the first to suggest that monkeys might exchange grooming for support in agonistic interactions. His argument was based on the notion that high-ranking animals make powerful coalition partners. He reasoned that females might groom higher-ranking monkeys who would in return provide support for them when they were harassed by other group members. Grooming and support are positively correlated among vervets in Amboseli (Seyfarth 1980) and white-faced capuchins in Costa Rica (Perry 1996). However, kinship was not known for these two groups, and the observed correlation between grooming and support might actually arise because females selectively support and groom close kin (Hemelrijk and Ek 1991). This is apparently the case among rhesus macaques on Cayo Santiago where grooming and support are correlated among related females but not among unrelated females (Kapsalis and Berman 1996b). However, grooming and support are correlated among male bonnet macaques (Silk 1992) and male chimpanzees (Mitani, Merriwether, and Zhang 2000) and these results are not confounded by maternal kinship. Researchers have failed to find consistent associations between grooming and support in several cases (Fairbanks 1980; Silk 1982; de Waal and Luttrell 1986; Silk, Alberts, and Altmann 2004).

Although the naturalistic data provide only tepid support for Seyfarth's model, two experimental studies demonstrate a direct link between grooming and support in Old World monkeys. Using tape-recorded vocalizations of females' screams, which signal distress and are often used to recruit support, Seyfarth and Cheney (1984) showed that free-ranging vervet females were more attentive to screams of unrelated females if they had been groomed by the screaming female shortly before they heard the scream than if they had not been groomed by her. Similarly, Hemelrijk (1994) artificially induced fights among unrelated female macaques housed temporarily in groups of three. When fights between two females occurred, aggressors sometimes received support from the third female. Support was more likely to be given to the aggressor if she had previously groomed the potential supporter.

Grooming may also be used to obtain other valuable benefits. Female bonnet macaques are less likely to be harassed while they are grooming higher-ranking females than when they are grooming lower-ranking females (Silk 1982), and grooming may confer protection. Female monkeys may also use grooming to obtain access to infants. For reasons that are not altogether clear, female monkeys are strongly attracted to newborn infants (Paul 1999; Maestripieri 1994; Silk 1999). Females gather around new mothers, attempting to smell, nuzzle, touch, and inspect the genitals of newborn infants. Macaque and baboon mothers do not seem to welcome this interest in their infants, even though most of the interactions seem relatively benign. In these species, new mothers are often approached and groomed at higher rates than they are at other times (Altmann 1980) and some researchers suggest that females trade grooming for access to newborn infants (Muroyama 1994; Henzi 2001).

2.5 Food Sharing

Food sharing plays a fundamental role in the organization of traditional human societies (Foley 1987). While gathered foods are generally redistributed only to family members, meat is typically shared with all members of the group. In primates, which rely mainly on plant foods, food sharing is generally uncommon and limited to offspring (Foley 1987; McGrew 1992). Chimpanzees represent a major exception to this rule—males hunt regularly and successfully, and share access to their kills (Boesch and Boesch-Achermann 2000; Goodall 1986; Mitani and Watts 2001; Stanford et al. 1994). This has generated considerable interest in the dynamics of hunting and food sharing among chimpanzees.

In chimpanzees, hunting is usually a collective activity. At some sites, hunters take different roles in stalking, ambushing, and snatching prey (Boesch 1994; Boesch and Boesch 1989; Boesch and Boesch-Achermann

2000). At other sites, hunting involves no obvious coordination (Stanford 1996; Busse 1978; Goodall 1986; Uehara et al. 1992). Surprisingly, there is little consensus about why male chimpanzees hunt. In some primates, predatory activity increases when plant foods become scarce (Dunbar 1983; Foley 1987). Chimpanzees rely heavily on ripe fruit, and they may hunt to compensate for seasonal shortages of their preferred foods (Teleki 1973; Takahata, Hasegawa, and Nishida 1984; Stanford 1996, 1998). In contrast, at Ngogo males hunt most when food is most abundant (Watts and Mitani 2002).

Hunting seems to have a social component as well. Males are most likely to hunt when they are in large groups, and hunting success generally increases with party size (Stanford 1996; Watts and Mitani 2002). This suggests that males may hunt to obtain meat that they can trade for sexual access to females (Stanford 1996, 1998; Stanford et al. 1994) or they may use meat to cultivate social bonds with other males (Nishida et al. 1992; Boesch and Boesch-Achermann 2000; Mitani and Watts 2001).

Careful analyses of the distribution of fruit, hunting effort, and food sharing at Ngogo, a site in the Kibale Forest of Uganda (Mitani and Watts 2001) suggest that hunting may enhance the quality of social bonds among males. In Ngogo, chimpanzees hunt most often when fruit is most abundant (Watts and Mitani 2002), ruling out the possibility that males hunt to compensate for food shortages. Males did not share selectively with sexually receptive females and receptive females did not mate selectively with males who shared food with them, suggesting that males do not trade meat for sex at Ngogo. However, males did share meat selectively with males who shared meat with them and with males who regularly supported them in agonistic interactions. Moreover, males who hunt together also tend to groom one another selectively, support one another, and participate in border patrols together (Mitani, Merriwether, and Zhang 2000). Frequent participation in border patrols is, in turn, linked to male mating success (Watts and Mitani 2001). It is not clear whether the patterns detected at Ngogo characterize chimpanzees at other sites.

In captivity, food sharing extends to provisioned plant foods. De Waal (1997a) observed chimpanzees for several hours before and after they were fed fresh cuttings of leaves and branches, delicacies that the chimpanzees clearly relished. Those that possessed leaves and branches were more likely to share their booty with animals that had previously groomed them than with animals who had not groomed them in the past few hours. Moreover, if there had been no grooming before provisioning, the possessor was more likely to respond aggressively to efforts to take food from their pile. The possessor's largesse was not simply a result of being groomed—the chimps limited their generosity to the animals that had just groomed them. Furthermore, the possessor's attitude was not simply a reflection of the quality of the relationship between the two animals—the chimps were more likely to share with those that groomed them than those that they had groomed themselves. However, the magnitude of the effect of prior grooming was influenced by the nature of the relationship between the two individuals—for pairs that rarely groomed, sharing was strongly contingent on recent grooming, while for pairs that groomed at higher rates, recent grooming had a smaller impact on sharing.

De Waal and his colleagues have also studied the mechanisms underlying food sharing in captive capuchin monkeys. In one set of experiments, a pair of familiar monkeys was held in adjacent cages separated by wire mesh (de Waal 1997a). The holes in the mesh were large enough to allow the monkeys to reach into the adjacent cage and take food items. The experimental design was simple. First, one monkey was given food. Later, the other monkey was given food. All transfers of food in both phases of the experiment were monitored by the observers.

In this experimental situation, a considerable amount of food changed hands. Owners virtually never handed food to their partners or pushed it through the holes in the wire mesh, but they often sat very near the mesh partition with their food. When they did so, the monkey in the adjacent cage was able to reach through the wire mesh and take pieces of food, often from within the owner's reach and in plain sight. For some animals, the rate of transfer from the owner to its partner in the first phase of the experiment was positively correlated with the rate of transfer when their roles were reversed in the second phase of the experiment. However, there was a wide range of values in the correlation coefficients across individuals. Transfer rates were affected by the quality of social relationships among females, as dyads that tended to associate frequently and fight infrequently had higher transfer rates than dyads that associated less often and fought more frequently.

De Waal (1997a) initially used the term "sharing" to refer to these food transfers, but subsequently suggested that "facilitated taking" might be a better label for them (de Waal 2000). He points out that the capuchins rarely gave food to their partners directly (de Waal 1997b), even though they did little to protect their food from theft. Thus, capuchins may be strongly motivated to be near particular partners, and food transfers may be an inadvertent side effect of their sociability. The fact that the quality of social bonds influences food transfer rates suggest that the capuchins may not share in a strictly contingent manner (de Waal 1997b). De Waal (2000) conducted a second set of experiments in which two females housed in adjacent cages were given food at the same time, but the food items differed in their desirability. Females spent more time near the mesh partition when a monkey was in the adjacent cage than when it was empty, but they dropped less food near the partition when it was occupied by another monkey. Moreover, females tended to spend less time near the partition (and within their partner's reach) when they had more desirable foods than their partners. Thus, females seem to be drawn to favored companions, but are also wary of losing desirable food items to them. Observed rates of food transfer are the product of a compromise between these competing motivations (de Waal 2000).

Using a different experimental paradigm, de Waal and Berger (2000) explored capuchins willingness to participate in cooperative tasks. As in the previous experiment, monkeys were held in adjacent cages separated by a wire mesh partition. Here, the monkeys had to pull a counterweighted bar to bring a tray holding a baited food bowl within reach. De Waal and Berger examined the monkeys' participation in this task under three different conditions. In the solo condition, only one food bowl was baited and a single monkey was able to pull the bowl to within reach. In the cooperative condition, only one food bowl was baited, but it required joint action by both monkeys to pull the bowl within reach. In the mutualistic condition, both bowls were baited and it required joint action by both monkeys to pull the bowl within reach. Monkeys were equally successful in the solo and mutualistic conditions, pulling the food bowl forward approximately 85 percent of the time. Monkeys succeeded on the cooperative task only 40 percent of the time. However, when monkeys did succeed on the cooperative task, more food was transferred than in the successful solo trials. Moreover, a larger fraction of food transfers were tolerated (in sight and reach of the owner) than in solo trials.

De Waal and Berger (2000) argue that these experiments show that "capuchins cooperate even if it is obvious that only one of them, and which one, will be rewarded," and that that capuchins "exchange labor for payment." Yet given the small size of the cages, the capuchins marked affinity for their partners, and the messiness of their eating habits, both parties may be relatively certain that they will obtain food if they cooperate in pulling the bowl forward. Moreover, it is not clear that food transfers reflect an exchange of payment for labor. Even in solo trials, some food is transferred and the incremental effects of cooperation on food transfers and tolerance is relatively small. In solo trials seven to nine pieces of food are transferred on average and 58 percent of those transfers are tolerated by the owner. In cooperative trials, these numbers increase only slightly—nine to eleven pieces are taken and 65 percent of these transfers are tolerated.

Primatologists have recently begun to explore the psychological predispositions that underly exchanges in primate groups. One of the key assumptions of reciprocity is that animals must be able to evaluate the value of the commodities or services that are being exchanged. Brosnan and de Waal (2003) conducted an intriguing experiment to explore how monkeys assess "value." In these experiments, capuchins were trained to exchange tokens for food rewards. When a monkey handed a token to the experimenter, it was given a piece of food. The experimenters then conducted a series of trials in which the subjects observed transfers involving other individuals. In some cases, monkeys saw others receive food without any exchange of tokens, and in some cases they saw other monkeys receive a higher quality food reward than they received themselves when they exchanged tokens for foods. Monkeys who observed others obtain rewards without exchange or obtain higher quality rewards than they received were significantly more likely to refuse the food rewards that they obtained themselves—sometimes flinging food back at the experimenters. Monkeys virtually never refused rewards unless they observed others who had gotten a better deal. The authors suggest that monkeys displayed an aversion to inequality, although this interpretation has been questioned (Henrich 2004). At the very least, the data suggest that monkeys have some ability to evaluate the value of commodities and react negatively when they perceive that an exchange is disadvantageous to themselves.

The psychology underlying exchange has also been explored in captive tamarins. Hauser et al. (2003) created an experimental paradigm in which one individual could pull a tool that would provide food for its partner but no food for itself. The researchers trained several tamarins to be "unconditional altruists" who always pulled and others to be "unconditional defectors" who never pulled. They paired these trained animals with untrained animals to determine whether the untrained tamarins would adjust their behavior in a contingent way. Tamarins pulled more when paired with unconditional altruists than when paired with unconditional defectors, indicating that cooperation was contingent on the behavior of the partner. However, Stevens and Hauser (2004) emphasize that the tamarins cooperated only half the time and that cooperation with unconditional altruists declined over the course of the experiments. They conclude that tamarins do not "demonstrate robust reciprocity" and conclude that "cognitive limitations such as temporal discounting, numerical discrimination, and memory make reciprocity difficult for animals" including nonhuman primates.

2.6 Evolutionary Mechanisms Underlying Reciprocity in Primates

Balanced exchanges between partners and interchange across currencies are often interpreted as evidence that monkeys practice reciprocal altruism. De Waal has questioned this interpretation, suggesting that balanced exchanges might simply arise from mutual tolerance or high rates of association between partners rather than from contingent exchanges that require careful record keeping (de Waal and Luttrell 1988; de Waal 1997b; de Waal 2000; de Waal and Berger 2000): "If members of a species were to direct aid preferentially to close associates, a reciprocal distribution would automatically result due to the symmetrical nature of association" (de Waal 2000). De Waal calls this "symmetry-based reciprocity" and suggests that proximity should be controlled in analyses of reciprocity (de Waal and Luttrell 1988).

There are both logical and empirical reasons to doubt that symmetry-based reciprocity accounts for the distribution of altruistic behavior in primate groups. Symmetry-based reciprocity implies that proximity can be treated as an independent variable that is not affected by the nature of interactions between individuals. It seems more likely that association patterns reflect the nature of affiliative relationships between individuals. Thus, animals preferentially associate with those that tolerate, groom, and help them; they do not preferentially tolerate, help, and groom those that they just happen to associate with. Second, it seems unlikely that symmetry-based reciprocity would be stable against invasion by cheaters. Those who accepted help from close associates but did not return it would be at a distinct advantage. In fact, there is no evidence for symmetry-based reciprocity in primate groups. Significant correlations between benefits given and received are maintained, even when proximity is controlled statistically (de Waal and Luttrell 1988). Moreover, several experimental studies demonstrate contingencies between benefits given and subsequently received (Seyfarth and Cheney 1984; Hemelrijk 1994; de Waal 1997a, 1997b, 2000).

De Waal's (2000) observations of fluctuations in the rate of food transfer within dyads over the course of successive experiments led him to suggest that reciprocity may be based on a tendency to mirror the social predispositions of partners, responding positively to positive social overtures and negatively to negative social overtures: "If facilitated taking is mediated by such general social predispositions, this would mean that, rather than keeping track of exact amounts of given and received food, the monkeys follow a simple tolerance-breeds-tolerance scheme" (de Waal 2000, 260). Attitudinal reciprocity is assumed to be less cognitively demanding than "calculated reciprocity," which relies on precise quantification of benefits given and received in different currencies.

Attitudinal reciprocity is analogous to strong reciprocity because both processes focus on the proximate motives that generate cooperation and assume that reciprocity could occur without concern for long-term consequences. However, it is not clear how evolution could sustain attitudinal reciprocity (or strong reciprocity) in primate groups. It seems likely that individuals who systematically returned somewhat less than they received would benefit at the expense of their partners. To avoid this, costs and benefits must be translated into affect, a process that may hide the calculus of reciprocal altruism, but does not eliminate it.

2.7 Punishment

Strong reciprocity relies on the tendency to punish noncooperators. Among nonhuman primates there is considerable evidence of negative reciprocity. Thus, animals use aggression or other forms of costly sanctions to shape the behavior of group members (Clutton-Brock and Parker 1995a, 1995b) or to exact revenge (de Waal and Luttrell 1988; Silk 1992). But there is very little evidence that monkeys and apes use aggression or negative sanctions to shape the behavior of third parties or to punish deviation from social norms.

Several researchers have reported episodes of aggressive behavior that could be interpreted as punishment. In the Mahale Mountains of Tanzania, a young adult male was brutally attacked by eight members of his own group (Nishida et al. 1995). The authors speculated that this young male may have been victimized because he did not conform to social rules—he did not defer to higher-ranking males and launched unprovoked attacks on adult females. The problem with these observations (and other anecdotal observations) is that they are based on a single event. In these cases, conspicuous aggressive responses to unusual types of behavior may be more salient than occasions in which unusual behaviors were ignored. Without systematic analyses of the consequences of aberrant behaviors, it is difficult to be certain that violations of social norms are consistently punished.

The only systematic evidence of third party punishment comes from an experimental study on rhesus macaques conducted by Hauser and Marler (1993a, 1993b, Hauser 1997). Rhesus macaques give characteristic calls when they discover food items (Hauser and Marler 1993a). Taking advantage of this situation, Hauser and Marler (1993b) conducted an experiment in which observers surreptitiously dropped handfuls of coconut or monkey chow and waited for monkeys to find it. When monkeys found the food, they sometimes called and sometimes remained silent. Calling had little effect on the likelihood of being detected after finding food, but calling significantly reduced the likelihood of being harassed after discovery by other group members. Monkeys who discovered food and subsequently called were less likely to be supplanted, chased, or attacked than monkeys who remained silent after they found food. In the published report, the authors did not control for the relative dominance of the original possessors and the discoverers, even though macaque females rarely initiate aggression toward more dominant animals. However, subsequent reanalyses of the data (Hauser personal communication) indicate that noncallers were more likely to be harassed when they were discovered by higher-ranking animals than callers were. Apparently, these rules apparently apply only to females. Males virtually never call when they find food and are rarely punished (Hauser and Marler 1993b; Hauser 1997).

These data provide intriguing evidence that rhesus macaques punish group members who violate social norms. However, the weight of this conclusion is limited by the fact that these results have not been replicated, and no other observers have reported similar findings in other groups or species.

2.8 Prospects for Finding Strong Reciprocity in Primate Groups

For primates, cooperation is bounded by kinship and reciprocity and involves pairs of animals who have long-term social bonds. Most primatologists have assumed that reciprocal altruism is ultimately responsible for reciprocity within dyads, an assumption that is bolstered by experimental evidence that cooperative behavior is contingent on the nature of previous interactions. However, de Waal (2000) has suggested that reciprocal exchanges in capuchins may be the product of attitudinal reciprocity—a tendency to mirror the predispositions of their partners. If he is right, then we have reason to believe that strong reciprocity is rooted in the behavior of nonhuman primates. However, it is also possible that the monkey's initial attitude toward its partner reflects the quality of their social relationship, and this is based on a long series of cooperative exchanges over time.

Good evidence of punishment would provide support for the idea that strong reciprocity operates in primate groups. Presently, systematic evidence for punishment rests on a single experiment. These data are quite provocative, but their significance will not be established until these experiments are replicated and extended to other species.

To understand the role of strong reciprocity in primate groups, we need to know more about the proximate factors that motivate cooperative behavior. Strong reciprocity in humans seems rooted in a deep sense of fairness and concern for justice that is extended even toward strangers, but we have no systematic evidence that other animals have similar sensibilities. Even those who have argued most forcefully for the emergence of moral sentiments in monkeys and apes have drawn their evidence from the interactions of close associates with long-term social bonds, not interactions among strangers (de Waal 1996; Flack and de Waal 2000).

The idea of strong reciprocity emerged from carefully designed experimental studies on humans that revealed surprisingly high levels of altruism in one-shot interactions with strangers. It is hard to imagine obtaining comparable data on interactions among strangers in nonhuman primates. Most primates live in stable social groups where they restrict peaceful social interactions mainly to known group members. Close associations with strangers are fraught with tension, generating aggression and avoidance, not cooperation. Aversions to strangers extend to captive settings. It might be possible to adapt de Waal's experimental studies of capuchins to assess cooperative behavior with anonymous partners, but it is not clear whether capuchins or other primates would tolerate this protocol.

In conclusion, the literature suggests that primates reserve cooperation mainly for kin and reciprocating partners, but punishment is apparently uncommon. While we know a lot about what nonhuman primates do, we know very little about what motivates them to do it. The patterning of cooperative interactions among nonrelatives could be the product of reciprocal altruism, but the same patterns could also arise from strong reciprocity. To identify the proximate mechanisms that generate cooperation in primate groups, we need to develop experimental procedures that allow us to assess the tendency to cooperate in one-shot interactions with strangers. The ability to interact peacefully in one-shot interactions with strangers may prove to be one of the most remarkable traits of our own species. We also need to know more about other primates' propensity to punish violations of social norms. Work addressing these issues in nonhuman primates is needed to assess the evolutionary roots of strong reciprocity.

References

Altmann, J. 1979. Age cohorts as paternal sibships. *Behav. Ecol. Sociobiol.* 6:161–169.

Altmann, J. 1980. *Baboon mothers and infants.* Harvard University Press, Cambridge, MA.

Altmann, J., Alberts, S. C., Haines, S. A., Dubach, J. D., Muruthi, P., Coote, T., Geffen, E., Cheesman, D. J., Mututua, R. S., Saiyalele, S. N., Wayne, R. K., Lacy, R. C., and Bruford, M. W. 1996. Behavior predicts genetic structure in a wild primate group. *Proc. Natl. Acad. Sci. USA* 93:5797–5801.

Altmann, J., Myles, B., and Combes, S. 1998. Grooming relationships in a primate group: Social cohesion or currying favors? Poster presented at the annual meetings of the American Primatological Society.

Aureli, F., and Smucny, D. A. 2000. The role of emotion in conflict and conflict resolution. In *Natural conflict resolution*, ed. F. Aureli and F. B. M. de Waal, 199–224. Berkeley, CA: University of California Press.

Axelrod, R., and Hamilton, W. D. 1981. The evolution of cooperation. *Science* 211:1390–1396.

Barrett, L., Henzi, S. P., Weingrill, T., Lycett, J. E., and Hill, R. A. 1999. Market forces predict grooming reciprocity in female baboons. *Proc. R. Soc. Lond.* 266:665–670.

Bearder, S. K. 1987. Lorises, bushbabies, and tarsiers: Diverse societies in solitary foragers. In *Primate societies*, eds. B. B. Smuts, D. L. Cheney, R. M. Seyfarth, R. W. Wrangham, and T. T. Struhsaker, 11–24. Chicago: University of Chicago Press.

Berman, C. M. 1980. Early agonistic experience and rank acquisition among free-ranging infant rhesus monkeys. *Int. J. Primatol.* 1:152–170.

Berman, C. M. 1983a. Early differences in relationships between infants and other group members based on the mother's status: Their possible relationship to peer-peer rank acquisition. In *Primate social relationships: An integrated approach*, ed. R. A. Hinde, 154–156. Sunderland, MA: Sinauer Associates.

Berman, C. M. 1983b. Influence of close female relations on peer-peer rank acquisition. In *Primate social relationships: An integrated approach*, ed. R. A. Hinde, 157–159. Sunderland, MA: Sinauer Associates.

Berman, C. M. 1983c. Matriline differences and infant development. In *Primate social relationships: An integrated approach*, ed. R. A. Hinde, 132–134. Sunderland, MA: Sinauer Associates.

Bernstein, I. S. 1991. The correlation between kinship and behaviour in non-human primates. In *Kin recognition*, ed. by P. G. Hepper, 6–29. Cambridge: Cambridge University Press.

Blaustein, A. R., Bekoff, M., and Daniels, J. 1987. Kin recognition in vertebrates (excluding primates): Empirical evidence. In *Kin recognition in animals*, eds. D. J. C. Fletcher and C. D. Michener, 287–331. New York: John Wiley and Sons.

Boesch, C. 1994. Cooperative hunting in wild chimpanzees. *Anim. Behav.* 48:653–667.

Boesch, C., and Boesch, H. 1989. Hunting of wild chimpanzees in the Taï National Park. *Amer. J. Phys. Anthropol.* 78:547–573.

Boesch, C., and Boesch-Achermann, H. 2000. *The Chimpanzees of the Taï Forest*. Oxford: Oxford Univesity Press.

Boinski, S. 1994. Affiliation patterns among male Costa Rican squirrel monkeys. *Behaviour* 130:191–209.

Brosnan, S. F., and de Waal, F. B. M. 2003. Monkeys reject unequal pay. *Nature* 425:297–299.

Buchan, J. C., Alberts, S. C., Silk, J. B., Altmann, J. 2003. True paternal care in a multi-male primate society. *Nature* 425:179–181.

Busse, C. 1978. Do chimpanzees hunt cooperatively? *Amer. Nat.* 112:767–770.

Chapais, B. 1983. Dominance, relatedness, and the structure of female relationships in rhesus monkeys. In *Primate social relationships: An integrated approach*, ed. R. A. Hinde, 209–219. Sunderland, MA: Sinauer Associates.

Chapais, B. 1992. The role of alliances in social inheritance of rank among female primates. In *Coalitions and alliances in humans and other animals*, eds. A. H. Harcourt and F. B. M. de Waal, 29–59. Oxford: Oxford Science Publications.

Chapais, B. 1995. Alliances as a means of competition in primates: Evolutionary, developmental, and cognitive aspects. *Yrbk. Phys. Anthropol.* 38:115–136.

Chapais, B., Girard, M., and Primi, G. 1991. Non-kin alliances and the stability of matrilineal dominance relations in Japanese macaques. *Anim. Behav.* 41:481–491.

Chapais, B., Prud'homme, J., and Teijeiro, S. 1994. Dominance competition among siblings in Japanese macaques: Constraints on nepotism. *Anim. Behav.* 48:1335–1347.

Chapais, B., Gauthier, C., Prud'homme, J., and Vasey, P. 1997. Relatedness threshold for nepotism in Japanese macaques. *Anim. Behav.* 53:1089–1101.

Cheney, D. L. 1977. The acquisition of rank and the development of reciprocal alliances among free-ranging immature baboons. *Behav. Ecol. Sociobiol.* 2:303–318.

Cheney, D. L. 1983. Extrafamilial alliances among vervet monkeys. In *Primate social relationships: An integrated approach*, ed. R. A. Hinde, 278–286. Sunderland, MA: Sinauer Associates.

Clutton-Brock, T. H., and Parker, G. A. 1995a. Punishment in animal societies. *Nature* 373:209–216.

Clutton-Brock, T. H., and Parker, G. A. 1995b. Sexual coercion in animal societies. *Anim. Behav.* 49:1345–1365.

Cords, M. 1987. Male-male competition in one-male groups. In *Primate societies*, eds. B. B. Smuts, D. L. Cheney, R. M. Seyfarth, R. W. Wrangham, and T. T. Struhsaker, 98–111. Chicago: University of Chicago Press.

Cords, M. 1995. Predator vigilance costs of allogrooming in wild blue monkeys. *Behaviour* 132:559–569.

Crockett, C. M. 1984. Emigration by female red howler monkeys and the case for female competition. In *Female primates: Studied by women primatologists*, ed. M. F. Small, 159–173. New York: Alan R. Liss.

Crockett, C. M., and Pope, T. R. 1988. Inferring patterns of aggression from red howler monkey injuries. *Amer. J. Primatol.* 14:1–21.

Crockett, C. M., and Pope, T. R. 1993. Consequences for sex difference in dispersal for juvenile red howler monkeys. In *Juvenile primates: Life history, development, and behavior*, eds. M. E. Pereira and L. A. Fairbanks, 104–118. Oxford: Oxford University Press.

Datta, S. B. 1983a. Relative power and the acquisition of rank. In *Primate social relationships: An integrated approach*, ed. R. A. Hinde, 93–103. Sunderland, MA: Sinauer Associates.

Datta, S. B. 1983b. Relative power and the maintenance of dominance. In *Primate social relationships: An integrated approach*, ed. R. A. Hinde, 103–112. Sunderland, MA: Sinauer Associates.

de Waal, F. B. M. 1977. The organization of agonistic relations within two captive groups of Java-monkeys (*Macaca fasicularis*). *Z. Tierpsychol.* 44:225–282.

de Waal, F. B. M. 1996. *Good natured: The origins of right and wrong in humans and other animals.* Cambridge, MA: Harvard University Press.

de Waal, F. B. M. 1997a. The chimpanzee's service economy: Food for grooming. *Evol. Hum. Behav.* 18:375–386.

de Waal, F. B. M. 1997b. Food transfers through mesh in brown capuchins. *J. Comp. Psychol.* 111:370–378.

de Waal, F. B. M. 2000. Attitudinal reciprocity in food sharing among brown capuchin monkeys. *Anim. Behav.* 60:253–261.

de Waal, F. B. M., and Luttrell, L. M. 1985. The formal hierarchy of rhesus monkeys: An investigation of the bared teeth display. *Amer. J. Primatol.* 9:73–85.

de Waal, F. B. M., and Luttrell, L. M. 1986. The similarity principle underlying social bonding among female rhesus monkeys. *Folia Primatol.* 46:215–34.

de Waal, F. B. M., and Luttrell, L. M. 1988. Mechanisms of social reciprocity in three primate species: Symmetrical relationship characteristics or cognition? *Ethol. Sociobiol.* 9:101–118.

de Waal, F. B. M., and Berger, M. L. 2000. Payment for labour in monkeys. *Nature* 404:563.

Di Bitetti, M. S. 1997. Evidence for an important social role of grooming in a platyrrhine primate. *Anim. Behav.* 54:199–211.

Dittus, W. P. J. 1979. The evolution of behaviors regulating density and age-specific sex ratios in a primate population. *Behaviour* 69:265–301.

Dittus, W. P. J. 1988. Group fission among wild toque macaques as a consequence of female resource competition and environmental stress. *Anim. Behav.* 36:1626–1645.

Dugatkin, L. A. 1997. *Cooperation among animals.* Oxford: Oxford University Press.

Dunbar, R. I. M. 1983. Theropithecines and hominids: Contrasting solutions to the same ecological problem. *J. Hum. Evol.* 12:647–658.

Dunbar, R. I. M. 1988. *Primate social systems.* London: Croom Helm.

Dunbar, R. I. M. 1991. The functional significance of social grooming in primates. *Folia Primatol.* 57:121–131.

Fairbanks, L. 1980. Relationships among adult females in captive vervet monkeys: Testing a model of rank-related attractiveness. *Anim. Behav.* 28:853–859.

Flack, J. C., and de Waal, F. B. M. 2000. "Any animal whatever." Darwinian building blocks of morality in monkeys and apes. *Journal of Consciousness Studies* 7(1–2), 1–29.

Foley, R. 1987. *Another Unique Species.* Essex, UK: Longman Scientific and Technical.

Gagneux, P., Woodruff, D., and Boesch, C. 1998. Furtive mating in female chimpanzees. *Nature* 387:358–359.

Gagneux, P, Boesch, C., and Woodruff, D. 1999. Female reproductive strategies, paternity, and community structure in wild West African chimpanzees. *Anim. Behav.* 57:19–32.

Galdikas, B. M. F. 1988. Orangutan diet, range, and activity at Tanjung Putting, Central Borneo. *Int. J. Primatol.* 9:1–35.

Garber, P. A. 1997. One for all and breeding for one: Cooperation and competition as a tamarin reproductive strategy. *Evol. Anthropol.* 5:187–199.

Gintis, H. 2000. Strong reciprocity and human sociality. *Journal of Theoretical Biology* 206:169–179.

Goldberg, T., and Wrangham, R. W. 1997. Genetic correlates of social behaviour in wild chimpanzees: Evidence from mitochondrial DNA. *Anim. Behav.* 54:559–570.

Goodall, J. 1986. *The chimpanzees of Gombe: Patterns of behavior.* Cambridge, MA: The Belknap Press.

Goodall, J., Bandura, A., Bergmann, E., Busse, C., Matamo, H., Mpongo, E., Pierece, A., and Riss, D. 1979. Inter-community interactions in the chimpanzee populations of Gombe. In *The great apes*, eds. D. A. Hamburg and E. McCown, 13–53. Menlo Park, CA: Benjamin/Cummings.

Gouzoules, S., and Gouzoules, H. 1987. Kinship. In *Primate societies*, eds. B. B. Smuts, D. L. Cheney, R. M. Seyfarth, R. W. Wrangham, and T. T. Struhsaker, 299–305. Chicago: University of Chicago Press.

Grafen, A. 1991. Modelling in behavioural ecology. In *Behavioural ecology*, eds. J. R. Krebs and N. B. Davies, 5–31. Oxford: Blackwell.

Hamilton, W. D. 1964. The genetical evolution of social behavior. I and II. *J. Theor. Biol.* 7:1–52.

Hamilton, W. D. 1987. Discriminating nepotism: Expectable, common, overlooked. In *Kin recognition in animals*, eds. D. J. C. Fletcher and C. D. Michener, 417–637. New York: John Wiley and Sons.

Harcourt, A. H. 1987. Dominance and fertility among female primates. *J. Zool. Lond.* 213:471–487.

Hauser, M. D. 1997. Minding the behaviour of deception. In *Machiavellian intelligence II* eds. A. Whiten and R. W. Byrne, 112–143. Cambridge: Cambridge University Press.

Hauser, M. D., and Marler, P. 1993a. Food-associated calls in rhesus macaques (*Macaca mulatta*): I. Socioecological factors. *Behav. Ecol.* 4:194–205.

Hauser, M. D., and Marler, P. 1993b. Food-associated calls in rhesus macaques (*Macaca mulatta*): II. Costs and benefits of call production and suppression. *Behav. Ecol.* 4:206–212.

Hauser, M. D., Chen, M. K., Chen, F., and Chuang, E. 2003. Give unto others: Genetically unrelated cotton-top tamarin monkeys preferentially give food to those who altruistically give food back. *Proc. Roy. Soc. London, B.* 270:2363–2370.

Hemelrijk, C. K. 1994. Support for being groomed in long-tailed macaques, *Macaca fasicularis*. *Anim. Behav.* 48:479–481.

Hemelrijk, C. K., and Ek, A. 1991. Reciprocity and interchange of grooming and "support" in captive chimpanzees. *Anim. Behav.* 41:923–935.

Henrich, J. 2004. Inequity aversion in capuchins? *Nature* 428:139.

Henzi, P. 2001. Baboons exchange grooming for tolerance around infants. Paper presented at the XVIIIth Congress of the International Primatological Society, Adelaide, Australia, 7–12 January 2001.

Henzi, S. P., and Barrett, L. 1999. The value of grooming to female primates. *Primates* 40:47–59.

Henzi, S. P., Lycett, J. E., and Weingrill, T. 1997. Cohort size and the allocation of social effort by female mountain baboons. *Anim. Behav.* 54:1235–1243.

Horrocks, J., and Hunte, W. 1983. Maternal rank and offspring rank in vervet monkeys: An appraisal of the mechanisms of rank acquisition. *Anim. Behav.* 31:772–782.

Hunte, W., and Horrocks, J. A. 1987. Kin and non-kin interventions in the aggressive disputes of vervet monkeys. *Behav. Ecol. Sociobiol.* 20:257–263.

Johnson, J. A. 1987. Dominance rank in olive baboons, *Papio anubis*: The influence of gender, size, maternal rank and orphaning. *Anim. Behav.* 35:1694–1708.

Kaplan, J. R. 1977. Patterns of fight interference in free-ranging rhesus monkeys. *Amer. J. Phys. Anthropol.* 47:279–288.

Kaplan, J. R. 1978. Fight interference and altruism in rhesus monkeys. *Amer. J. Phys. Anthropol.* 49:241–249.

Kapsalis, E., and Berman, C. M. 1996a. Models of affiliative relationships among free-ranging rhesus monkeys (*Macaca mulatta*) I. Criteria for kinship. *Behaviour* 133:1209–1234.

Kapsalis, E., and Berman, C. M. 1996b. Models of affiliative relationships among free-ranging rhesus monkeys (*Macaca mulatta*) II. Testing predictions for three hypothesized organized principles. *Behaviour* 133:1235–1263.

Kurland, J. A. 1977. *Kin selection in the Japanese monkey. Contributions to primatology*, vol. 12. Basel: Karger.

Lee, P. C. 1983a. Context-specific unpredictability in dominance interactions. In *Primate social relationships: An integrated approach*, ed. R. A. Hinde, 35–44. Sunderland, MA: Sinauer Associates.

Lee, P. C. 1983b. Effects of the loss of the mother on social development. In *Primate social relationships: An integrated approach*, ed. R. A. Hinde, 73–79. Sunderland, MA: Sinauer Associates.

Lee, P. C., and Oliver, J. I. 1979. Competition, dominance, and the acquisition of rank in juvenile yellow baboons (*Papio cynocephalus*). *Anim. Behav.* 27:576–585.

Linn, G. S., Mase, D., Lafrancois, D., O'Keefe, R. T., and Lifshitz, K. 1995. Social and menstrual cycle phase influences on the behavior of group-housed *Cebus apella*. *Amer. J. Primatol.* 35:41–57.

Maestripieri, D. 1993. Vigilance costs of allogrooming in macaque mothers. *Amer. Nat.* 141:744–753.

Maestripieri, D. 1994. Social structure, infant handling, and mother styles in group-living Old World monkeys. *Int. J. Primatol.* 15:531–553.

Manson, J. H., Rose, L. M., Perry, S., and Gros-Louis, J. 1999. Dynamics of female-female relationships in Wild *Cebus capucinus*: Data from two Costa Rican sites. *Int. J. Primatol.* 20:679–706.

Manson, J. H., Navarette, C. D., Silk, J. B., and Perry, S. 2004. Time-matched grooming in female primates? New analyses from two species. *Anim. Behav.* 67(3):493–500.

Mason, W. A. 1966. Social organization of the South American monkey, *Callicebus molloch*: A preliminary report. *Tulane Studies in Zoology* 13:23–28.

Massey, A. 1977. Agonistic aids and kinship in a group of pig-tail macaques. *Behav. Ecol. Sociobiol.* 2:31–40.

McGrew, W. C. 1992. *Chimpanzee material culture*. Cambridge: Cambridge University Press.

McGrew, W. C., and McLuckie, E. C. 1986. Philopatry and dispersion in the cotton-top tamarin, *Saguinus (o.) oedipus*: An attempted laboratory simulation. *Int. J. Primatol.* 7:401–422.

Mitani, J. C., and Watts, D. P. 2001. Why do chimpanzees hunt and share meat? *Anim. Behav.* 61:915–924.

Mitani, J. C., Merriwether, D., and Zhang, C. 2000. Male affiliation, cooperation and kinship in wild chimpanzees. *Anim. Behav.* 59:885–893.

Mitani, J. C., Watts, D. P., Pepper, J. W., and Merriwether, D. A. 2002. Demographic and social constraints on male chimpanzee behaviour. *Anim. Behav.* 64:727–737.

Muroyama, Y. 1991. Mutual reciprocity of grooming in female Japanese macaques (*Macaca fuscata*). *Behaviour* 119:161–170.

Muroyama, Y. 1994. Exchange of grooming for allomothering in female patas monkeys. *Behaviour* 128:103–119.

Netto, W. J., and van Hooff, J. A. R. A. M. 1986. Conflict interference and the development of dominance relationships in immature *Macaca fasicularis*. In *Primate ontogeny, cognition and social behaviour*, eds. J. G. Else and P. C. Lee, 291–300. Cambridge: Cambridge University Press.

Nishida, T., Hiraiwa-Hasegawa, M., and Takahata, Y. 1985. Group extinction and female transfer in wild chimpanzees in the Mahale Mountains. Z. Tierpsychol. 67:284–301.

Nishida, T., Hosaka, K., Nakamura, M., and Hamai, M. 1995. A within-group gang attack on a young adult male chimpanzee: Ostracism of an ill-mannered member? *Primates* 36:207–211.

Nishida, T., Hasegawa, T., Hayaki, H., Takahata, Y., and Uehara, S. 1992. Meat-sharing as a coalition strategy by an alpha male chimpanzee? In *Topics in primatology:* Volume 1. *Human origins*, ed. T. Nishida, W. C. McGrew, P. Marler, M. Pickford, and F. de Waal, 159–174. Basel: Karger.

Noë, R., and Hammerstein, P. 1995. Biological markets. *Trends Ecol. Evol.* 10:336–340.

O'Brien, T. 1993. Allogrooming behavior among adult female wedge-capped capuchins. *Anim. Behav.* 46:499–510.

Palombit, R. 1994. Dynamic pair bonds in hylobatids: Implications regarding monogamous social systems. *Behaviour* 128(1–2):65–101.

Parr, L. A., Matheson, M. D., Bernstein, I. S., and de Waal, F. B. M. 1997. Grooming down the hierarchy: Allogrooming in captive brown capuchin monkeys, *Cebus apella*. *Animal Behaviour* 54:361–367.

Paul, A. 1999. The socioecology of infant handling in primates: Is the current model convincing? *Primates* 40:33–46.

Paul, A., and Kuester, J. 1987. Dominance, kinship, and reproductive value in female Barbary macaques (*Macaca sylvanus*) at Affenberg, Salem. *Behav. Ecol. Sociobiol.* 21:323–331.

Pérez, A., and Veà, J. J. 2000. Functional implications of allogrooming in *Cercocebus torquatus*. *Int. J. Primatol.* 212:255–268.

Pereira, M. E. 1989. Agonistic interactions of juvenile savannah baboons II. Agonistic support and rank acquisition. *Ethology* 80:152–171.

Perry, S. 1996. Female-female social relationships in wild white-faced capuchin monkeys (*Cebus capucinus*). *Amer. J. Primatol.* 40:167–182.

Pfennig, D. W., and Sherman, P. W. 1995. Kin recognition. *Scientific American* 272(6):98–103.

Pope, T. R. 1990. The reproductive consequences of male cooperation in the red howler monkey: Paternity exclusion in multi-male and single-male troops using genetic markers. *Behav. Ecol. Sociobiol.* 27:439–446.

Pope, T. R. 2000a. The evolution of male philopatry in neotropical monkeys. In *Primate males*, ed. P. M. Kappeler, 219–235. Cambridge: Cambridge University Press.

Pope, T. R. 2000b. Reproductive success increases with degree of kinship in cooperative coalitions of female red howler monkeys (*Alouatta seniculus*). *Behav. Ecol. Sociobiol.* 48:253–267.

Pusey, A. E., and Packer, C. 1987. Dispersal and philopatry. In *Primate societies*, eds. B. B. Smuts, D. L. Cheney, R. M. Seyfarth, R. W. Wrangham, T. T. Struhsaker, 250–266. Chicago: University of Chicago Press.

Pusey, A., and Wolf, M. 1996. Inbreeding avoidance in animals. *Trends Ecol. Evol.* 11:201–206.

Radespiel, U., Lutermann, H., Schmelting, B., Bruford, M. W., and Zimmermann, E. 2003. Patterns and dynamics of sex-biased dispersal in a nocturnal primates, the grey mouse lemur, *Microcebus murinus*. *Anim. Behav.* 65(4):709–719.

Reeve, H. K., and Keller, L. 1999. Levels of selection: Burying the units-of-selection debate and unearthing the crucial new issues. In *Levels of selection in evolution*, ed. L. Keller, 3–14. Princeton, NJ: Princeton University Press.

Reichard, U. 1995. Extra-pair copulations in a monogamous gibbon (*Hylobates lar*). *Ethology* 100:99–112.

Sambrook, T. D., Whiten, A., and Strum, S. C. 1995. Priority of access and grooming patterns of females in a large and small group of olive baboons. *Animal Behaviour* 50:1667–1682.

Saunders, C. D. 1988. Ecological, social, and evolutionary aspects of baboon (*Papio cynocephalus*) grooming behavior. Ph.D. dissertation, Cornell University.

Seyfarth, R. M. 1977. A model of social grooming among adult female monkeys. *J. Theor. Biol.* 65:671–98.

Seyfarth, R. M. 1980. The distribution of grooming and related behaviours among adult female vervet monkeys. *Anim. Behav.* 28:798–813.

Seyfarth, R. M., and Cheney, D. L. 1984. Grooming, alliances, and reciprocal altruism in vervet monkeys. *Nature* 308:541–43.

Seyfarth, R. M., and Cheney, D. L. 1988. Empirical tests of reciprocity theory: Problems in assessment. *Ethol. Sociobiol.* 9:181–188.

Seyfarth, R. M., Cheney, D. L., and Marler, P. 1980. Monkey responses to three different alarm calls: Evidence for predator classification and semantic communication. *Science* 210:801–803.

Silk, J. B. 1982. Altruism among female *Macaca radiata*: Explanations and analysis of patterns of grooming and coalition formation. *Behaviour* 79:162–8.

Silk, J. B. 1987. Social behavior in evolutionary perspective. In *Primate societies*, eds. B. B. Smuts, D. L. Cheney, R. M. Seyfarth, R. W. Wrangham, and T. T. Struhsaker, 318–329. Chicago: University of Chicago Press.

Silk, J. B. 1992. The patterning of intervention among male bonnet macaque: Reciprocity, revenge, and loyalty. *Curr. Anthropol.* 33:318–325.

Silk, J. B. 1993. The evolution of social conflict among primate females. In *Primate social conflict*, eds. W. A. Mason and S. Mendoza, 49–83. Albany: SUNY Press.

Silk, J. B. 1999. Why are infants so attractive to others? The form and function of infant handling in bonnet macaques. *Anim. Behav.* 57:1021–1032.

Silk, J. B. 2002. Kin selection in primate groups. *Intl. J. Primatol.* 23(4):849–875.

Silk, J. B., Cheney, D. L. and Seyfarth, R. M. 1999. The structure of social relationships among female savannah baboons in Moremi Reserve, Botswana. *Behaviour* 136:679–703.

Silk, J. B., Alberts, S. C., and Altmann, J. 2004. Patterns of coalition formation by adult female baboons in Amboseli, Kenya. *Anim. Behav.* 67:573–582.

Simpson, M. 1973. The social grooming of male chimpanzees. In *Comparative ecology and behavior in primates*, eds. R. Michael and J. Crook, 411–505. New York: Academic Press.

Smith, K. L., Alberts, S. C., and Altmann, J. A. 2003. Wild female baboons bias their social behavior toward paternal half-sisters. *Proc. Roy. Soc. Lond. B.* 270:503–510.

Smuts, B. B., Cheney, D. L., Seyfarth, R. M., Wrangham, R. W., and Struhsaker, T. T. (eds.) 1987. *Primate societies*. Chicago: University of Chicago Press.

Stammbach, E. 1978. On social differentiation in groups of captive female hamadryas baboons. *Behaviour* 67:322–338.

Stanford, C. B. 1996. The hunting ecology of wild chimpanzees: implications for the evolutionary ecology of pliocene hominids. *Amer. Anthropol.* 98:96–113.

Stanford, C. B. 1998. *Chimpanzees and red colobus: The ecology of predator and prey.* Cambridge, MA: Harvard University Press.

Stanford, C. B., Wallis, J., Matama, H., and Goodall, J. 1994. Patterns of predation by chimpanzees on red colobus monkeys in Gombe National Park, Tanzania, 1982–1991. *Amer. J. Phys. Anthropol.* 94:213–229.

Starin, E. D. 1994. Philopatry and affiliation among red colobus. *Behaviour* 130:252–270.

Stevens, J. R., and Hauser, M. D. 2004. Why be nice? Psychological constraints on the evolution of cooperation. *Trends Cog. Sci.* 8:60–65.

Strier, K. B. 1992. *Faces in the forest.* Cambridge, MA: Harvard University Press.

Strier, K. B. 2000. From binding brotherhoods to short-term sovereignty: The dilemma of male Cebidae. In *Primate males*, ed. P. M. Kappeler, 72–83. Cambridge: Cambridge University Press.

Struhsaker, T. T. 1967. Auditory communication among vervet monkeys (*Cercopithecus aethiops*). In *Social communication among primates*, ed. S. A. Altmann, 281–324. Chicago: University of Chicago Press.

Struhsaker, T. T. 2000. Variation in adult sex ratios of red colobus monkey social groups: Implications for interspecific comparisons. In *Primate males*, ed. P. Kappeler, 108–119. Cambridge: Cambridge University Press.

Symington, M. M. 1990. Fission-fusion social organization in *Ateles* and *Pan*. *Int. J. Primatol.* 11:47–62.

Takahata, Y., Hasegawa, T., and Nishida, T. 1984. Chimpanzee predation in the Mahale Mountains from August 1979 to May 1982. *Int. J. Primatol.* 5:213–233.

Teleki, G. 1973. *The predatory behavior of wild chimpanzees*. Lewisburg, PA: Bucknell University Press.

Trivers, R. L. 1971. The evolution of reciprocal altruism. *Q. Rev. Biol.* 46:35–57.

Uehara, S., Nishida, T., Hamai, M., Hasegawa, T., Hayaki, H., Huffman, M., Kawanaka, K., Kobayashi, S., Mitani, J., Takahata, Y., Takasaki, H., and Tsukahara, T. 1992. Characteristics of predation by the chimpanzees in the Mahali Mountains National Park, Tanzania. In *Topics in primatology:* Volume 1. *Human origins*, ed. T. Nishida, W. C. McGrew, P. Marler, M. Pickford, and F. de Waal, 143–158. Basel: Karger.

van Schaik, C. P., and Janson, C. H. 2000. Infanticide by males: Prospectus. In *Infanticide by males and its implications*, eds. C. P. van Schaik and C. H. Janson, 1–6. Cambridge: Cambridge University Press.

Walters, J. R. 1980. Interventions and the development of dominance relationships in female baboons. *Folia Primatol.* 34:61–89.

Walters, J. R. 1987. Kin recognition in non-human primates. In *Kin recognition in animals*, eds. D. J. C. Fletcher and C. D. Michener, 359–393. New York: John Wiley and Sons.

Watanabe, K. 1979. Alliance formation in a free-ranging troop of Japanese macaques. *Primates* 20:459–474.

Watts, D. P. 1998. Coalitionary mate guarding by male chimpanzees at Ngogo, Kibale National Park, Uganda. *Behav. Ecol. Sociobiol.* 44:43–55.

Watts, D. P. 2000. Grooming between male chimpanzees at Ngogo, Kibale National Park. I. Partner number and diverity and grooming reciprocity. *Int. J. Primatol.* 21:189–210.

Watts, D. P., and Mitani, J. C. 2001. Border patrols and intergroup encounters in wild chimpanzees. *Behaviour* 138(3):299–327.

Watts, D. P., and Mitani, J. C. 2002. Hunting behavior of chimpanzees at Ngogo, Kibale National Park, Uganda. *Int. J. Primatol.* 23(1):1–28.

Widdig, A., and Nürnberg, P. 2001. Paternal kin discirimination in adult female rhesus macaques at Cayo Santiago. Paper presented at the XVIIIth Congress of the International Primatological Society, Adelaide, Australia, 7–12 January 2001.

Wilson, D. S. 1997. Altruism and organism: disentangling the themes of multilevel selection theory. *Am. Nat.* 150:S122–134.

Wimmer, B., Tautz, D., and Kappeler, P. M. 2002. The genetic population structure of the grey mouse lemur (*Microcebus murinus*), a basal primate from Madagascar. *Behav. Ecol. Sociobiol.* 52:166–175.

Wrangham, R. W. 1980. An ecological model of female-bonded primate groups. *Behaviour* 75:262–300.

Wrangham, R. W., and Smuts, B. B. 1980. Sex differences in the behavioral ecology of chimpanzees. *J. Reprod. Fertil. Suppl.* 28:13–31.

3

The Natural History of Human Food Sharing and Cooperation: A Review and a New Multi-Individual Approach to the Negotiation of Norms

Hillard Kaplan and Michael Gurven

3.1 Introduction

Humans share food unlike any other organism does. Many other animals, including eusocial insects (bees, ants, termites); social carnivores (lions, wolves, wild dogs); some species of birds (e.g., ravens) and vampire bats actively share food. However, the patterning and complexity of food sharing among humans is truly unique. Unlike other mammals, for which food sharing between mothers and offspring is limited largely to lactation during infancy, human parents provision their children until adulthood.[1] Moreover, the sharing of food between human parents and their children continues bidirectionally until death in most traditional non-market societies. Additionally, marriage is universal among human societies, and husbands and wives regularly share food with one another throughout their marriage. Food sharing within human families is based upon a division of labor in subsistence effort by age and sex, where tasks are divided and the proceeds of work are shared. In fact, within-family transfers of food are so universal among humans that they are largely taken for granted and have rarely been systematically studied. This gap in anthropological research is ironic, since the sexual division of labor and the concomitant sharing of food between spouses and between parents and offspring have figured prominently in several models of hominid evolution (e.g., Isaac 1978; Lancaster and Lancaster 1983).

In addition to within-family food transfers, food sharing sometimes extends beyond the nuclear family in many societies. Most recent research on food sharing has focused on food transfers among adults living in different households. The majority of this research has been conducted in small-scale societies, particularly hunter-gatherers and groups that combine simple horticulture with hunting and gathering (forager-horticulturalists). There are two reasons for this focus. First, interfamilial food sharing is pervasive among hunter-gatherers and many forager-horticulturalists; they are often referred to as "egalitarian societies." Second, hominids lived as hunter-gatherers for the vast majority of their evolutionary history (which has lasted over two million years). Agriculture originated only about 10,000 years ago and has been practiced by the majority of the world's population for only two or three millennia. Since most hunter-gatherers share food on a daily basis, studies of food transfers among foragers may provide important insights into the evolutionary basis of human food sharing and more generally, about the origins of human hyper-sociality.

This chapter has three principal objectives. The first is to provide a brief overview of existing theory and research about food sharing in small-scale societies for nonspecialists. In the first part of the chapter, we outline the principal hypotheses proposed to account for variation in food sharing and evaluate available evidence pertaining to these hypotheses. The second objective is to present evidence regarding why we consider it necessary to rethink existing approaches to food sharing. In this second part of the chapter, we argue that intrafamilial resource flows are critical to the understanding of interfamilial sharing and that neither the human life course nor human intelligence could have evolved without long-term imbalances in flows of food between families. We suggest that future research on this topic should consider small-group decision processes and the emergence of institutionalized sharing norms. In the third part of the chapter, we review several case studies of food sharing in different societies and across contexts within societies as a preliminary step towards building a theory of how these norms may correspond to local ecological conditions. The chapter concludes with a discussion of new directions for research and some major unresolved questions that should be addressed.

3.2   Part I: Theories and Empirical Evidence

Six different theories have been proposed to explain the existence and patterning of intragroup food sharing.

I. *Reciprocal altruism*
Several investigators have proposed that reciprocal altruism (Trivers 1971), where food is exchanged at one point in time for food at some later time, may explain many or most cases of human food sharing

(Kaplan and Hill 1985; Winterhalder 1986; Smith 1988). The pervasiveness of reciprocal food sharing among humans is commonly explained in terms of the kinds of foods they acquire and their inherently "risky" nature (Kaplan and Hill 1985; Winterhalder 1986; Smith 1988). Human hunter-gatherers tend to specialize on the largest, highest-quality, most nutrient-dense foods available in their environments (Kaplan et al. 2000), and as a result, they experience high variance in foraging luck due to the difficulty in acquiring these items. For example, individual Ache hunters return empty-handed on 40 percent of the days they hunt, but on some days return with several hundred thousand calories of meat (Hill and Hawkes 1983). Hunting success is even more sporadic among large-game hunters, such as the Hadza, who only acquire meat on about 3 percent of their hunting days (Hawkes, O'Connell, and Blurton Jones 1991).

Since there are diminishing returns to consumption of large quantities of food (especially in environments where spoilage is a problem) and because food portions are very valuable to hungry individuals, reciprocal sharing can significantly reduce variation in day-to-day consumption and maximize the intertemporal utility of food. Reciprocal altruism therefore allows people to devote time and energy to the pursuit of large, asynchronously acquired, high-quality packages. Trade is a special form of reciprocal altruism where the return benefits of giving are in another currency, such as meat for sex, food for labor, or fish for yams. However, when the return benefit is a non-food currency, such as increased mate access, such sharing does not serve the goal of risk-reduction.

II. *Cooperative acquisition and byproduct mutualism*
Sharing may also enable individuals to achieve gains from cooperative pursuits of food. The acquisition of difficult-to-acquire foods, especially wild game, often requires the coordinated efforts of several individuals. However, usually only a single individual is identified as the owner of the acquired resource, determined by cultural-specific norms of ownership (e.g., the hunter who makes first lethal shot, the finder, the killer [Dowling 1968]). In many groups, sharing among task group members occurs as an initial wave of sharing (e.g., Pygmies [Bailey 1991; Harako 1976]). Owners may reward nonowners for their current cooperation by giving them shares of the resource, but this sharing may also act as a means of insuring future cooperation in similar food production activities. Thus, sharing is a form of trade-based reciprocal altruism, where labor is rewarded with food.

An alternative interpretation of the same phenomenon is that engaging in group production when there is sharing provides participants with higher per capita returns than if they produced food by themselves. Thus, group production may represent a form of byproduct mutualism (Clements and Stephens 1995; Dugatkin 1997; Alvard and Nolin 2002). Once rigid sharing norms exist in a population, the decision to participate in, say, a group whale hunt or cooperative monkey hunt should depend only on the higher per capita return rates relative to those that could be gained in solitary subsistence activities (see Alvard 2002). Thus, an advantage of strong sharing norms is that they act to transform the payoff structure of group food production strategies from that of a Prisoner's Dilemma to that of mutualism.

III. *Tolerated theft or scrounging*

Building on the same insights regarding large asynchronously acquired food packages and diminishing returns to consumption of large food quantities, others have proposed that much apparent voluntary sharing may actually be "theft" or scrounging of food from food acquirers by individuals who have little or none (Blurton Jones 1984, 1987). This hypothesis is based upon the assumption that asymmetries between individuals in the marginal value of additional food can lead to contests over packages. The hungry person is more motivated to fight, while the person with more should relinquish some food because the lost food value is not worth the fight (Blurton Jones 1987; Winterhalder 1996). When power or "resource holding potential" is equal among contestants, a simple prediction of tolerated scrounging is that distributions will be highly egalitarian—such that any additional food portions have the same marginal value for each contestant (Winterhalder 1996).

Proponents of this view have pointed out that tolerated theft in the context of large, highly variable foods raises a secondary problem. Why do people spend time foraging for large packages if they know that much of what they acquire will be taken from them? Scrounging of large packages may effectively reduce their per capita consumption return rate below several other food production options in the environment, especially the pursuit of small packages (Hawkes 1993). To answer this question, Hawkes (1991, 1992, 1993) proposed that the pursuit of large packages, particularly hunted foods, is very sex-biased and that men acquire large packages to "show off" and garner attention. Men focus their efforts on acquiring large packages, precisely because others will scrounge from them. As a result, these men will gain the attention and support of scroungers, many of whom will be women. The payoffs to this attention presumably come in the form of increased access to mates and an increased number of offspring.

IV. *Costly signaling*

Costly signaling is an extension of the show-off hypothesis that may explain why certain individuals (usually men) pursue difficult-to-acquire foods that often yield suboptimal caloric return rates (Smith and Bliege Bird 2000; Gurven, Allen-Arave et al. 2000; Bliege Bird, Smith, and Bird 2001). The costliness of the signal insures the honesty of the information being advertised (Zahavi and Zahavi 1997; Grafen 1990; Johnstone 1997). The signal might provide information about phenotypic quality (such as disease-resistance) or about intentions to cooperate in the future. Recipients of the signal confer benefits on the generous donor not as payback for food given, but because information about the donor's phenotypic quality makes that donor a desirable partner, mate, or ally. Costly signaling differs from showing off because it does not rely on tolerated theft to explain food transfers. Additionally, because the honesty of the signal makes the signaler an attractive partner, costly signaling avoids the second-order–collective action problem of who should pay prestige back to good hunters.

V. *Nepotism based on kin selection*

Because biologically related individuals share genes by descent, any behavior that sufficiently benefits kin can be favored by natural selection. According to models developed by Hamilton (1964), natural selection will favor altruism to kin when the benefits to the recipient, discounted by Wright's coefficient of genetic relatedness between donor and recipient, outweigh the costs of giving. A simple prediction is that, all else being equal, close kin should receive shares either more frequently or in greater quantities than distantly related and unrelated individuals (Feinman 1979). It has also been argued we should expect to find greater imbalances in quantities given and received among close kin than among nonkin or distant kin (Hames 1987; Feinman 1979), who, presumably, would only share reciprocally. However, this might not be true if close kin are also reciprocity partners and if reciprocal altruism is an important factor influencing food transfers among kin (Gurven, Hill et al. 2000).

VI. *Trait-group selection*

Selection among groups has also been proposed in order to explain cooperation and food sharing within human groups (Wilson 1998; Boyd and Richerson in press; Boehm 1993). In group selection models, the relative fitness of altruists is lower than that of selfish individuals within groups, but the average fitness of individuals in groups containing more altruistic members is greater than those in groups containing fewer altruists. Group selection could favor costly food sharing if the increased absolute fitness of altruists among groups in a metapopulation outweighs the decrease in relative fitness within groups, where "group" refers to any congregation of individuals (Wilson 1990, 1998). While the conditions favoring trait-group selection are much less stringent than those of older group selection models, its overall influence is still limited by grouping patterns and migration, and ultimately may be no more revealing than egoistic models (Harpending 1998; Krebs 1987). However, given the conflict between group and individual interests, cultural means of encouraging individuals to share food may increase the frequency of giving within groups (Simon 1990; Boyd and Richerson in press), leading to socially enforced egalitarian behavior (Boehm 1993).

3.2.1 Cross-cultural Evidence

There is a great deal of cross-cultural evidence that sharing is most common for large packaged resources characterized by high acquisition variance, especially wild game. Widespread pooling of large game animals is common among the Hadza (Hawkes 1993; Marlowe n.d.), Dobe !Kung (Lee 1979; Marshall 1976), G/wi (Silberbauer 1981), Ifaluk (Sosis, Feldstein, and Hill 1998), Ache (Kaplan and Hill 1985), Yanomamo (Hames 1990), and Gunwinggu (Altman 1987). While such pooling can significantly reduce variation in daily meat consumption, the outcome of risk reduction is consistent with all six models, even though risk reduction is only explicitly incorporated as a goal within the reciprocal altruism and group selection frameworks. This is because widespread sharing of relatively large sized game items, characterized by high within- and across-individual variability in acquisition, can be explained by future reciprocation (reciprocal altruism), demands and threats of hungry individuals (tolerated theft), honest signals of phenotypic quality (costly signaling), and the Pareto-optimal distribution solution maximizing group benefit (trait-group selection). Because the costs of sharing decrease with increased package size of the resource (assuming diminishing returns), it is not surprising that large package size is a significant predictor of sharing for meat and other food items such as fruits, cultigens, and market foods (Hames 1990; Gurven, Hill et al. 2000; Gurven, Hill, and Kaplan 2002; Kitanishi 1998).

Thus the observation that the sharing of large packages is widespread does not help distinguish between the models discussed in section 3.2. The empirical findings relevant to understanding which models are most appropriate for explaining much of the variance in sharing within and across groups are generally concerned with three issues: contingency of giving upon receiving, producer control over distributions, and imbalances between families in what is given and received.

3.2.1.1 Contingency Contingency is the feature of sharing relationships that is critical for distinguishing between reciprocal altruism and other models (Rothstein and Pierroti 1988; Hill and Kaplan 1993). *General* contingency requires that all giving be balanced by all receiving, while *specific* contingency requires that giving to specific others be balanced by receipts from those same individuals (Hames 2000; Gurven, Hill et al. 2000). Specific contingency is usually estimated as the correlation between the percentage or quantity of food given by A to B with the percentage or quantity given by B to A over some appropriate sample period. Contingency can be measured within food categories (such as meat for meat, roots for roots, and so forth) or for all food, which includes exchange across food types. In order for reciprocal altruism to be beneficial to a donor, donors should preferentially give to those who are likely to share with them in the future (specific contingency). Costly signaling, on the other hand, requires that the prestige-related benefits from signaling outweigh the costs of producing food that is widely shared (general contingency). Neither tolerated theft, kin selection, nor trait-group selection predict that food donations will be conditional upon expected return.

Specific contingency has only been measured in four groups, all of which are in South America—the Yanomamo (Hames 2000), Hiwi (Gurven, Hill et al. 2000), Ache (Gurven, Allen-Arave et al. 2000), and Pilaga (Henry 1951). Correlations which describe specific contingency for all foods are significantly greater than zero, but not very high (between 0.2 and 0.5 [Gurven in press], see discussion of imbalances in section 3.2.1.3), while within resource categories, contingency is often highest for cultivated and collected foods. These results are most consistent with reciprocal altruism and least consistent with tolerated theft, because tolerated theft predicts that there should be no relationship between giving and receiving.[2] Among the Ache, however, there is no evidence of specific contingency for wild game over the duration of single foraging trips, nor for game items brought back to the permanent colony. This is inconsistent with reciprocal altruism, unless sharing among the Ache rewards group work effort (cooperative acquisition and mutualism, discussed in part III). Nevertheless, further research is needed to determine whether these significant positive correlations imply that the time-discounted value of food returns is sufficient to offset the present costs of giving.

Anecdotal evidence that giving is balanced by future receiving and that those who do not give do not receive is found in many traditional societies. As one Maimande explained, "If one doesn't give, one doesn't get in return ... Some people are specifically excluded from most distributions because they never or only rarely give any of their products to us" (Aspelin 1979, 317). Similar anecdotes exist among the Agta (Peterson 1978; Bion Griffin personal communication), Pintupi (Myers 1988), Siriono (Holmberg 1969, 45), and G/wi (Silberbauer 1981, 463). Although there is an emphasis on peoples' expectations for future receipt in these and other ethnographies, the extent of time depth separating episodes of giving and receiving is often unclear. Indeed, Sahlins' (1972) use of the term "generalized reciprocity" was meant to reflect short-term imbalances, especially among kin, that are eventually balanced over the span of peoples' lives.

General contingency or balance has been measured in five societies—the Ache (Gurven, Hill, and Kaplan 2002), Hiwi (Gurven, Hill et al. 2000), Meriam (Bliege Bird and Bird 1997), Pilaga (our analysis of Henry 1951), and Yanomamo (Hames 2000). These studies showed mixed support for general balance. While the lack of specific balance contradicts reciprocal altruism, the presence of general balance is consistent with indirect reciprocity (Alexander 1987; Boyd and Richerson 1989) or costly signaling, where the return benefit to the donor is food. If the return benefit is in another currency, such as increased mating opportunities, then a lack of general balance is not inconsistent with costly signaling.

3.2.1.2 Producer Control Reciprocal altruism and kin selection require that producers maintain some control over the distribution of foods they acquire, whereas tolerated theft assumes no producer "rights." If producers have no control over the distribution of certain items, then those food items may act as partial public goods (Dowling 1968; Hawkes 1993). Despite observations of widespread game distributions in some groups (e.g., Ache [Kaplan and Hill 1985], G/wi [Silberbauer 1981], Hadza [Hawkes 1993], Western Desert Aborigines

[Gould 1980]), several lines of evidence indicate that producers often maintain significant control over distributions in many—if not most—cultures. First, as shown in the previous section, there is often a bias in sharing towards those who shared with the producer. Additionally, there are clear biases in distributions towards close kin living in other families at the expense of distant kin and unrelated families (Gunwinggu [Altman 1987], Copper and Netsilik Eskimo [Damas 1972], Pilaga [Henry 1951], Hiwi [Gurven, Hill et al. 2000], Kaingang [Henry 1941], Batek [Endicott 1988], Pintupi [Myers 1988], Washo [Price 1975], Yanomamo [Hames 1990], Machiguenga [Kaplan 1994], Ache [Kaplan and Hill 1985; Gurven, Hill, and Kaplan 2002], Ifaluk [Sosis 1997], Basarwa [Cashdan 1985]), and to those participating in the hunting party (Netsilik Eskimo [Damas 1972], Nyae Nyae !Kung [Marshall 1976], Ifaluk [Sosis 1997], Pintupi [Myers 1988], Washo [Price 1975], Mbuti [Ichikawa 1983], Aka [Bahuchet 1990; Kitanishi 1998], Efe [Bailey 1991], Lamalera [Alvard 2002], Northwest Coast Indians [Gould 1980]). Among the Hiwi and Ache at the settlement, there are clear kin biases in sharing, even when controlling for residential distance. Finally, several ethnographies are explicit about the ownership of shares after an initial distribution, even if others still have not received any meat (Efe [Bailey 1991, 100]; Nyae Nyae !Kung [Marshall 1976, 363]).

Second, hunters frequently consume portions of kills (e.g., internal organs and marrow) at the kill site and usually no one begrudges them this right (Batek [Endicott 1988]; Hadza [Marlowe n.d.]; Nyae Nyae !Kung [Marshall 1976]; G/wi [Silberbauer 1981]). Third, producers often keep significantly more than $1/n$ of the game packages they acquire, even though others in the camp or village may not possess any meat (Gunwinggu [Altman 1987]; Yora [Hill and Kaplan 1989]; Yuqui [Stearman 1989]; Yanomamo [Hames 2000]; Hadza [Hawkes et al. 2001]; Ache [Gurven, Allen-Arave et al. 2001]; Hiwi [Gurven, Hill et al. 2000]). Finally, the frequent observations of incessant demands for food in many foraging societies (Peterson 1993; Chagnon 1983) does not mean that producers are powerless to ignore or reject requests for food made by other group members. There is evidence that nonproducers do not possess automatic claims to shares among the Pintupi (Myers 1988), the Aka (Bahuchet 1990, 38), Agta (Griffin 1984), Pilaga (Henry 1951), and Sirionó (Holmberg 1969, 88).

3.2.1.3 Imbalances: Relative Need, Bargaining, and Signaling Several ethnographies have reported large short-term between-family imbalances, but long-term balance in food transfers, consistent with generalized reciprocity (e.g., Batek [Endicott 1988, 118]; Kaingang [Henry 1941, 101]). While short-term imbalances are relatively easy to measure, the existence of long-term balances in terms of lifelong symbiosis is much more difficult to confirm. Nepotistic food sharing based on kin selection can predict imbalances in food sharing, even though kinship is a symmetrical relationship. Food given to dependent and unskilled offspring and relatives can have a large benefit at a relatively small cost to a skilled producer ($B > C$ in Hamilton's Rule). Similarly, the downward flow of food provides useful calories to younger kin of higher reproductive value (Rogers 1993). Over the course of an individual's lifetime, current evidence suggests that among the Ache, Piro, Machiguenga, and perhaps other traditional groups, children are net costs to parents, and thus children's debt is never repaid directly, but is instead redirected to grandchildren (Kaplan 1994; see part II of this chapter). We should expect to find smaller short-term imbalances in transfers among kin of similar age. Allen-Arave et al. (n.d.) find that among the Ache, imbalances over a four-month sample period are smaller among kin of similar ages (e.g., siblings) than among kin of disparate ages (e.g., between older parents and their adult offspring).

Apart from kinship, there is good evidence that large short-term and long-term exchange imbalances among individuals and families occur among foragers and forager-horticulturalists. The highest food producers among the Ache, Efe, Pilaga, and Yuqui consistently gave away more than they received as compared to low producers (Kaplan and Hill 1985; Gurven, Allen-Arave et al. 2000; Bailey 1991; Henry 1941; Stearman 1989). Indeed, observations that high producing Ache and Hadza hunters often do not receive in-kind compensation for their generosity initially led to the proposition that reciprocal altruism was an inadequate model of human food sharing (Hawkes 1991, 1993).

Imbalances in quantities transferred across individuals or families can be interpreted in several ways. First, the short-term nature of most field studies places an arbitrary horizon on the delayed time for reciprocation, and the sampling bias associated with any brief series of snapshots of interfamily exchange relations is likely to result in some degree of imbalance. Hames (2000) argues that meticulous scorekeeping meant to ensure balance should be found across pairs of distantly interacting individuals, where trust is weak (e.g., market transactions), while imbalances might be quite common among individuals who interact over extensive periods of time.

Second, an imbalance may be intentional if sharing is based on the signaling of phenotypic or genotypic quality. Imbalances in turtle meat exchanges, where hunters expend a great deal of energy to provide community feasts, are most likely due to costly signaling (Bliege Bird and Bird 1997; Smith and Bliege Bird 2000). Similarly, an imbalance is expected if the return benefits of reciprocal altruism or costly signaling are in other currencies. High-producing Ache hunters may give away more than they receive, but they obtain greater mating opportunities and higher offspring survivorship (Hill and Hurtado 1996). Yuqui and Tsimane hunters sometimes trade portions of their kills for garden products (Stearman 1989; Chicchón 1992), while Kuikuyu with unsuccessful gardens will trade labor for access to a neighbor's manioc patches (Carneiro 1983).

As mentioned above, contingency estimates well below 1.0 suggest a relatively high occurrence of exchange imbalances among pairs of families. It is important to mention that all measures of contingency are based on *quantities* of food shared among families. Bargaining theory, however, can lead to outcomes consistent with reciprocal altruism but inconsistent with strong balance in food quantities (Ståhl 1972; Hill and Kaplan 1993; Sosis, Feldstein, and Hill 1998; Gurven, Hill et al. 2000). If donors continue giving portions to others as long as the expected future benefits outweigh the current costs of giving relative to other options, there is no reason to expect the exchange of equal quantities over time. The extent of imbalance should be a function of differential wealth holdings, influence, status, and need. One calculation of contingency that measured the balance in "value" transferred across families—by incorporating the frequency and sizes of shares—found a slightly higher level of balance among Hiwi and Ache foragers (Gurven 2004).

There has been much written on the importance of "need" and the direction of food flows (Woodburn 1982; Barnard and Woodburn 1988; Winterhalder 1996), supporting the notion that "if there is hunger, it is commonly shared" (Marshall 1976, 357) and possibly the group selection hypothesis. Among the Ache, Maimande, G/wi, and Hiwi, shares are often given in proportion to the number of consumers within the recipient family (Gurven, Hill, and Kaplan 2002; Aspelin 1979; Silberbauer 1981; Gurven, Hill et al. 2000). Batek families with high dependency tend be net consumers while those with low dependency are net producers (Cadelina 1982). There is additional evidence that older men, with larger families, preferentially benefit from sharing networks at the expense of younger men's labor, especially if one considers brideservice payments (Efe [Bailey 1991], Gunwinggu [Altman 1987], Kutse [Kent 1993], Yanomamo [Ritchie 1996], and Agta [Bion Griffin 1984]). Differential need among families leads to different costs and benefits of giving across families, and should therefore influence bargaining outcomes and observed levels of balance. We explore this issue further in part II of this chapter.

Although certain levels of imbalance may be due to differential need, there is much evidence to suggest that such imbalances are sometimes tolerated only within limits. Those who do not produce or share enough are often subject to criticism, either directly or through gossip, and social ostracism. Anecdotes of shirkers being excluded from distributions until they either boosted their production or sharing levels are found among the Maimande (Aspelin 1979), Pilaga (Henry 1951, 199), Gunwinggu (Altman 1987, 147), Washo (Price 1975, 16), Machiguenga (Baksh and Johnson 1990), Agta (Griffin 1984, 20), and Netsilik Eskimo (Balikci 1970, 177). However, other ethnographies report the persistence of long-term imbalances without any obvious punishment, exclusion, or ostracism (Chácobo [Prost 1980, 52]; Kaingang [Henry 1941, 101]; Batek [Endicott 1988, 119]), although these anecdotes suggest that such imbalances are due to a small number of low producers within the group.

In summary, there is substantial cross-cultural evidence supporting the view that reciprocal altruism of some sort underlies much food-sharing behavior. First, in many societies producers appear to exert control over the distribution of resources. Second, although specific contingency of giving upon receiving has been measured in only a few cases, there is evidence over the short term that people form preferential food-sharing partnerships with high rates of giving and receiving and share less with those who give less (meat sharing in the forest among the Ache is one exception, however) (Kaplan and Hill 1985). There are also a plethora of qualitative reports suggesting that giving and receiving are contingent in many or most cultures and in different contexts.

At the same time, persistent imbalances in amounts given and received between families suggest that strict reciprocal altruism cannot account for all food sharing between families. Some of those imbalances may be due to kin selection, costly signaling, tolerated theft, trait-group selection or some combination of these four forces. In the next section, we sketch the importance of food sharing in the evolution of human life. We show that the evolved life history of humans required long-term imbalances in food flows. We also present a new way to understand imbalances in terms of multi-individual decision processes and long-term mutual benefit.

3.3   Part II: Human Life History and Food Sharing

3.3.1   Features of Our Human Life History

The distinctive life history of humans is related to their unique foraging niche relative to that of other mammals (and even primates). Five distinctive features of the human life course are noteworthy.

1) an exceptionally long lifespan

2) an extended period of juvenile dependence

3) support of reproduction by older post-reproductive individuals

4) male support of reproduction through the provisioning of females and their offspring

5) a large brain and its associated capacities for learning, cognition, and insight

Humans have a very flexible foraging strategy, consuming different foods in different environments, and this flexibility has allowed us to survive successfully in all of the world's terrestrial environments. In another sense, however, the human foraging niche is very specialized. In every environment, human foragers consume the largest, most nutrient-dense, highest-quality, and most difficult-to-acquire foods, using techniques that often take years to learn (Kaplan et al. 2000, Kaplan 1997).

This foraging niche is related to human life history because high levels of knowledge, skill, coordination, and strength are required to exploit the suite of high-quality, difficult-to-acquire resources humans consume. The attainment of those abilities requires time, a significant commitment to development, and a large brain to support the learning, information processing, and planning underlying those skills. This extended learning phase during which productivity is low can be compensated by higher productivity during the adult period and subsidized by an intergenerational flow of food from old to young. Since productivity increases with age, the time investment in skill acquisition and knowledge leads to selection for lowered mortality rates and greater longevity, because the returns on the investments in development occur at older ages.

There are three foraging groups (the Ache, Hadza, and Hiwi) and two groups of forager-horticulturalists (the Machiguenga and Piro) for whom quantitative data are available regarding age-profiles of food consumption and production. All of these groups display similar age-profiles of net food production. Children are largely supported by their parents until about age eighteen (when food production approximately equals consumption), after which productivity rises steeply through the twenties until the mid-thirties. The more skill-intensive the task, the greater is the delay to peak performance and the greater the increase in productivity with "on-the-job-training" (Bock 2002). High productivity is maintained until the mid-sixties when the deleterious effects of senescence become significant. This pattern of development and aging bears a striking resemblance to modern societies, where wages depend on education-based capital and the ages eighteen and sixty-five have similar significance.

Figure 3.1 shows survival probabilities and net production by age for wild chimpanzees, our closest living relatives, and modern human hunter-gatherers living under conditions similar to our evolutionary

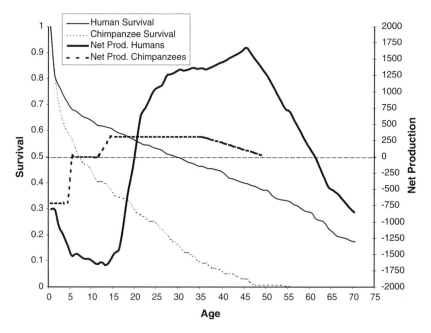

Figure 3.1
Survival and net food production: Human foragers and chimpanzees. Adapted from Kaplan, Lancaster, and Robson 2003.

past (see Kaplan et al. 2000, 2001 for details on data sources). It is evident that the chimpanzee net production curve shows three distinct phases. The first phase, to about age five, is the period of complete to partial dependence upon mother's milk and of negative net production. The second phase is independent juvenile growth, lasting until adulthood, during which net production is zero. The third phase is reproductive, during which females, but not males, produce a surplus of calories that they allocate to nursing. Humans, in contrast, produce less than they consume for about twenty years. Net production becomes increasingly negative until about age fourteen and then begins to climb. Net production in adulthood in humans is much higher than in chimpanzees and peaks at a much older age, reflecting the payoff of long dependency. More precisely, human peak net production is about 1,750 calories per day, reached at about age forty-five. Among chimpanzee females, peak net production is only about 250 calories per day and, since fertility decreases with age, net productivity probably decreases throughout adulthood. By age fifteen, chimpanzees have consumed 43 percent and produced 40 percent of their expected lifetime calories, respectively; in contrast, humans have consumed 22 percent and produced only 4 percent of their expected lifetime calories! In fact, the human production profile requires a long lifespan and would not be viable with chimpanzee survival rates, since expected lifetime net production would be negative (Kaplan et al. 2000).

These results imply a highly structured life course in which physiological and behavioral processes are coordinated. The greater proliferation of neurons in early fetal development among humans, as compared to monkeys and apes, has cascading effects, extending other phases of brain development and ultimately resulting in a larger, more complex, and effective brain. From a behavioral point of view, although cognitive development is largely complete among chimpanzees by about eight years of age, formal abstract logical reasoning does not emerge in humans until age sixteen to eighteen. This is the age when productivity begins to increase dramatically among human foragers.

3.3.2   The Evolutionary Role of Sharing

A central thesis of this chapter is that the human life course could not have evolved without long-term imbalances in food transfer within and among families. First, it is clear from the above figures that if children are eating more than they produce for some twenty years, those deficits must be subsidized. Surplus food provided by older people and those with few dependents can be utilized to finance this long developmental period.

Second, those data represent average production and consumption by age, combining data from both sexes. Men and women, however, specialize in different forms of skill acquisition with correspondingly different foraging niches and activity budgets and then share the fruits of their labor. The specialization generates two forms of complementarity. Hunted foods acquired by men complement gathered foods acquired by women, because protein, fat, and carbohydrates complement one another with respect to their nutritional functions (see Hill 1988 and Hames 1989 for a review) and because most gathered foods, such as roots, palm fiber, and fruits are low in fat and protein (nuts are an exception). The fact that male specialization in hunting produces high delivery rates of large, shareable packages of food leads to another form of complementarity. The meat inputs of men shift the optimal mix of activities for women, increasing time spent in childcare and decreasing time spent in food acquisition. They also shift women's time to foraging and productive activities that are compatible with childcare and away from activities that are dangerous to them and their children.

There are data on the productivity of adults for ten foraging societies (see Kaplan et al. 2000 for details). On average, men acquired 68 percent of the calories and almost 88 percent of the protein; women acquired the remaining 32 percent of calories and 12 percent of protein. After subtracting their own consumption (31 percent of total calories), women supply only 3 percent of their offspring's caloric deficit (i.e., children's consumption minus their production), while men provide the remaining 97 percent! Men not only supply all of the protein to offspring, but also the bulk of the protein consumed by women. This contrasts sharply with most mammalian species (> 97 percent), where the female supports all of the energetic needs of the offspring until it begins eating solid foods (Clutton-Brock 1991) and the male provides little or no investment.

In addition to specialization among men and women, specialization in productive activities by age is equally important. Foragers and forager-horticulturalists typically assign low skill/low strength activities (such as collecting fruits or fetching water) to children, high strength/high skill activities (such as hunting and extractive foraging) to prime-aged adults, and low strength/high skill activities (such as child care and craft manufacture) to elderly people (Bock 2002; Gurven and Kaplan n.d.; Kramer 1998). In this way, family returns from labor are maximized. It also appears to be the case that there is some specialization in activities within age-sex classes. Although this is less documented, anecdotal reports suggest that some men spend more time gathering or farming and others more time hunting (Tsimane [Chicchón 1992], Yuqui [Stearman 1989]), and there is even specialization in hunting roles and in prey types pursued.

There are also imbalances between families that support this intensive mothering characteristic of human life histories. Figure 3.2 (adapted from Lancaster et al. 2000) compares the acquisition of calories and reproductive status of baboons (Altmann 1980) with Ache foragers (Hill and Hurtado 1996). Time spent foraging during the day is presented in relation to reproductive status for female baboons, where foraging time includes both travel and feeding time. Baboon mothers are hard pressed to meet the demands of lactation. When they must produce energy beyond their own maintenance needs, their daily time budget is stretched to the limit. They cannot afford to increase their

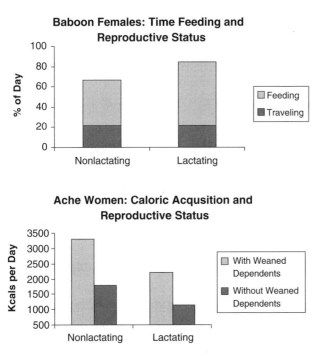

Figure 3.2
Production and reproductive status. Adapted from Lancaster et al. 2000.

travel time, which would be energetically costly, especially since they must carry their infants. Instead they increase their feeding time by reducing resting and socializing to about 15 percent of the day. Lactating baboons thus work harder. In fact, female baboons have higher mortality rates when lactating than when cycling or pregnant (Altmann 1980).

In contrast, when lactating and even when they have dependent juveniles to be fed, Ache, Efe, and Hadza women reduce their time spent foraging for food (Hurtado et al. 1985; Ivey 2000; Hawkes, O'Connell, and Blurton Jones 1997). It appears that human females are able to reduce time spent in energy production when they are nursing, even though their caloric consumption must increase to support lactation. Among the Ache, most of women's food production is derived from pounding the pulp of palms to produce starch. About 60 percent of the starch that women produce on extended foraging trips is shared outside the nuclear family (Kaplan and Hill 1985) with no bias towards close kin. Since lactating women produce much less palm starch than women without a baby, this pattern of sharing means that there are net food transfers from women to other women over periods of several months to several years.

Third, and most important for the present discussion, even with such extensive cooperation within families, additional flows of food between families are necessary to support this life history pattern. The fact that parental provisioning does not cease when children are weaned means that the caloric burden on parents increases as they produce more children. The diamonds show how the net demand on Ache parents changes with age as they produce additional children (viewed in terms of the man's age). Demands peak between forty and fifty years of age and remain significant until age sixty. Even though food production increases with age to about age thirty-five or forty and remains high, demands increase faster than food production. The triangles show how net family food production (calories produced minus calories consumed by self and offspring) changes with the age of the man.[3] These data show that there must be net transfers from the families of younger men to the families of older men! Moreover, there is a great deal of variance among men in both family size and productivity. Family size is inherently stochastic, due to both infant and child mortality and to individual differences in fecundity (see Hill and Hurtado 1996). There are also large differences in hunting ability among men. For example, there is a five-fold difference in the long

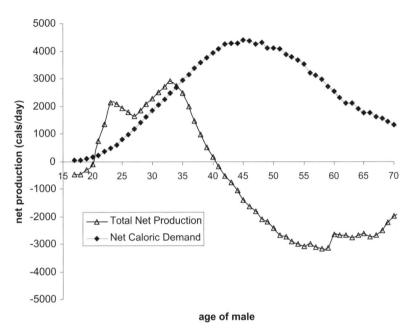

Figure 3.3
Family demands and net family production.

term average hunting returns between the best and worst hunter in the sample of Ache men (Hill et al. 1987). Similar discrepancies in hunting ability across men have been found among the !Kung (Lee 1979), Hadza (Hawkes, O'Connell, and Blurton Jones 2001), Hiwi (Gurven, Hill et al. 2000), Gunwinggu (Altman 1987), Agta (Bion Griffin 1984), and Machiguenga (Kaplan unpublished data).[4] Therefore, even among men of the same age, there must be net transfers over the long term from families producing a surplus to families producing a deficit.

These food transfers provide great reproductive benefits. The ability to "borrow" and "lend" across the life course is necessary for subsidizing the juvenile learning period (see Kaplan and Robson 2002 and Robson and Kaplan 2003 for theoretical models of the evolution of such age transfers and their relationship to learning). If families had to "balance their budget" at every period, they would either have had to lower their fertility or force their older children to fend for themselves. This would most likely increase childhood and adolescent mortality and lower rates of skills acquisition. Adolescent males could not afford to hunt, because their returns are so low during the learning period. Moreover, there would be no way to buffer the risks associated with the stochasticity of family size and child demands. If families needed to support all of their individual food needs, regardless of whether few or many children survived, they would be forced to lower fertility or reduce child subsidies. Similarly, the ability of women to shift production across time without changing consumption probably increases infant survival and decreases the length of interbirth intervals, thereby increasing the total reproductive success of women. When the opportunity costs of food acquisition are high due to the need to care for infants, women may produce less when they have infants and then work harder when those opportunity costs are low (i.e., when they have no infant to nurse and protect).

3.3.3   The Problem with Dyadic Reciprocal Altruism

It is unlikely that such a system of sharing would be stable with strictly dyadic reciprocal altruism. Reciprocal altruism will only emerge among self-interested actors if there is repeated interaction that rewards cooperation and punishes defection. In terms of reciprocal altruism, there is no incentive for young or older adults with small families to support older adults with large families. Those older adults with large families will never produce a surplus to "pay back" those subsidies, because they are likely to die before the young adults reach the age in which they need assistance to support their families. While it might be argued that there is intergenerational reciprocity where the children of the older adults, in turn, support the families of those who helped them, the long time periods between changes in directional flows would make such arrangements inherently risky. There is a great deal of mobility between hunter-gatherer bands and residential arrangements are not stable over long periods. There is no guarantee that children who are helped when they are young will live in the same band as those who helped them. The same argument applies to sharing between non-nursing and nursing women. Additionally, time discounting of benefits received in the distant future (relative to the present consumption payoffs from not sharing) also makes intergenerational reciprocity unstable (Hawkes 1992).

Similarly, reciprocal arrangements regarding the stochasticity of family size are unlikely to emerge with dyadic relationships. If family size variation is due primarily to random luck, it may be beneficial for two individuals to agree at the start of their reproductive careers to an arrangement in which the individual who ends up with fewer surviving offspring agrees to support the one with more surviving offspring.

However, once the outcome is known, there is no incentive for the one with fewer children to provide the support, since his family will never need the payback and there is no way to enforce the bargain.

Our thesis is that humans have found ways to take advantage of the gains from such trades, even though these gains would not emerge through dyadic reciprocal altruism. We propose that multi-individual negotiations result in the emergence of social norms that are collectively enforced. We base this proposal on a result obtained by Boyd and Richerson (1992), and treated more recently by Bowles and Gintis (2000), in which cooperation is modeled with punishment. These four researchers found that cooperation can be stable in large groups, if noncooperators are punished and if those who do not punish noncooperators are also punished. In fact, they found that any social norm could be stable as long as both those who disobey and those who fail to punish those who disobey are punished. However, we suggest that self-interested actors also negotiate these norms, weighing the individual costs and benefits of different social norms.

3.3.4   Two Thought Experiments

Imagine the following scenario. A woman returns from collecting berries and pounding palm fiber with her bawling infant. A wingless wasp stung her baby while she had put him down to pound the fiber, and the baby is in great pain. She is frustrated and says to the other women in camp, "This is crazy for me to go out and pound fiber when I have such a young baby. I would gladly work twice as hard when he is a little older if I could concentrate on watching him now." A few days later when the baby's wound is infected and the child has a fever, another woman, remembering a similar incident she experienced a few years ago, says, "You know, Singing Deer is right. We should work hard when we have no baby on the breast and allow those with a young one to care for it well." Another woman, who has not had a child in the last ten years, says, "Why should we work to feed other people's babies? If you have a baby, you must feed it." Other men and women consider their own situation (as well as the situation of their children) and present their opinions. Eventually a consensus (or at least, an agreement) is reached, with those in the minority either agreeing to go along with the new norm or leaving to live with "less foolish" people. However, one woman, who is not nursing, hardly pounds fiber at all. Other women begin to gossip about her, remarking upon how lazy she is, because she has no child to care for. She notices that the shares she receives in food distributions start to become less generous and begins to suspect that others are talking about her behind her back. She leaves and pounds a large quantity of fiber, which she generously shares with the rest of the group. She can feel the warmth of others return and has learned her lesson.

We consider another similar scenario. A fifty-year old man turns to another older man and exclaims, "Look at these lazy young men! They come back to camp at midday and play around. Yet you and I have lots of children to feed and no food to give them. What will those boys do when they have big families to feed?" The other older man agrees, adding, "How do I know if that lazy one is good enough for my daughter? How do I know if he will get enough food to keep her children healthy? He should come to my fire and bring me lots of meat— then I will know."

The young men are not very enthusiastic, because they do not like hunting all day long, but they are reluctant to anger the men whose daughters they favor. One young man, who is a good hunter for his age, realizes that he could take advantage of such a system and starts to hunt longer hours, giving the older men generous shares from his hunt. The other young men, afraid of being outdone, also begin to hunt longer hours and share the fruits of their labor more generously.

While admittedly hackneyed, these scenarios are meant to reflect the ongoing discussions and commentaries about sharing, work effort, and laziness that are so pervasive in foraging societies. We do not mean to suggest that all social norms are explicitly negotiated with words or that norms solidify over a short period as a result of a few conversations. In some circumstances, lack of compliance and "voting with one's feet" are almost surely involved in those negotiations. In fact, we know virtually nothing about how standards for appropriate behavior emerge and change in small-scale societies without official means of enforcement. It is likely that majority-rule voting arrangements are not adhered to in a strict sense, since some individuals exercise undue influence (e.g., *kombeti* among Aka, *kapita* among Efe [Hewlett and Walker 1990], and chiefs among Yuqui [Stearman 1989]). Nevertheless, we propose that such multi-individual negotiations, partly verbal and partly nonverbal, do result in social norms and that the weight of collective opinion, based upon the individual costs and benefits of norms in given contexts, determines accepted patterns of behavior. In the next section, we develop a preliminary framework for explaining variation in norms regarding cooperation.

3.4   Part III: A Preliminary Framework for Explaining Sharing Norms

We propose that social norms of sharing reflect the relative strengths of two opposing forces: gains from cooperation and possibilities for free-riding. Socioecological variation in potential benefits of cooperation and possibilities to free-ride on cooperative behavior determine cultural variability in norms of sharing and cooperative labor.

We also propose that in the course of our evolutionary history, natural selection has shaped our psychology to possess certain traits.

1) perceptual sensitivity to potential gains from cooperation

2) motivation to take advantage of those gains

3) perceptual sensitivity to opportunities for free-riding

4) motivation to avoid being a victim of free-riding

5) motivation to take advantage of opportunities for free-riding

6) perceptual sensitivity to the short- and long-term personal costs and benefits of social norms regarding cooperative behavior (from the perspectives of both the self and others)

7) motivation to negotiate social norms so that one's own personal benefits from cooperation and free-riding are maximized

8) motivation to obey and enforce social norms so that punishment is avoided, and those who disobey norms or fail to enforce them are punished

Our proposal is that this psychology, the complex analytical brain, and the extended life history coevolved in the hominid line—all because of the dietary shift towards large, high-quality food packages and hunting. It is this feeding adaptation that generates the gains from group cooperation. The large size of the packages and the difficulty of their acquisition through hunting

a) facilitate sharing (imagine sharing blades of grass back and forth)

b) increase short-term variation in acquisition luck, since large packages are not abundant

c) require significant learning and experience

d) increase the disparity between production and consumption at the individual and family levels over the medium and long term

e) increase the benefits of collective action and cooperative pursuits, especially in hunting

f) generate economies of scale, since foods are often distributed in larges patches distant from residential locations.

These qualities generate large gains from intertemporal substitution in consumption and production over the short, medium, and long term; gains from specialization by age, sex, and perhaps individual qualities; gains from joint production and cooperative acquisition; and gains from turn-taking in acquisition of patchily distributed foods. The distribution and relative importance of each of those gains is likely to vary with local ecology and the foods exploited.

Possibilities for, and gains from, free-riding act against cooperation. Three factors are likely to influence the threat of free-riding. First, a larger number of individuals in cooperative networks is likely to increase the threat, because the ability to detect and punish free-riders probably diminishes with partner number. As group size increases, the probability that more than one individual free-rides may also increase (Boyd 1988). As the number of free-riders increases, costs of punishment increase and the incentive to cooperate decreases. Second, the quality of information about behavior is also likely to affect opportunities for free-riding. If work effort is difficult to monitor and if it is difficult to determine whether variance in productivity is due to acquisition luck or work effort, opportunities for free-riding may increase (Cosmides and Tooby 1992). Third, gains from free-riding are also likely to vary according to kinship relationships between participants. As overall relatedness decreases, the differences among optimal allocations of work and distribution across individuals are likely to increase.

Those opposing forces may have led to the evolution of some general moral sentiments—supported both by the motivational psychology of individuals and common cultural norms. Variation in need and production among individuals due to stochasticity should engender generosity and cultural norms emphasizing the value of generosity— perhaps mediated through costly signaling and reciprocal altruism. Sharing sentiments and norms would favor those who were unfortunate over the short or long run and require generosity from the more fortunate. Virtually every investigator who seeks to establish friendships with members of traditional subsistence populations, who are much poorer, feels the pressures associated with those sentiments. Similarly, temporary states affecting production or need—such as illness, nursing, and high dependency ratios—would also promote generosity. As mentioned above, the rule that larger families deserve and receive larger shares is very widespread. Conversely, variation due to lack of effort or laziness would not generate generosity and perhaps invoke ridicule or punishment. Indeed, laziness and stinginess are constant themes for gossip in traditional societies. Other things being equal, people should feel more generous towards (and trusting of) close kin, because of the reduced scope of conflicting interests.

At the same time that moral systems are likely to have such general guiding principles, there is scope for considerable variation in the norms of cooperation and sharing, depending upon the specific constellation of gains from cooperation and possibilities for free-riding. Of critical importance is the relationship between the size and composition of residential groups and the optimal size of cooperating units. In general, people will tend to organize residential groups so that they can take maximal advantage of the gains from cooperation and reduce risks of free-riding. Thus, many forager-horticultirists in South America—such as the Machiguenga, Piro, and Tsimane—settle in extended family units, characterized by an older couple, their adult sons and/or daughters, and the founding couple's grandchildren. Labor is divided by age and sex, and food is eaten communally. This system of communal production and consumption maximizes gains from specialization and from spreading consumption and production needs through the entire age-structure, while kinship and shared genetic interests in the young children minimize conflicts of interest.

Several factors may cause residential groups to differ in size and composition from their optimal structure for cooperation. Aggregation of larger groups is common, because of threats of violence (e.g., Yanomamo [Chagnon 1983]), lack of resources such as water or groves of trees (e.g., Dobe !Kung [Lee 1979]), and now schools and delivery points of social services (e.g., Chácobo [Prost 1980]). In these cases, restricted sharing—where some or all foods are shared with only a subset of the residential group—is the norm.

Restricted sharing systems appear to be particularly common when the primary gains from sharing derive from variance reduction in consumption and when gains from cooperative pursuits are small or restricted to only some resources or times of the year. A common principle evidenced in restricted sharing systems is that the breadth and depth of resource sharing depends on the size of food packages available. When food packages are small, they are shared with a few special

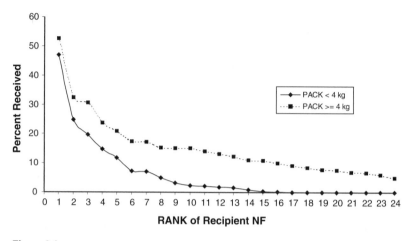

Figure 3.4
Aché sharing by package size.

partners, with whom reciprocal sharing is very common. As package size increases, the size of sharing networks grows (increased breadth) and the percentage of the food kept by the acquirer's family is reduced (increased depth).

Figures 3.4 and 3.5 illustrate features of this system. Figure 3.4 shows the percentage of sharing events by resource package size, in which specific Ache families receive shares at their permanent horticultural settlement. For each individual, sharing partners were rank-ordered from those who received most often to those who received least often. The x-axis displays the rank order and the y-axis gives the average percentage of occasions in which partners of each rank received shares. The data show that small packages are repeatedly shared with few individuals and that the size of sharing networks expands with large packages. Figure 3.5 (derived from data collected among the Hiwi and adapted from Gurven, Hill et al. 2000) is a path analysis predicting the total accumulation of food transferred between families over a six-month sample period, giving additional information about how partners are selected and about the size of shares given. Kinship predicts the spatial proximity between givers and receivers, which, in turn, predicts both how much was received in the past and the amount given in the present. In addition to kinship and proximity, the past history of sharing also predicts the amount given, suggesting that giving is contingent upon past receipts when controlling for these other factors.

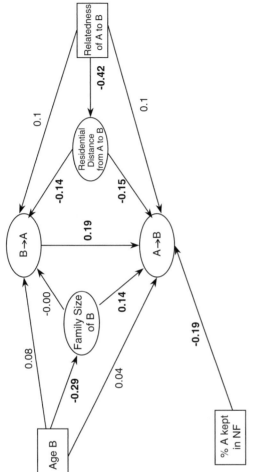

Figure 3.5
What affects how much nuclear family A gives to nuclear family B among Hiwi foragers?

Larger families also receive larger shares, as would be expected if need is being taken into account. Qualitative and quantitative reports from other societies suggest that similar patterns—kin bias, differential rules for sharing different resources (with increased breadth and depth of sharing with increased package size), contingency of sharing on the basis of past receipts, and larger shares to larger families—are found in other societies (Ifaluk [Sosis 1997], Eskimo [Damas 1972], Batak [Cadelina 1982], Yora [Hill and Kaplan 1989]). It is not always the case, however, that the residential group is larger than the optimal sharing network for all resources acquired. In cases where very large packages are sometimes acquired (e.g., giraffe among the !Kung), it is sometimes necessary to inform members of neighboring groups about kills because the optimal sharing group size is larger than the optimal residential unit (Lee 1979).

Such systems tend to take advantage of the gains from cooperation while minimizing risks of free-riding. Reducing daily variation in the consumption of small packages requires fewer partners than in the case of larger packages. Thus, a small circle of trusted partners, frequently kin and neighbors, is most efficient. As package size increases, the benefits of a greater number of partners increase, but so too do the costs of free-riding.

Another important principle of restricted sharing systems is that work effort in cooperative activities is rewarded. Thus, when cooperative task groups form, food is often shared equally among the participants. When those task groups do not include members from all the families in the residential group, a system of primary and secondary sharing is very common. In the primary distribution, all participants in the cooperative activity receive approximately equal shares of the total catch (see part I of this chapter for a list of groups engaging in this practice). In secondary distributions, each individual that received shares redistributes his or her share to families that did not participate. Those shares are smaller and tend to be shared according to the size of the packages acquired in the manner discussed earlier in this section. Figure 3.6 from the Yora illustrates this pattern (see Hill and Kaplan 1989). The first two bars show the primary distribution to members of the foraging party and the second two bars show the secondary distribution. This is an "incentive compatible" system in which work effort is rewarded in the primary distribution and the other benefits of sharing (e.g., intertemporal substitution in consumption and production) are handled in the secondary distribution. In cases where representa-

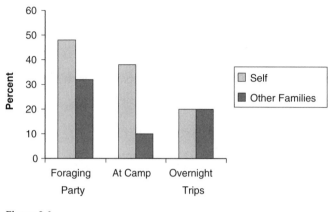

Figure 3.6
Yora meat sharing.

tives from every family in the residential group become involved in co-operative pursuits, such as the Ache when living in the forest and the Yora on trek (the third set of bars), food tends to be eaten communally.

In addition to rewarding work effort, sharing systems also appear to reward special capital contributed to cooperative efforts. For example, cooperative fishing and whaling among some coastal groups (e.g., Ifaluk [Sosis 1997], Lamalera [Alvard and Nolin 2002], and Makah [Singleton 1998]) requires boats and large work parties. Again, there is a primary distribution to all those who worked and secondary distributions for further sharing. However, in this case, boat owners receive larger or preferential shares. This suggests that not all individuals are weighted equally in the negotiation of sharing norms. While it is possible that those without boats could form a coalition to enforce equal sharing (since they are greater in number), it appears that those with special capital have more to offer in the market for cooperative partners and use this leverage to their advantage. Similarly, among Mbuti pygmies who hunt with large nets, net owners receive more food (Turnbull 1965) and among Efe and Aka Pygmie hunters, food shares depend upon the task performed in the cooperative hunt (Ichikawa 1983; Kitanishi 1998).

Finally, sharing systems undergoing transition also illustrate important principles in the negotiation of sharing norms. For example, the Ache have experienced several changes in food sharing and labor organization. Their economy transformed from full reliance on hunting and gathering in small groups to a mixed economy of foraging, farming, and wage labor in larger settlements after their establishment of permanent peaceful contact with the larger Paraguayan society. For the first five or so years following settlement, agricultural fields were cleared and planted communally. All able-bodied men were expected to contribute labor in large work parties. This pattern resembled the cooperative economy of the past. However, within a few years, it became apparent that some people were often absent from work parties and resentments began to build. Some men tired of this system and cleared their own personal gardens. Communal fields became smaller and a system of private fields, with fewer friends helping each other, came to predominate. Similarly, even with hunted and gathered foods, the system changed from communal sharing of all game to a restricted pattern resembling the Hiwi one shown in figure 3.5. It is interesting to note that the Ache still retain the traditional sharing pattern when trekking in the forest, even though they revert to the new pattern when residing in the settlement. Similarly, the !Kung San appear to have undergone major changes in their system of food distribution, since becoming involved in a mixed economy and the larger state society. Again, the trend seems to be from more communal distributions towards more restricted sharing, with a great deal of bickering and strife during the transition (see Shostak 1981 and the associated N/ai film for qualitative accounts).

The transition to horticulture among the Ache and !Kung was very rapid, and encouraged through missionary assistance. As mentioned above, the establishment of private fields was quickly advocated and voted upon in local Ache meetings. This contrasts with the pattern in other groups such as the Hadza (Woodburn 1982) and the Batek (Myers 1988), where initial attempts at horticulture by a minority of the population met with abrupt failure. The first harvests of the few transitional farmers were exploited by incessant demands from those who did not farm, ultimately making farming an unproductive activity due to mutual adherence to more traditional norms of sharing.

3.5   Conclusion

We have proposed that in addition to individual reciprocal arrangements, humans appear to be able to take advantage of gains from cooperation in ways that are unexpected by pair-wise game models. We suggested that people engage in multi-individual processes of norm negotiation (both verbal and nonverbal) that allow gains from cooperation and minimize risks of free-riding. The framework we proposed, however, is qualitative and far from fully specified. It clearly requires formal models to evaluate its plausibility.

We suspect that given the absence of state controls, the systems of exchange and cooperation found in traditional societies would not be stable without the complex web of kinship connections characterizing their residential groups. Those connections have two effects. First, as discussed earlier in this chapter, they reduce conflicts of interest between individuals and families. In fact, the marriage alliances between families (observed and commented on since the earliest days of anthropology) may be a way to minimize such conflicts of interest through the production of descendents sharing genes from both sets of families. Second, kinship connections lower the variance in the payoffs associated with norms of sharing and cooperation. For example, norms that allocate larger shares to families with more children to feed may be disadvantageous for individuals in small families, but because, members of small families are likely to have close kin (nieces, nephews, brothers, sisters, and grandchildren) in large families, the total net results of the norm for their genetic lineage may be positive. Since most other species that have elaborate systems of resource sharing and cooperation—such as social insects and group-hunting predators—organize cooperation along kinship lines, it is likely that kinship played an important role in the evolution of cooperation in humans. Models of multi-individual norm negotiation with and without kinship will be particularly useful in evaluating this intuition.

In part III of this chapter, we suggested that norms of sharing and cooperation would reflect the ecology of subsistence, as well as the associated variability in the gains from cooperation and possibilities for free-riding. However, it is possible that similar ecologies may result in very different equilibria, depending upon historical conditions and perhaps even essentially random perturbations. Formal models would also be useful for evaluating this possibility. If multiple equilibria are possible, then cultural or trait group selection may determine which equilibria come to dominate over time. Given the kinship relations organizing the formation of groups in traditional societies, cultural and genetic selection among groups and lineages may occur simultaneously.

Finally, informal observation (and the results of behavioral genetics studies) suggest that there may be significant individual differences within groups in terms of free-riding and obedience to group norms.

The existence of varying degrees of free-riding by individual members of social groups may be an inevitable outcome of cooperative norms that can only be partially enforced. The optimal amount of effort allocated to police free-riding may itself be subject to negotiation, as are allocations to law enforcement in state societies.

This chapter represents a first step in a developing a multi-individual approach to cooperation among traditional human societies and to the psychology that underlies it. Our hope is that this paper will help stimulate the development of formal analyses of those processes.

Notes

1. Chimpanzee mothers do share some difficult-to-acquire solid foods with weaned offspring (Silk 1979), but chimpanzee young are largely self-sufficient after they are weaned.

2. While computer simulations reveal that significant correlations between individuals in amounts given and received are possible when tolerated theft is the sole cause of food sharing, correlations greater than 0.2 were only found in groups of fewer individuals than was common in the above groups.

3. The consumption and production of women is not included in this calculation since, on average, women produce just enough to support their own consumption or a bit less.

4. Among the Machiguenga of Yomiwato, the best hunter produced more than half of the meat for the whole village over a year period.

References

Alexander, R. 1987. *The Biology of Moral Systems*. New York: Aldine de Gruyter.

Allen-Arave, W., M. Gurven, and K. Hill. n.d. Is Food Sharing Among Close Kin Maintained by Kin Selection or Reciprocal Altruism? Evidence from Ache Food Transfers. University of New Mexico. Ms.

Altman, J. 1987. *Hunter-Gatherers Today: An Aboriginal Economy of North Australia*. Canberra: Australian Institute of Aboriginal Studies.

Altman, J. 1980. *Baboon Mothers and Infants*. Cambridge: Harvard University Press.

Alvard, M. 2002. Carcass ownership and meat distribution by big-game cooperative hunters. *Research in Economic Anthropology*, 99–131.

Alvard, M., and D. Nolin. n.d. Rousseau's whale hunt? Coordination among big game hunters. *Current Anthropology* 43(4):533–559.

Aspelin, P. 1979. Food distribution and social bonding among the Mamainde of Mato Grosso, Brazil. *Journal of Anthropological Research* 35:309–327.

Bahuchet, S. 1990. Food sharing among the pygmies of Central Africa. *African Study Monographs* 11:27–53.

Bailey, R. C. 1991. *The Behavioral Ecology of Efe Pygmy Men in the Ituri Forest, Zaire*. Anthropological Papers, No. 86, Museum of Anthropology, University of Michigan.

Baksh, M., and A. Johnson. 1990. Insurance policies among the Machiguenga: An ethnographic analysis of risk management in a non-Western society. In *Risk and Uncertainty in Tribal and Peasant Economics*. Ed. Elizabeth Cashdan, Boulder, CO: Westview Press.

Balikci, A. 1970. *The Netsilike Eskimo*. New York: Natural History Press.

Barnard, A., and J. Woodburn. 1988. Property, power and ideology in hunting-gathering societies: An introduction. In *Hunter-Gatherers, Volume II: Property, Power and Ideology*. Eds. Tim Ingold, David Riches, and James Woodburn. 4–31. Oxford: Berg.

Bion Griffin, P. 1984. The acquisition and sharing of food among Agta foragers. The sharing of food: From phylogeny to history conference. Homburg, Germany.

Bliege Bird, R. L., and D. W. Bird. 1997. Delayed reciprocity and tolerated theft: The behavioral ecology of food-sharing strategies. *Current Anthropology* 38:49–77.

Bliege Bird, R., E. A. Smith, and D. W. Bird. 2001. The hunting handicap: costly signaling in male foraging strategies. *Behavioral Ecology and Sociobiology* 50:9–19.

Blurton Jones, N. 1984. A selfish origin for human food sharing: Tolerated theft. *Ethology and Sociobiology* 5:1–3.

Blurton Jones, N. 1987. Tolerated theft, suggestions about the ecology and evolution of sharing, hoarding, and scrounging. *Social Science Information* 26:31–54.

Bock, J. 2002. Learning, Life History, and Productivity: Children's lives in the Okavango Delta of Botswana. *Human Nature* 13(2):161–198.

Boehm, C. 1993. Egalitarian society and reverse dominance hierarchy. *Current Anthropology* 34:227–254.

Boyd, R. 1988. The evolution of reciprocity in sizable groups. *Journal of Theoretical Biology* 132:337–356.

Boyd, R., and P. Richerson. 1989. The evolution of indirect reciprocity. *Social Networks* 11:213–236.

Boyd, R., and P. J. Richerson. In press. Solving the puzzle of human cooperation, In *Evolution and Culture*. Ed. S. Levinson. Cambridge MA: MIT Press.

Boyd, R., and P. Richerson. 1992. Punishment allows the evolution of cooperation (or anything else) in sizable groups. *Ethology and Sociobiology* 13:171–195.

Cadelina, R. V. 1982. Batak Interhousehold Food Sharing: A Systematic Analysis of Food Management of Marginal Agriculturalists in the Philippines. Ph.D. dissertation. University of Hawaii, Honolulu.

Carneiro, R. L. 1983. The cultivation of manioc among the Kuikuru of the Upper Xingú. In *Adaptive Responses of Native Amazonians*. Eds. R. Hames and W. Vickers, 65–111. New York: Academic Press.

Cashdan, E. 1985. Coping with risk: Reciprocity among the Basarwa of Northern Botswana. *Man* (N.S.) 20:454–474.

Chagnon, N. 1983 [1968]. *Yanomamo: The Fierce People*. New York: Holt, Rinehart and Winston.

Chicchón, A. 1992. Chimane Resource Use and Market Involvement in the Beni Biosphere Reserve, Bolivia. Ph.D. dissertation. University of Florida.

Clements, K. C., and D. W. Stephens. 1995. Testing models of animal cooperation: Feeding bluejays cooperate mutualistically, but defect in a massively iterated Prisoner's Dilemma. *Animal Behaviour* 50:527–535.

Clutton-Brock, T. H. 1991. *The Evolution of Parental Care*. Princeton, NJ: Princeton University Press.

Cosmides, L., and J. Tooby. 1992. Cognitive adaptations for social exchange. In *The Adapted Mind: Evolutionary Psychology and the Generation of Culture*. Eds. J. H. Barkow, L. Cosmides, and J. Tooby. New York: Oxford University Press, 163–228.

Damas, D. 1972. Central Eskimo systems of food sharing. *Ethnology* 11:220–240.

Dowling, J. 1968. Individual ownership and the sharing of game in hunting societies. *American Anthropologist* 70:502–507.

Dugatkin, L. A. 1997. *Cooperation among Animals: An Evolutionary Perspective*. New York: Oxford University Press.

Endicott, K. 1988. Property, sharing, and conflict among the Batek of Malaysia. In *Hunter-Gatherers, Volume II: Property, Power and Ideology*. Eds. Tim Ingold, David Riches, and James Woodburn. Oxford: Berg, 110–128.

Feinman, S. 1979. An evolutionary theory of food sharing. *Social Science Information* 18:695–726.

Frank, R. 1988. *Passions within Reason*. New York: Norton.

Gintis, H. 2000. Strong Reciprocity and Human Sociality. *Journal of Theoretical Biology* 206:169–179.

Gould, R. A. 1980. Comparative ecology of food-sharing in Australia and northwest California. In *Omnivorous Primates*. Ed. R. Harding and G. Teleki. New York: Columbia University Press, 422–454.

Grafen, A. 1990. Biological signals as handicaps. *Journal of Theoretical Biology* 144:517–546.

Gurven, M. 2004. Reciprocal altruism and food sharing decisions among Hiwi and Ache hunter-gatherers. *Behavioral Ecology and Sociobiology* 56(4):366–380.

Gurven, M. 1999. Transitions in food sharing patterns from nomadic foragers to sedentary horticulturalists. Society for Cross-Cultural Research, Santa Fe, NM.

Gurven, M., and H. Kaplan. n.d. Determinants of Time Allocation to Production across the Lifespan among the Machiguenga and Piro Indians of Peru. University of New Mexico. Ms.

Gurven, M., K. Hill, and H. Kaplan. 2002. From forest to reservation: transitions in food sharing behavior among the Ache of Paraguay. *Journal of Anthropological Research* 58(1):91–118.

Gurven, M., W. Allen-Arave, K. Hill, and A. M. Hurtado. 2000. "It's a Wonderful Life": Signaling generosity among the Ache of Paraguay. *Evolution and Human Behavior* 21:263–282.

Gurven, M., W. Allen-Arave, K. Hill, and A. M. Hurtado. 2001. Reservation sharing among the Ache of Paraguay. *Human Nature* 12(4):273–298.

Gurven, M., K. Hill, H. Kaplan, A. M. Hurtado, and R. Lyles. 2000. Food transfers among Hiwi foragers of Venezuela: Tests of reciprocity. *Human Ecology* 28(2):171–218.

Hames, R. 1987. Garden labor exchange among the Ye'kwana. *Ethology and Sociobiology* 8:354–392.

Hames, R. 1989. Time, efficiency, and fitness in the Amazonian protein quest. *Research in Economic Anthropology* 11:43–85.

Hames, R. 1990. Sharing among the Yanomamo: Part I, The effects of risk. In *Risk and Uncertainty in Tribal and Peasant Economies*. Ed. E. Cashdan. Boulder, CO: Westview Press.

Hames, R. 2000. Reciprocal altruism in Yanomamo food exchange. In *Human Behavior and Adaptation: An Anthropological Perspective*. Eds. N. Chagnon, L. Cronk, and W. Irons. New York: Aldine de Gruyter.

Hamilton, W. D. 1964. The genetical evolution of social behavior. *Journal of Theoretical Biology* 7:1–52.

Harako, R. 1976. The Mbuti as hunters. A study of ecological anthropology of the Mbuti Pygmies (Ituri, Zaire). *Kyoto University African Studies* 10:37–99.

Harpending, H. 1998. Comment. *Current Anthropology* 39:88–89.

Hawkes, K. 1991. Showing off: Tests of an hypothesis about men's foraging goals. *Ethology and Sociobiology* 12:29–54.

Hawkes, K. 1992. Sharing and collective action. In *Evolutionary Ecology and Human Behavior*. Eds. E. A. Smith and B. Winterhalder. Aldine de Gruyter, New York: 269–300.

Hawkes, K. 1993. Why hunter-gatherers work: An ancient version of the problem of public goods. *Current Anthropology* 34:341–361.

Hawkes, K., J. F. O'Connell, and N. G. Blurton Jones. 1989. Hardworking Hadza grandmothers. In *Comparative Socioecology of Mammals and Man*. Eds. R. Foley and V. Standen. London: Basil Blackwell, 341–366.

Hawkes, K., J. F. O'Connell, and N. G. Blurton Jones. 1991. Hunting income patterns among the Hadza: Big game, common goods, foraging goals and the evolution of the human diet. *Phil. Trans. R. Soc. Lond. B* 334:243–251.

Hawkes, K., J. F. O'Connell, and N. G. Blurton Jones. 1997. Hadza women's time allocation, offspring provisioning, and the evolution of long post-menopausal life spans. *Current Anthropology* 38:551–577.

Hawkes, K., J. F. O'Connell, and N. G. Blurton Jones. 1998. Hadza Hunting and the Evolution of Nuclear Families. University of Utah. Ms.

Hawkes, K., J. F. O'Connell, and N. G. Blurton Jones. 2001. Hadza meat sharing. *Evolution and Human Behavior* 22:113–142.

Hawkes, K., H. Kaplan, K. Hill, and A. M. Hurtado. 1987. Ache at the settlement: Contrasts between farming and foraging. *Human Ecology* 15:133–161.

Henry, J. 1941. *Jungle people: A Kaingáng tribe of the highlands of Brazil*. New York: J. J. Augustin.

Henry, J. 1951. The economics of Pilagá food distribution. *American Anthropologist* 53:187–219.

Hewlett, B., and P. Walker. 1990. Dental health, diet and social status among Central African Pygmies and Bantu. *American Anthropologist* 92:383–398.

Hill, K. 1988. Macronutrient modifications of optimal foraging theory: An approach using indifference curves applied to some modern foragers. *Human Ecology* 16:157–197.

Hill, K., and K. Hawkes. 1983. Neotropical hunting among the Ache of eastern Paraguay. In *Adaptive Responses of Native Amazonians*. Eds. R. Hames and W. Vickers. New York: Academic Press, 139–188.

Hill, K., and A. M. Hurtado. 1996. *Ache Life History: Ecology and Demography of a Foraging People*. New York: Aldine De Gruyter.

Hill, K., and H. Kaplan. 1988. Tradeoffs in male and female reproductive strategies among the Ache: Part 1. In *Human Reproductive Behavior*. Eds. L. Betzig, P. Turke, and M. Borgerhoff Mulder. 277–290. Cambridge: Cambridge University Press.

Hill, K., and H. Kaplan. 1989. Population description and dry season subsistence patterns among the newly contacted Yora (Yaminahua) of Manu National Park, Peru. *National Geographic Research* 3:317–324.

Hill, K., and H. Kaplan. 1993. On why male foragers hunt and share food. *Current Anthropology* 34:701–710.

Hill, K., K. Hawkes, H. Kaplan, and A. M. Hurtado. 1987. Foraging decisions among Ache hunter-gatherers in eastern Paraguay. *Human Ecology* 12:145–180.

Hoffman, E., K. McCabe, and V. Smith. 1998. Behavioral foundations of reciprocity: Experimental economics and evolutionary psychology. *Economic Inquiry* 36:335–352.

Holmberg, A. R. 1969 [1941]. *Nomads of the Long Bow: The Sirionó of Eastern Bolivia*. New York: Natural History Press.

Hurtado, A. M., K. Hawkes, K. Hill, and H. Kaplan. 1985. Female subsistence strategies among Ache hunter-gatherers of eastern Paraguay. *Human Ecology* 13:1–28.

Ichikawa, M. 1983. An examination of the hunting-dependent life of the Mbuti pygmies, eastern Zaïre. *African Study Monographs*, 4:55–73.

Isaac, G. 1978. The food-sharing behavior of protohuman hominids. *Scientific American* 238:90–108.

Ivey, P. K. 2000. Cooperative reproduction in Ituri Forest hunter-gatherers: Who cares for Efe infants? *Current Anthropology* 41:856–866.

Johnstone, R. 1997. The evolution of animal signals. In *Behavioural Ecology: An Evolutionary Approach*. Eds. J. R. Krebs and N. B. Davies. London: Blackwell Scientific, 155–178.

Kaplan, H. 1994. Evolutionary and wealth flows theories of fertility: Empirical tests and new models. *Population and Development Review* 20:753–791.

Kaplan, H., and K. Hill. 1985. Food sharing among Ache foragers: Tests of explanatory hypotheses. *Current Anthropology* 26:223–245.

Kaplan, H. and Robson, A. 2002. The co-evolution of intelligence and longevity and the emergence of humans. *Proceedings of the National Academy of Sciences* 99:10221–10226.

Kaplan, H., K. Hill, and A. M. Hurtado. 1990. Risk, foraging, and food sharing among the Ache. In *Risk and Uncertainty in Tribal and Peasant Economies*. Ed. E. Cashdan. Boulder, CO: Westview Press, 107–144.

Kaplan, H., K. Hill, K. Hawkes, and A. M. Hurtado. 1984. Food sharing among the Ache hunter-gatherers of eastern Paraguay. *Current Anthropology* 25:113–115.

Kaplan, H., K. Hill, A. M. Hurtado, and J. B. Lancaster. 2001. The embodied capital theory of human evolution. In *Reproductive Ecology and Human Evolution*. Ed. P. T. Ellison. Hawthorne, NY: Aldine de Gruyter.

Kaplan, H., K. Hill, J. Lancaster, and A. M. Hurtado. 2000. A theory of human life history evolution: Diet, intelligence, and longevity. *Evolutionary Anthropology* 9:156–185.

Kaplan, H. S., Lancaster, J. B., and Robson, A. 2003. Embodied capital and the evolutionary economics of the human lifespan. In: *Lifespan: Evolutionary, Ecology, and Demographic Perspectives*. Eds. J. R. Carey and S. Tuljapakur. *Population and Development Review* 29, supplement, 152–182.

Kent, S. 1993. Sharing in an egalitarian Kalahari community. *Man* (N.S.) 28:479–514.

Kitanishi, K. 1998. Food sharing among the Aka hunter-gatherers in northeastern Congo. *African Study Monographs* 25:3–32.

Kramer, K. L. 1998. Variation in Children's Work among Modern Maya Subsistence Agriculturalists. Ph.D. dissertation. University of New Mexico.

Krebs, D. 1987. The challenge of altruism in biology and psychology. In *Sociobiology and Psychology: Ideas, Issues, and Applications*. Eds. C. Crawford, M. Smith, and D. Krebs. Hillsdale, NJ: Lawrence Erlbaum Associates, 81–118.

Lancaster, J. B., and C. S. Lancaster. 1983. Parental investment: The hominid adaptation. In *How Humans Adapt*. Ed. D. Ortner. Washington, DC: Smithsonian Institute Press, 33–69.

Lancaster, J. B., H. Kaplan, K. Hill, and A. M. Hurtado. 2000. The evolution of the human life course and investment in human capital. In *Perspectives in Ethology: Evolution, Culture and Behavior*, vol. 13. Eds. F. Tonneau and N. S. Thompson. Plenum, NY.

Lee, R. B. 1979. *The !Kung San: Men, Women, and Work in a Foraging Society*. Cambridge: Cambridge University Press.

Marlowe, F. n.d. Sharing among Hadza Hunter-Gatherers. Harvard University Department of Anthropology. Ms.

Marshall, L. 1976. Sharing, talking, and giving: Relief of social tensions among the !Kung. In *Kalahari Hunter-Gatherers*. Eds. R. Lee and I. Devore, 350–371.

Myers, F. 1988. Burning the truck and holding the country: Property, time and the negotiation of identity among Pintupi Aborigines. In *Hunter-Gatherers, Volume II: Property, Power and Ideology*. Eds. Tim Ingold, David Riches, and James Woodburn. Oxford: Berg, 52–74.

Peterson, J. T. 1978 [1974]. The Ecology of Social Boundaries: Agta Foragers of the Philippines. Urbana: University of Illinois Press.

Peterson, N. 1993. Demand sharing: Reciprocity and the pressure for generosity among foragers. *American Anthropologist* 95:860–874.

Price, J. A. 1975. Sharing: The integration of intimate economies. *Anthropologica* 17:3–27.

Prost, G. 1980. Chácobo: Society of Equality. University of Florida. M.A. thesis.

Ritchie, M. A. 1996. *Spirit of the Rainforest*. Chicago: Island Lake Press.

Robson, A., and Kaplan, H. 2003. The evolution of human life expectancy and intelligence in hunter-gatherer economies. *American Economic Review* 93:150–169.

Rogers, A. R. 1993. Why menopause? *Evolutionary Ecology* 7:406–420.

Rothstein, S. I., and R. Pierroti. 1988. Distinctions among reciprocal altruism, kin selection, and cooperation and a model for the initial evolution of beneficient behavior. *Ethology and Sociobiology* 9:189–209.

Sahlins, M. 1972. *Stone Age Economics*. London: Tavistock.

Shostak, M. 1981. *Nisa: The Life and Words of a !Kung Woman*. New York: Random House.

Silberbauer, G. 1981. Hunter/gatherers of the central Kalahari. In *Omnivorous Primates*. Ed. R. Harding and G. Teleki. New York: Columbia University Press, 455–498.

Silk, J. 1979. Feeding, foraging, and food sharing of immature chimpanzees. *Folia Primatologica* 31:123–142.

Simon, H. 1990. A mechanism for social selection and successful altruism. *Science* 250:1665–1668.

Singleton, S. 1998. *Constructing Cooperation: The Evolution of Institutions and Comanagement*. Ann Arbor: University of Michigan Press.

Smith, E. A. 1988. Risk and uncertainty in the "original affluent society": Evolutionary ecology of resource-sharing and land tenure. In *Hunter-Gatherers, Volume 1: History, Evolution and Social Change*. Eds. Tim Ingold, David Riches, and James Woodburn. New York: Berg, 222–251.

Smith, E. A., and R. Bliege Bird. 2000. Turtle hunting and tombstone opening: Public generosity as costly signaling. *Evolution and Human Behavior* 21:245–261.

Sosis, R. H. 1997. The Collective Action Problem of Male Cooperative Labor on Ifaluk Atoll. University of New Mexico. Ph.D. thesis.

Sosis, R., S. Feldstein, and K. Hill. 1998. Bargaining theory and cooperative fishing participation on Ifaluk Atoll. *Human Nature* 9(2):163–203.

Speth, J. D. 1990. Seasonality, resource stress, and food sharing in so-called egalitarian foraging societies. *Journal of Anthropological Archaeology* 9(2):148–188.

Ståhl, I. 1972. *Bargaining Theory*. Economic Research Institute at Stockholm School of Economics, Stockholm.

Stanford, C. B. 1995. Chimpanzee hunting behavior and human evolution. *American Scientist* 83:256–261.

Stearman, A. M. 1989. Yuquí foragers in the Bolivian Amazon: Subsistence strategies, prestige, and leadership in an acculturating society. *Journal of Anthropological Research* 45:219–244.

Tanaka, J. 1980. *The San Hunter-Gatherers of the Kalahari*. Tokyo: University of Tokyo Press.

Trivers, R. L. 1971. The evolution of reciprocal altruism. *Quarterly Review of Biology* 46:35–57.

Turnbull, C. M. 1965. *Wayward Servants: The Two Worlds of the African Pygmies*. Westport, CT: Greenwood Press.

Wilson, D. S. 1990. Weak altruism, strong group selection. *Oikos* 59:135–140.

Wilson, D. S. 1998. Hunting, sharing, and multilevel selection: The tolerated-theft model revisited. *Current Anthropology* 39:73–97.

Winterhalder, B. 1986. Diet choice, risk, and food sharing in a stochastic environment. *Journal of Anthropological Archaeology* 5:369–392.

Winterhalder, B. 1996. A marginal model of tolerated theft. *Ethology and Sociobiology* 17:37–53.

Winterhalder, B. 1997. Social foraging and the behavioral ecology of intragroup resource transfers. *Evolutionary Anthropology* 5:46–57.

Woodburn, J. 1982. Egalitarian societies. *Man* 17:431–451.

Zahavi, A., and A. Zahavi. 1997. *The Handicap Principle: A missing Piece of Darwin's Puzzle*. New York: Oxford University Press.

4 Costly Signaling and Cooperative Behavior

Eric A. Smith and Rebecca
Bliege Bird

There is, deep down within all of us, an instinct. It's a kind of drum major instinct—a desire to be first ... We all want to be important, to surpass others, to achieve distinction, to lead the parade ... Don't give it up. Keep feeling the need for being first. But I want you to be first in love. I want you to be first in moral excellence. I want you to be first in generosity.

(From a sermon by Dr. Martin Luther King, Jr.)

4.1 Introduction

The last few decades have witnessed an increasing convergence and interaction between economic and evolutionary approaches to human behavior, a trend certainly exemplified in the present volume. In this chapter, we draw on a framework we will refer to as costly signaling theory (CST) that has been elaborated more or less independently in both economics (e.g., Veblen 1899; Spence 1973) and evolutionary biology (e.g., Zahavi 1975; Grafen 1990). In keeping with the theme of the present volume, we explore the ways in which CST might illuminate strong reciprocity and other forms of cooperative behavior.[1] In contrast to most of the contributors to this volume, we argue that many of the phenomena classed as strong reciprocity (as defined in chapter 1) might be individually optimal (i.e., produce a net fitness benefit) and thus not require cultural or genetic group selection, at least not for their evolutionary origins.

This chapter is organized as follows. Section 4.2 summarizes the fundamental features of costly signaling theory, and section 4.3 outlines a game-theoretical model of cooperative behavior based on this theory. Section 4.4 discusses the conditions under which we might expect group-beneficial signaling to be favored over neutral or "selfish" signaling. We then apply these arguments to a variety of contexts in which cooperative behavior is commonly observed, and for which standard models of conditional reciprocity seem inadequate. First, we consider cases of unconditional generosity involving the provisioning of collective goods, such as public feasts or fighting on behalf of one's community. Section 4.5.5 considers the special, but crucial, case of enforcement of group-beneficial norms and punishment of those who defect from them. We then discuss ways in which CST may illuminate situations involving trust and commitment (section 4.6). In each of these sections, we present a variety of ethnographic and historical examples that illustrate the application of CST to understanding cooperative behavior. Section 4.7 offers a brief set of conclusions that both review the material presented in this chapter and suggest the areas where major questions remain.

4.2   Costly Signaling Theory

Costly signaling theory proposes that expensive and often seemingly arbitrary or "wasteful" behavioral or morphological traits are designed to convey honest information benefiting both signalers and observers (Zahavi 1975; Grafen 1990; Johnstone 1997). These signals reveal information about underlying qualities of the signaling individuals (or groups). By "qualities," we mean characteristics of the signaler that are of importance to observers (i.e., elements that will affect their payoffs from social interaction with the signaler), but that are directly observable only with difficulty or not at all (e.g., disease resistance, competitive ability, resource endowment, dedication to an ongoing social relationship). Readers unfamiliar with CST should note that it is relevant to a much wider range of behavioral and morphological features than are considered here (see for example Johnstone 1995; Zahavi and Zahavi 1997).

There are two key conditions required for evolutionary stability of such signaling. First, both signalers and receivers must benefit from sharing information about signaler variation in the underlying quality. The second condition is that signals impose a cost on the signaler that is linked to the quality being advertised. This link can take one of two forms: either lower-quality signalers pay higher marginal costs for signaling or they reap lower marginal benefits. These two conditions are related, since quality-dependent cost (the second condition) serves to ensure that the signal honestly advertises the relevant underlying qualities of the signaler (the first condition).

CST provides a powerful framework for explaining how honest communication can be evolutionarily stable despite the pervasive conflicts of interest generated by natural selection. When the conditions outlined above are met, honest signals will be of benefit to both signaler and observer, even when their interests overlap very little. The payoff to the observer derives from the information inferred from the signal—he or she should be able to evaluate the signaler's qualities as competitor, mate, or ally by attending to the signal rather than through more costly means of assessing the signaler's abilities, qualities, or motivations. The payoff to the signaler results from the observer's response. Note that the mutuality of interest in information sharing can exist even when in a broad sense signaler and observer have strongly opposed interests and hence incentives to engage in deceit—for example, interactions between predator and prey, or between enemy soldiers.

It bears emphasizing that the logic of CST is not based on standard conditional reciprocity (see table 4.1). For example, when we say that signal observers may use the information they have received to choose someone as a (future) ally, we are *not* proposing that this is a favor reciprocated to the signaler, any more than a peahen that chooses the peacock with the showiest tail is "paying back" the cock for having expended high signaling costs. Rather, CST explanations propose that responding to signals in a way that benefits the signaler is simply the best move the responder can make given the available information. The mere fact that a costly action (e.g., hosting an expensive feast) results in a beneficial response (e.g., an increase in social status) does not entail conditional reciprocity. It is important to keep this distinction

Table 4.1
Comparison of conditional reciprocity and costly signaling accounts of cooperation.

Are features below expected with:	Conditional reciprocity?	Costly signaling?
Donor obtains net gain in the long run	Yes	Yes
Donor is paid back by recipients	Yes	Not necessarily
Unilateral provisioning of public good	No	Possibly
Donors have higher status than recipients	No	Yes
Requires punishment of free riders	Yes	No
Stability less likely with larger group size	Yes	No

in mind when considering the special case of group-beneficial signaling.

4.3 Group-Beneficial Signaling

In most cases, CST is applied to contexts where the benefits in question are privately consumed (e.g., mating opportunities) and any wider social benefits absent or incidental. In principle, signaler-observer relations can range from highly cooperative to blatantly antagonistic, as in the case of prey signaling their vigor to predators (Caro 1994), or individuals or social groups competing for social dominance (Neiman 1997). The situation that concerns us here is when costly signaling ensures that competitors for various social goods (e.g., alliances, mating opportunities, leadership positions) advertise their relevant qualities honestly, thus allowing observers to discriminate amongst the signalers and make their best move (such as ally with, mate with, or defer to those signaling more often or more intensely).

Several authors (Zahavi 1977, 1995; Boone 1998; Roberts 1998; Wright 1999) have proposed that costly signaling could provide an explanation for cooperation and group-beneficial behavior. In an earlier set of papers (Bliege Bird, Smith, and Bird 2001; Smith and Bliege Bird 2000), we argued that unconditionally providing a collective good when it was otherwise not in the provider's best interest to do so could be favored if such provisioning served as a reliable signal of the provider's quality. Those who provide this group benefit, or who provide more of it (i.e., signaling more intensively), assume costs greater than their personal share of the collective good, but in doing so honestly advertise their quality as allies, mates, or competitors. This information could then alter the behavior of other group members to act (for purely selfish motives) in ways that provide positive payoffs to signalers—for example, preferring them as allies or mates, or deferring to them in competitive situations (Smith and Bliege Bird 2000).

A formal model of this proposal, framed as an n-player public goods game, has been developed by Gintis, Smith, and Bowles (2001); we will refer to this as the GSB model.[2] In this model, cooperation involves providing a benefit to all members of the group regardless of any reciprocation in kind. Given the public goods game payoff structure and non-repeated interactions, the unique equilibrium of this game involves universal defection as the dominant strategy, and hence individually costly cooperation could not evolve (unless there were strong group selection in its favor). Even if interactions among group members were repeated, cooperation among more than a few individuals would require implausible forms of coordination (Boyd and Richerson 1988). The GSB model is meant to apply to such cases, where conditional reciprocity is unlikely to emerge and is vulnerable to free-riding.

It seems reasonable to suppose, however, that providing the group benefit serves as an honest signal of the provider's underlying quality (as defined in section 4.2). Specifically, suppose that providing the group benefit is differentially costly as a function of the provider's quality. For simplicity, GSB assume that members of the social group come in two types, high quality and low quality. The model further assumes that every individual knows his or her own quality (but not that of others) and that any other group member has probability p of being high quality (and probability $q = 1 - p$ of being low quality).

In the GSB game, each member plays two roles in any given period: signaler and responder. The signaler role takes two forms: providing the collective benefit (e.g., hosting a feast) or not providing it. The responder role consists of observing signalers (including partaking in any collective benefits they may provide) and then making a decision whether or not to interact with one of them. This interaction, like the signal, is stated in the most general terms here, but could involve such things as mate choice, coalition formation, partner choice, deference in competitive situations, and so on.

With these options, in each role a player can use one of four strategies, as listed in table 4.2. Specifically, signalers can chose to signal (provide the collective benefit) (1) always, regardless of their quality;

Table 4.2
Strategies in the n-person signaling game.

Signalers:
AS = always signal, regardless of quality
SH = signal only if one is high quality
SL = signal only if one is low quality
NS = never signal

Responders:
AR = always respond, whether or not signaler signals
RS = respond by interacting only with a signaler who signals
RN = respond by interacting only with those who do not signal
NR = never respond

or they can make signaling conditional on their type—signaling (2) only if high quality, or (3) only if low quality; or (4) decide to never signal.

Similarly, responders can interact with an individual chosen at random (1) from all the other $n - 1$ group members; (2) from the subset of other members who provided the benefit; (3) from the subset of other members who did not provide the benefit; or (4) the responder can forgo interacting with any group member in this period.

A signaling equilibrium will occur if all players chose to a) signal only if high quality, and b) respond by interacting only with those who signal. Following the labels in table 4.2, this means that all play "SH" as signalers, and "RS" as responders. To determine if this signaling equilibrium will be favored (i.e., if it will be a strict Nash equilibrium), we need to specify some assumptions about payoffs from the various strategies. First, following the standard logic of CST, we assume that high-quality individuals pay a lower cost to signal than low-quality ones and that interacting with high-quality individuals will yield a higher payoff to responders than if they interact with low-quality individuals. We also assume that any signaler who interacts with a responder will gain a positive benefit from this interaction; in the GSB model, this benefit is the same irrespective of the signaler's type and regardless of whether or not the Signaler in fact signaled (provided the collective good).[3]

These assumptions produce the payoff matrix outlined in table 4.3 (for a full explication, see Gintis, Smith, and Bowles 2001). The analytical results discussed in GSB reveal that three conditions are necessary and sufficient for honest signaling (SH, RS) to be a strict Nash equilibrium. First, the benefits of signaling must exceed its expected cost for the high-quality type. Second, the opposite must hold for low-quality types. Finally, responders must gain greater benefits from interacting with a high-quality type than with a low-quality type. Note that these conditions are essentially the minimal assumptions needed to apply a costly signaling framework.

In addition, as long as p (responder's payoff from interacting with a high-quality individual) $+ q$ (responder's payoff from interacting with a low-quality individual) > 0, there is a non-signaling equilibrium (NS, AR) in which no one signals and responders choose randomly from all other group members. Similarly, if the above inequality is reversed, there is a non-signaling equilibrium (NS, NR) in which no

Table 4.3
Payoff matrix for the n-person signaling game. Adapted from Gintis, Smith, and Bowles 2001. See table 4.2 for key to strategy abbreviations.

	AR	RS	RN	NR
AS	$s - pc - qc'$ $ph + ql$	$s/p - pc - qc'$ $ph + ql$	$-pc - qc'$ 0	$-pc - qc'$ 0
SH	$s - pc$ $ph + ql$	$s - pc$ h	$s - pc$ l	$-pc$ 0
SL	$s - qc'$ $ph + ql$	$qs/p - qc'$ l	$s - qc'$ h	$-qc'$ 0
NS	s $ph + ql$	0 0	s $ph + ql$	0 0

Note:
s = signaler's payoff from interacting with a responder
c = signaling cost for a high-quality type
c' = signaling cost for a low-quality type
h = responder's payoff from interacting with a high-quality type
l = responder's payoff from interacting with a low-quality type
p = proportion of n group members who are high-quality types
$q = 1 - p$ = proportion of n group members who are low-quality types

one signals and responders never choose interaction partners. The GSB analysis indicates that the honest signaling equilibrium will have higher payoffs than either non-signaling equilibria when, holding all other parameters of the model fixed, (a) high quality types are sufficiently rare (p is small); (b) the responder's benefit from consuming the collective good provided by the Signaler is sufficiently large; (c) the advantage of interacting with high quality types is sufficiently large; and (d) the cost of signaling is sufficiently small (for high-quality types).

GSB also show that the form of signaling outlined in the previous paragraphs will proliferate when rare and be evolutionarily stable, as long as the cost of signaling is sufficiently greater for low-quality than for high-quality players, and high-quality individuals are neither too common nor too rare. The reason for the latter condition is that if high-quality individuals become too common (p is very high), responders have a very high probability of interacting with such individuals even if they choose randomly, and thus those who avoid the costs of signaling will still have a high probability of being chosen for beneficial interactions. GSB provide an analysis showing that p will attain an equilibrium value under a range of plausible conditions.

In summary, the n-player costly signaling model developed by Gintis, Smith and Bowles (2001) shows that cooperative acts can function as ordinary costly signals and be favored by selection acting on either cultural or genetic variation. Over a broad range of parameter values, honest signaling of high quality by providing collective benefits is a strict Nash equilibrium, and a large basin of attraction grants it robust evolutionary stability. The conditions for this equilibrium are simply that (a) low-quality types pay greater marginal signal costs than do high-quality types; (b) other group members benefit more from interacting with high-quality than with low-quality types; and (c) this interaction provides benefits to high-quality signalers that exceed the signaling cost.

All of these results, however, apply equally to ordinary noncooperative signals, and thus the GSB model in itself specifies only necessary, but not sufficient, conditions for understanding why cooperative signaling might be favored over other forms with equivalent individual costs and benefits. The remainder of this chapter examines this last issue, both theoretically and empirically.

4.4   Why Group-Beneficial Signaling?

Honest signaling of quality need not be beneficial to the signaler's group. Indeed, the GSB model applies equally well to socially neutral or harmful forms of costly signaling. This raises the question of why costly signaling should ever take the form of providing collective goods. After all, in other species such signaling generally involves displays such as peacock's tails, roaring contests between red deer, or ritualized struggles between male elephant seals, which provide no overall group benefits. Furthermore, there appear to be numerous human examples of such socially wasteful displays: foot-binding, headhunting, various forms of conspicuous consumption, duels, violent brawling, and even the conspicuous flouting of social norms.

We can think of three possible answers to this question. One—invoking group selection among alternative evolutionarily stable equilibria (Boyd and Richerson 1990)—will be discussed briefly in a later section of this chapter. First, we explore two other explanations in greater detail, one involving the superiority of collective goods in attracting a larger audience and the other proposing that such provisioning is a superior signal of group-beneficial qualities (i.e., that cooperation is an intrinsic element of the qualities being signaled).

4.4.1 Broadcast Efficiency and Signal Escalation

Because signals evolve not only to convey honest information, but also to attract the attention of observers, advertising levels can escalate as a result of competition among signalers over such attention (Arak and Enquist 1995; Guilford and Dawkins 1993). Signal design may thus be directly related to competition over observer attention. This process could transform a socially neutral signal, such as an individual showing off his skill by spearing a few small fish, into a socially beneficial one, such as investing in construction of a stone fish weir allowing hundreds of kilograms of fish to be caught and shared throughout the community. Providing larger amounts of food than a competitor for "no-strings-attached" public consumption will tend to attract more attention from more observers (Hawkes 1993). This argument could easily be generalized to a wide range of public goods and corresponding appetites.

Put another way, one of the advantages *to the signaler* of providing a collective good over some more "wasteful" display of handicap may lie in the broadcast efficiency of the signal (Smith and Bliege Bird 2000). By "broadcast efficiency," we mean the number of observers attracted per unit of signaling effort. A man who expends a given amount of energy and risk in fighting with his neighbor might broadcast his abilities to far fewer people than one who assumes the same costs in publicly defending his village against an attack. We would expect individuals to take advantage of any means for increasing broadcast efficiency when they can benefit from increasing the number of observers and thus to signal by providing collective goods if doing so has such an effect. Furthermore, we expect that competition among such signalers will often result in increasing quantities of collective goods being provided to attract larger audiences (up to some equilibrium level, of course).

Grafen (1990) has modeled the role of differential quality in setting levels of competition in costly signaling games. His analysis indicates that as differences among competitors become more acute (e.g., as the differences in quality between the best and worst males increases), the level of advertising effort among all competitors increases correspondingly. Individuals near the low end invest heavily in advertising to distinguish themselves from slightly worse males; those of higher quality have no choice but to increase their effort to outdo those below them. This effect will be strongest when there are many competitors, especially if quality is continuously varying, rather than discrete. For example, male frogs will call more frequently and produce calls of longer duration when the number or density of competitive callers increases (Wells 1988). Levels of advertising tend to spiral upward under these conditions, in an arms race to outdo one's competitors.

Note that this broadcast efficiency argument does not reduce to saying that signalers gain benefits by providing goods that attract an audience. For CST to apply, there must also be a relation between the signal (in this case, the goods used to attract an audience) and variation in the underlying qualities being signaled. If signaling were simply a matter of attracting audiences by supplying collective goods, we would expect that quantity of goods supplied would be the only relevant dimension. Yet this fails to account for observations that only certain resources—and often relatively scarce ones at that—are provided for public consumption. The argument we are making here is that certain types of collective goods yield greater signal value per unit produced because they reveal relevant underlying qualities of the signaler. Resources that are more sensitive to marginal differences in levels of skill, strength, knowledge, or leadership will allow observers to discriminate amongst competing signalers in terms of these qualities more effectively.

For example, in a foraging economy, large game (e.g., marine turtles) is usually harder to locate and capture than smaller, more abundant game (e.g., sardines) or most plant resources. When the amount of a resource harvested does not reflect differences in underlying quality, the marginal payoff to the signaler of harvesting enough to provide a public good might not be high enough to justify the increased labor costs. In addition, if observers are interested in qualities such as skill or dedication, harvests of gathered resources or low-variance game should generally attract a smaller audience than an equivalent amount of a more challenging resource that does facilitate such discrimination. This would further increase the difference in payoff to the signaler of producing and providing quality-correlated collective goods versus other resources. This may explain why the marine foragers we have studied (see section 4.5.3) voluntarily assume higher labor costs and failure rates to provision a feast with 50 kilograms of turtle meat, rather than providing 50 kilograms of sardines with greater reliability and at lower labor costs.

4.4.2 Signaling Cooperative Qualities

Ordinarily, CST views signals as "indicator traits" of underlying qualities, with simply a contingent connection between signal and quality.

Thus, a signal such as a peacock's tail is an indicator of male vigor and hence (on average) genetic quality; only those cocks who are vigorous, disease-resistant, and excellent foragers can afford the cost of producing, maintaining, and dragging around a heavy and showy tail (Petrie 1994). But any trait that reliably indicated genetic quality would serve as well; there is no inherent reason that peahens should favor showy tails over some other equally reliable indicator. However, signal observers may value cooperative traits in themselves. Consequently, such traits may have intrinsic value to observers that extends beyond their role as indicator traits.

We can expect that responders will prefer signals that provide a collective good worth G over some equally informative signal that provides no collective good because, in addition to the gains from the information transferred in the signal, each of the n responders' payoffs will also be increased by G/n. Note, however, that this responder preference will not be enough to favor group-beneficial signaling if (as assumed earlier in this chapter) the interaction is a one-shot game, and all group members receive a share of the collective good whether they ally with the signaler producing it or not. In a more realistic model, however, group-beneficial signals may enhance the signaler's value to a potential ally because they strongly predict the signaler's ability to produce such signals in the future. For instance an individual who punishes wrongdoers within the group has honestly signaled his ability to also punish enemies of the political alliances of which he is part. Similarly, one who harvests surplus resources and generously shares them with others rather than conspicuously consuming them personally has honestly signaled his ability to do the same with an ally or mate. In both cases, we are proposing that a high-quality individual is more likely to provide the social benefit because the cost of doing so is lower than the cost for a low-quality one. The quality being signaled might be anything that lowers the cost of behaving in a cooperative manner, such as superior strength or greater foraging skills.

The important point here is that the potential ally may prefer not just good indicator traits, but ones that will provide additional benefits to him or her. In many cases, group-beneficial signals will be more likely to have this quality than other types of signals. Note that this explanation, like the broadcast efficiency one in the previous section, relies solely on individual advantages (to signaler and to observer) of group-beneficial signaling; it is based on mutualism rather than altruism and thus provides an alternative to both reciprocal altruism and strong reciprocity.

4.5   Signaling and Collective Action

4.5.1   The Problem of Collective Goods

Generosity—such phenomena as sharing food outside the immediate family, giving gifts, hosting public events, or helping neighbors in need, all at some cost to one's self—seems to be a ubiquitous cross-cultural feature of human social life. But generosity is not universally nor randomly extended. Instead, it appears to be strategic—the contexts in which such acts occur, as well as the characteristics of donors and recipients, seem to be highly constrained and patterned. Some of this variability may be adaptive and therefore explicable using theory from evolutionary ecology. Such explanations have most frequently been framed in terms of conditional reciprocity, involving such concepts as reciprocal altruism, tit-for-tat, iterated Prisoner's Dilemma, and the like (Trivers 1971; Axelrod and Hamilton 1981; Cosmides and Tooby 1989). Others have argued that sharing or other forms of putative generosity are due to coercion on the part of recipients and hence are a form of "tolerated theft" (Blurton Jones 1984; Hawkes 1992). CST provides a third explanation, involving mutualism rather than reciprocity or coercion (Dugatkin 1997), although as we will argue, these need not be mutually exclusive and indeed can work in concert.

One classic example of public generosity is the widespread practice among hunter-gatherers of sharing individually harvested resources with nonkin. This practice is commonly explained as a means of reducing the risk associated with acquiring productive but highly variable resources such as big game (Smith 1988). Pooling individually harvested resources smoothes out consumption variance for all participants, a considerable benefit when harvests are so unpredictable that individual hunters can expect many days or weeks to elapse between successes (Winterhalder 1990). While risk-reduction effects are plausible and can be demonstrated to exist (Cashdan 1985; Kaplan, Hill, and Hurtado 1990), these effects might be an outcome rather than a cause of food-sharing. Sharing in order to reduce consumption variance involves a Prisoner's Dilemma payoff structure (Smith and Boyd 1990) and thus creates incentives to slack off and free-ride on the efforts of others (Blurton Jones 1986; Hawkes 1993). This insight has led to an active debate about how to explain the undisputed fact of extensive food-sharing by hunter-gatherers (Winterhalder 1996).

We believe that while conditional reciprocity may explain some cases of hunter-gatherer food sharing, it cannot explain them all. When all group members have rights to consume the resource regardless of their past contribution, and the number partaking is dozens or more, the conditions for conditional reciprocity are not met (Hawkes 1992). Such lack of contingency (failure to direct shares so as to repay debts or create indebtedness) occurs where there are strong social norms governing the distribution of shares and when resources are distributed to individuals regardless of whether they ever repay the donor. This situation applies most obviously in public ceremonial contexts such as funerary rites (Smith and Bliege Bird 2000), big-man feasting (Wiessner and Schiefenhövel 1995), Northwest Coast Indian potlatching (Boone 1998), or charity galas in capitalist society (Veblen 1899). Here, generosity takes place within a broad social arena, and resources are distributed as a collective good simultaneously to large numbers of recipients. The generous individual cannot ensure that the targets of his generosity will return the favor. If sharing or generosity cannot be made contingent upon reciprocation, then the fundamental condition for evolutionarily stable reciprocity is absent.

Lack of attention to a recipient's past history or future probability of reciprocating has been described as part of food sharing patterns in many hunter-gatherer societies, such as the Ache Indians of the Paraguayan forest (Kaplan and Hill 1985a), and the Hadza of the East African savanna (Hawkes 1993). In these cases (and others), at least some types of harvested resources are shared unconditionally with most or all members of the community, and some hunters consistently provide more than others while sharing more or less equally in the catch. These "altruistic" providers in fact enjoy higher social status and reproductive success than their less productive peers, despite the absence of any conditional exchange of "meat for mates" (Kaplan and Hill 1985b; Marlowe 2000; Bliege Bird, Smith, and Bird 2001; Smith in press). Enhanced reputations, social status, and its subsequent mating advantages could be the "selective incentive" (Olson 1965) that motivates certain individuals to provide collective goods. But why should recipients reward generous providers with high status? Is this not just another form of reciprocity? If so, we would seem to have solved one collective action problem by posing another (Smith 1993).

4.5.2   Is "Indirect Reciprocity" a Solution?

Early social theorists analyzing public generosity interpreted some of its many forms as an outgrowth of social competition, a rivalry in divesting oneself of goods where the most generous individual gains the highest prestige, and the recipients of goods gain material benefit at the expense of their reputations (Veblen 1899; Mauss 1926; Fried 1967). Recently, behavioral biologists have begun to modify models of reciprocal altruism to account for reputation enhancement and status benefits associated with giving, what Alexander (1987, 85) termed "indirect reciprocity." Indirect reciprocity, in Alexander's scheme, results when "the return explicitly comes from someone other than the recipient of the original beneficence."

Nowak and Sigmund (1998) proposed that the benefit gained from advertising one's cooperative tendencies through costly acts of altruism is the increased chance of becoming the recipient of another's altruistic act at a later date. They constructed computer simulations in which one of a pair of players could choose whether or not to donate help based on the potential recipient's behavior in previous pairings with others, as measured in their "image score." While their simulation showed that reputations did matter in choosing partners, others have demonstrated that the particular form by which the "image score" is instantiated in Nowak and Sigmund's analysis is not evolutionarily stable (Leimar and Hammerstein 2001). However, a related form of indirect reciprocity, the "standing strategy" (Sugden 1986), can both invade a noncooperative population and resist invasion by other strategies, even when errors and incomplete information are allowed (Panchanathan and Boyd 2003).

While this work illuminates theoretical possibilities, it will take empirical research to determine if altruists are indeed preferred targets of the altruism of third parties. For example, experiments conducted by Wedekind and Milinski (2000) showed that those who were more generous in dyadic semi-anonymous interactions received more donations in return, which the experimenters interpret as support for the "image scoring" version of indirect reciprocity. However, the more generous players preferred to give indiscriminately, rewarding the generous and stingy alike. This is precisely the behavior one would predict if generosity were a costly signal of the ability to donate resources. Milinski, Semmann, and Krambeck (2002) report experimental results showing that players who donated more to a charity (information which was known to other players in the game) received both more aid from fellow players in an indirect reciprocity game and more votes for election to a student organization. As the authors note (p. 883), "Donating to those who are in need might serve as an honest and efficient (because it is done in public) signal for one's reciprocity reliability."

Boyd and Richerson (1989) also modeled indirect reciprocity and concluded that strategies based on the principle "be nice to people who are nice to others" were relatively successful. However, they and others have noted that the evolutionary stability of indirect reciprocity is likely only in small groups, where there is some way of keeping score of one's giving and receiving and of targeting cooperation conditionally at reciprocators—precisely the same limitations faced in direct conditional reciprocity. Roberts (1998) proposed a solution to this problem by arguing that reputation could be an indirect benefit of altruistic behavior if interactions are modeled in two stages: (1) an assessment stage, in which individuals establish reputations for generosity through public and non-reciprocal displays; and (2) a subsequent stage involving dyadic interactions, where individuals choose a cooperating partner based on reputations previously established. Like Milinski et al., Roberts is thus proposing essentially a costly signaling argument, where the key function of establishing reputations through costly public displays of altruism is to facilitate trust in dyadic partnerships.

While "indirect reciprocity" models tend to focus on benefits gained through subsequent pair-wise cooperative interactions following display, CST helps us see that these may not be necessary in order for both signalers and observers to benefit. As we have pointed out (Smith and Bliege Bird 2000), observers might respond to signals by subsequently avoiding the signaler altogether, in much the same way as red deer roaring provides a way for competitors to evaluate the probability of winning a fight without actually risking injury (Clutton-Brock and Albon 1979). Indirect reciprocity explanations also overlook the possibility that there may be benefits gained simply as a function of the display, both by those who display and those who observe.

4.5.3   The Costly Signaling Solution: An Ethnographic Example

Meriam turtle hunting provides an interesting test of the ability of CST to explain seemingly inefficient (and costly) foraging and food distribution patterns (Smith and Bliege Bird 2000; Bliege Bird, Smith, and Bird 2001). There are two primary types of marine turtle acquisition on Mer (an island in Torres Strait, northern Australia)—hunting and collecting. Turtle hunting occurs primarily in the context of public feasting events; hunters choose to hunt in response to a request from feast organizers to provide turtles for consumption at a previously announced feast. Among Meriam turtle hunters, there are three distinct roles: hunt leader, jumper, and driver. In addition, turtles are also collected, primarily in the context of household provisioning, but also for feasts, by men of all ages, women, and children. This occurs only when they can be harvested on beaches during the nesting season (October through April).

Hunting turtles is a competitive pursuit, with a very different complement of participants than collecting. As the Meriam put it, "*Anyone can collect turtle in the nesting season, but only certain men have the ability to succeed at turtle hunting.*" Compared to collecting, hunting is more costly (in terms of time, energy, and risk), provides meat less efficiently (due to higher travel, search, and pursuit costs), and is associated with wider distributions of meat (figure 4.1). Hunters keep no meat for themselves, except in the rare occasion when they are hunting for household consumption, in which case they still keep less and share more than turtle collectors. Hunters take on a variety of costs for which they are not materially compensated, including time and energy

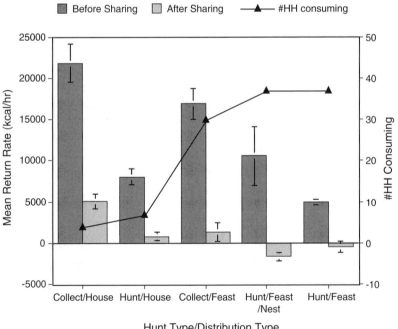

Figure 4.1
Meriam turtle hunting versus collecting returns before and after sharing, and number of households consuming for each hunt/distribution type.

in hunting, money for fuel, and time organizing and preparing the hunting team and its equipment prior to the hunt. The ability to bear such costs appears to be linked to hunter quality: because a hunt leader is an organizer and decision-maker, his abilities peak as he gains skill and experience. The signals sent by hunting also are efficiently broadcast: hunts are associated with larger numbers of consumers and thus attract a broader audience than collections during the nesting season and during household consumption events (figure 4.1). When quizzed, most feast-goers (audience members) know the identity of hunters, while the identity of jumpers seems to be common knowledge only among their own peer group of young males.

The benefits hunters receive from generously providing turtle for public consumption do not appear to come in the form of increased shares of collected turtle or other foods, as we might predict if risk reduction reciprocity were structuring the payoffs for hunting (Bliege Bird et al. 2002). Those who acquire turtle (both hunted and collected) more frequently and share more widely (figure 4.2) or acquire turtle in greater quantity (figure 4.3) do not receive turtle more frequently as compared to those who share less or not at all. In addition, generous turtle sharing does not appear to be repaid through receiving shares of fish or other foods (figure 4.4).

The CS explanation of collective goods provisioning as applied to the Meriam turtle hunting case proposes that turtle hunters benefit from unconditional sharing because their harvesting success sends honest signals about their quality to the community in which they will

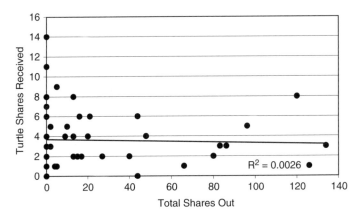

Figure 4.2
Do those who give turtle to more households receive turtle more frequently?

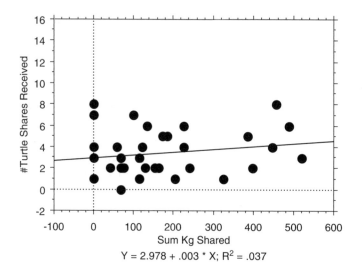

Y = 2.978 + .003 * X; R² = .037

Regression Coefficients
#Turtle Shares Received vs. Sum Kg Shared

	Coefficient	Std. Error	Std. Coeff.	t-Value	P-Value
Intercept	2.978	.541	2.978	5.506	<.0001
Sum Kg Sh	.003	.002	.192	1.127	.2680

Figure 4.3
Do those who share more kilograms of turtle receive more frequently?

play out their lives as mates, allies, and competitors. Paying attention to such signals can benefit observers because the costs and potential for complete failure inherent in the signal guarantee that it is an honest measure of the underlying qualities at issue. Only those endowed with the necessary skills will succeed and be asked to serve regularly on crews or as hunt leaders. The benefits accruing to signalers (hunters) will depend upon the specific signal and audience. For hunt leaders, they might consist of being deferred to by elders or obtaining benefits of a hard working wife's labor (Smith, Bliege Bird, and Bird 2003). For jumpers, they might include a means of establishing social dominance among peers and hence preferential access to various social resources, including enhanced mating opportunities.

Interestingly, the Meriam themselves interpret unconditional generosity such as donating turtles to feasts or sharing collected turtles with neighbors as different from conditional reciprocity (which also has a

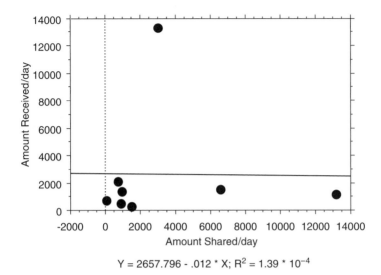

$$Y = 2657.796 - .012 * X; R^2 = 1.39 * 10^{-4}$$

Regression Coefficients
Amt Rec/day vs. Amt Sh/day

	Coefficient	Std. Error	Std. Coeff.	t-Value	P-Value
Intercept	2657.796	2139.059	2657.796	1.243	.2604
Amt Sh/day	-.012	.399	-.012	-.029	.9779

Figure 4.4
Do those who share more food receive more food?

place in their social and economic lives). The Meriam conception of generosity involves reference to a concept called "*debe tonar*," which means "the good way." *Debe tonar* is a set of principles for everyday social interactions, and adhering to those principles is considered a signal of Meriam identity. Following *debe tonar* is said to provide long-term benefits in the form of an enhanced social reputation as a "good person." Subsistence decisions intersect with that aspect of *debe tonar* that incorporates generosity with food. There are strong social sanctions against conditional or contingent sharing of "table food" (*derapeili*—to share portions out) between households following the harvesting of wild or cultivated foods. Similarly, there are social norms governing the provisioning of food to feasts: such foods are explicitly designated public goods (*kies*), open to unconditional consumption. *Debe tonar* states that such unconditional sharing is its own reward; to share with the expectation of a return in kind is to share selfishly, and to return a portion given freely is to imply that the giver had selfish motives. A Meriam adage goes, "When you expect payment back, you do not *esak gem blo em*" (make an lasting impression). Sharing selfishly is equivalent to not sharing at all: both are referred to as being "*gobar*," greedy with food. While *derapeili* and *kies* sharing are explicitly unconditional, there are conditional sharing contexts within which reciprocal exchange is considered proper: markets (*tama*), labor exchange/work party feasts (*irapu*), ceremonial exchange partners (*wauri tebud*), and repayments (*bodomelam*) for use-rights to certain individually or corporately owned items (land, foraging areas, boats, or tools).

4.5.4   Why Does Crowding Out Occur?

As discussed in chapter 1 and elsewhere in this volume, it often happens that voluntary contributions to a public good will decrease when such contribution is supplemented or replaced by direct material incentives (e.g., payments to blood donors). The costly signaling framework can be used to generate the hypothesis that this "crowding out" may be due to a dilution of signaling value. If the social value of donating blood is cheapened by an increased supply from sellers or if blood donation might be conflated with blood selling, the signaling value of donating is likely to fall, perhaps sufficiently to lie below the donation cost for many former donors.

We are not arguing that all examples of "crowding out" can be explained by costly signaling processes, nor that we are certain that some can be so explained. However, it appears to be a plausible hypothesis, supported by a formal model and empirically testable under the right circumstances. The alternative explanations in terms of strong reciprocity and histories of group selection proposed elsewhere in this volume are equally testable, but it appears in most cases that the data to distinguish between the explanatory efficacy of the two explanations are lacking.

4.5.5   Signaling and Group-Beneficial Enforcement

Another type of collective good that may be a form of costly signaling involves punishing those who free-ride on the group's cooperative activities or otherwise violate group-beneficial norms. It is well known that although enforcing cooperation by punishing defectors will solve collective action problems, such enforcement is costly to those who carry out the enforcement and is itself a collective good, thus posing a second-order collective action problem (Hardin 1982)—albeit a less demanding one at the cooperative (low–enforcement-frequency) equilibrium (Boyd et al. 2003). Boyd and Richerson (1992) demonstrated that if enforcement takes the form of punishing both noncooperators and nonpunishers, then cooperation (or anything else) can be evolutionarily stable, even in large groups and even if enforcement is only carried out by a small fraction of the group's members. Such enforcement may be a potent element in stabilizing cooperation in many types of social systems (Clutton-Brock and Parker 1995; Frank 1995; Richerson and Boyd 1998; chapter 7 in this volume).

Note, however, that enforcement can serve as a costly signal in its own right, as long as the costs of enforcement are quality-dependent. If the qualities that make one a good (low-cost) enforcer also make one attractive as a potential ally or someone it will pay to defer to in other contexts, enforcement costs can be recouped by signaling benefits. This costly signaling dynamic can then provide a private benefit to the enforcer and thus in principle solve the second-order collective action problem. The GSB model provides one mechanism for the evolution of such a system. In this version, enforcement—punishment of noncooperators—is itself the behavior that signals high quality. This model readily allows such punishment or enforcement to serve as the costly signal and hence to be maintained when the conditions for evolutionary stability specified in the model are met.

Here is a brief account to show how the model captures this form of signaling (adapted from Gintis, Smith, and Bowles 2001). Suppose that a group of n members can cooperate to provide some collective good. By cooperating, each member contributes a total benefit of γ to others at a fitness cost of δ to himself. Thus, the gain from defecting is δ, and to prevent this, members must be punished at least δ for defecting. Now suppose that a high-quality individual can impose δ on defectors at a personal cost of c, whereas a low-quality individual must incur cost $c' > c$ to achieve the same effect. Following the model summarized in section 4.3, under the range of parameter values noted, there will be an equilibrium in which high-quality individuals will punish and low-quality ones will not. In turn, observers will benefit by using such punishment behavior as a signal of underlying qualities that will provide useful information for future social interactions. And of course, all group members will benefit from the effect of punishment in enforcing cooperation in collective action. To our knowledge, this argument has not been directly applied to any empirical cases of group-beneficial punishment. However, it does seem to be consistent with a variety of ethnographic observations (e.g., Boehm 1999, chapter 5 of this volume).

A common observation that can be experimentally replicated (see chapter 5 of this volume), is that in many circumstances people enforce a norm of fairness or equity. Of course, the specific meaning of "fairness" is culturally variable and often highly contested within any given culture or society (compare the arguments of U.S. Democratic versus Republican lawmakers on tax policy, for example). Nevertheless, even if subject to conflicting interpretations and strategies of deception and manipulation, enforcement of fairness or redistributive equity in division of the social product is a pervasive feature of human social life (see various chapters of the present volume for evidence and discussion). While models of strong reciprocity (chapter 6) and conditional reciprocity (chapter 3) offer plausible hypotheses to explain this phenomenon, in the spirit of theoretical pluralism we want to sketch how CST might have something to contribute to this topic.

In brief, we suggest that fairness norms allow assessment of the ability (or willingness) of individuals or coalitions to "pay their share"— that is, to pay the cost that ensures signal reliability. This could apply equally (but with different forms and signaling details) to both egalitarian systems—where fairness means contributing equally—and to hierarchical systems—where some are allowed to possess more wealth and power than others but are expected to contribute to the common good (e.g., hosting ceremonial events) according to their greater abilities. In either case, norms that require members of a collective to donate their surplus to have-nots (Boone 1998) or to contribute equally to production of a public good could be motivated by signaling concerns.

Given this multiplicity of social contexts and underlying qualities being signaled, failure to pay one's share could have one of several distinct meanings and consequences, including:

1) inability to do so (a signal of low quality, leading to reduced social status),

2) defection from the game (a decision to withdraw from a given arena of status competition), and

3) flaunting the norm (a signal of social power or superior status, reliable to the extent that norm violation is more costly than simply "paying one's share," and hence not viable for low-status or subordinate individuals).

Thus, we suggest that the meaning of fairness-norm violations must be interpreted in light of contextual information. In any case, the CS framework suggests that attention must be paid to the information value of fairness norms, and that enforcement of these norms may be aimed at ensuring signal reliability and solving status-competition games as much as (or more than) ensuring equity *per se*.

4.5.6   Signaling and Inter-Group Conflict

A related set of phenomena involve individually costly contributions to violent conflict between social groups. Participating in group raiding or defense is common among chimpanzees as well as human societies (Boehm 1992; Manson and Wrangham 1991), yet this kind of activity poses some thorny challenges to evolutionary analysis. Such behavior provides benefits that are available to all group members and cannot be hoarded or individually consumed, and therefore approach the classic definition of a pure public good. Yet the costs to contributors can be extraordinarily high (including of course death), which means that the payoffs to free-riding should be considerable. Some have argued that the widespread occurrence of organized intergroup violence thus can only be explained as the result of a history of genetic group selection (Alexander 1979, 1987; Hamilton 1975; Eibl-Eibesfeldt 1982). Others suggest that group selection acting on *cultural* variation could be responsible for favoring self-sacrificial aspects of intergroup conflict (Peoples 1982; Richerson and Boyd 1998; chapter 7 of this volume). CST offers a possible alternative to both of these views, with participation in group military defense and offense serving as a display of underlying qualities useful for status competition within one's group.

The evidence that military contribution and self-sacrificial bravery is a primary avenue to male status enhancement in small-scale societies is substantial (Chagnon 1990; Otterbein 1970; Patton 2000). It is easy to see that status enhancement may ensure the spread of even dangerous status-enhancing behavior if it has sufficient benefits to material, reproductive, or cultural success. The key question, as we saw with the issue of unconditional generosity, is *why* others grant such status to warriors. The CS explanation is that success in warfare signals underlying qualities that are valued by prospective allies and deferred to by prospective competitors. In turn, females may mate preferentially with successful warriors (Chagnon 1988) because they benefit from the social dominance of such individuals, even if the particular qualities signaled are not of direct benefit to a spouse.

The group-level benefits of status-seeking by warriors is thus incidental to the CS explanation, and indeed the CS dynamic could produce an oversupply of military adventuring as well as an undersupply of dedicated warriors. We read the ethnographic and historical record as providing ample evidence of both (e.g., Boone 1983; Keeley 1996; Mesquida and Wiener 1996; Otterbein 1970). Of course, CS dynamics could work in concert with multilevel selection of either genetic or cultural variation. For example, depending on initial conditions, CS might yield a variety of equilibria in the intensity of intergroup conflict, and those equilibria that happen to optimize the supply of belligerence (as measured by enhanced persistence and/or spread of the social group) would then be favored. This would be an example of the process of group selection among alternative local equilibria modeled by Boyd and Richerson (1990) (see also chapter 7 in this volume).

4.6   Signaling and Commitment

4.6.1   Signaling and Common Goals

The presence of conflicting interests among social organisms often sets high barriers to cooperation. Gender can be a source of profound disparities in reproductive interests such that "even when cooperating in a joint task, male and female interests are rarely identical" (Trivers 1972, 174). Even the most closely related groups of cooperating individuals have imperfectly coincident genetic interests and can therefore exhibit intense conflict and competition. Although siblings share a considerable degree of common genetic interest, they also often compete more with each other (for parental investment and other resources) than with other individuals in the social group (Sulloway 1996). Conflicting genetic interests between mother and fetus institute a form of maternal-fetal warfare during gestation, even though by cooperating each could maintain an outcome better for both (Haig 1993).

Individuals often come into conflict about working toward a shared goal when each faces different tradeoffs and gains different benefits from working toward that goal. For example, given the fact that males and females have different reproductive strategies and life histories, they will often face conflicts between working toward a common goal of household provisioning (in effect, an investment in self-maintenance and the rearing of children) and alternative productive and reproductive goals, such as gaining status in the wider community, producing children with other mates, acquiring more mates, or accumulating wealth. To have an incentive to cooperate, however, partners must have goals in common to some degree, such that both benefit more from the partnership than each would if they acted independently.

In choosing a partner for a dyadic cooperative endeavor—such as a mate to cooperatively raise offspring, a research colleague, or a coauthor—each partner must be convinced that he or she will gain a net benefit from the interaction. This is particularly important if the association will be a long-term one, with opportunities for cheating or periods of one-sided costs for one partner (e.g., carrying a child to term or writing the first draft of a manuscript) that would allow the other partner to maximize short-term returns by defecting. How can the potential partners discern each other's intentions with any degree of reliability?

One way they might do so is by sending honest signals of commitment to common goals for the project or relationship in question. Pursuing our coauthorship example, conflict can occur when one partner seeks individual status over the collective status achieved through coauthorship or seeks to free-ride on the efforts of a harder-working coauthor. In order to honestly signal his commitment to common goals, he must show that when given the opportunity to gain individual status at the expense of his partner, he chooses to forgo this in favor of promoting the interests of the partnership. For example, one partner might be approached by a publisher interested in securing the rights to a book deal based on jointly conducted research. If this partner accepts the deal and promotes himself as sole author, he gains individual benefits but jeopardizes the continuation of the partnership. If he declines the publisher's offer (or brings the partner into the deal), he pays an opportunity cost in terms of his own individual status but signals his ongoing commitment to the partnership. Since the tempted partner can only expect the short-term cost of forgoing sole authorship to be repaid if he expects the relationship to last long enough to produce benefits greater than these costs, his actions are an honest signal of commitment. Thus, the cost paid by not defecting (if sufficiently high) guarantees the honesty of the signal.

4.6.2   Coalition Commitment

Signaling of common goals applies not only to dyadic partnerships, but might also help solve multi-agent cooperative dilemmas. Relationships among members of relatively stable social groups often involve such interactions; for example, some of the most important interactions are cooperative behaviors involving group territorial defense. When challenges by neighboring groups come at unpredictable times, periodic testing of the commitment of group members to engage in costly territorial defense helps ensure that they can be relied upon when the time comes to fight. Zahavi and Zahavi (1997) suggest that among Arabian Babblers (a group-living bird), many social behaviors such as huddling, grooming, and group dances serve to test the social bond and, by extension, demonstrate commitment to group defense. Dances and ceremonies in many human groups that are performed prior to heading into battle might serve much the same function. However, plausibility arguments such as this one need to be stated in a more directly falsifiable manner and then subjected to careful empirical tests.

Cooperative dilemmas also arise in the context of within-group competition, involving political coalitions and alliances. Most models of political power assume that politicians gain power as part of a reciprocal exchange: a politician promises "pork" to his constituents in return for the favor of their vote. Given the delayed return here ("If I support you now, you will return the favor by providing collective goods in the future"), defection is always a distinct possibility. Costly signaling may not eliminate the risk of defection, but it could help in predicting which individuals are less likely to do so. If a politician can reliably signal a superior ability to obtain resources for redistribution during period 1, he should be more likely to actually do so in period 2.

Here, costly signaling does not guarantee honesty of intent to deliver collective goods, but it may guarantee honest advertisement of the ability to do so. A variety of political systems, ranging from the semi-egalitarian "big-man" systems of Melanesia to the stratified chiefdoms of the Northwest Coast Indians, appear to display various elements of this costly signaling dynamic of garnering and maintaining political support through magnanimity (Boone 1998). In these cases, and arguably in many instances of electoral politics in modern industrialized democracies, political candidates use distributions of goods to honestly signal their ability to benefit supporters in the future. The big man, chief, or congressional candidate encourages others to donate wealth or labor in his support by displaying honest signals of his skill in accumulating resources, thus ameliorating the most problematic aspect of delayed reciprocity: the risk of default.

4.7   Conclusions

Costly signaling theory provides the basis for arguing that generosity—incurring the costs of providing collective goods (including those shared with partners in dyadic relationships)—is one means by which individuals and coalitions compete for status, and ultimately for the material and fitness-enhancing correlates of status (such as political power, mates, and economic resources). The quality-dependent cost of providing the collective good guarantees the honesty of the signaler's claim to such qualities as resource control, leadership abilities, kin-group solidarity, economic productivity, or good health and vigor—information that is useful to the signaler's potential mates, allies, and competitors (Boone 1998; Smith and Bliege Bird 2000). If this explanation is correct, it means that those who engage in acts of unconditional generosity by providing collective goods are not acting in hope of reciprocation in kind, nor sacrificing for the good of the group or their partner, but rather are competing for status and its perquisites. We extended these arguments to address the issue of *commitment* in cases of both dyadic reciprocity and n-person coalitions and argued that signaling might provide an alternative to (or at least strengthen) more conventional analyses of these phenomena.

The n-player game-theoretical model summarized earlier in this chapter (and developed more fully in Gintis, Smith, and Bowles 2001) specifies conditions under which an honest-signaling equilibrium will be stable. At this equilibrium, only high-quality individuals signal while observers respond only to signalers (these being the player's respective best moves). This model shows that group-beneficial signals (such as unconditionally providing a collective good) can meet the conditions for a signaling equilibrium. However, these results apply equally well to socially neutral or even harmful signals, and hence this model alone cannot tell us why group-beneficial signals would be favored over other signals.

To address this last question, we briefly discussed three distinct (but not mutually exclusive) hypotheses. One of these involves equilibrium selection among alternative (some more group-beneficial, some less) signaling equilibria, possibly through a process of cultural group selection. A second proposes that the value *to the signaler* of providing a collective good over some more "wasteful" display may lie in the broadcast efficiency of the signal in competing for observer attention, given that observers are more likely to be attracted to signals that provide an additional consumption benefit. Our third hypothesis is that when members of a social group benefit directly from cooperative signals, these signals can be favored because they serve as reliable indicators that the signaler's allies have an increased probability of receiving similar private benefits from the signaler in the future.

While the costly-signaling approach to cooperation and collective action opens up some exciting vistas, it raises many questions that will require extensive theoretical and empirical work. Of these, we will mention three major ones: figuring out (1) what underlying qualities are being signaled, (2) who the intended signal recipients are, and (3) under what conditions signaling to the field is a better strategy than targeting specific signal recipients. The first two questions are primarily empirical, although potentially very difficult ones to answer in particular cases. The third question is one that is side-stepped in the GSB model—which simply presumes that attracting a large audience by providing a collective good will increase the payoff to the signaler. This is likely to be the case under at least two circumstances: 1) when each signaler can benefit from attracting multiple partners of a single type (e.g., multiple potential mates), and 2) when each signaler can benefit from influencing multiple types of observers (e.g., attracting allies and mates, intimidating competitors).

Another issue that presents intriguing possibilities for theoretical development is to extend the one-shot analysis of the GSB model to situations of repeated signaling and extended interaction. Repeated signaling is likely to occur when reputations need to be built or maintained. We suspect that this is likely to be important under two main (but not mutually exclusive) conditions: (1) where there is lots of "noise" (i.e., variation in signaling that is not due to underlying qualities), and (2) where the qualities being signaled are likely to change quickly over time (e.g., due to ecological and economic variations). The first situation is exemplified by the hunting of large game. In this scenario, elements not controlled by the hunter can have a large but unpredictable effect on success, yet underlying qualities (such as ethological knowledge, visual acuity, stamina, and so forth) can lead to consistent differences between individuals in long-term average returns. The second situation—where underlying qualities are subject to rapid decay—is characteristic of a variety of economic situations, ranging from subsistence regimes subject to severe ecological fluctuation (e.g., pastoralists in arid lands) to a speculative capitalist economy, where entrepreneurs and members of the underclass are subject to boom-and-bust conditions. We can expect the first situation to feature repeated signaling early in an individual's career, in order to establish a reputation that will then be relatively stable and require little or no future reinforcement (e.g., the turtle-hunting careers of Meriam that typically take a decade or so to establish and may then persist for only a few years more, yet result in long-term social and reproductive gains). The second situation is likely to be much more dynamic, with signalers' fortunes (and signaling intensities) rising and falling rapidly with changing circumstances; this scenario will presumably present a more challenging arena for formal modeling.

4.8 Acknowledgments

For many fruitful discussions that have strongly influenced the ideas developed in this paper, we thank Doug Bird, Carl Bergstrom, Sam Bowles, Herb Gintis, Kristen Hawkes, Hillard Kaplan, and Joan Silk. The n-player signaling model outlined in this chapter was developed in collaboration with Gintis and Bowles and a more detailed version is published elsewhere (Gintis, Smith, and Bowles 2001). Fieldwork among the Meriam was carried out in close collaboration with Doug Bird, Craig Hadley, and many Meriam friends, especially members of the Passi family. This fieldwork was supported by grants from the National Science Foundation, the Leakey Foundation, the Wenner-Gren Foundation, and the Australian Institute of Aboriginal and Torres Strait Islander Studies.

Notes

1. By "cooperative behavior" we mean any actions by Ego that enhance the well-being of members of Ego's social group beyond his or her immediate kin. Such actions need not impose a net cost on Ego in the short term, and the social benefits need not be evenly distributed among Ego's social group, though these special cases are of particular interest in this chapter and elsewhere in the present volume.

2. Lotem, Fishman and Stone (2002) subsequently published a model of the evolution of cooperation via costly signaling that shares some aspects of the GSB model. However, Lotem et al. model only dyadic interactions, and start with a population containing high frequencies of conditional reciprocators, whereas Gintis et al. (2001) develop a multiplayer game with no initial (pre-signaling) levels of cooperation.

3. GSB show that the results are unchanged if (following Johnstone 1997 and Getty 1998) signaling benefits rather than signaling costs are made quality-dependent. They did not, however, analyze the effect of allowing Responders to vary in ways that affect the

interaction payoff to Signalers. This two-sided matching problem is difficult to model, and has not been attempted in the costly signaling framework, though it has been developed for marriage markets and mate choice (e.g., Bergstrom and Real 2000).

References

Alexander, Richard D. (1979) *Darwinism and Human Affairs*. Seattle: University of Washington Press.

Alexander, Richard D. (1987) *The Biology of Moral Systems*. Hawthorne, NY: Aldine de Gruyter.

Arak, A., and M. Enquist. (1995) Conflict, receiver bias, and the evolution of signal form. *Phil Trans R Soc Lond B* 1355:337–344.

Axelrod, Robert, and William D. Hamilton. (1981) The evolution of cooperation. *Science* 211:1390–1396.

Bergstrom, Carl, and Leslie A. Real. (2000) Towards a theory of mutual mate choice: Lessons from two-sided matching. *Evolutionary Ecology Research* 2:493–508.

Bliege Bird, Rebecca L., Eric A. Smith, and Douglas W. Bird. (2001) The hunting handicap: Costly signaling in human foraging strategies. *Behavioral Ecology and Sociobiology* 50:9–19.

Bliege Bird, Rebecca L., Douglas W. Bird, Eric A. Smith, and Geoffrey Kushnick. (2002) Risk and reciprocity in Meriam food sharing. *Evolution and Human Behavior* 23(4):297–321.

Blurton Jones, Nicholas G. (1984) A selfish origin for human food sharing: Tolerated theft. *Ethology and Sociobiology* 5:1–3.

Blurton Jones, Nicholas G. (1986) Fitness returns from resources and the outcome of contests: Some implications for primatology and anthropology. In *Primate Ontogeny, Cognition and Social Behaviour*, vol. 3. Ed. J. G. Else and P. Lee. Proceedings of the 10th Congress of the International Primatology Society. Cambridge: Cambridge University Press, 393–406.

Boehm, Christopher. (1992) Segmentary warfare and management of conflict: A comparison of East African chimpanzees and patrilineal-patrilocal humans. In *Coalitions and Alliances in Humans and Other Animals*. Ed. A. Harcourt and F. B. M. de Waal. Oxford: Oxford University Press, 137–173.

Boehm, Christopher. (1999) *Hierarchy in the Forest: The Evolution of Egalitarian Behavior*. Cambridge, MA: Harvard University Press.

Boone, James L. (1983) Noble family structure and expansionist warfare in the late Middle Ages: A socioecological approach. In *Rethinking Human Adaptation*. Ed. R. Dyson-Hudson and M. A. Little. Boulder, CO: Westview Press, 79–96.

Boone, James L. (1998) The evolution of magnanimity: When is it better to give than to receive? *Human Nature* 9:1–21.

Boyd, Robert, and Peter J. Richerson. (1988) The evolution of reciprocity in sizable groups. *Journal of Theoretical Biology* 132:337–356.

Boyd, Robert, and Peter J. Richerson. (1989) The evolution of indirect reciprocity. *Social Networks* 11:213–236.

Boyd, Robert, and Peter J. Richerson. (1990) Group selection among alternative evolutionarily stable strategies. *J. of Theoretical Biology* 145:331–342.

Boyd, Robert, and Peter J. Richerson. (1992) Punishment allows the evolution of cooperation (or anything else) in sizable groups. *Ethology and Sociobiology* 13:171–195.

Boyd, Robert, Herbert Gintis, Samuel L. Bowles, and Peter J. Richerson. (2003) The evolution of altruistic punishment. *Proceedings of the National Academy of Sciences, USA* 100:3531–3535.

Caro, Tim M. (1994) Ungulate antipredator behaviour: Preliminary and comparative evidence from African bovids. *Behaviour* 128:189–228.

Cashdan, Elizabeth A. (1985) Coping with risk: Reciprocity among the Basarwa of northern Botswana. *Man* 20:454–474.

Chagnon, Napoleon A. (1988) Life histories, blood revenge, and warfare in a tribal population. *Science* 239:985–992.

Chagnon, Napoleon A. (1990) Reproductive and somatic conflicts of interest in the genesis of violence and warfare among tribesmen. In *The Anthropology of War*. Ed. J. Hass. Cambridge: Cambridge University Press, 77–104.

Clutton-Brock, T. H., and S. D. Albon. (1979) The roaring of red deer and the evolution of honest advertisement. *Behaviour* 69:145–170.

Clutton-Brock, T. H., and G. A. Parker. (1995) Punishment in animal societies. *Nature* 373:209–216.

Cosmides, Leda, and John Tooby. (1989) Evolutionary psychology and the generation of culture, part II: Case study: A computational theory of social exchange. *Ethology and Sociobiology* 10:51–97.

Dugatkin, Lee Alan. (1997) *Cooperation among Animals: An Evolutionary Perspective*. New York: Oxford University Press.

Eibl-Eibesfeldt, Iraneus. (1982) Warfare, man's indoctrinability, and group selection. *Zeitschrift für Tierpsychologie* 67:177–198.

Frank, Steven A. (1995) Mutual policing and repression of competition in the evolution of cooperative groups. *Nature* 377:520–522.

Fried, Morton H. (1967) *The Evolution of Political Society*. New York: Random House.

Getty, Thomas. (1998) Handicap signalling: When fecundity and viability do not add up. *Animal Behaviour* 56:127–130.

Gintis, Herbert, Eric A. Smith, and Samuel Bowles. (2001) Cooperation and costly signaling. *Journal of Theoretical Biology* 213:103–119.

Grafen, Alan. (1990) Biological signals as handicaps. *J. of Theoretical Biology* 144:517–546.

Guilford, Tim, and Marian Stamp Dawkins. (1993) Receiver psychology and the design of animal signals. *Trends in the Neurosciences* 16:430–436.

Haig, David. (1993) Genetic conflicts in human pregnancy. *Quarterly Review of Biology* 68:495–532.

Hamilton, William D. (1975) Innate social aptitudes of man: An approach from evolutionary genetics. In *Biosocial Anthropology*. Ed. R. Fox. London: Malaby, 133–155.

Hardin, Russell. (1982) *Collective Action*. Baltimore: John Hopkins University Press.

Hawkes, Kristen. (1992) Sharing and collective action. In *Evolutionary Ecology and Human Behavior*. Ed. E. A. Smith and B. Winterhalder. Hawthorne, New York: Aldine de Gruyter, 269–300.

Hawkes, Kristen. (1993) Why hunter-gatherers work. *Current Anthropology* 34(4):341–362.

Johnstone, Rufus A. (1995) Sexual selection, honest advertisement and the handicap principle: Reviewing the evidence. *Biological Reviews* 70:1–65.

Johnstone, Rufus A. (1997) The evolution of animal signals. In *Behavioural Ecology: An Evolutionary Approach*. Ed. John R. Krebs and Nicholas B. Davies. Oxford: Blackwell, 155–178.

Kaplan, Hillard, and Kim Hill. (1985a) Food sharing among Ache foragers: Tests of explanatory hypotheses. *Current Anthropology* 26(2):223–246.

Kaplan, Hillard, and Kim Hill. (1985b) Hunting ability and reproductive success among male Ache foragers: preliminary results. *Current Anthropology* 26(1):131–133.

Kaplan, Hillard, Kim Hill, and A. Magdalena Hurtado. (1990) Fitness, foraging and food sharing among the Ache. In *Risk and Uncertainty in Tribal and Peasant Economies*. Ed. E. Cashdan. Boulder, CO: Westview Press.

Keeley, Lawrence H. (1996) *War before Civilization: The Myth of the Peaceful Savage*. New York: Oxford University Press.

Leimar, Olof, and Peter Hammerstein. (2001) Evolution of cooperation through indirect reciprocity. *Proceedings of the Royal Society of London, Series B* 268(1468):745–753.

Lotem, Arnon, Michael A. Fishman, and Lewi Stone. (2002) From reciprocity to unconditional altruism through signalling benefits. *Proceedings of the Royal Society of London B* 270:199–205.

Manson, Joseph H., and Richard W. Wrangham. (1991) Intergroup aggression in chimpanzees and humans. *Current Anthropology* 32:360–390.

Marlowe, Frank. (2000) The patriarch hypothesis: An alternative explanation of menopause. *Human Nature* 11:27–42.

Mauss, Marcel. (1967[1926]) *The Gift: Forms and Functions of Exchange in Archaic Societies*. New York: Norton.

Mesquida, Christian G., and Neil I. Weiner. (1996) Human collective aggression: A behavioral ecology perspective. *Ethology and Sociobiology* 17:247–263.

Milinski, Manfred, Dirk Semmann, and Hans-Jürgen Krambeck. (2002) Donors to charity gain in both indirect reciprocity and political reputation. *Proceedings of the Royal Society of London, Series B* 269:881–883.

Neiman, Fraser D. (1997) Conspicuous consumption as wasteful advertising: A Darwinian perspective on spatial patterns in Classic Maya terminal monument dates. In *Redis-

covering Darwin: Evolutionary Theory and Archeological Explanation. Ed. C. Michael Barton and Geoffrey A. Clark. Washington, D.C.: Archeological papers of the American Anthropological Association, No. 7, 267–290.

Nowak, Martin A., and Karl Sigmund. (1998) Evolution of indirect reciprocity by image scoring. *Nature* 393:573–577.

Olson, Mancur. (1965) *The Logic of Collective Action: Public Goods and the Theory of Groups.* Cambridge: Harvard University Press.

Otterbein, Keith. (1970) *The Evolution of War: A Cross-Cultural Study.* New Haven: HRAF.

Panchanathan, Karthik, and Robert Boyd. (2003) A tale of two defectors: The importance of standing for evolution of indirect reciprocity. *Journal of Theoretical Biology* 224:115–126.

Patton, John Q. (2000) Reciprocal altruism and warfare: A case from the Ecuadorian Amazon. In *Adaptation and Human Behavior: An Anthropological Perspective.* Ed. Lee Cronk, Napoleon Chagnon, and William Irons. Hawthorne, New York: Aldine de Gruyter, 417–436.

Peoples, James G. (1982) Individual or group advantage? A reinterpretation of the Maring ritual cycle. *Current Anthropology* 23:291–310.

Petrie, M. (1994) Improved growth and survival of offspring of peacocks with more elaborate trains. *Nature* 371:598–599.

Richerson, Peter J., and Robert Boyd. (1998) The evolution of human ultra-sociality. In *Ideology, Warfare, and Indoctrinability.* Ed. I. Eibl-Eibesfeldt and F. Salter. Oxford: Berghahn, 71–95.

Roberts, Gilbert. (1998) Competitive altruism: From reciprocity to the handicap principle. *Proceedings of the Royal Society of London B* 265:427–431.

Smith, Eric Alden. (1988) Risk and uncertainty in the "original affluent society": Evolutionary ecology of resource sharing and land tenure. In *Hunters and Gatherers: History, Evolution, and Social Change.* Ed. T. Ingold, D. Riches, and J. Woodburn. Oxford: Berg, 222–252.

Smith, Eric Alden. (1993) Comment on Hawkes. *Current Anthropology* 34:356.

Smith, Eric Alden. In press. Why do good hunters have higher reproductive success? *Human Nature.*

Smith, Eric Alden, and Robert Boyd. (1990) Risk and reciprocity: Hunter-gatherer socioecology and the problem of collective action. In *Risk and Uncertainty in Tribal and Peasant Economies.* Ed. E. Cashdan. Boulder, CO: Westview Press, 167–191.

Smith, Eric Alden, and Rebecca L. Bliege Bird. (2000) Turtle hunting and tombstone opening: Public generosity as costly signaling. *Evolution and Human Behavior* 21(4):245–261.

Smith, Eric Alden, Rebecca L. Bliege Bird, and Douglas W. Bird. (2003) The benefits of costly signaling: Meriam turtle hunters. *Behavioral Ecology* 14(1):116–126.

Spence, Michael. (1973) Job market signaling. *Quarterly J. of Economics* 87:355–374.

Sugden, R. (1986) *The Economics of Rights, Co-operation and Welfare.* Oxford: Basil Blackwell.

Sulloway, F. (1996) Born to Rebel: Birth Order, Family Dynamics, and Creative Lives. New York: Vintage.

Trivers, Robert L. (1971) The evolution of reciprocal altruism. *Quarterly Review of Biology* 46:35–57.

Trivers, Robert L. (1972) Parental investment and sexual selection. In *Sexual Selection and the Descent of Man, 1871–1971*. Ed. B. G. Campbell. Chicago: Aldine, 136–179.

Veblen, Thorstein. (1994 [1899]) *The Theory of the Leisure Class*. New York: Dover.

Wedekind, Claus, and Manfred Milinski. (2000) Cooperation through image scoring in humans. *Science* 288:850–852.

Wells, K. D. (1988) The effect of social interactions on anuran vocal behavior. In *The Evolution of the Amphibian Auditory System*. Ed. B. Fritzch. New York: Wiley, 433–454.

Wiessner, Polly, and Wulf Schiefenhövel, eds. (1995) *Food and the Status Quest: An Interdisciplinary Perspective*. Oxford: Berghahn Books.

Winterhalder, Bruce. (1990) Open field, common pot: Harvest variability and risk avoidance in agricultural and foraging societies. In *Risk and Uncertainty in Tribal and Peasant Economies*. Ed. E. Cashdan. Boulder, CO: Westview Press, 67–87.

Winterhalder, Bruce. (1996) Social foraging and the behavioral ecology of intragroup resource transfers. *Evolutionary Anthropology* 5(2):46–57.

Wright, Jonathan. (1999) Altruism as signal—Zahavi's alternative to kin selection and reciprocity. *J. of Avian Biology* 30:108–115.

Zahavi, Amotz. (1975) Mate selection—A selection for handicap. *J. of Theoretical Biology* 53:205–214.

Zahavi, Amotz. (1977) Reliability in communication systems and the evolution of altruism. In *Evolutionary Ecology*. Ed. B. Stonehouse and C. M. Perrins. London: Macmillan Press, 253–259.

Zahavi, Amotz. (1995) Altruism as handicap—the limitations of kin selection and reciprocity. *J. of Avian Biology* 26:1–3.

Zahavi, Amotz, and Avishag Zahavi. (1997) *The Handicap Principle: A Missing Piece of Darwin's Puzzle*. New York: Oxford University Press.

III

**Modeling and Testing
Strong Reciprocity**

5   The Economics of Strong Reciprocity

Ernst Fehr and Urs Fischbacher

5.1   Introduction

The purpose of this chapter is to show that economists and other so-cial scientists fail to understand core questions in economics and social theory if they insist on the self-interest hypothesis and rule out hetero-geneity in the realm of social preferences. Two developments support our argument. First, during the previous decades, experimental psy-chologists and economists have gathered overwhelming evidence that systematically refutes the self-interest hypothesis and suggests that a substantial fraction of the people demonstrate social motives in their preferences—in particular, preferences for strong reciprocity. Second, there is also strong evidence indicating that deviations from self-interest have had a fundamental impact on core issues in economics and social theory.

Social preferences are other-regarding preferences in the sense that individuals who exhibit them behave as if they value the payoff of rel-evant reference agents positively or negatively. Depending on the situ-ation, the relevant reference agents may be a person's colleagues, relatives, trading partners, or neighbors. It is important to keep in mind that a person may have different reference agents indifferent domains. Strong reciprocity means that individuals behave as if their positive or negative valuation of the reference agent's payoff depends on the actions of the reference agent. If the actions of the agent are per-ceived as kind, a strong reciprocator values the payoff of the reference agent positively. If the actions are perceived as hostile, the payoff of the reference agent is valued negatively. As we will see, strong reci-procity is a particularly important form of social preference.[1]

One core question is to understand the workings of competition and the interplay of competition and cooperation in markets, organizations, and politics. Other core questions pertain to understanding the conditions for successful collective actions, the prevailing structure of contracts and property rights, and, above all, the workings of economic incentives, because the workings of incentives constitute the essence of economics. We claim that a satisfactory understanding of these questions is impeded by the self-interest hypothesis. In particular, we provide evidence suggesting that preferences for strong reciprocity shape the functioning of competition, govern the laws of cooperation and collective action, and have a decisive impact on how economic incentives are constituted and how they function. The evidence we present also indicates that, by changing the incentives for selfish types, strong reciprocity affects the prevailing interaction patterns and the constraints on individual behavior, that is, the prevailing contracts and institutions.

The structure of this chapter is as follows. In "The Nature of Social Preferences," we shortly describe the most important types of social preferences. We then illustrate the preference for strong reciprocity by means of two simple one-shot experiments and discuss whether reciprocal behavior in these experiments can be interpreted as a cognitive mistake—that is a kind of habit that is learned in the repeated interactions outside the laboratory and inappropriately applied to one-shot situations—or whether reciprocal behavior is better interpreted as rational behavior driven by a preference for strong reciprocity. "Competition" then shows that if one neglects strong reciprocity, one cannot understand the important effects of competition on market prices. "Cooperation" deals with cooperation and shows that decisive determinants of cooperation cannot be understood on the basis of the self-interest hypothesis. "Economic Incentives and Property Rights" deals with economic incentives, contracts, and property rights. We present evidence indicating that neither the effects nor the determinants of economic incentives can be adequately understood if one neglects strong reciprocity and that the interaction between economic incentives and strong reciprocity is likely to have important effects on the optimality of different types of contracts and property rights. "Proximate Models of Strong Reciprocity" discusses some problems in the modeling of strong reciprocity and fairness preferences, and to what extent it is possible to mimic preferences for strong reciprocity by simpler and more tractable models of inequity aversion.

5.2   The Nature of Social Preferences

The last fifteen years have seen a large number of studies indicating that—in addition to economic self-interest—social preferences shape the decisions of a substantial fraction of people. A person exhibits social preferences if the person does not only care about the economic resources allocated to her but also cares about the economic resources allocated to relevant reference agents. In this chapter, we do not attempt to summarize the empirical evidence on social preferences (for surveys, see Fehr and Schmidt 2003, Sobel 2001, and chapter 6). Instead, we are interested in the social and economic implications of people's social preferences. Before we proceed, it is nevertheless useful to mention the quantitatively most important types of social preferences that have been established.

A particularly important type of social preference is the preference for *strong reciprocity*. A strongly reciprocal individual responds kindly toward actions that are perceived to be kind and hostilely toward actions that are perceived to be hostile. Whether an action is perceived to be kind or hostile depends on the fairness or unfairness of the intention underlying the action. The fairness of the intention, in turn, is determined by the equitability of the payoff distribution (relative to the set of feasible payoff distributions) caused by the action. It is important to emphasize that strong reciprocity is not driven by the expectation of future economic benefit. It is, therefore, fundamentally different from "cooperative" or "retaliatory" behavior in repeated interactions. These behaviors arise because actors expect future economic benefits from their actions. In the case of reciprocity, the actor is responding to friendly or hostile actions even if no economic gains can be expected. Models of strong reciprocity have been developed by Rabin (1993), Levine (1998), Falk and Fischbacher (chapter 6, this volume), Dufwenberg and Kirchsteiger (2004), and Segal and Sobel (1999).[2]

A second type of social preference is *inequity aversion* as modeled in Fehr and Schmidt (1999) and Bolton and Ockenfels (2000). Fehr and Schmidt (1999) assume, for example, that inequity-averse persons want to achieve an equitable distribution of economic resources. This means that they are altruistic towards other persons—that is, they want to increase other persons' economic payoff if the other persons' economic payoffs are below an equitable benchmark. However, inequity-averse persons also feel envy—that is, they want to decrease the other persons' payoffs when these payoffs exceed the equitable level. In many

situations, strongly reciprocal persons and inequity-averse persons behave in similar ways. For example, both strong reciprocity and inequity aversion imply the desire to reduce the payoff of another person if
that person made a decision such that the payoff of the strongly reciprocal or inequity-averse person is much lower than the payoff of the
other person. Recent evidence (Falk, Fehr, and Fischbacher [henceforth
FFF] 2000 and 2001; Offerman 2002) suggests, however, that strong
reciprocity is the quantitatively more important motive.

The similarity in the behavior of reciprocal and inequity-averse persons is due to the fact that both concepts depend in important ways on
the notion of a fair or equitable payoff. Since models of inequity aversion are much simpler and more tractable than models of strong reciprocity, it is often convenient to "mimic" or to "black box" reciprocal
behavior by inequity aversion (see the section on proximate models of
strong reciprocity later in the chapter). Some authors (e.g., Charness
and Rabin 2002) have also found evidence suggesting that subjects
tend to help the least well off. Such behavior is, however, often not distinguishable from inequity aversion, in particular, nonlinear inequity
aversion. Recently, Neilson (2000) provided an axiomatic characterization of a nonlinear version of Fehr-Schmidt type inequality aversion.

Strong reciprocity and inequity aversion are very different from *unconditional altruism*, which constitutes a third type of social preference.
Unconditional altruists do not condition their behavior on the actions
of others—that is, altruism given does not emerge as a response to
altruism received (Andreoni 1989; Andreoni and Miller 2002; Cox,
Sadiraj, and Sadiraj 2001). In technical terms, unconditional altruism
means that a person values the economic resources allocated to a relevant reference agent positively. An unconditional altruist, therefore,
never takes an action that decreases the payoff of a reference agent.
Yet, as we will see later in the chapter, an important stylized fact concerns people's willingness to punish other people for unfair or hostile
actions. Unconditional altruism also cannot explain the phenomenon
of conditional cooperation, that is, the fact that many people are willing to increase their voluntary cooperation in response to the cooperation of the others.

Finally, research has also shown that a fraction of the people exhibits
spiteful or envious preferences (FFF 2001). A spiteful or envious person
always values the economic payoff of relevant reference agents negatively. The person is, therefore, willing to decrease the economic payoff
of a reference agent at a personal cost to himself (Kirchsteiger 1994;

Mui 1995), irrespective of the payoff distribution and irrespective of the reference agent's fair or unfair behavior. Spiteful choices seem to be quantitatively less important than reciprocal choices. Moreover, spitefulness (as well as unconditional altruism) cannot explain why the *same* people often are willing to help others at a personal cost in one situation while they harm other people in other situations (FFF 2000).

Although previous research clearly indicates that many people exhibit social preferences it is important to keep in mind that not everybody exhibits social preferences. In fact, most studies indicate that there is also a substantial number of people who behave in a purely *selfish* manner. A key question, therefore, is how the heterogeneity of motives at the individual level can be captured by parsimonious models and how the different individual motivations interact. In this chapter, we concentrate on the existence of strongly reciprocal and selfish types. The reason for this is three-fold. First, empirical evidence clearly suggests that in the domain of payoff-decreasing or punishing behavior, strong negative reciprocity is the dominant motive (FFF 2000, 2001; Kagel and Wolfe 2001; Offerman 2002). Second, in the domain of helping or rewarding behavior, strong positive reciprocity also plays an important role—although other motives like unconditional altruism, inequity aversion, and efficiency-seeking behavior play a role as well (Cox 2000; Charness and Rabin 2002; FFF 2000; Offerman 2002). For reasons of parsimony we will, however, neglect these other motives in this chapter.

Theory as well as empirical evidence suggest that the interaction between strongly reciprocal and selfish types is of first-order importance for many economic questions. The reason for this is that the presence of reciprocal types often changes the economic incentives for the selfish types, which induces the selfish types to make "nonselfish" choices. For example, a selfish person is deterred from behaving opportunistically if the person expects to be punished by the reciprocators. Likewise, a selfish person may be induced to behave in a cooperative and helpful manner because she expects the reciprocators to return the favor. Since the presence of strongly reciprocal types changes the pecuniary incentives for the selfish types, the strongly reciprocal types often have a significant impact on the aggregate outcome in markets and organizations.

We focus our presentation on laboratory experiments because it is impossible to unambiguously isolate the impact of strong reciprocity in most real-life situations. A skeptic may always discount field evidence with the argument that, in the field, the notion of fairness is only used for rhetorical purposes that disguise purely self-interested behavior in an equilibrium of a repeated game.[3] The experimental evidence on ultimatum games (Güth, Schmittberger, and Schwarze 1982) and the gift exchange games (Fehr, Kirchsteiger, and Riedl 1993) provides transparent illustrations of strong positive and negative reciprocity.[4] Since both games have been described in the introductory chapter to this volume, we do not describe the experiments in detail here. It suffices to mention that the rejection of positive offers by the responders in the ultimatum game can be interpreted as strong negative reciprocity, whereas the generous effort choices by the employees in response to generous wage offers in the gift exchange game can be interpreted as strong positive reciprocity. These results have been replicated in numerous studies—in many countries and across a variety of differing conditions.[5] It is also worth mentioning that strong reciprocity has been observed in the ultimatum and the gift exchange game even when the stake size in the experiment has been raised to the level of three months income (Cameron 1999; Fehr, Tougareva, and Fischbacher 2002).

5.2.1   One-Shot and Repeated Interactions

Sometimes it is argued that reciprocal behavior in anonymous one-shot experiments is due to subjects' inability to adjust properly to one-shot interactions. One idea (see Binmore 1998) is that outside the laboratory, subjects are typically involved in a network of repeated interactions. It is well-known from repeated game theory that in repeated interactions, rewarding and punishing may be in the long-term self-interest of an individual. According to this argument, subjects who routinely interact in the repeated game of life import routines and habits that are appropriate for repeated interactions into the laboratory's one-shot situation because they do not understand the strategic differences between one-shot and repeated interactions. Therefore, the observation of reciprocal behavior in one-shot interactions should not be interpreted as a deviation from self-interest but merely as a form of rule-of-thumb behavior, that is, as a cognitive failure to properly distinguish between one-shot and repeated interactions.

Our response to this argument is twofold. First, and most importantly, the argument is refuted by evidence indicating that the vast majority of the subjects understand the strategic differences between one-shot and repeated interactions quite well. Later in this chapter we discuss the experiment reported by Fehr and Fischbacher (2003) that explicitly tested for this phenomenon. Second, even if the argument were correct, social scientists would have strong reasons to take the habits and routines that shape people's behavior into account. The importance of reciprocal behavior for the social sciences does not depend on whether it is interpreted as a deviation from self-interest or as a form of bounded rationality. Reciprocal behavior is important because it affects the functioning of markets, organizations, incentives, and collective actions in fundamental ways.

In principle, it is testable whether people have the ability to distinguish temporary one-shot play from repeated play. Fehr and Fischbacher (2003) investigated this problem in the context of the ultimatum game, and Gächter and Falk (2002) provided evidence for the gift exchange game. Fehr and Fischbacher conducted a series of ten ultimatum games in two different conditions. In both conditions, subjects played against a different opponent in each of the ten iterations of the game. In each iteration of the *baseline condition*, the proposers knew nothing about the past behavior of their current responders. Thus, the responders could not build up a reputation for being "tough" in this condition. In contrast, in each iteration of the *reputation condition*, the proposers knew the full history of the behavior of their current responders, that is, the responders could build up a reputation for being "tough." In the reputation condition, a reputation for rejecting low offers is, of course, valuable because it increases the likelihood to receive higher offers from the proposers in future periods.

If the responders understand that there is a pecuniary payoff from rejecting low offers in the reputation condition, one should in general observe higher acceptance thresholds in this condition. This is the prediction of the social preferences approach that assumes that subjects derive utility from both their own pecuniary payoff and a fair payoff distribution. If, in contrast, subjects do not understand the logic of reputation formation and apply the same habits or cognitive heuristics to both conditions, one should observe no systematic differences in responder behavior across conditions. Since the subjects participated in both conditions, it was possible to observe behavioral changes at the individual level. It turns out that the vast majority (slightly more than 80 percent, $N = 72$) of the responders *increase* their acceptance thresholds in the reputation condition relative to the baseline condition.[6] This contradicts the hypothesis that subjects do not understand the difference between one-shot and repeated play.

5.3   Competition

In this section, we illustrate our claim that it is not possible to understand the effects of competition if concerns for fairness and strong reciprocity are neglected. We will show, in particular, that the self-interest hypothesis hinders social scientists from understanding important comparative static effects of competition. In addition, we present results indicating that competition may sometimes have much less impact than predicted by models based on the self-interest hypothesis.

5.3.1   The Effects of Competition under Exogenous Contract Enforcement

Consider the following slightly modified ultimatum game. Instead of one responder, there are now two competing responders. When the proposer has made his offer, the two responders simultaneously accept or reject the offer. If both accept, a random mechanism determines with probability 0.5 which one of the responders will get the offered amount. If only one responder accepts, he will receive the offered amount of money. If both responders reject, the proposer and both responders receive nothing.

This version of the ultimatum game—with responder competition—can be interpreted as a market transaction between a seller (proposer) and two competing buyers (responders) who derive the same economic payoff from an indivisible good. Moreover, if the parties' pecuniary valuations of the good are public information, all involved parties know the surplus. Since there is a known fixed surplus, there is no uncertainty regarding the quality of the good provided by the seller. The situation can thus be viewed as a market in which the contract (the quality of the good) is enforced exogenously.

If all parties are selfish, competition among the responders does not matter because the proposer is already predicted to receive the whole surplus in the bilateral case. Adding competition to the bilateral ultimatum game therefore has no effect on the power of the proposer. It is also irrelevant whether there are two, three, or more competing responders. The self-interest hypothesis thus implies a very counterintuitive result—namely, that increasing the competition among the responders does not affect the share of the surplus that the responders receive. Fischbacher, Fong, and Fehr (2003) tested this prediction by conducting ultimatum games with one, two, and five responders. To allow for convergence and learning effects, in each experimental session a large group of subjects played the same game for twenty periods. For example, in the case with two responders, one-third of the subjects were always in the role of the proposer and two-thirds of the subjects were in the role of the responder. In every period the proposers and the responders were randomly rematched to ensure the one-shot nature of the interactions. All subjects knew that the experiment would end after period twenty. The results of these experiments are presented in figure 5.1.

Figure 5.1 shows the responder's average share of the surplus in each period across conditions. In the bilateral case, the average share is—except for period 1—very close to 40 percent. Moreover, the share does not change much over time. In the final period, the responder still appropriates slightly more than 40 percent of the surplus. In the case of two responders, however, the situation changes dramatically. Already in period 1 the responder's share is reduced by 16.5 percentage points relative to the bilateral case. Moreover, from period 1 until period 12

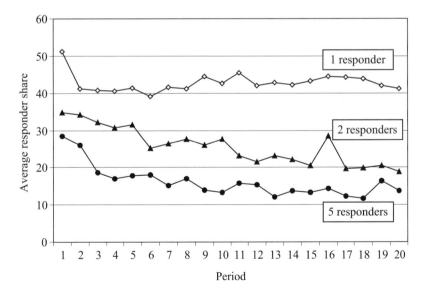

Figure 5.1
Responder share in the ultimatum game with one, two, and five competing responders.
Source: Fischbacher, Fong, and Fehr 2003.

responder competition induces a further reduction of the responder's share by 14 percentage points (from 35 percent to 21 percent) and in the final period the share is even below 20 percent. Thus, the addition of just one more responder has a dramatic impact on the responder's share. If we add three additional responders, the share goes down even further. From period 3 onwards, it is below 20 percent and comes close to 10 percent in the second half of the session.[7]

The reason why the responder's share decreases when competition increases is that the rejection probability of the responders declines when there are more competing responders. These facts can be parsimoniously explained if one takes the presence of strongly reciprocal or inequity averse responders into account (Falk and Fischbacher this volume, chapter 6; Fehr and Schmidt 1999). Recall that strongly reciprocal responders reject low offers in the bilateral ultimatum game because by rejecting they are able to punish the unfair proposers. They can always ensure this punishment in the bilateral case, while in the competitive case this is no longer possible. In particular, if one of the other responders accepts a low offer, it is impossible for a reciprocal responder to punish the proposer. Since there is a substantial fraction of selfish responders, the probability that one of the other responders is selfish increases with a larger number of competing responders. This means, in turn, that the expected non-pecuniary return from the rejection of a low offer is smaller when the number of competing responders increases. Therefore, strongly reciprocal responders will reject less frequently as more competing responders are added.

5.3.2   The Effects of Competition under Endogenous Contract Enforcement

The previous example illustrates that the self-interest model underestimates the power of competition. This example should not, however, make us believe that sufficient competition will in general weaken or remove the impact of fairness on market outcomes. Quite the contrary. In this section, we will show that the presence of strongly reciprocal individuals may completely nullify the impact of competition on market outcomes. Whether competition does have the effects illustrated in figure 5.1 depends critically on the enforceability of the contracts.

The double auction experiments conducted by Fehr and Falk (1999) help to illustrate this argument. Fehr and Falk deliberately chose the double auction as the trading institution because a large body of research has shown the striking competitive properties of experimental double auctions. In hundreds of such experiments, prices and quantities quickly converged to the competitive equilibrium predicted by standard self-interest theory (see Davis and Holt 1993, for a survey of important results). Therefore, showing that strong reciprocity renders competition completely powerless in an experimental double auction provides a strong piece of evidence in favor of the importance of strong reciprocity in markets.

Fehr and Falk use two treatment conditions: a competitive condition and a bilateral condition in which competition is completely removed. In the competitive condition, they embed the gift exchange framework into the context of an experimental double auction that is framed in labor market terms.[8] The crucial difference between the competitive condition and the gift exchange game described earlier in this chapter is that in the competitive condition, both experimental firms and experimental workers can make wage bids in the interval [20, 120] because the workers' reservation wage is 20 and the maximum revenue from a trade is 120. If a bid is accepted, a labor contract is concluded and the worker has to choose the effort level. As in the gift exchange game, the workers ("responders") can freely choose any feasible effort level. They have to bear effort costs while the firm ("proposer") benefits from the effort. Thus, the experiment captures a market in which the quality of the good traded ("effort") is not exogenously enforced but is chosen by the workers. Workers may or may not provide the effort level that is expected by the firms. In the competitive double auction, there are 8 firms and 12 workers. Each firm can employ at most 1 worker. A worker who enters into a contract has costs of 20. Therefore, due to the excess supply of labor, the competitive wage level is 20. A double auction lasts for ten periods and each period lasts for three minutes.[9]

In contrast to the double auction, firms in the bilateral condition are exogenously matched with a worker. If a worker rejects the firm's offer, both parties earn nothing. The bilateral condition consists of a series of ten one-shot gift exchange games that are also framed in labor market terms. There are ten firms (proposers) and ten workers (responders). In each of the ten periods, each firm is matched with a different worker. Firms have to make an offer to the matched worker in each period. If the worker accepts, he has to choose the effort level. As in the competitive condition, a worker who accepts a wage offer has costs of 20, and the maximum revenue from a trade is 120. The self-interest model predicts that in both conditions the workers will only provide the minimum effort so that the firms will pay a wage of 20 or 21 in equilibrium. However, we know already from bilateral ultimatum games that firms (proposers) cannot reap the whole surplus—that is, wages in the bilateral gift exchange game can also be expected to be much higher than predicted by the self-interest model. Moreover, since in the gift exchange game the effort is in general increasing in the wage level, firms have even an additional reason to offer workers a substantial share of the surplus. The task, therefore, is to determine what extent competition in the double auction pushes wages below the level in the bilateral condition.

Figure 5.2 shows the evolution of wages in both conditions. This figure indicates the startling result that competition has no long-term impact on wage formation in this setting. Wages in the double auction are slightly lower than the wages in the bilateral condition only in the beginning periods but since workers responded to lower wages with lower effort levels, firms raised their wages from period four onwards. In the last five periods, firms paid even slightly higher wages in the double auction than in the bilateral condition; this difference is not significant, however. It is also noteworthy that competition among the

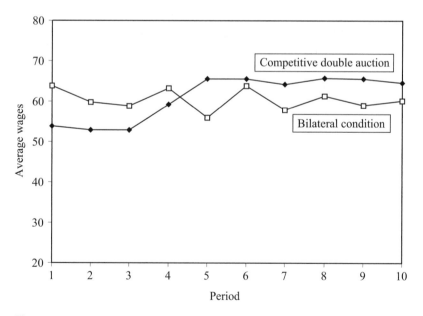

Figure 5.2
Wage levels in the competitive double auction and the bilateral condition. Source: Fehr and Falk 1999.

workers was extremely intense in the double auction. In each period, many workers offered to work for wages below 30 but firms preferred instead to pay workers on average wages around 60. It was impossible for the workers to get a job by underbidding the going wages because the positive effort-wage relation made it profitable for the firms to pay high, noncompetitive, wages.[10]

The previous evidence in this section indicates that strong reciprocity severely limits the impact of competition in markets in which effort or quality is not enforced exogenously. It restricts the impact of competition on wages by generating an efficiency wage effect that renders it profitable for the firms to pay noncompetitive wages. As is well-known, such noncompetitive wages may in turn cause involuntary unemployment (Akerlof 1982). In addition, the existence of strongly reciprocal types may endogenously generate a distinction between insiders and outsiders. Firms are of course interested in workers who do not exploit every opportunity to shirk—workers who are loyal and who also perform when they are unobserved. Since workers are heterogeneous in this regard (and since a worker's type may be difficult to ascertain), firms are generally reluctant to replace existing workers with new workers even if the new workers are willing to work for less than the going wage. This protects firms' existing workforce from outside competition.

Finally, strong reciprocity may also contribute to the existence of noncompetitive wage differentials. In the 1980s and the early 1990s, there has been a heated debate about whether inter-industry wage differentials should be interpreted as noncompetitive job rents. The debate did not result in a consensus because the results could also be interpreted as reflecting unobservable heterogeneity in working conditions and unobservable heterogeneity in skill levels.[11] Laboratory experiments can help resolve some of the open issues because it is possible to rule out heterogeneity in working conditions and skill levels in the laboratory. This situation was done by Fehr, Gächter, and Kirchsteiger (1996), who embedded the gift exchange framework into a competitive market environment in which experimental firms differed according to their profit opportunities. Under their experiment, once a worker has accepted a firm's wage offer and before she makes her effort choice, she is informed about the firm's profit opportunity. This procedure ensured that only the effort decision—but not the contract acceptance decision—of the worker is affected by the firm's profit opportunity. Both firms and workers know this information revelation procedure in advance. The experiment shows that firms with better profit opportunities pay systematically higher wages and higher job rents. This wage policy is quite rational because a given effort increase leads to a larger profit increase for a more profitable firm. Hence, high-profit firms have a stronger incentive to appeal to the workers' reciprocity by paying high wages.

5.4   Cooperation

Free-riding incentives are a pervasive phenomenon in social life. Participation in collective actions against a dictatorship or in industrial disputes, collusion among firms in oligopolistic markets, the prevention of negative environmental externalities, workers' effort choices under team-based compensation schemes, or the exploitation of a common resource are typical examples. In these cases, the free rider cannot be excluded from the benefits of collective actions or the public good even though he does not contribute. In view of the ubiquity of cooperation problems in modern societies, it is crucial to understand the forces shaping people's cooperation. In this section, we will show that the neglect of strong reciprocity may induce economists to completely misunderstand the nature of many cooperation problems. As we will see, a key to the understanding of cooperation problems is again the interaction between selfish and strongly reciprocal types and how this interaction is shaped by the institutional environment.

5.4.1   Conditional Cooperation

Strong reciprocity changes the typical cooperation problem for two reasons. First, strongly reciprocal subjects are willing to cooperate if they are sure that the other people who are involved in the cooperation problem will also cooperate. If the others cooperate—despite pecuniary incentives to the contrary—they provide a gift that induces strongly reciprocal subjects to repay the gift, that is, reciprocators are conditionally cooperative. Second, strongly reciprocal subjects are willing to punish free-riders because free-riders exploit the cooperators. Thus, if potential free-riders face reciprocators, they have an incentive to cooperate in order to prevent being punished.

The impact of strong reciprocity on cooperation can be demonstrated in the context of the Prisoner's Dilemma (PD) in the following situation. Subject A and Subject B both posses £10. Each person can either keep her 10 pounds or transfer it to the other person. If either subject transfers the money, the experimenter triples the transferred amount, that is, the recipient receives £30 from the transfer. A and B each have to decide simultaneously whether to keep or whether to transfer her £10. If both subjects transfer their money, both earn £30. If they both keep their own money, both earn only £10. Moreover, irrespective of whether the other subject transfers the money, it is always in the subject's self-interest to keep the £10.[12] The self-interest hypothesis predicts, therefore, that both subjects will keep their money. In fact, however, many subjects cooperate in situations like this one (see Ledyard 1995; Dawes 1980). For example, in one-shot PDs cooperation rates are frequently between 40 and 60 percent.

In the presence of sufficiently reciprocal subjects, cooperative outcomes in the PD can be easily explained because the above game—although a PD in terms of material payoffs—is not a PD in utility payoffs. It is, instead, a coordination game with two equilibria. If both subjects are reciprocators and if A believes that B will cooperate (i.e., transfer the money), A *prefers* to cooperate. The same holds true for B if B believes that A will cooperate. Thus, the strategy combination (cooperate, cooperate) constitutes an equilibrium. Similarly, if both believe that the other person will defect (i.e., keep the money), A and B both prefer to defect as well. Therefore, the combination (defect, defect) is also an equilibrium.[13]

The fact that the PD is transformed into a coordination game in the presence of strongly reciprocal players can explain two further facts. It has been shown dozens of times that communication leads to much higher cooperation rates in PDs and other social dilemma games (Sally 1995).[14] If all subjects were completely selfish, the positive impact of communication would be difficult to explain. If, however, the PD in economic terms is in fact a coordination game, communication allows the subjects to coordinate on the superior equilibrium. It has also been shown that cooperation is affected by how the PD is framed. If the PD is framed in "cooperative" terms, subjects are more likely to cooperate than if it is framed in "competitive" terms. Since it is likely that the "cooperative" framework induces more optimistic beliefs about the behavior of the other player than the "competitive" framework, subjects are more likely to coordinate on the good equilibrium while working within the "cooperative" framework.

If the actual preferences of the subjects do transform social dilemma situations like the PD game into a coordination game, the self-interest hypothesis induces economists to fundamentally misperceive social dilemma problems. In view of the importance of this claim, it is desirable to have more direct evidence on this. Fischbacher, Gächter, and Fehr (2001) and Croson (1999) elicited subjects' willingness to cooperate conditional on the average cooperation of others' in the context of four-person public good games in which the dominant strategy for each subject was to free-ride completely. It was in the selfish interest of each subject to free-ride, although the socially optimal decision required the contribution of each individual's whole endowment to the public good.

Both studies found considerable evidence for the presence of conditional cooperators.[15] The results of the Fischbacher, Gächter, and Fehr study are presented in figure 5.3. This figure shows that 50 percent of the subjects are willing to increase their contributions to the public good if the other group members' average contribution increases, even though the pecuniary incentives always implied full free-riding. The behavior of these subjects is consistent with models of strong reciprocity (or inequity aversion). The figure also reminds us that a substantial fraction of the subjects (30 percent) are complete free-riders while 14

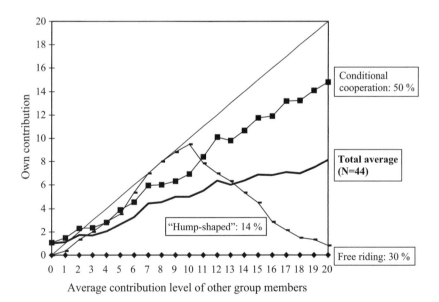

Figure 5.3
Contributions of individual subjects as a function of the contribution of other members' average contribution. Source: Fischbacher, Gächter, and Fehr 2001.

percent exhibit a hump-shaped response. Yet taken together, there are sufficiently many conditional cooperators such that an increase in the other group members' contribution level causes an increase in the contribution of the "average" individual (see the bolded line in figure 5.3).

The coexistence of conditional cooperators and selfish subjects has important implications. It implies, for example, that subtle institutional details may cause large behavioral effects. To illustrate this, assume that a selfish and a strongly reciprocal subject are matched in the *simultaneous* PD and that the subjects' type is common knowledge. Since the reciprocal type knows that the other player in question is selfish, he knows that this other player will always defect. Therefore, the reciprocal type will also defect—that is, (defect, defect) is the unique equilibrium. Now consider the *sequential* PD in which the selfish player decides first whether to cooperate or to defect. Then the strongly reciprocal player observes what the first-mover did and chooses his action. In the sequential case, the unique equilibrium outcome is that both players cooperate because the reciprocal second-mover will match the choice of the first-mover. This means that the selfish first-mover essentially has the choice between the (cooperate, cooperate)-outcome and the (defect, defect)-outcome. Since mutual cooperation is better than mutual defection, the selfish player will cooperate. Thus, while in the simultaneous PD the selfish player induces the reciprocal player to defect, in the sequential PD the reciprocal player induces the selfish player to cooperate. This example neatly illustrates how institutional details interact in important ways with the heterogeneity of the population.

Since there are many conditional cooperators, the problem of establishing and maintaining cooperation involves the management of people's beliefs. If people believe that the others cooperate to a large extent, cooperation will be higher compared to a situation where they believe that others rarely cooperate. Belief-dependent cooperation can be viewed as a social interaction effect that is relevant in many important domains. For example, if people believe that cheating on taxes, corruption, or abuses of the welfare state are widespread, they themselves are more likely to cheat on taxes, take bribes, or abuse welfare state institutions. It is therefore important that public policy prevents the initial unraveling of civic duties, because once people start to believe that most others engage in unlawful behavior, the belief-dependency of individuals' behavior may render it very difficult to reestablish lawful behavior.

In an organizational context, the problem of establishing cooperation among the members of the organization also involves the selection of the "right" members. A few shirkers in a group of employees may quickly spoil the whole group. Bewley (1999), for example, reports that personnel managers use the possibility of firing workers mainly as a means to remove "bad characters and incompetents" from the group and not as a threat to discipline the workers. The reason is that explicit threats create a hostile atmosphere and may even reduce the workers' general willingness to cooperate with the firm. Managers report that the employees themselves do not want to work with lazy colleagues because these colleagues do not bear their share of the burden, which is viewed as unfair. Therefore, the firing of lazy workers is mainly used to protect the group from "bad characters and incompetents,"—to establish internal equity and to prevent the unraveling of cooperation. This supports the view that conditional cooperation is also important inside firms.

Strong reciprocity and conditional cooperation are also likely to shape the structure of social policies regarding the poor (Fong, Bowles, and Gintis this volume, chapter 10; Bowles and Gintis 1998; Wax 2000). The reason is that the political support for policies regarding the poor depends to a large extent on whether the poor are perceived as "deserving" or as "undeserving." If people believe that the poor are poor because they do not *want* to work hard, support for policies that help the poor is weakened because the poor are perceived as undeserving. If, on the other hand, people believe that the poor try hard to escape poverty but that for reasons beyond their control have not been able to make it, the poor are perceived as deserving. This indicates that the extent to which people perceive the poor as deserving is shaped by strong reciprocity. If the poor exhibit good intentions, try to contribute to society's output, or if they are poor for reasons that have nothing to do with their intentions, they are perceived as deserving. In contrast, if the poor are perceived as lacking the will to contribute to society's output, they are perceived as undeserving. This means that social policies that enable the poor to demonstrate their willingness to reciprocate the generosity of society will mobilize greater political support than social policies that do not allow the poor to exhibit their good intentions. Wax (2000) convincingly argues that an important reason for the popularity of former president Bill Clinton's 1996 welfare reform initiative was that the initiative appealed to people's sense of strong reciprocity.[16]

5.4.2   Cooperation and Punishment

We argued above that the presence of a selfish subject will induce the strongly reciprocal subject in the simultaneous PD to defect. This proposition also holds more generally in the case of n-person social dilemma situations. It can be shown theoretically that even a small minority of selfish subjects induces a majority of reciprocal (or inequity averse) subjects to free-ride in simultaneous social dilemmas (Fehr and Schmidt 1999, proposition 4). In an experiment with anonymous interactions, subjects of course do not know whether the other group members are selfish or strongly reciprocal. If they interact repeatedly over time, however, they may learn the others' types. Therefore, one would expect that cooperation will eventually unravel in (finitely repeated) simultaneous social dilemma experiments. This unraveling of cooperation has indeed been observed in dozens of experiments (Ledyard 1995; Fehr and Schmidt 1999).

This raises the question of whether there are social mechanisms that can prevent the decay of cooperation. A potentially important mechanism is social ostracism and peer pressure stemming from reciprocal subjects. Recall that strongly reciprocal subjects exhibit a willingness to punish unfair behavior and it is very likely that cooperating reciprocators view free-riding as very unfair. Yamagichi (1986), Ostrom, Gardner, and Walker (1994), and Fehr and Gächter (2000a) studied the impact of punishment opportunities in public goods and social dilemma games where the same players could stay together in the same group for several periods. In the experiments conducted by Fehr and Gächter, there were two stages. Stage one was the same public goods game as described in Fischbacher, Gächter, and Fehr (2001). In particular, the dominant strategy of each player is to free-ride completely in the stage game, although the socially optimal decision requires each player to contribute her whole endowment to the public good. In stage two, after the group has been informed of the contributions of each group member, each player can assign up to ten punishment points to any of the other group members. The assignment of one punishment point reduces the first-stage income of the punished subject by three points on average, but it also reduces the income of the punisher.[17] This kind of punishment mimics an angry group member scolding a free-rider or spreading the word so that the free-rider is ostracized— there is some cost to the punisher, but a larger cost to the free-rider. Note that since punishment is costly for the punisher, the self-interest hypothesis predicts zero punishment. Moreover, since rational players will anticipate this, the self-interest hypothesis predicts no difference in the contribution behavior between a public goods game without punishment and the game with a punishment opportunity. In both conditions, zero contributions are predicted.

The experimental evidence completely contradicts this prediction (see figure 5.4).[18] In contrast to the game without a punishment opportunity, where cooperation declines over time and is close to zero in the final period, the punishment opportunity causes a sharp jump in cooperation (compare period 10 with period 11 in figure 5.4). Moreover, in the punishment condition, there is a steady increase in contributions until almost all subjects contribute their whole endowment. This sharp increase occurs because free-riders often get punished, and the less they give, the more likely punishment is. Cooperators feel that free-riders take unfair advantage of them and, as a result are willing to punish them. This induces the punished free-riders to increase cooperation in the following periods. A nice feature of this design is that the actual rate of punishment is very low in the last few periods—the mere threat of punishment, and the memory of the pain from previous punishments, is enough to induce potential free-riders to cooperate.

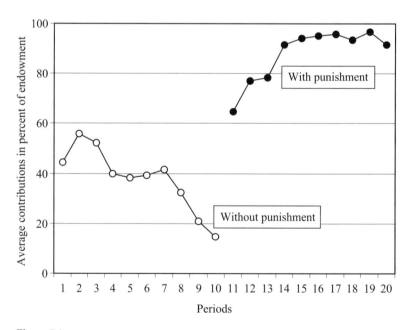

Figure 5.4
Average contributions to the public good. Source: Fehr and Gächter 2000a.

5.4.3   Strategic Versus Nonstrategic Punishment

Peer pressure, social ostracism, and the cooperation-enhancing punishment of free-riders in general play a key role in the enforcement of social norms. They are also important in industrial disputes between workers and firms, in team production settings, in the management of common property resources, or as an enforcement device for collusion in oligopolistic industries. For example, striking workers often ostracize strike breakers (Francis 1985) or, under a piece rate system, violators of production quotas are punished by those who try to maintain effort-withholding norms (Roethlisberger and Dickson 1947; Whyte 1955).[19] During World War I, British men who did not volunteer for the army faced strong public contempt and were called "whimps." Ostrom, Gardner, and Walker (1994) also report that punishment is frequently imposed on those who excessively use common property resources. They convincingly argue that the successful management of such resources requires institutions that render the excess extraction of common resources visible or easy to detect. This enables the users of the resource to impose sanctions on the wrongdoers.

A further interesting example is provided by Slade (1990), who analysed the behavior of firms during price wars in oligopolistic industries. She shows that during price wars, firms sell their products far below their marginal costs. While this behavior may be rationalized as part of a complicated punishment strategy in a repeated game involving only self-interested players, it seems more likely that players get angry and that their punishment behavior is driven by non-selfish forces. Anecdotal evidence from oil company marketers supports this view. According to Slade (personal communication), the marketers stated that they would follow a rival's price cut right down to zero if that rival started a price war. Yet, anecdotal evidence alone, as suggestive as it might be, is not fully convincing.

All of the examples in this section raise similar questions. To what extent is the punishment observed strategically motivated—that is, caused by the expectation of future economic benefit—and to what extent is it due to the mere (nonstrategic) desire to punish? Moreover, what are the implications of the existence of nonstrategic sanctions over and above what repeated game theory already tells us?

Our answer to these questions is as follows. *First*, repeated game theory tells us in fact very little about the actual behavior in infinitely repeated interactions because for sufficiently high discount factors there is typically a plethora of equilibria, including equilibria with no punishment and no cooperation. Thus, at a minimum, the results on punishment-based cooperation show that people do punish and they typically coordinate on cooperative outcomes. *Second*, there are in fact many situations in which interactions are only one-shot, finitely repeated, or where people's discount factors are so low that self-interested agents cannot sustain cooperation in equilibrium. The results of Fehr and Gächter (2000a) show that in these situations nonstrategic punishment is a powerful cooperation-enforcement device. *Third*, if fairness considerations are an important driving force of nonstrategic sanctions, it is quite likely that strategic sanctioning is also shaped in important ways by fairness concerns. In particular, we believe that many people will forgo the possibility of sanctioning others for purely pecuniary reasons if the sanction is viewed as unfair. They may refrain from sanctioning for intrinsic reasons or because they fear that the sanctioned player will retaliate.[20] Thus, unfair punishments are quite unlikely even if they yield economic benefits, while fair punishments will occur even if they cause a net decrease in the punisher's payoff. *Finally*, although it is true that due to the ambiguity of most field situations it is not possible to unambiguously attribute the sanctions to non-pecuniary motives, this does not mean that sanctions are automatically driven by strategic reasons. In fact, we do not know of any rigorous evidence that free-riders are punished for strategic reasons.

The lack of evidence in favor of strategic sanctions led Falk, Fehr, and Fischbacher (2001) to examine this question. They conducted a public goods experiment with a punishment opportunity in two conditions. In the partner condition, three group members stay together for six periods. In the perfect stranger condition, the game also lasts for six periods, but it is ensured that nobody meets any of the other participants more than once. Thus, in the partner condition, subjects can benefit in economic terms from their punishments because the punished group members typically raise their contributions in the following periods; in the perfect stranger condition, no such benefits can accrue. If there are more sanctions in the partner condition, we have evidence in favor of strategic sanctions. The results of this experiment are displayed in figure 5.5.

Figure 5.5 shows the sanctioning behavior as a function of the deviation of the contribution of the sanctioned subject from the contribution of the sanctioning subject. It indicates that in the first five periods, the sanctioning pattern and the strength of the sanctions are very similar in both conditions. The sanctions in the partner condition are only

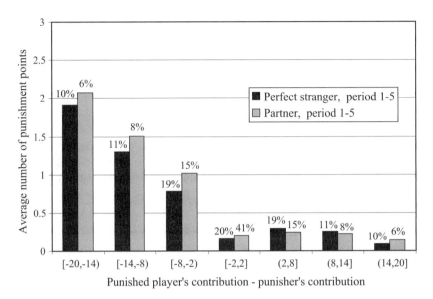

Figure 5.5
Punishment pattern in the public goods game—partners versus perfect strangers. Source: Falk, Fehr, and Fischbacher 2001.

slightly stronger and the difference is not significant. Thus, the bulk of the sanctions already exists when there are no pecuniary benefits from sanctioning—so there is little or no evidence in favor of strategic sanctioning. Moreover, it turns out that in the final (sixth) period of the partner treatment, the sanctions are even slightly higher than in the previous five periods of this treatment.[21] Since subjects know in advance that the experiment ends after period six, this result also indicates a lack of evidence in favor of strategic sanctions. Although we do not regard our experiment as the last word on this question, this evidence should remind us that the mere fact that strategic punishments can be part of an equilibrium does not yet mean that strategic punishments will actually occur in the real world or in the laboratory.[22]

In view of the ubiquity of opportunities for free-riding, the existence of a substantial amount of nonstrategic punishment of free-riders is quite important. It suggests that even in one-shot situations or when the discount factor is low, collusive practices in output and labor markets are much more likely than predicted by the self-interest hypothesis. It also lends support to the insider-outsider theory of involuntary unemployment developed by Lindbeck and Snower (1988). This theory is based on the idea that the firm's existing workforce will harass outsiders and will not cooperate with them if the outsiders are employed below the going wage. Our evidence indicates that insiders will harass outsiders even if this is costly for the insiders and brings them no economic benefits.

5.5   Economic Incentives and Property Rights

In this section, we show that the neglect of strong reciprocity prevents the understanding of crucial determinants and effects of economic incentives. We will show, in particular, that economic incentives may reduce efficiency in situations in which they are predicted to be efficiency-enhancing by the self-interest model. In addition, we show that strong reciprocity may have strong consequences for the optimal provision of incentives in a moral hazard context. Incentive contracts that are optimal when there are only selfish actors become inferior when some agents prefer strong reciprocity. Conversely, contracts that are doomed to fail when there are only selfish actors provide powerful incentives and become superior when there are also strongly reciprocal players.

5.5.1   Economic Incentives May Be Harmful

In the gift exchange game described earlier in the chapter, there are no economic incentives to provide nonminimal effort levels. Despite this, many responders (workers) put forward nonminimal effort levels in case of fair wage offers. In reality, economic incentives are, of course, also used to induce workers to provide high effort. How do explicit performance incentives interact with motivations of fairness and strong reciprocity? One possibility is that strong reciprocity gives rise to extra effort on top of what is enforced by economic incentives alone. However, it is also possible that explicit incentives may cause a hostile atmosphere of threat and distrust, which reduces any reciprocity-based extra effort. Bewley (1999, 431), for example, reports that many "managers stress that punishment should seldom be used to obtain cooperation" because of the negative effects on work atmosphere.

In a series of experiments, Fehr and Gächter (2000b) examined this possibility. They implemented a baseline gift exchange game with a slight modification. In addition to the wage, experimental employers also stipulate a desired effort level. However, the desired effort represents merely "cheap talk"—it is not binding for the workers. This means that workers still face no economic incentives in this treatment. Fehr and Gächter (2000b) also implemented a treatment with explicit performance incentives. This treatment keeps everything constant relative to the baseline treatment, except employers now have the possibility to fine an employee in case of verified shirking. The probability of verification is given by 0.33, and the fine is restricted to an interval between zero and a maximum fine. The maximum fine is fixed at a level such that a selfish risk-neutral worker will choose an effort level of 4 when faced with this fine.[23]

Figure 5.6 presents the results of this experiment. The line with the black dots in figure 5.6 shows workers' effort behavior in the baseline treatment. It depicts the average effort on the vertical axis as a function of the rent offered to the workers. The offered rent is implied by the original contract offer. It is defined as the wage minus the cost of providing the desired effort level. Due to the presence of many reciprocal workers, the average effort level is strongly increasing in the offered rent and rises far above the selfish level of $e = 1$.

The line with the white dots in figure 5.6 shows the relationship of rent to effort in the presence of the explicit performance incentive. Except at the low-rent levels, the average effort is *lower* in the presence of

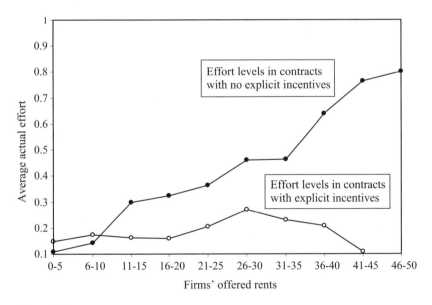

Figure 5.6
Average effort levels and explicit incentives. Source: Fehr and Gächter 2000b.

the explicit incentives! This result suggests that reciprocity-based effort elicitation and explicit performance incentives may indeed be in conflict with each other. Performance incentives that are perceived as hostile can provoke hostile responses from workers. In the context of our incentive treatment, this meant that strongly reciprocal workers were no longer willing to provide nonminimal effort levels.[24]

In the experiments of Fehr and Gächter (2000b), the average effort taken over all the different trades (and hence the aggregate monetary surplus) is lower in the incentive treatment than in the baseline treatment. However, employers' profits are higher because in the incentive treatment they infrequently rely on the carrot of generous wage offers. Instead, they threaten the workers with the maximal fine in most cases. For the employers, the savings in wage costs more than offset the reductions in revenues that are caused by the lower effort in the incentive treatment. However, while the wage savings merely represent a transfer from the workers to the firms, the reduction in effort levels reduces the aggregate surplus. This shows that in the presence of reciprocal types, efficiency questions and questions of distribution are inseparable. Since the perceived fairness of the distribution of the gains from trade affects the effort behavior of the reciprocal types, different distributions are associated with different levels of the aggregate gains. Thus, lump-sum transfers between trading parties have efficiency consequences.

5.5.2 Reciprocity-based Incentives Versus Explicit Incentives

Standard principal-agent models predict that contracts should be made contingent on all verifiable measures that are informative with regard to the agent's effort. But in reality, we often observe highly incomplete contracts. For example, as noted earlier in the chapter, wages are often paid without explicit performance incentives. On this point, the discussion has focused on demonstrating that strong reciprocity has powerful economic effects in situations where explicit incentives are absent. This section seeks to explore underlying causes for the absence of explicit incentives. Strong reciprocity plays a twofold role in this context. First, as the previous experiment has shown, certain kinds of explicit incentives have negative side effects because they reduce reciprocity-based voluntary cooperation. Second, it renders contracts that do not rely on explicit incentives more efficient relative to the prediction of the self-interest model because strong reciprocity itself constitutes a powerful contract enforcement device. Each of these two reasons may induce the principals to prefer contracts without explicit incentives.

To study the impact of strong reciprocity on contractual choices, Fehr, Klein, and Schmidt (2001) conducted an experiment in which principals had the choice between an explicit incentive contract and an implicit contract without explicit incentives. In a typical session of this experiment, there are 12 principals and 12 agents who play for ten periods. In each of the 10 periods, an agent faces a different principal, which ensures that all matches are one-shot. A period consists of three stages. At stage one, the principal has to decide whether to offer the agent an implicit or an explicit contract. The implicit contract specifies a fixed wage and a desired effort level (where effort choices can range from 1 to 10). In addition, the principal can promise a bonus that may be paid after the actual effort has been observed. In the implicit contract, there is no contractual obligation to pay the announced bonus, nor is the agent obliged to choose the desired effort level. The principal is, however, committed to pay the wage. An explicit contract also specifies a binding fixed wage and a desired effort level between 1 and 10. Here, however, the principal can impose a fine on the agent that has to be paid to the principal in case of verified shirking. Except for one detail, the explicit contract is identical to the performance contract discussed in the previous section. The difference concerns the fact that the choice of the explicit contract involves a fixed verification cost of 10 units. This reflects the fact that the verification of effort is, in general, costly. Note that the implicit contract does not require third-party verification of effort. It is only necessary that effort is observable by the principal.[25]

At stage two, the agent observes which contract has been offered and decides whether to accept or reject the offer. If the agent rejects the offer, the game ends and both parties get a payoff of zero. If the agent accepts, the next step is for the agent to choose the actual level of effort.

At stage three, the principal observes the actual effort level. If the principal has offered an implicit contract, the next decision is whether the agent should be awarded the bonus payment. If the principal offered an explicit contract and if the agent's effort falls short of the agreed effort level, a random draw decides with probability 0.33 whether shirking is verifiable, in which case the agent has to pay the fine.

If all players have purely selfish preferences, the analysis of this game is straightforward. A selfish principal would never pay a bonus. Anticipating this, there is no incentive for the agent to spend more than the minimum effort. If the principal chooses the explicit contract, the principal should go for the maximum punishment because this is the best deterrence for potential shirkers. The parameters of the experiment are chosen such that a risk-neutral and selfish agent maximizes expected utility by choosing an effort level of 4 if faced with the maximum fine. Since the enforceable effort level is 4 under the explicit contract, while it is only 1 under an implicit contract, the self-interest model predicts that principals prefer the explicit contract.

The experimental evidence is completely at odds with these predictions. In total, the implicit contract was chosen in 88 percent of the cases. In view of the relative profitability of the different contracts, the popularity of the implicit contract is not surprising. Those principals choosing the explicit contract made an average loss of 9 tokens per contract, while those preferring the implicit contract made an average profit of 26 tokens per contract. Since the fixed verification cost in the explicit contract was 10 tokens, the explicit contract would have been much less profitable even in the absence of these costs. For both contracts, the average income of the agents was roughly 18 tokens. Implicit contracts were more profitable because—contrary to the standard prediction—they induced much higher effort levels. The effort level in the implicit contract was 5.2 on the average (on a scale of 1 to 10), while the effort level in the explicit contract was 2.1 on the average.

How did implicit contracts induce much higher effort levels than predicted? A major reason is that in the presence of strongly reciprocal principals, the promised bonus does not merely represent cheap talk, because reciprocal principals can—and actually do—condition the bonus payment on the effort level. The average data clearly reflect this impact of the reciprocal types because the actual average bonus rises steeply with the actual effort level. The principal's capability to commit himself to paying a conditional bonus is based on his reciprocal inclinations. Conditional bonus payments, in turn, provide a strong pecuniary incentive for the agents to perform as desired by the principals. Why did explicit contracts induce lower effort levels than predicted? A likely reason is that these contracts are perceived as hostile and even induce negative reciprocity, as shown in the previous section.

One might also conjecture that the preference for implicit contracts in this particular experiment is solely caused by the fact that the explicit contract involves a punishment while the implicit contract involves a reward. Further experiments by Fehr, Klein, and Schmidt (2001), however, cast doubt on this explanation. If the implicit contract described in this section competes with a piece-rate contract, the vast majority of principals still prefer the implicit contract.

5.5.3 Individual Versus Joint Ownership

The impact of strong reciprocity on contractual choices suggests that it may not only cause substantial changes in the functioning of given economic institutions, but that it may also have a powerful impact on the selection and formation of institutions. To provide a further example: The present theory of property rights (Hart 1995) predicts that joint ownership will in general severely inhibit relations-specific investments so that it emerges only under very restrictive conditions. This may no longer be true in the presence of strongly reciprocal actors who are willing to cooperate if they expect the trading partner to cooperate as well and who are willing to punish even at a cost to themselves.

To illustrate this point, consider two parties, A and B, who are engaged in a joint project (a "firm") to which they have to make some relationship specific investments today in order to generate a joint surplus in the future. An important question that has received considerable attention in recent years is who should own the firm. In a seminal paper, Grossman and Hart (1986) argued that ownership rights allocate residual rights of control to the physical assets that are required to generate the surplus. For example, if A owns the firm, then he will have a stronger bargaining position than B in the renegotiation game in which the surplus between the two parties is shared *ex post facto*, because he can exclude B from using the assets which make B's relationship specific investment less productive. Grossman and Hart showed that there is no ownership structure that implements first best investments, but some ownership structures do better than others, and there is a unique second-best optimal allocation of ownership rights. They also show that joint ownership is, in general, not optimal. This result is at odds with the fact that there are many jointly-owned companies, partnerships, or joint ventures. Furthermore, the argument neglects that strong reciprocity may be an important enforcement mechanism to induce the involved parties to invest more under joint ownership than otherwise predicted.

In order to test this hypothesis, Fehr, Kremhelmer, and Schmidt (2001) conducted a series of experiments on the optimal allocation of ownership rights. The experimental game is a simplified version of Grossman and Hart (1986): There are two parties, A and B, who have to make investments, $a, b \in \{1, \ldots, 10\}$, respectively, in order to generate a joint surplus $v(a, b)$. Investments are sequential: B has to invest first and her investment level b is observed by A, who has to invest thereafter. We consider two possible ownership structures: Under A-ownership, A hires B as an employee and pays her a fixed wage w. In this case, monetary payoffs are $v(a, b) - w - a$ for A and $w - b$ for B. Under joint ownership, each party gets half of the gross surplus minus her investment cost—$\frac{1}{2}v(a, b) - a$ for A and $\frac{1}{2}v(a, b) - b$ for B. The gross profit function has been chosen such that maximal investments are efficient—that is, $a^{FB} = b^{FB} = 10$, but if each party gets only 50 percent of the marginal return of his or her investment, then it is a dominant strategy for a purely self-interested player to choose the minimum level of investment, $\underline{a} = \underline{b} = 1$. Finally, in the first stage of the game, A can decide whether to be the sole owner of the firm and make a wage offer to B, or whether to have joint ownership.

The prediction of the self-interest model is straightforward. Under A-ownership, B has no incentive to invest and will choose $b = 1$. On the other hand, A is the residual claimant, so she will invest efficiently. Under joint ownership each party gets only 50 percent of the marginal return, which is not sufficient to induce any investments. In this case, B's optimal investment level is unchanged, but A's investment level is reduced to $\underline{a} = 1$. Thus, A-ownership outperforms joint ownership and A should hire B as an employee.

In the experiments just the opposite happens. Party A chooses joint ownership in more than 80 percent (187 out of 230) of all observations and gives away 50 percent of the gross return to B. Moreover, the fraction of joint ownership contracts increases from 74 percent in the first two periods to 89 percent in the last two periods. With joint ownership, B players choose on the average an investment level of 8.9, and A responds with an investment of 6.5 (on the average). On the other hand, if A-ownership is chosen and A hires B as an employee, B's average investment is only 1.3, while all A players choose an investment level of 10. Furthermore, A players earn much more on the average if they choose joint ownership rather than A-ownership.

These results are inconsistent with the self-interest model, but it is straightforward to explain them with concerns for strong reciprocity. Under joint ownership, the investments are associated with positive externalities and, hence, joint ownership favors positively reciprocal behavior. If, under joint ownership, B expects A to behave reciprocally, even a selfish B player has a strong incentive to make high investments because this induces the reciprocal players A to invest, too. Under A-ownership, the incentives for B are quite different because B does not benefit from the investments of A. Hence, the selfish Bs choose the

minimal investment under A-ownership. If there is sufficient complementarity between the investments of A and B, the joint surplus is
therefore much higher under joint ownership. This makes it profitable
for A to choose joint ownership.

5.6 Proximate Models of Strong Reciprocity

The evidence from this chapter indicates that strong reciprocity has a
deep impact on fundamental economic issues. It is an important behavioral force that shapes the functioning of competition, governs the
laws of cooperation, and has a decisive impact on how incentives
work. Strong reciprocity creates implicit incentives and renders some
explicit incentives quite inefficient. By changing the incentives for the
selfish types, it also affects the prevailing interaction patterns and constraints on individual behavior—the prevailing contracts and institutions relative to a world that is exclusively populated by self-interested
people.

We believe that—in view of the importance of strong reciprocity—
mainstream economics as well as the social sciences in general have
much to gain by routinely incorporating concerns for strong reciprocity
into the analysis. This means that when analyzing an economic or social problem, one should routinely try to derive the implications of
the assumption that, in addition to the purely self-interested types,
roughly 40 to 50 percent of the people exhibit strongly reciprocal preferences. It is obvious that to achieve this a precise mathematical model
of strongly reciprocal preferences is desirable. In the past few years,
several authors have worked on models of strong reciprocity (Rabin
1993; Levine 1998; Dufwenberg and Kirchsteiger 2004; Falk and Fischbacher, this volume, chapter 6; Segal and Sobel 1999; Charness and
Rabin 2002). These papers are very useful because they sharpen the notion of strong reciprocity. However, they also show that it is extremely
difficult to build simple and tractable models of strong reciprocity. The
problem is that the explicit modeling of intention-based or type-based
strong reciprocity quickly renders these models very complex and difficult to handle.

The first best solution to the modeling problem would surely be a
simple and tractable model of strong reciprocity. However, since this
solution is not presently available, there is also a need for simpler
models that mimic the outcomes of strong reciprocity models in a
wide variety of circumstances but that do not explicitly model strong

reciprocity. Such models have been developed by Fehr and Schmidt (1999), and Bolton and Ockenfels (2000). They are based on the assumption that "fair" types dislike an inequitable distribution of economic resources. The impressive feature of these models is that although they are much simpler than strong reciprocity models, they correctly predict the outcome of experiments in a wide variety of games. The model of Fehr and Schmidt (1999), for example, is consistent with the stylized facts in scenarios presented earlier in the chapter—the bilateral ultimatum and gift exchange game, market games under exogenous and endogenous contract enforcement, cooperation games with and without a punishment opportunity, and contract choice and property rights experiments. This suggests that it is possible in many instances to capture the behavioral predictions of strong reciprocity with simpler models of fairness.

However, the black-boxing of strong reciprocity via simple fairness models must be done with a background knowledge about the limits of these models. Mindless application of these models may lead to wrong predictions, as is demonstrated in the experiments of Brandts and Sola (2001), and Falk, Fehr, and Fischbacher (2003). In the Falk, Fehr, and Fischbacher (2003), paper, the rejection rates of the (8/2)-offer (8 for the proposer and 2 for the responder) in four different mini-ultimatum games are compared. The games differ only with regard to the available alternative to the (8/2)-offer. In one game the alternative was (5/5), in the second game it was (2/8), in the third game it was (8/2), and in the last game it was (10/0). Note that if the responder cares only about the distribution of payoffs, the rejection rate of the (8/2)-offer should be the same in all four games.

In fact, however, the rejection rate is monotonically declining across the four games. It is highest in the (5/5)-game, where (5/5) was the alternative, and lowest in the (10/0)-game. A plausible interpretation of this result is that in the (5/5)-game an offer of (8/2) indicates an unfair intention or an unfair type, while in the (10/0)-game this is not the case. Thus, if responders punish unfair intentions or unfair types, they should exhibit a higher rejection rate in the (5/5)-game. This example indicates that if the set of feasible alternatives changes across situations such that the possibilities for expressing good or bad intentions changes, simple fairness models do not capture important aspects of behavior.

It is, however, interesting that even in these situations, a simple model can be useful because the prediction of the model provides hints when intention- or type-based strong reciprocity is likely to matter. The prediction thus alerts the researcher about the limits of the model. For instance, if (5/5) instead of (10/0) is the alternative to (8/2), the Fehr-Schmidt model (1999) predicts that for reasonable rejection rates, the population of proposers who make the (8/2)-offer is less fair. Thus responders will make different inferences about the type or the intention of the population who made the (8/2)-offer when (5/5) is the alternative compared to when (10/0) is the alternative. This inference induces strongly reciprocal responders to reject the (8/2)-offer more frequently when (5/5) is the alternative.[26]

It is also important to keep in mind that models that have been developed to explain a diverse set of facts in laboratory experiments must be used with care and need perhaps some adaptations when applied to field situations. For example, it is often not possible to determine the relevant reference agents in the field without further empirical analysis, while in an experiment, the set of the other players in the group is often a good first approximation. Likewise, it does not seem likely that the effort-relevant fairness judgements of a worker are based on a comparison between the worker's income and the income of the top managers of the firm. Instead, the behaviorally relevant comparisons tend to be more local—that is, comparisons with her coworkers or comparisons with the average value of the output she generates.

5.7 Conclusion

The self-interest hypothesis assumes that all people are exclusively motivated by their economic self-interest. This hypothesis is sometimes a convenient simplification and there are, no doubt, situations in which almost all people behave *as if* they were strictly self-interested. In particular, for comparative static predictions of aggregate behavior, self-interest models may make empirically correct predictions because models with more complex motivational assumptions predict the same outcome. However, the evidence presented in this paper also shows that fundamental issues in economics and the social sciences in general cannot be understood solely on the basis of the self-interest model. The evidence indicates that concerns for fairness and strong reciprocity are important for bilateral negotiations, for the functioning of markets and incentives, for the structure of property rights and contracts, and for the laws governing collective action and cooperation.

Notes

1. Economists and biologists defined the term "reciprocity" in the past in different ways. Biologists think of reciprocity, or "reciprocal altruism," as tit-for-tat strategies in repeated interactions (Trivers 1971; Axelrod and Hamilton 1981). Some economists (Binmore 1998) use the term in a similar way. During the last ten years, however, an increasing number of contributions show that reciprocal behavior also exists in sequentially structured one-shot interactions. Reciprocity in one-shot interactions cannot be explained on the basis of selfish motives. Therefore, we use the term "strong reciprocity" to describe these non–self-interested behaviors to distinguish them from reciprocal behaviour of self-interested agents in a repeated game.

2. Strictly speaking, Levine's model of reciprocity is not based on intentions, but on the reciprocation to the other players' preferences. A subject with Levine-type preferences is more altruistic (or less spiteful) towards an altruistic player and more spiteful (or less altruistic) towards a spiteful player. The model thus captures a kind of type-based reciprocity.

3. For evidence suggesting that fairness and reciprocity is important in the field see, for example, Agell and Lundborg (1995), Bewley (1999), Frey and Weck-Hanneman (1984), Frey and Pommerehne (1993), Greenberg (1990), Kahneman, Knetsch, and Thaler (1986), Lind and Tyler (1988), Ostrom (1990, 2000), Seidl and Traub (1999), and Zajac (1995).

4. In the experiments, human subjects make decisions with real monetary consequences in carefully controlled laboratory settings. In particular, the experimenter can implement one-shot interactions between the subjects so that long-term self-interest can be ruled out as an explanation for what we observe. As we will see, in some experiments the monetary stakes involved are quite high—amounting up to the income of three months' work. In the experiments reviewed in this chapter, subjects do not know each other's identities, interact anonymously, and sometimes even the experimenter cannot observe their *individual* choices. Due to the anonymity conditions, the laboratory environment is quite unfavorable to the emergence of reciprocal behavior. Yet, if we observe reciprocal behavior under such unfavorable conditions, it is even more likely to prevail in non-anonymous interactions between people who know each other.

5. For surveys on ultimatum games, see Roth (1995) or Camerer (2003). Gift exchange games have been conducted by scholars such as Brandts and Charness (forthcoming), Charness (2000, forthcoming), Fehr and Falk (1999), Gächter and Falk (2002), Falk, Gächter, and Kovàcs (1999), and Hannan, Kagel, and Moser (2002).

6. The remaining subjects, except one, exhibit no significant change in the acceptance threshold. Only 1 out of 70 subjects exhibits a significant decrease in the threshold relative to the baseline. Note that if a subject places a very high value on fairness, the acceptance threshold may already be very high in the baseline condition so that there is little reason to change the threshold in the reputation condition. Identical thresholds across conditions are, therefore, also compatible with a social preference approach. Only a decrease in the acceptance threshold is incompatible with theories of social preferences.

7. In the study of Roth et al. (1991), competition led to an even more extreme outcome. However, in their market experiments, 9 competing proposers faced only 1 responder, and the responder was forced to accept the highest offer.

8. In the meantime, the gift exchange game has been framed in goods market terms, labor market terms, and in a completely neutral language. The results indicate that there are no framing effects.

9. In each period the same stationary situation is implemented—there are 12 workers, 8 firms, and each worker's reservation wage is 20. In a given period, employers and workers can make as many wage bids as they like, as long as they have not yet been signed on. Trading is anonymous. Every worker can accept an offer made by a firm and every firm can accept an offer made by a worker.

10. A variety of studies have found that one major reason why managers are reluctant to cut wages in a recession is the fear that wage cuts may hamper work performance. Among others, Bewley (1999, this volume, chapter 11) reports that managers are afraid that pay cuts "express hostility to the work force" and will be "interpreted as an insult." For similar results see Agell and Lundborg (1995), and Campbell and Kamlani (1997).

11. For the severe difficulties created by unobservable heterogeneity in this context, see Murphy and Topel (1990), and Gibbons and Katz (1992).

12. This situation mimics a classic exchange problem in the absence of exogenous contract enforcement. A would like to have the good that B possesses, because she values that good more than B does and vice versa. Since A and B cannot write a contract that is enforced by a third party and since both have to send their goods simultaneously to the other person, they have a strong incentive to cheat.

13. For rigorous proofs that reciprocity (or inequity aversion) transform the PD into a co-ordination game, see section IV in Fehr and Schmidt (1999).

14. Social dilemma games are generalised PD-games in the following sense: There is a Pareto-superior cooperative outcome that renders everybody strictly better off relative to the Nash equilibrium.

15. Social psychologists have also found evidence that people who believe that others cooperate more will themselves cooperate more (Dawes 1980; Messick and Brewer 1983; Hayashi et al. 1999). Some of them have interpreted this in terms of a false consensus effect. According to the false consensus effect, the causality runs from a subject's cooperativeness to the subject's belief that others cooperate. However, the evidence in Fischbacher, Gächter and Fehr (2001) and in Hayashi et al. (1999) shows that the causality goes the other way round: If the other players contribute more strongly, reciprocal subjects contribute more on average.

16. The official title of former president Clinton's reform initiative—"The Personal Responsibility and Work Opportunity Reconciliation Act"—is telling in this regard.

17. The written instructions for the subjects do not use value-laden terms such as "punishment points." Instead, the instructions are framed in neutral terms. For example, subjects do not assign "punishment points" but just "points" to the other players.

18. In the experiments, subjects first participate in the game without a punishment opportunity for ten periods. After this, they are told that a new experiment takes place. In the new experiment, which lasts again for ten periods, the punishment opportunity is implemented. In both conditions, subjects remain in the same group for ten periods and they know that after ten periods the experiment will be over.

19. Francis' (1985, 269) description of social ostracism in communities of the British miners provides a particularly vivid example. During the 1984 miners' strike, which lasted for several months, he observed the following: "To isolate those who supported the 'scab union,' cinemas and shops were boycotted, there were expulsions from football teams, bands, and choirs, and 'scabs' were compelled to sing on their own in their chapel services. 'Scabs' witnessed their own 'death' in communities which no longer accepted them."

20. Suppose we offer you £100 for hitting a stranger in the face. Even if the stranger had no possibility to hit back, most people would probably reject this offer.

21. A plausible reason for this is that if subjects cooperate successfully for five periods and then some group members try to cheat (free-ride) in the final period, the cooperators may be more angry than when they face free-riding in earlier periods. Being cheated by a "friend" might make people angrier than being cheated by a "stranger."

22. There is an interesting difference between the ultimatum game experiments with reputation formation discussed in this chapter and the punishment of free-riders in the partner treatment. Recall that responder's acceptance thresholds were significantly higher in the reputation treatment of the ultimatum game relative to the baseline treatment. In the reputation treatment, a responder could aqcuire an *individual* reputation for being a tough bargainer and he could reap the full benefits of his reputation. In the partner treatment of the public goods game, the punishment of free-riders constitutes a second-order public good because all group members benefit from the cooperation-enhancing effect of the punishment. This may be one reason why we observe so little strategic punishment in the partner treatment.

23. To prevent hostility from being introduced merely by the use of value-laden terms, we avoided terms like "fine," "performance," and so forth. Instead we used a rather neutral language—for example, "price deduction."

24. Note that according to this interpretation, there is no crowding out of an intrinsic (reciprocal) motivation here. Instead, the preference for reciprocity implies that workers respond in a hostile manner to incentives that are perceived as hostile.

25. Employers are, in general, not free to cut a worker's wage for shirking, while they have few legal problems when they refuse to pay a promised bonus.

26. One way to explain this evidence is to modify the Fehr-Schmidt (1999) model of inequity aversion such that the disutility from disadvantageous inequality is lower if a person faces a subject with a high preference against advantageous inequality. This basically boils down to a type-based model of reciprocity. The model by Falk and Fischbacher (this volume, chapter 6) can also explain this evidence.

References

Agell, Jonas, and Per Lundborg. 1995. "Theories of Pay and Unemployment: Survey Evidence from Swedish Manufacturing Firms." *Scandinavian Journal of Economics* 97:295–308.

Akerlof, George. 1982. "Labor Contracts as Partial Gift Exchange." *Quarterly Journal of Economics* 97:543–569.

Andreoni, James. 1989. "Giving with Impure Altruism: Applications to Charity and Ricardian Equivalence." *Journal of Political Economy* 97:1447–1458.

Andreoni, James, and John Miller. 2002. "Giving According to GARP: An Experimental Test of the Rationality of Altruism." *Econometrica* 70:737–753.

Axelrod, Robert, and William D. Hamilton. 1981. "The Evolution of Cooperation." *Science* 211:1390–1396.

Bewley, Truman. 1999. *Why Wages Don't Fall During a Recession.* Cambridge, MA: Harvard University Press.

Bewley, Truman. 2003. "Fairness, Reciprocity, and Wage Rigidity," chapter 11, this volume.

Binmore, Ken. 1998. *Game Theory and the Social Contract: Just Playing*. Cambridge, MA: MIT Press.

Bolton, Gary E., and Axel Ockenfels. 2000. "A Theory of Equity, Reciprocity and Competition." *American Economic Review* 100:166–193.

Bowles, Samuel, and Herbert Gintis. 1998. "Is Equality Passé." *Boston Review* 23(6).

Brandts, Jordi, and Gary Charness. Forthcoming. "Do Labor Market Condition Affect Gift-Exchange?" *Economic Journal*.

Brandts, Jordi, and Carles Sola. 2001. "Reference Points and Negative Reciprocity in Simple Sequential Games." *Games and Economic Behavior* 36:138–157.

Camerer, Colin F. 2003. *Behavioral Game Theory*. Princeton, NJ: Princeton University Press.

Cameron, Lisa. 1999. "Raising the Stakes in the Ultimatum Game: Experimental Evidence from Indonesia." *Economic Inquiry* 37:47–59.

Campbell, Carl M., and Kunal S. Kamlani. 1997. "The Reasons for Wage Rigidity: Evidence from a Survey of Firms." *Quarterly Journal of Economics* 112:759–789.

Charness, Gary. 2000. "Responsibility and Effort in an Experimental Labor Market." *Journal of Economic Behavior and Organization* 42:375–384.

Charness, Gary. Forthcoming. "Attribution and Reciprocity in an Experimental Labor Market." *Journal of Labor Economics*.

Charness, Gary, and Matthew Rabin. 2002. "Understanding Social Preferences with Simple Tests." *Quarterly Journal of Economics* 117:817–869.

Cox, Jim. 2000. "Trust and Reciprocity: Implications of Game Triads and Social Contexts." Mimeo. Tucson: University of Arizona.

Cox, Jim, Klarita Sadiraj, and Vjollca Sadiraj. 2001. "A Theory of Fairness and Competition without Inequality Aversion." Mimeo.

Croson, Rachel T. A. 1999. "Contributions to Public Goods: Altruism or Reciprocity." Discussion Paper. Wharton School of Business, University of Pennsylvania.

Davis, Douglas D., and Charles A. Holt. 1993. *Experimental Economics*. Princeton, NJ: Princeton University Press.

Dawes, Robin. 1980. "Social Dilemmas." *Annual Review of Psychology* 31:169–193.

Dufwenberg, Martin, and Georg Kirchsteiger. 2004. "A Theory of Sequential Reciprocity." *Games and Economic Behavior* 47:268–298.

Falk, Armin, and Urs Fischbacher. 2003. "Modelling Strong Reciprocity," chapter 6, this volume.

Falk, Armin, Ernst Fehr, and Urs Fischbacher. 2000. "Testing Theories of Fairness—Intentions Matter." Working Paper No. 63. Institute for Empirical Research in Economics, University of Zurich.

Falk, Armin, Ernst Fehr, and Urs Fischbacher. 2001. "Driving Forces of Informal Sanctions." Institute for Empirical Research in Economics, University of Zurich, Working Paper No. 59.

Falk, Armin, Ernst Fehr, and Urs Fischbacher. 2003. "On the Nature of Fair Behaviour." *Economic Inquiry* 41:20–26.

Falk, Armin, Simon Gächter, and Judit Kovàcs. 1999. "Intrinsic Motivation and Extrinsic Incentives in a Repeated Game with Incomplete Contracts." *Journal of Economic Psychology* 20:251–284.

Fehr, Ernst, and Armin Falk. 1999. "Wage Rigidity in a Competitive Incomplete Contract Market." *Journal of Political Economy* 107:106–134.

Fehr, Ernst, and Urs Fischbacher. 2003. "The Nature of Human Altruism." *Nature* 425:785–791.

Fehr, Ernst, and Simon Gächter. 2000a. "Cooperation and Punishment in Public Goods Experiments." *American Economic Review* 90:980–994.

Fehr, Ernst, and Simon Gächter. 2000b. "Do Incentive Contracts Crowd out Voluntary Contribution?" Working Paper No. 34. Institute for Empirical Research in Economics, University of Zurich.

Fehr, Ernst, and Klaus M. Schmidt. 1999. "A Theory of Fairness, Competition and Cooperation." *Quarterly Journal of Economics* 114:817–868.

Fehr, Ernst, and Klaus M. Schmidt. 2003. "Theories of Fairness and Reciprocity— Evidence and Economic Applications." In *Advances in Economic Theory, Eigth World Congress of the Econometric Society*. Eds. M. Dewatripont, L. P. Hansen, S. Turnovski. Cambridge: Cambridge University Press.

Fehr, Ernst, Simon Gächter, and Georg Kirchsteiger. 1996. "Reciprocal Fairness and Noncompensating Wage Differentials." *Journal of Institutional and Theoretical Economics* 152(4):608–640.

Fehr, Ernst, Georg Kirchsteiger, and Arno Riedl. 1993. "Does Fairness prevent Market Clearing? An Experimental Investigation." *Quarterly Journal of Economics* 108:437–460.

Fehr, Ernst, Alexander Klein, and Klaus M. Schmidt. 2001. "Fairness, Incentives and Contractual Incompleteness." Working Paper No. 72. Institute for Empirical Research in Economics, University of Zurich.

Fehr, Ernst, Susanne Kremhelmer, and Klaus Schmidt. 2001. "Fairness and the Optimal Allocation of Property Rights." Mimeo. University of Munich.

Fehr, Ernst, Elena Tougareva, and Urs Fischbacher. 2002. "Do High Stakes and Competition Undermine Fairness? Evidence from Russia." Working Paper No. 120. Institute for Empirical Economic Research, University of Zurich.

Fischbacher, Urs, Christina Fong, and Ernst Fehr. 2003. "Fairness and the Power of Competition." Working Paper No. 133. Institute for Empirical Economic Research, University of Zurich.

Fischbacher, Urs, Simon Gächter, and Ernst Fehr. 2001. "Are People Conditionally Cooperative? Evidence from a Public Goods Experiment." *Economics Letters* 71:397–404.

Fong, Christina, Samuel Bowles, and Herbert Gintis. "Egalitarian Redistribution and Reciprocity," chapter 10, this volume.

Francis, Hywel. 1985. "The Law, Oral Tradition and the Mining Community." *Journal of Law and Society* 12:267–271.

Frey, Bruno S., and Werner W. Pommerehne. 1993. "On the Fairness of Pricing—An Empirical Survey among the General Population." *Journal of Economic Behavior and Organization* 20:295–307.

Frey, Bruno, and Hannelore Weck-Hannemann. 1984. "The Hidden Economy as an 'Unobserved' Variable." *European Economic Review* 26:33–53.

Gächter, Simon, and Armin Falk. 2002. "Reputation and Reciprocity: Consequences for the Labour Relation." *Scandinavian Journal of Economics* 104:1–26.

Gibbons, Robert, and Lawrence Katz. 1992. "Does Unmeasured Ability Explain Inter-Industry Wage Differentials?" *Review of Economic Studies* 59:515–535.

Greenberg, Jerald. 1990. "Employee Theft as a Reaction to Underpayment Inequity: The Hidden Cost of Pay Cuts." *Journal of Applied Psychology* 75:561–568.

Grossman, Sanford, and Oliver Hart. 1986. "The Costs and Benefits of Ownership: A Theory of Vertical and Lateral Integration." *Journal of Political Economy* 94(1):691–719.

Güth, Werner, Rolf Schmittberger, and Bernd Schwarze. 1982. "An Experimental Analysis of Ultimatium Bargaining." *Journal of Economic Behavior and Organization* 3:367–388.

Hannan, Lynn, John Kagel, and Donald Moser. 2002. "Partial Gift Exchange in Experimental Labor Markets: Impact of Subject Population Differences, Productivity Differences and Effort Requests on Behavior." *Journal of Labor Economics* 20:923–951.

Hart, Oliver. 1995. *Firms, Contracts, and Financial Structure.* Oxford: Clarendon Press.

Hayashi, Nehoko, Elinor Ostrom, James Walker, and Toshio Yamagichi. 1999. "Reciprocity, Trust, and the Sense of Control—A Cross Societal Study." *Rationality and Society* 11:27–46.

Kagel, John, and Katherine Wolfe. 2001. "Tests of Fairness Models based on Equity Considerations in a Three Person Ultimatum Game." *Experimental Economics* 4:203–220.

Kahneman, Daniel, Jack L. Knetsch, and Richard Thaler. 1986. "Fairness as a Constraint on Profit Seeking: Entitlements in the Market." *American Economic Review* 76:728–741.

Kirchsteiger, Georg. 1994. "The Role of Envy in Ultimatum Games." *Journal of Economic Behavior and Organization* 25:373–389.

Ledyard, John. 1995. "Public Goods: A Survey of Experimental Research." In *Handbook of Experimental Economics.* Ed. Alvin Roth and John Kagel. Princeton, NJ: Princeton University Press.

Levine, David. 1998. "Modeling Altruism and Spitefulness in Experiments." *Review of Economic Dynamics* 1:593–622.

Lind, Allan, and Tom Tyler. 1988. *The Social Psychology of Procedural Justice.* New York and London: Plenum Press.

Lindbeck, Assar, and Dennis J. Snower. 1988. "Cooperation, Harassment, and Involuntary Unemployment: An Insider-Outsider Approach." *American Economic Review* 78(1):167–189.

Messick, David, and Marylin Brewer. 1983. "Solving Social Dilemmas—A Review." In *Review of Personality and Social Psychology*. Ed. L. Wheeler. Beverly Hills: Sage Publications.

Mui, Vai-Lam. 1995. "The Economics of Envy." *Journal of Economic Behavior and Organization* 26:311–336.

Murphy, Kevin M., and Robert H. Topel. 1990. "Efficiency Wages Reconsidered: Theory and Evidence." In *Advances in the Theory and Measurement of Unemployment*. Ed. Y. Weiss and G. Fischelson. London: Macmillan.

Neilson, William S. 2000. "An Axiomatic Characterization of the Fehr-Schmidt Model of Inequity Aversion." Working Paper. Texas A&M University.

Offerman, Theo. 2002. "Hurting Hurts More than Helping Helps." *European Economic Review* 46:1423–1437.

Ostrom, Elinor. 1990. *Governing the Commons—The Evolution of Institutions for Collective Action*. New York: Cambridge University Press.

Ostrom, Elinor. 2000. "Collective Action and the Evolution of Social Norms." *Journal of Economic Perspectives* 14:137–158.

Ostrom, Elinor, Roy Gardner, and James Walker. 1994. *Rules, Games, and Common Pool Resources*. Ann Arbor: The University of Michigan Press.

Rabin, Matthew. 1993. "Incorporating Fairness into Game Theory and Economics." *American Economic Review* 83(5):1281–1302.

Roethlisberger, Fritz F., and William J. Dickson. 1947. *Management and the Worker: An Account of a Research Program Conducted by the Western Electric Company, Hawthorne Works, Chicago*. Cambridge, MA: Harvard University Press.

Roth, Alvin E. 1995. "Bargaining Experiments." In *Handbook of Experimental Economics*. Eds. J. Kagel and A. Roth. Princeton, NJ: Princeton University Press.

Roth, Alvin E., Vesna Prasnikar, Masahiro Okuno-Fujiwara, and Shmuel Zamir. 1991. "Bargaining and Market Behavior in Jerusalem, Ljubljana, Pittsburgh, and Tokyo: An Experimental Study." *American Economic Review* 81:1068–1095.

Sally, David. 1995. "Conversation and Cooperation in Social Dilemmas: A Meta-Analysis of Experiments from 1958 to 1992." *Rationality and Society* 7(1):58–92.

Segal, Uzi, and Joel Sobel. 1999. "Tit for Tat: Foundations of Preferences for Reciprocity in Strategic Settings." Mimeo. University of California at San Diego.

Seidl, Christian, and Stefan Traub. 1999. "Taxpayers' Attitudes, Behavior, and Perceptions of Fairness in Taxation." Mimeo. Institut für Finanzwissenschaft und Sozialpolitik, University of Kiel.

Slade, Margret. 1990. "Strategic Pricing Models and Interpretation of Price-War Data." *European Economic Review* 34:524–537.

Sobel, Joel. 2001. "Social Preferences and Reciprocity." Mimeo. University of California San Diego.

Trivers, Robert. 1971. "Evolution of Reciprocal Altruism." *Quarterly Review of Biology* 46:35–57.

Wax, Amy L. 2000. "Rethinking Welfare Rights: Reciprocity Norms, Reactive Attitudes, and the Political Economy of Welfare Reform." *Law and Contemporary Problems* 63(1–2):257–298.

Whyte, William. 1955. *Money and Motivation*. New York: Harper and Brothers.

Yamagichi, Toshio. 1986. "The Provision of a Sanctioning System as a Public Good." *Journal of Personality and Social Psychology* 51:110–116.

Zajac, Edward. 1995. *Political Economy of Fairness*. Cambridge, MA: MIT Press.

6　Modeling Strong Reciprocity

Armin Falk and Urs Fischbacher

6.1　Introduction

In this chapter, we discuss how preferences for reciprocity can be modeled in a game-theoretic framework. The fact that people have a taste for fairness and reciprocity implies that their utility does not only depend on their own monetary payoff but also on the payoffs of the other players. This means that we have to distinguish between the *payoff* subjects receive (for instance, in an experimental game) and the *utility*, which not only consists of the own payoff but also on the payoff relative to the payoffs of the other players. We denote by π_i the material payoff player i gets while U_i denotes utility.

The basic structure of reciprocal behavior consists of the *reward of kind actions* and the *punishment of unkind ones*. This structure can be expressed in the following formula:

$$U_i = \pi_i + \rho_i \varphi \sigma \tag{1}$$

According to definition (1) player i's utility is the sum of the following two terms: The first summand is simply player i's *material payoff* π_i. This material payoff corresponds to the material payoffs that are induced by the experimenter. The second summand—which we call *reciprocity utility*—is composed of the following terms:

• The positive constant ρ_i is called the *reciprocity parameter*. This constant is an individual parameter that captures the strength of player i's reciprocal preferences. The higher ρ_i, the more important is the reciprocity utility as compared to the utility arising from the material payoff. Note that if ρ_i equals zero, player i's utility is equal to his material payoff. Put differently, if $\rho_i = 0$, the player has *Homo economicus* preferences just as assumed in standard game theory.

• The *kindness term* φ measures the kindness player i experiences from another player j's actions. The kindness term can be positive or negative. If φ is positive, the action of player j is considered as kind. If φ is negative, the action of player j is considered as unkind.

• The *reciprocation term* σ measures player i's reciprocal response. As a first approximation, σ is simply player j's payoff.

• The product of the *kindness* term (φ) and the *reciprocation term* (σ) measures the reciprocity utility. If the kindness term is greater than zero, player i can *ceteris paribus* increase his utility if he chooses an action that increases player j's payoff. The opposite holds if the kindness term is negative. In this scenario, player i has an incentive to reduce player j's payoff. As an example of this phenomenon, consider the ultimatum game (Güth, Schmittberger, and Schwarze 1982). If the proposer's offer was very low, the kindness term is negative and a reciprocal player i can increase his utility by rejecting the offer, which reduces player j's payoff.

To make the strong reciprocity model more concrete, we have to clarify two questions: *How do people evaluate whether a treatment is kind or unkind* and *how do people react towards that kindness or unkindness?* Both questions are much more subtle than it may seem on the surface. For example, in order to evaluate kindness, do people care only for the consequences of an action or do they also look at the motives imputed to that action? Or, what exactly is the primary aim of a reciprocating subject, to retaliate or to decrease payoff differences between him and the other person? And, who is the relevant other person? These and many other questions need to be answered before a concise modeling of reciprocity is possible.

To better understand the determination of kindness and the aim of the reciprocal act, we present new questionnaire data and report on a series of experiments that were designed to answer the most relevant questions:

1. What determines the *sign* of φ? This question is intimately related to the question of what *reference standard* is applied for the comparison of payoffs. An intuitive anchor for comparisons is an *equitable* share of payoffs. In fact, we show that many people consider an equitable share as an important reference standard.

2. How important are the fairness *intentions* attributed to other players' actions? This question has attracted a lot of attention. It

touches on the fundamental issue of consequentialistic versus non-consequentialistic fairness judgments: Is it only the material payoff consequence that determines the perception of fairness, or do people also take into account the motivation that underlies a particular action? The answer to this question is not only important for the correct modeling of fairness preferences, but also for the consequentialistic practice in standard economic theory that defines the utility of an action solely in terms of the consequences of this action.

3. What is the aim of a reciprocating agent? Do people punish in order to reduce *distributional inequity* between themselves and their opponent(s) or in order to reduce the other players' payoffs—that is, to *retaliate*? This question allows a clear distinction between so-called inequity aversion approaches and reciprocity approaches. According to the former, reciprocal actions are triggered by the desire to reduce an unfair payoff distribution. This implies, for example, that we should observe no reciprocal actions if the rewarding or punishing act cannot reduce inequity. Reciprocity, on the other hand, understands reciprocal actions as the desire to reward or to retaliate—meaning one should observe punishments and rewards even in situations where inequity cannot be reduced.

4. Who is the relevant *reference agent*? This question arises immediately if persons interact in groups and not only in bilateral relationships. Do people evaluate fairness towards individuals separately or towards the group as a whole? This question is of obvious importance, for example, in the context of social dilemma situations. If kindness is evaluated towards each of the other group members, reciprocal reactions are also targeted individually. Only if this dynamic holds it is guaranteed that the "right" persons (the defectors) receive the punishments. As a consequence, reciprocally driven sanctions can function as a disciplinary device to promote cooperative outcomes.

The chapter is organized as follows. In the next section, we discuss the determinants of kindness and reciprocation with the help of a questionnaire study and various experiments. Section 6.3 summarizes the arguments and presents a formal model of reciprocity that takes the facts presented in section 6.2 into account. The final section discusses related literature and gives a short conclusion.

6.2   Determinants of Kindness and Reciprocation

6.2.1   Equity as a Reference Standard

To investigate how people perceive the kindness or unkindness of an action, it is a natural starting point to simply *ask* people. We therefore conducted a questionnaire study with 111 students from the University of Zurich and the Polytechnical University of Zurich. The study was performed under anonymous conditions in our experimental computer lab during the months of May and June in 1998.

In the study, each subject i was in a hypothetical bilateral exchange situation with another subject j. Subjects i were asked to indicate how *kind* or *unkind* they perceive different divisions of an endowment of 10 Swiss Francs, where it was always j who divides the pie between herself and i. To measure kindness, subjects could use numbers ranging from -100 (very unkind) to $+100$ (very kind). In total, subjects were given nine different decision situations with different strategy sets for j.

In this section we concentrate on the first decision situations, where j could choose among 11 different allocations (see figure 6.1). If j offers 0 to i (and keeps everything to herself), i perceives this as very unkind (-95.4). If j offers 1 (and keeps 9 to herself), this is regarded as slightly less unkind (-84.5). This progression continues to the situation where

Figure 6.1
Kindness dependent on player j's offer.

j keeps nothing to herself and offers i 10, which is viewed as very kind (+72.3). Figure 6.1 reveals various important insights. First, it demonstrates kindness is monotonically increasing in the offer. The more j is willing to share with i, the more kind this is perceived by i. Second, an equitable share serves as an anchor for the determination of a fair or unfair offer. This can be concluded from the fact that as the offer approaches the equitable figure of 5, the perception changes from "unkind" to "kind."

A similar questionnaire study was conducted by Loewenstein, Thompson, and Bazerman (1989). They also found strong evidence for the importance of an equity based reference standard.

6.2.2   How Important Are Intentions?

There is an ongoing debate whether intentions are behaviorally relevant. The consequentialistic perspective claims that intentions are irrelevant for the evaluation of kindness. According to this conception, the distributive consequences of an action are sufficient to trigger behavior and no consideration of intentions is needed. Alternatively, it has been argued that the kindness or unkindness of an action crucially depends on the motives and intentions that can be attributed to that action. According to this perspective, actions that cause the same consequences might be perceived very differently, depending on the underlying intentions. As a result, they also might be reciprocated very differently.

To examine whether intentions matter, Falk, Fehr, and Fischbacher (2003) conducted four mini-ultimatum games (see figure 6.2). As figure 6.2 indicates, the proposer can choose between two allocations, x and y. In all four games, the allocation x is the same while the allocation y (the "alternative" to x) differs from game to game. If the proposer chooses x and the responder accepts this offer, the proposer gets 8 points while the responder receives 2 points. In game (a), the alternative offer y is (5/5). This game is therefore called the (5/5)-game and so forth.

Let us concentrate on the (8/2)-offer. The standard model with selfish preferences predicts that in all games, the offer (8/2) is never rejected. Fairness theories that rely on the consequentialistic perspective predict that this offer may be rejected, but that the rejection rate of the (8/2)-offer is the *same* across all games. Since outcomes following the (8/2)-offer are identical across games, different rejection rates of the (8/2)-offer are impossible to reconcile with a consequentialistic perspective.

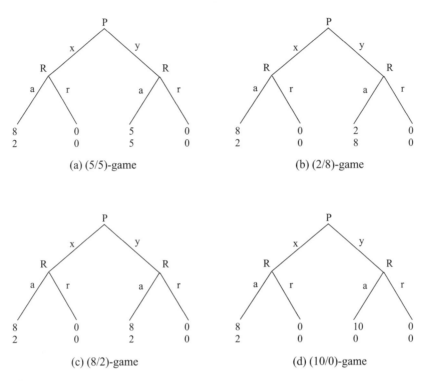

Figure 6.2
The mini-ultimatum games that test the importance of intentions.

Intuitively, one would expect that in the (5/5)-game, a proposal of (8/2) is clearly perceived as unfair because the proposer could have proposed the egalitarian offer (5/5). In the (2/8)-game offering, (8/2) may still be perceived as unfair—but probably less so than in the (5/5)-game, because the only alternative available to (8/2) gives the proposer much less than the responder. In a certain sense, therefore, the proposer has an excuse for not choosing (2/8) because one cannot unambiguously infer from his unwillingness to propose an unfair offer to himself that he wanted to be unfair to the responder.

Thus, one could expect that the rejection rate of the (8/2)-offer in the (5/5)-game is higher than in the (2/8)-game. In the (8/2)-game, the proposer has no choice at all so that the proposer's behavior cannot be judged in terms of fairness. Responders can only judge the fairness of the outcome (8/2), and if they exhibit sufficient aversion against ineq-uitable distributions, they will reject this distribution of money. Since any attribution of unfairness to the proposer's behavior is ruled out in this situation, one might expect an even lower rejection rate compared to the (2/8)-game. Finally, offering (8/2) in the (10/0)-game may even be perceived as fair (or less unfair) since, after all, the proposer could have chosen an even more unfair payoff. Therefore, the rejection rate of (8/2) is likely to be the lowest in this game.

In fact, the rejection rate in the (5/5)-game is highest: 44.4 percent rejected the (8/2)-offer in this game. Meanwhile, 26.7 percent rejected the (8/2)-offer in the (2/8)-game, 18 percent in the (8/2)-game and 8.9 percent in the (10/0)-game. These results clearly reject the consequentialistic perspective and suggest that intentions play a major role in the determination of kindness. Since rejection rates are not zero in the (8/2)-game (where intentions cannot play a role because the proposer has no choice), it seems, however, that kindness comprises both intentions *and* consequences of an action. This finding is corroborated by experiments by Brandts and Sola (2001), McCabe, Rigdon, and Smith (2003), Blount (1995), and Charness (forthcoming). The latter two studies investigate experiments in which the first mover's choice is made by a random device. This excludes any intention from this choice. They show that the reciprocal response of the second mover is weaker but not absent. For a dissenting view on the role of intentions see Cox (2000), and Bolton, Brandts, and Ockenfels (1998).

The discussion of the experiment shown in figure 6.2 has pointed at the question how people infer intentions from their opponents. We have argued that the *alternatives* the opponent can choose from are essential in this determination. To better understand *how* the set of alternative actions of an opponent j alters i's perception of j's kindness, we conducted the questionnaire study mentioned earlier in this section. In particular, we changed the set of alternatives of j could choose from and asked players i how kind they perceived different actions of j to be. Table 6.1 contains all variants. As a benchmark for our discussion, we use column (i) where player j has a rather unlimited action space—where j's action set allows the choice between fair and unfair actions, and therefore each action clearly signals (fair or unfair) intentions. In columns (ii) to (ix), we systematically vary the strategy set of j. In column (ii), for example, j can offer only 2, 5, or 8 to player i, while in column (iii), j can offer only 2, and so on. Table 6.1 reveals *five* interesting observations. In our discussion we focus primarily on the two payoff combinations (2/8) and (8/2).

First, if j's strategy set contains only one element—that is, if j has no alternative to choose, the kindness of an advantageous offer and the

Table 6.1
Player i's estimation of j's kindness (average values, $n = 111$).

(π_j, π_i)	i	ii	iii	iv	v	vi	vii	viii	ix
(0, 10)	72.3					79.9	73.4		80.3
(1, 9)	68					73.3	62		72.5
(2, 8)	62	75.3		41.1	61.2	61.9	40.8		62.2
(3, 7)	51.4								
(4, 6)	40								
(5, 5)	29.4	33.4							27.9
(6, 4)	−23.2								
(7, 3)	−52.9								
(8, 2)	−71.9	−70.6	−31.5		−47.7	−50.5		−9.1	−60.9
(9, 1)	−84.5					−80.3		−56.4	−82.6
(10, 0)	−95.4					−97.3		−88.8	−97.3

unkindness of a disadvantageous offer is much weaker, compared to a situation where j can choose between fair and unfair offers. This can be seen by comparing the perceived kindness of the (2/8)-offer in columns (i) and (iv) (+62 versus +41.1), and the unkindness of the (8/2)-offer in columns (i) and (iii) (−71.9 versus −31.5). The fact that the *same* payoff consequences are perceived differently, depending on the strategy set of player j, clearly contradicts the consequentialistic view of fairness.

Second, even if j has no alternatives and therefore cannot signal any intentions, perceived kindness or unkindness is not zero (see columns (iii) and (iv)). People dislike the disadvantageous (8/2)-outcome (−31.5) and like the advantageous (2/8)-outcome (+41.1), even if this outcome was unintentionally caused. This finding is in contradiction to a *purely* intention-based notion of fairness.

Third, even if j's strategy space is limited, the kind (2/8)-offer is viewed as similarly kind as in column (i), as long as j could have made *less kind offers* to i (compare columns (i) with columns (ii), (v), (vi), and (ix)). This means that a fair offer signals fair intentions if j could have been less fair. By the same token, the kindness of the (2/8)-offer is lower than in column (i) and similarly low as in column (iv) if player j does not have the chance to make a less fair offer (compare column (vii)). The intuition for the latter result is straightforward. If j has no chance to behave more "opportunistically," how should i infer from a fair action that j really wanted to be fair? After all, he took the least fair action.

Fourth, a comparison between columns (viii) and (i) shows that the unkindness of an offer depends on j's possibility to choose a less unkind offer. In column (viii), the (8/2)-offer is the least unfriendly offer and players i indicate a much lower perceived unkindness compared to column (i). The intuition for the different kindness scores parallels the one given in case of a kind offer: You cannot blame a person for being mean if—after all—he did the best he could.

Fifth, there is an asymmetry between the perception of kind and unkind offers. We saw that as long as j could have made a worse offer to i, the kind (2/8)-offer is viewed as similarly kind as in column (i) (see our third observation). Things look different for unkind offers, however. Take a look at column (ii). In this situation, j could have made more friendly offers than to offer (8/2)—namely, (5/5) and (2/8). The perceived unkindness of the (8/2) offer is very similar to the one in column (i) (-70.6 and -71.9, respectively). If we move on to columns (v) and (vi), however, the perceived unkindness drops to -47.7 and -50.5, respectively—even though player j could have made better offers to i.

The difference between the perceived unkindness in columns (ii) and (v) and (vi) points at the question of "how reasonable" it is to expect that j chooses an offer that puts herself in a disadvantageous position. In column (ii), j has the option to offer (5/5), an offer that is reasonable to expect. In columns (v) and (vi) on the other hand, a more friendly offer for i than (8/2) implies that player j puts herself in a very disadvantageous position (8 to i and 2 to j). In this situation, players i seem to understand that it is an unreasonable sacrifice for j to make a more friendly offer. Therefore, they consider the (8/2) as less unkind compared to a situation where j does have a reasonable alternative (as in column (ii)). In our formal model later in this chapter, we use these five observations to formalize intentions.

The results of this questionnaire data match very nicely the rejection behavior in the mini ultimatum games (UGs) in figure 6.2. Consider for instance the (8/2)-offer in the (8/2)-game. The rejection rate of this offer is lower in the (8/2)-game than in the (5/5)-game. This corresponds to the lower indicated unkindness of the corresponding offer in table 6.1 (-31.5 in column (iii) compared to -70.6 in column (ii)). However, an (8/2)-offer is also perceived as unkind if there is no alternative (-31.5 in column (iii) is negative). This explains why there are rejections of the (8/2)-offer in the (8/2)-game.

6.2.3   Reciprocation Target

So far, we have analyzed important motives for the evaluation of kindness. In this section, we address the question how people react to perceived kindness, that is, to what end do they reward or punish? There are two principal motives that may account for performing punishments: (i) retaliation and (ii) inequity aversion. According to the latter, a person will punish another person only if this reduces the inequity between the person and his opponent(s). Retaliation, on the other hand, dictates to punish in order to reciprocate an unkind act. In retaliation, the aim of the reciprocating subject is not to reduce distributional inequity but to lower the (unkind) opponent's payoff. Retaliation-driven punishments are therefore not restricted to situations where inequity can be reduced. Instead it occurs whenever a person is treated unkindly and is given a chance to "pay back."

With the help of the following three experiments, Falk, Fehr, and Fischbacher (2001) directly tested the importance of inequity aversion and retaliation motives for the performance of punishments. In the first experiment, the prediction depends on the way inequity is measured. In discussing this experiment, we also bring attention to the question whether inequity aversion should be measured as a difference between payoffs or in terms of relative payoff shares. The first two games described here are simple ultimatum games, and the third is a public goods game with a subsequent punishment stage. The two ultimatum games are presented in figure 6.3.

In both games presented in figure 6.3, the proposer can choose between the offer x and y, where x is the unfair offer (8/2) and y the fair offer (5/5). The consequences arising from the rejection of an offer

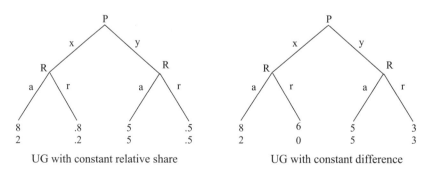

Figure 6.3
Ultimatum games (UGs) where a rejection does not reduce inequity.

are different, however. In the game *UG with constant relative share*, a rejection of an offer leaves the ratio between the players' payoffs unchanged. In the game *UG with constant difference*, it is the difference between the payoffs that remains unchanged following a rejection. The standard economic prediction for the two ultimatum games dictates the proposers to choose the offer x which is accepted by the responders. Assuming that people have fairness preferences, the predictions depend on the nature of these preferences.

Let us start our discussion with the *UG with constant relative share*. In this game, the retaliation motive predicts that the unfair offer x is rejected. After all, the offer (8/2) is very unkind and the proposer "deserves" the punishment. The predictions put forward by a fairness concept based on inequity aversion depend on the way inequity is measured. If inequity is measured as the difference between the own payoff and the payoff of the other player $(\pi_i - \pi_j)$, inequity aversion predicts rejection because the difference between 0.8 and 0.2 is smaller than the difference between 8 and 2. If inequity aversion is measured on the basis of the relative share of own payoff to (the sum of all) others' payoffs $(\pi_i/\Sigma\pi_j)$, no rejections are expected—since the share of 0.2/1 is exactly the same as that of 2/10. In the *UG with constant differences*, inequity aversion predicts no punishments *independent* on how inequity aversion is measured. The retaliation motive, on the other hand, does not preclude punishments in this game because the offer (8/2) is quite unfair and the responder's payoff can be reduced by a rejection.

The results of the *UG with constant relative share* cast serious doubts on the validity of the inequity aversion motive if modeled as relative share. Even though the relative share argument predicts a rejection rate of zero, 38 percent of all players reject the unfair offer (8/2). Inequity aversion as measured by the difference between payoffs seems to fit the data better. However, in the *UG with constant differences*, the rejection rate of the unfair offer (8/2) is still 19 percent. Thus, even if modeled in terms of differences of payoffs, inequity aversion does not account for about 20 percent of the observed punishment in our reduced ultimatum game.

To further test the importance of inequity aversion as a motivational factor that drives punishments, we studied a public goods game with a subsequent punishment opportunity (Falk, Fehr, and Fischbacher 2001). In the first stage of this one-shot game, three players first decide simultaneously on a voluntary provision to a linear public good. The decision amounts to an investment of either 0 or 20 points to the public good. Payoffs in the first stage are 20 − *own provision* + 0.6 ∗ *sum of all provisions*. During the second stage, each player has to decide whether or not he wants to sanction the other players in his group. Deducting points is costly—deducting 1 point from another player is associated with a cost of 1 point.

Assuming selfish preferences, the predicted outcome is straightforward. Since deducting points is costly, the second stage is basically irrelevant and hence nobody invests into the public good. As a consequence, total group income amounts to 60 points. Social surplus, on the other hand, is maximized if each player invests his 20 points. In this case, total group income equals 60 ∗ 1.8 = 108. What do we expect if people have a preference for fairness? The most obvious prediction can be derived for the situation where a cooperator faces two defectors. In this situation, a cooperator *cannot reduce inequality* by punishing the defectors (independent of how inequality is measured). In fact, to reduce the payoff of each of the two defectors by one point, a cooperator has to invest two points. Hence, inequity aversion predicts zero punishments in this situation. Quite to the contrary, retaliation is compatible with punishments in this situation since a defector has acted in an unkind fashion and "deserves" a punishment.

As it was the case with the two UGs discussed in the previous paragraphs, inequity aversion cannot account for the observed reciprocal actions in the public goods game with costly punishments: here 46.8 percent of the cooperators punish even if they are facing two defectors, where as the inequity aversion motive predicts zero punishment. We therefore conclude that much of the observed punishment behavior is incompatible with inequity aversion and should rather be understood as a desire to retaliate. Even if cooperators cannot reduce the inequity between cooperators and defectors, they want to *lower* the payoffs of the unkind defectors.

6.2.4   Is Kindness Evaluated towards Individuals or towards the Group?

In the questionnaire study outlined above, as well as in many *bilateral* bargaining situations, the question "who is the relevant reference agent" is trivial. This does not hold, however, if players interact in a group. Here it is far from obvious whether people determine kindness towards each of the other group members or, for example, towards the group on average. To investigate this question, Falk, Fehr, and Fischbacher (2001) conducted a variant of the public goods game with punishment opportunity discussed in the previous section. The only difference concerns the cost of punishment: The cost of deducting points now depends on the first stage behavior. Deducting one point from another player who has cooperated in the first stage is slightly more expensive (0.4 points per point deducted) than deducting a point from a defector (0.3 points per point deducted). Thus, punishing a cooperator is more expensive than punishing a defector.

Defecting in this game is clearly an unfair act. If people are sufficiently reciprocally motivated, they will therefore punish this unfair behavior. The precise punishment pattern, however, depends on whether people evaluate kindness towards each other as individuals or towards the group on average. Let us concentrate on the situation where player i cooperated while one of the other two players cooperated and the other defected. Theories that assume individual comparisons predict that if cooperators punish in this situation, they will only punish defectors: The other cooperator acted in a fair way and therefore there is no reason to punish him. The defector, however, acted in an unfair manner and therefore deserves the punishment.

Theories that rest on group comparison, however, predict that if cooperators punish, they will punish the other cooperator. The reason is simple: Before punishing, the cooperator has a lower payoff than the average group payoff. This is so because defectors have a higher payoff than cooperators. If the cooperator wants to reduce the disadvantageous inequity between his payoff and the average group payoff, it is cheapest to punish the cooperator because punishing the other cooperator is cheaper (0.3 per deduction point) than punishing the defector (0.4 per deduction point). Thus, if the cooperator punishes, he strictly prefers to *punish the cooperator*.

The experimental results clearly indicate that people perform *individual* comparisons. In the situation where a cooperator faces a defector and another cooperator, cooperators punish defectors quite frequently and almost never punish other cooperators. On average, cooperators allocate 6.6 punishment points to defectors and 0.3 punishment points to cooperators. This is in clear contradiction to the idea that cooperators want to improve their situation towards the group average, which would have dictated them to punish cooperators.

6.3 Modeling Reciprocity

The preceding sections suggest that a theory of reciprocity should incorporate the following four motives: (i) Equitable shares serve as a reference standard. (ii) The evaluation of kindness rests on intentions and consequences of an action. (iii) The desire to retaliate is much more important for a reciprocating person than the desire to reduce inequity. (iv) People evaluate kindness not towards a group average, but individually towards each person with whom they interact.

In the following section, we sketch a model of reciprocity that tries to take account of motives (i) through (iv). The purpose of the presentation in this section is only expositional. We restrict our presentation to the key aspects of our model and omit all technical details. The reader interested in technical details should refer to Falk and Fischbacher (1999) where the model is explained and discussed in detail.

6.3.1 Notations

Recall the sketch of the reciprocity model in section 6.1. We pointed out that reciprocity consists of a kind (or unkind) treatment by another person (represented by the *kindness term* φ) and a behavioral reaction to that treatment (represented by the *reciprocation term* σ). We will now define these terms and start the outline of the model with the two-player case.

Consider a two-player extensive form game with a finite number of stages and with complete and perfect information. Let i and j be the two players in the game. N_i denotes the set of nodes where player i has the move. Let n be a node of this player. Let A_n be the set of actions in node n. Let F be the set of end nodes of the game. The payoff function for player i is given by $\pi_i : F \to \mathbb{R}$.

Let S_i be the set of mixed behavior strategies of player i. For $s_i \in S_i$ and $s_j \in S_j$ and for a player $k \in \{i, j\}$, we define $\pi_k(s_i, s_j)$ as player k's expected payoff, given strategies s_i and s_j. Furthermore, we define $\pi_k(n, s_i, s_j)$ as the expected payoff conditional on node n: It is the expected payoff of player k in the subgame starting from node n, given that the strategies s_i and s_j are played.

6.3.2 The Kindness Term

Let $n \in N_i$. The kindness term $\varphi_j(n, s_i, s_j)$ is the central element of our model. It measures how kind a player i perceives the action by a player j and depends on both outcomes and intentions of this action. The outcome is measured with the *outcome term* $\Delta_j(n, s_i, s_j)$, where $\Delta_j(n, s_i, s_j) > 0$ expresses an advantageous outcome and $\Delta_j(n, s_i, s_j) < 0$ expresses a disadvantageous outcome. In order to determine the overall kindness, $\Delta_j(n, s_i, s_j)$ is multiplied with the *intention factor* $\vartheta_j(n, s_i, s_j) \geq 0$. This factor is a number between a small and positive ε

and 1, where $\vartheta_j(n, s_i, s_j) = 1$ captures a situation where $\Delta_j(n, s_i, s_j)$ is induced fully intentionally, and $\vartheta_j(n, s_i, s_j) < 1$ expresses a situation where intentions are absent or where it was not *fully* intentionally fair or unfair. The kindness term $\varphi_j(n, s_i, s_j)$ is simply the product of $\Delta_j(n, s_i, s_j)$ and $\vartheta_j(n, s_i, s_j)$.

First, we define the *outcome term*:

$$\Delta_j(n, s_i, s_j) := \pi_i(n, s_i, s_j) - \pi_j(n, s_i, s_j) \tag{2}$$

For a given $\vartheta_j(n, s_i, s_j)$, the outcome term $\Delta_j(n, s_i, s_j)$ measures the kindness of player j towards player i. It captures the knowledge of player i in node n about the two players' expected payoffs. Since $\vartheta_j(n, s_i, s_j)$ is always positive, the sign of the kindness term, that is, whether an action is considered as kind or unkind, is determined by the sign of $\Delta_j(n, s_i, s_j)$. The term $\Delta_j(n, s_i, s_j)$ is positive if player i thinks he gets more than j. It is negative if player i thinks he gets less than j.

This definition captures motive (i). We use equity as a reference standard—that is, kindness equals zero, if both players get the same payoff.

The answer to question (ii) showed that a purely outcome-oriented model is not in line with many experimental findings. This fact is implemented in the model with the intention factor $\vartheta_j(n, s_i, s_j)$. It measures to what extent there is a reasonable alternative for player j. This factor is 1 if there is a reasonable alternative—that is, in a situation where player i can conclude that the move of player j was *intentionally* kind or unkind. If there were no reasonable alternative, for instance if there were no alternative at all, this factor is positive but smaller than 1. The detailed definition of the θ term incorporates the results that followed from our discussion of table 6.1 and figure 6.2. Since the definition is a little bit tedious, the interested reader should refer to Falk and Fischbacher (1999).

Definition: Let strategies be given. We define the *kindness term* $\varphi(n, s_i, s_j)$ in a node $n \in N_i$ as:

$$\varphi_j(n, s_i, s_j) = \vartheta_j(n, s_i, s_j)\Delta_j(n, s_i, s_j) \tag{3}$$

From (3) it immediately follows that a given outcome is perceived as more kind or unkind depending on the size of $\vartheta_j(n, s_i, s_j)$. Put differently, if player j has, for example, no alternative to choose another outcome or if he was forced to choose a particular outcome, perceived kindness is smaller compared to a situation where $\vartheta_j(n, s_i, s_j) = 1$ (that is, where j had a reasonable alternative). The condition that

$\vartheta_j(n, s_i, s_j) > 0$ captures the fact that even if intentions are absent, players experience the outcome *per se* as either kind or unkind: If we would allow $\vartheta_j(n, s_i, s_j) = 0$, this would imply that in the absence of intentions, there would be no reciprocal actions anymore. As our discussion about the games in figure 6.2 and table 6.1 have shown, however, people reward and punish even in these situations.

6.3.3 The Reciprocation Term

The second ingredient of our model concerns the formalization of reciprocation. Let us fix an end node f that follows node n. Then we denote $v(n, f)$, as the unique node directly following the node n on the path leading from n to f.

Definition: Let strategies be as given in the previous section. Let i and j be the two players and n and f be defined as in the previous paragraph. Then we define

$$\sigma_i(n, f, s_i, s_j) := \pi_j(v(n, f), s_i, s_j) - \pi_j(n, s_i, s_j) \tag{4}$$

as the **reciprocation term** of player i in node n.

The *reciprocation term* expresses the response to the experienced kindness—that is, it measures how much player i alters the payoff of player j with his move in node n. The reciprocal impact of this action is represented as the *alteration* of player j's payoff from $\pi_j(n, s_i, s_j)$ to $\pi_j(v(n, f), s_i, s_j)$.

With this approach, we take into account finding (iii). Players do not attempt to reduce inequity. Instead, players in our model gain utility from punishing unkind behavior (or rewarding kind behavior)—that is, by lowering or increasing their opponent's payoff.

6.3.4 Utility and Equilibrium Concept

Notation: Let n_1 and n_2 be nodes. If node n_2 follows node n_1 in the game tree (directly or indirectly), we denote this by $n_1 \rightarrow n_2$.

Having defined the kindness and reciprocation term, we can now derive the players' utility of the transformed "reciprocity game":

Definition: Let player i and j be the two players of the game. Let f be an end node of the game. We define the utility in the transformed reciprocity game as:

$$U_i(f, s_i, s_j) = \pi_i(f) + \rho_i \sum_{\substack{n \to f \\ n \in N_i}} \varphi_j(n, s_i, s_j)\sigma_i(n, f, s_i, s_j)$$ (5)

For fixed (s_i, s_j), this utility function defines a new game $\Gamma(s_i, s_j)$. If (s_i, s_j) is a subgame perfect Nash equilibrium in $\Gamma(s_i, s_j)$, we call (s_i, s_j) a **reciprocity equilibrium**.

The strategies s_i and s_j in the game $\Gamma(s_i, s_j)$ can be interpreted as the beliefs of the players. For instance, player i believes player j will use strategy s_j, and he thinks player j expects him to use strategy s_i. Given this belief, player i chooses an optimal strategy. A reciprocity equilibrium can then be considered as a combination of strategies and beliefs in which the strategies are optimal and consistent with the beliefs. The presentation of our theory in this form (without beliefs) follows an idea of Gintis (2000).

6.3.5   Games with More than Two Players

There seem to be two ways for generalizing the model to more than $N > 2$ players. We could define aggregated kindness and reciprocation terms, for instance, in the form $\varphi_{-i}(n, s) = \vartheta_j(n, s)(\pi_i(n, s) - \frac{1}{N-1}\sum_{j \neq i} \pi_i(n, s))$. Or we could sum up the reciprocity utility towards each of the other players. From our analysis of question (iv), we know that the second way is the right way to go, because people perform individual comparisons instead of making comparisons to the group average. This is also how the model is generalized in Falk and Fischbacher (1999). We define $\varphi_{j \to i}(n)$ as player j's kindness towards player i and $\sigma_{i \to j}(n, f)$ as player i's reciprocation towards player j. The utility of player i is then defined as

$$U_i(f) = \pi_i(f) + \rho_i \sum_{j \neq i} \sum_{\substack{n \to f \\ n \in N_i}} \varphi_{j \to i}(n)\sigma_{i \to j}(n, f)$$ (6)

The model just outlined explains the relevant stylized facts of a wide range of experimental games (see Falk and Fischbacher 1999). Among them are the ultimatum game, the gift exchange game, the reduced best-shot game, the dictator game, the Prisoner's Dilemma, and public goods games. Furthermore, the theory explains why the same consequences trigger different reciprocal responses in different environments. Finally, the theory explains why in bilateral interactions outcomes tend to be "fair," whereas in competitive markets even extremely unfair distributions may arise.

6.4 Other Approaches

Several other theoretical models have been developed to account for observed reciprocal behavior. The models make very different assumptions about how people evaluate the fairness of an action and how they respond to perceived fairness or unfairness. In this section, we briefly discuss the most important models and relate their main assumptions to the four motives discussed in section 6.2.

Two well-known models rest on the premise that reciprocal actions are driven by the desire to reduce inequity (Fehr and Schmidt 1999 (henceforth FS), and Bolton and Ockenfels 2000 (henceforth BO)). In the specification of FS, it is assumed that in general, subjects suffer more from inequity that is to their material disadvantage than from inequity that is to their material advantage. Formally, consider a set of N players indexed by $i \in \{1, \ldots, N\}$ and let $\pi = (\pi_1, \ldots, \pi_n)$ denote the vector of monetary payoffs. In the FS model, the utility function of player i is given by

$$U_i = \pi_i - \frac{\alpha_i}{N-1} \sum_{j, \pi_j > \pi_i} (\pi_j - \pi_i) - \frac{\beta_i}{N-1} \sum_{j, \pi_i > \pi_j} (\pi_i - \pi_j) \qquad (7)$$

with

$$\alpha_i \geq \beta_i \geq 0 \quad \text{and} \quad \beta_i < 1.$$

The first term in (7), π_i, is the material payoff of player i. The second term in (7) measures the utility loss from disadvantageous inequality, while the third term measures the loss from advantageous inequality. Given his own monetary payoff π_i, player i's utility function obtains a maximum at $\pi_j = \pi_i$. The utility loss from disadvantageous inequality $(\pi_j < \pi_i)$ is larger than the utility loss if player i is better off than player j $(\pi_j < \pi_i)$. In a similar spirit, BO model inequity aversion. According to model BO's specification, a player i's utility is weakly increasing and concave in player i's material payoff and—for a given material payoff—utility is strictly concave in player i's share of total income and maximal if the share equals $1/N$. Both models, FS and BO, are able to correctly predict experimental outcomes in a wide variety of experimental games. This includes two-person bargaining games where outcomes tend to be "fair," as well as market games where the model (correctly) predicts that very unfair outcomes can emerge. Moreover, both models are quite tractable and are therefore well-suited as predictive tools if fairness issues have to be analyzed in complex environments.

In light of the presented evidence, it seems to us that the FS model has two major advantages over the BO model. First, according to the FS model, inequity is evaluated towards each individual with whom a player is interacting (see equation (7)). The BO model on the other hand, measures inequity considerations of a person towards some aggregate measure. As a consequence, the BO model predicts that in the public goods game outlined in section 6.2.4, cooperative players punish defectors. However, the data shows that it is just the other way round. Another drawback of the BO model is the measurement of inequity in terms of relative share. Even though this is appropriate for some games, it seems that the FS approach, which relies on the difference of payoffs, does a bit better in general (see section 6.2.4).

The strongest objections against both approaches concern the missing account of intentions and the fact that the strongest motives for punishments are retaliation motives and not the desire to reduce inequity. Both models take a consequentialistic perspective—for example, they predict the exact same rejection rates of the (8/2)-offer across all games in figure 6.2. While distributive consequences clearly matter, we have seen that the attribution of fairness intentions also plays a major role. The fact that much of the observed punishment (in UG games as well as in public goods games with punishment) are incompatible with the desire to reduce inequity further limits the validity of the inequity aversion approach.

Another class of models assumes that intentions are important and that reciprocal responses are not driven by the desire to reduce inequity aversion, but by the desire to retaliate and to reward. These so-called "reciprocity models" include Rabin (1993), Dufwenberg and Kirchsteiger (2004, henceforth DK), Levine (1998), Charness and Rabin (2002, henceforth CR), and Falk and Fischbacher (1999, henceforth FF), which we have sketched in section 6.4. Common to these approaches is a strong emphasis on the concept of *reciprocated kindness*. All models point out the importance of intentions for the evaluation of kindness. According to Rabin, DK, and FF, intentions depend on the different alternatives available to players. As we have outlined in our discussion on table 6.1 and the mini-ultimatum games in figure 6.2, players infer different intentions by looking at the available alternatives. An important difference between the models of FF, on one hand, and Rabin and DK on the other concerns the interaction of outcomes and intentions.

While DK and Rabin model kindness as *solely* determined by intentions, the FF approach combines distributive concerns with the importance of intentions. In the light of the experimental evidence (see section 6.2.2) this is important because many people care about both outcomes and intentions.

A completely different approach for measuring kindness is suggested by Levine (1998). As opposed to the reciprocity model explained earlier, the players in Levine's model do not reward or punish kind or unkind *actions*. They reward or punish kind or unkind *types*. They reward altruistic types and punish spiteful types. Levine assumes that players differ with respect to their other-regarding preference. This preference is described by a parameter α_i. It measures the relative importance of the payoff of another person compared to one's own payoff. If $\alpha_i > 0$, player i has some altruistic preference. If $\alpha_i < 0$, he is spiteful. Secondly, players like to reward players with high α_j and punish players with a low (negative) α_j.

The utility in Levine's model is given by $U_i = \pi_i + \sum_{j \neq i}((\alpha_i + \rho\alpha_j)/(1+\rho))\pi_j$. The parameter ρ is a universal reciprocity parameter—that is, all players are assumed to have the same reciprocity parameter. The model is an incomplete information model, since people have an initial prior about the type of their opponent. After observing their opponent's action, players update their beliefs. If the action was "friendly," the belief that the person is altruistic gets larger, which implies a friendly response and vice versa.

This approach is very elegant and offers interesting insights. However, it has also some serious limitations: Since the reciprocity parameter is universal, there are no selfish players in this model. This is not only theoretically unsatisfactory, but also empirically wrong. A further problem stems from the fact that in this model, the equilibria are difficult to find. Moreover, the use of an incomplete information approach implies the existence of many equilibria. This limits its use as a predictive tool.

The CR model combines a consequentialistic model of positive reciprocity with a type-based model of negative reciprocity. In this model, players care, in addition to the own payoff π_i, about the social benefit (modeled as $\sum \pi_j$), and about the payoffs of "those who need it" (modeled as $\min\{\pi_j\}$). This part captures a new motive—the search for efficiency—a motive that is neglected in all previous models. In this part of the model, all payoffs are weighted positively, meaning this part of the model accounts only for positive reciprocity. How is negative reciprocity modeled? In CR, the weight for social welfare in a player's utility function is expressed as a number. If this number is lower than a certain threshold, then the weight of this player's payoff in the utility function of the other players is reduced. (It can even be reduced to a negative number.)

The CR model is very rich and captures much of the experimental data. It does this at the cost of many parameters (six) and at the cost of a high complexity. In particular, the reciprocity part of the model is hard to solve for a particular game. Furthermore, this model shares with Levine and DK models the problem of multiple equilibria. However, the CR model is particularly interesting because it models positive and negative reciprocity in a different way. While positive reciprocity is modeled in a consequentialistic way, negative reciprocity is modeled in a purely intentional way. If a player does not deserve positive reciprocity, positive reciprocity is reduced or even negative reciprocity applies.

Taken together, all models have certain advantages and disadvantages. As it is usually the case, more realistic features imply a higher degree of complexity. As the predictive power and the psychological richness of a model increases, the tractability suffers. Therefore, a researcher's purpose will determine the model he or she uses.

References

Blount, S. 1995. "When Social Outcomes Aren't Fair: The Effect of Causal Attributions on Preferences," *Organizational Behavior & Human Decision Processes* 63:131–144.

Bolton, G. E., J. Brandts, and A. Ockenfels. 1998. "Measuring Motivations for the Reciprocal Responses Observed in a Simple Dilemma Game," *Experimental Economics* 1:207–219.

Bolton, G., and A. Ockenfels. 2000. "ERC—A Theory of Equity, Reciprocity and Competition," *American Economic Review* 90:166–193.

Brandts, J., and C. Sola. 2001. "Reference Points and Negative Reciprocity in Simple Sequential Games," *Games and Economic Behavior* 36:138–157.

Charness, G. Forthcoming. "Attribution and Reciprocity in a Simulated Labor Market: An Experimental Investigation," *Journal of Labor Economics*.

Charness, G., and M. Rabin. 2002. "Understanding Social Preferences with Simple Tests," *Quarterly Journal of Economics* 117, 817–869.

Cox, J. 2000. "Trust and Reciprocity: Implications of Game Triads and Social Contexts," Mimeo. University of Arizona at Tucson.

Dufwenberg, M., and G. Kirchsteiger. 2004. "A Theory of Sequential Reciprocity," *Games and Economic Behavior* 47:268–298.

Falk, A., and U. Fischbacher. 1999. "A Theory of Reciprocity," Working Paper No. 6. University of Zurich.

Falk, A., E. Fehr, and U. Fischbacher. 2001. "Driving Forces of Informal Sanctions," Working Paper No. 59. University of Zurich.

Falk, A., E. Fehr, and U. Fischbacher. 2003. "On the Nature of Fair Behavior," *Economic Inquiry* 41(1):20–26.

Fehr, E., and K. Schmidt. 1999. "A Theory of Fairness, Competition, and Cooperation," *Quarterly Journal of Economics* 114:817–868.

Gintis, H. 2000. *Game Theory Evolving*. Princeton: Princeton University Press.

Güth, W., R. Schmittberger, and B. Schwarze. 1982. "An Experimental Analysis of Ultimatum Bargaining," *Journal of Economic Behavior and Organization* 3:367–388.

Levine, D. 1998. "Modeling Altruism and Spitefulness in Experiments," *Review of Economic Dynamics* 1:593–622.

Loewenstein, G. F., L. Thompson, and M. H. Bazerman. 1989. "Social Utility and Decision Making in Interpersonal Contexts," *Journal of Personality and Social Psychology* 57:426–441.

McCabe, K., M. Rigdon, and V. Smith. 2003. "Positive Reciprocity and Intentions in Trust Games," *Journal of Economic Behavior & Organization* 52:267–275.

Rabin, M. 1993. "Incorporating Fairness into Game Theory and Economics," *American Economic Review* 83:1281–1302.

7

The Evolution of Altruistic Punishment

Robert Boyd, Herbert Gintis,
Samuel Bowles, and Peter J.
Richerson

7.1 Introduction

Cooperation among nonkin is commonly explained by one of two
mechanisms: repeated interactions (Axelrod and Hamilton 1981;
Trivers 1971; Clutton-Brock and Parker 1995) or group selection (Sober
and Wilson 1998). Neither allows the evolution of altruistic cooperation in large groups of unrelated individuals. While repeated interactions may support cooperation through the use of tit-for-tat and
related strategies in dyadic relations, this mechanism is ineffective unless the number of individuals interacting strategically is very small
(Boyd and Richerson 1988). Group selection can lead to the evolution
of altruism only when groups are small and migration infrequent
(Eshel 1972; Aoki 1982; Rogers 1990). A third recently proposed mechanism (Hauert et al. 2002) requires that asocial, solitary types outcompete individuals living in uncooperative social groups, an implausible
assumption for humans.

Altruistic punishment provides one solution to this puzzle. As we
have seen in previous chapters of this volume, in laboratory experiments, people punish noncooperators at a cost to themselves even in
one-shot interactions, and ethnographic data suggest that altruistic
punishment helps to sustain cooperation in human societies (Boehm
1993). It might seem that invoking altruistic punishment simply creates a new evolutionary puzzle: Why do people incur costs to punish
others and provide benefits to nonrelatives? However, in this chapter
we show group selection can lead to the evolution of altruistic punishment in larger groups because the problem of deterring free-riders
in the case of altruistic cooperation is fundamentally different from
the problem deterring free-riders in the case of altruistic punishment.
This asymmetry arises because the payoff disadvantage of altruistic

cooperators relative to defectors is independent of the frequency of defectors in the population, while the cost disadvantage of those engaged in altruistic punishment declines as defectors become rare, because acts of punishment become very infrequent (Sethi and Somanathan 1996). Thus, when altruistic punishers are common, selection operating against them is weak.

To see why this is the case, consider a model in which a large population is divided into groups of size n. There are two behavioral types, contributors and defectors. Contributors incur a cost c to produce a total benefit b that is shared equally among group members. Defectors incur no costs and produce no benefits. If the fraction of contributors in the group is x, the expected payoff for contributors is $bx - c$ and for defectors the expected payoff is bx—so the payoff disadvantage of the contributors is a constant c independent of the distribution of types in the population. Now add a third type, altruistic punishers, who cooperate and then punish each defector in their group, reducing each defector's payoff by p at a cost k to the punisher. If the frequency of altruistic punishers is y, the expected payoffs become $b(x + y) - c$ to contributors, $b(x + y) - py$ to defectors, and $b(x + y) - c - k(1 - x - y)$ to altruistic punishers. Contributors have higher fitness than defectors if altruistic punishers are sufficiently common that the cost of being punished exceeds the cost of cooperating ($py > c$). Altruistic punishers suffer a fitness disadvantage of $k(1 - x - y)$ compared to nonpunishing contributors. Thus, punishment is altruistic and mere contributors are "second-order free-riders." Note, however, that the payoff disadvantage of altruistic punishers relative to contributors approaches zero as defectors become rare because there is no need for punishment.

In a more realistic model (like the one later in the chapter), the costs of monitoring or punishing occasional mistaken defections would mean that altruistic punishers have slightly lower fitness levels than contributors, and that defection is the only one of these three strategies that is an evolutionarily stable strategy in a single isolated population. That is, a population of defectors cannot be successfully invaded by a small number of cooperators or altruistic punishers, whereas a population of cooperators can be successfully invaded by a few defectors, and a population of altruistic punishers can be invaded by a small number of cooperators, assuming there is a positive level of punishment due, for instance, to error in perception.

However, the fact that altruistic punishers experience only a small disadvantage when defectors are rare means that weak within-group evolutionary forces—such as mutation (Sethi and Somanathan 1996) or a conformist tendency (Henrich and Boyd 2001; Bowles 2001; Gintis 2003)—can stabilize punishment and allow cooperation to persist. But neither produces a systematic tendency to evolve toward a cooperative outcome. Here we explore the possibility that selection among groups leads to the evolution of altruistic punishment when selection is too weak to ensure the emergence of altruistic cooperation.

Suppose that more cooperative groups are less prone to extinction. This may be because more cooperative groups are more effective in warfare, more successful in co-insuring, more adept at managing commons resources, or other similar reasons. All other things being equal, group selection will tend to increase the frequency of cooperation in the population. Because groups with more punishers will tend to exhibit a greater frequency of cooperative behaviors (by both contributors and altruistic punishers), the frequency of punishing and cooperative behaviors will be positively correlated across groups. As a result, punishment will increase as a "correlated response" to group selection that favors more cooperative groups. Because selection within groups against altruistic punishers is weak when punishment is common, this process might support the evolution of substantial levels of punishment and maintain punishment once it is common.

To evaluate the plausibility of this argument, we studied the following more realistic model using simulation methods. There are N groups. Local density-dependent competition maintains each group at a constant population size n. Individuals interact in a two-stage game. During the first stage, contributors and altruistic punishers cooperate with probability $1 - e$ and defect with probability e. Cooperation reduces the payoff of cooperators by an amount c and increases the ability of the group to compete with other groups. For simplicity, we begin by assuming that cooperation has no effect on the individual payoffs of others but does reduce the probability of group extinction. We also assume that defectors always defect. During the second stage, altruistic punishers punish each individual who defected during the first stage. After the second stage, individuals encounter another individual from their own group with probability $1 - m$ and an individual from another randomly chosen group with probability m. An individual i who encounters an individual j, imitates j with probability $W_j/(W_j + W_i)$ where W_x is the payoff of individual x in the game, including the costs of any punishment received or delivered.

As a result, behaviors (like defection) that lead to higher payoffs will tend to spread within groups and diffuse from one group to another at a rate proportional to m. Group selection occurs through intergroup conflict (Bowles 2001). Because cooperation has no individual level effects, there is no tendency for group beneficial behaviors to spread by imitation of more successful neighbors. Each time period, groups are paired at random, and, with probability ε, intergroup conflict results in one group defeating and replacing the other group. The probability that group i defeats group j is $(1 + (d_j - d_i))/2$ where d_q is the frequency of defectors in group q. This means that the group with more defectors is more likely to lose a conflict. Finally, with probability μ individuals of each type spontaneously change into one of the two other types. The presence of mutation and erroneous defection insure that punishers will incur some punishment costs, even when they are common, thus placing them at a disadvantage with respect to the contributors.

7.2   Methods

Two simulation programs implementing the model just described were independently developed, one by Boyd in Visual Basic and a second by Gintis in Pascal. (These programs are available on request.) Results from the two programs are very similar. In all simulations, there were 128 groups. Initially, one group consisted of all altruistic punishers, and the other 127 groups were all defectors. Simulations were run for 2,000 consecutive time periods. The "steady state" results plotted in figures 7.1, 7.2, and 7.3 represent the average of frequencies over the last 1,000 time periods of ten simulations.

Base case parameters were chosen to represent cultural evolution in small-scale societies. The cost of cooperation, c, determines the time scale of adaptive change. With $c = 0.2$ and $k = p = e = 0$, "defection" becomes a simple individually advantageous trait that spreads from low to high frequency in about fifty time periods. Since individually beneficial cultural traits, such as technical innovations, diffuse through populations in 10 to 100 years (Rogers 1983; Henrich 2001) setting $c = 0.2$ means that the simulation time period can be interpreted as approximately one year. The mutation rate was set to 0.01, so the steady state value of such a simple individually advantageous trait was about 0.9. This means that considerable variation is maintained, but not so much as to overwhelm adaptive forces. The probability that contributors and altruistic punishers mistakenly defect, e, was set to 0.02. In the base case $k = 0.2$, so that the cost of altruistic cooperation and altruistic punishment are equivalent.

We set $p = 0.8$ to capture the intuition that in human societies punishment is more costly to the punishee than the punisher. With $\varepsilon = 0.015$, the expected waiting time to a group extinction is twenty years, which is close to a recent estimate of cultural extinction rates in small-scale societies (Soltis, Boyd, and Richerson 1995). With $m = 0.02$, passive diffusion (i.e., $c = p = k = e = 0$) will cause initially maximally different neighboring groups to achieve the same trait frequencies in approximately fifty time periods. Results of simulations using this model indicate that group selection can maintain altruistic punishment and altruistic cooperation over a wider range of parameter values than group selection will sustain altruistic cooperation without altruistic punishment.

7.3   Results

Our simulations indicate that group selection can maintain altruistic cooperation over a much wider range of conditions than group selection will maintain cooperation alone. Figures 7.1, 7.2, and 7.3 compare the steady state levels of cooperation with and without punishment for a range of parameter values. If there is no punishment, our simulations replicate the standard result—group selection can support high frequencies of cooperative behavior only if groups are quite small. However, adding punishment sustains substantial amounts of cooperation in much larger groups. As one would expect, increasing the rate of extinction increases the steady state amount of cooperation (figure 7.1).

In the model described in the last few paragraphs, group selection leads to the evolution of cooperation only if migration is sufficiently limited to sustain substantial between-group differences in the frequency of defectors. Figure 7.2 shows that when the migration rate increases, levels of cooperation fall precipitously. When altruistic punishers are common, defectors do badly, but when altruistic punishers are rare, defectors do well. Thus, the imitation of high-payoff individuals creates a selection-like adaptive force that acts to maintain variation between groups in the frequency of defectors. However, if there is too much migration, this process cannot maintain enough variation between groups for group selection to be effective. This means that the process modeled here is likely to be much less important for genetic evolution than for cultural evolution—because genetic adaptation by natural selection is likely to be weaker compared to migration than is cultural adaptation by biased imitation, and thus less able to maintain variation.

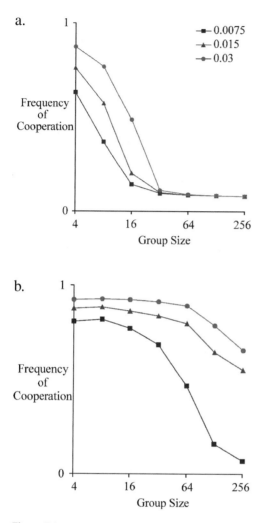

Figure 7.1

The evolution of cooperation is strongly affected by the presence of punishment. Part (a) plots the long run average frequency of cooperation (i.e., the sum of the frequencies of contributors and punishers) as a function of group size when there is no punishment ($p = k = 0$) for three different conflict rates. Group selection is ineffective unless groups are quite small. Part (b) shows that when there is punishment ($p = 0.8$, $k = 0.2$), group selection can maintain cooperation in substantially larger groups.

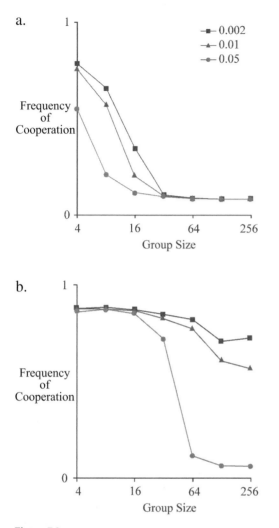

Figure 7.2
The evolution of cooperation is strongly affected by rate of mixing between groups. Part (a) plots the long run average frequency of cooperation (i.e., the sum of the frequencies of contributors and punishers) as a function of group size when there is no punishment ($p = k = 0$) for three mixing rates. Group selection is ineffective unless groups are quite small. Part (b) shows that when there is punishment ($p = 0.8$, $k = 0.2$), group selection can maintain cooperation in larger groups for all rates of mixing. However, at higher rates of mixing, cooperation does not persist in the largest groups.

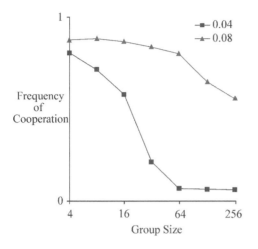

Figure 7.3
The evolution of cooperation is sensitive to the cost of being punished (p). Here we plot the long run average frequency of cooperation with the base case cost of being punished ($p = 0.8$) and with a lower value of p. Lower values of p result in much lower levels of cooperation.

The long run average amount of cooperation is also sensitive to the cost of being punished (figure 7.3). When the cost of being punished is at base case value ($p = 4c$), even a modest frequency of punishers will cause defectors to be selected against, and, as a result, there is a substantial correlation between the frequency of cooperation and punishment across groups. When the cost of being punished is the same as the cost of cooperation ($p = c$) punishment does not sufficiently reduce the relative payoff of defectors, and the correlation between the frequency of cooperators and punishers declines. Lower correlations mean that selection among groups cannot compensate for the decline of punishers within groups, and eventually both punishers and contributors decline.

It is important to see that punishment leads to increased cooperation only to the extent that the costs associated with being an altruistic punisher decline as defectors become rare. Monitoring costs, for example, must be paid whether or not there are any defectors in the group. When such costs are substantial—or when the probability of mistaken defection is high enough that altruistic punishers bear significant costs even when defectors are rare—group selection does not lead to the evolution of altruistic punishment (figure 7.4). However, because people live in long-lasting social groups, and language allows the spread

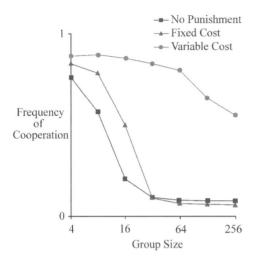

Figure 7.4
Punishment does not aid in the evolution of cooperation when the costs borne by punishers are fixed, independent of the number of defectors in the group. Here we plot the long run average frequency of cooperation when the costs of punishing are proportional to the frequency of defectors (variable cost), fixed at a constant cost equal to the cost of cooperating (c), and when there is no punishment.

of information about who did what, it is plausible that monitoring costs may often be small compared to enforcement costs. This result also leads to an empirical prediction: People should be less inclined to pay fixed rather than variable punishment costs if the mechanism outlined here is responsible for the psychology of altruistic punishment.

The effectiveness of group selection is especially sensitive to the rate of mutation when there is punishment. For example, decreasing the mutation rate from 0.05c to 0.005c leads to very high levels of cooperation even when groups include 256 individuals. Random drift-like processes have an important effect on trait frequencies in this model. Standard models of genetic drift suggest that lower mutation rates will cause groups to stay nearer the boundaries of the state space (Crow and Kimura 1970), and our simulations confirm this prediction (figure 7.5). When the mutation rate is low, there are very few groups in which defectors are common; most of the groups lie very close to the contributor-punisher boundary. In contrast, when the mutation rate is higher, groups with a wide range of defector frequencies are present. Thus, an increasing mutation rate, on average, increases the amount of punishment that must be administered and therefore increases the

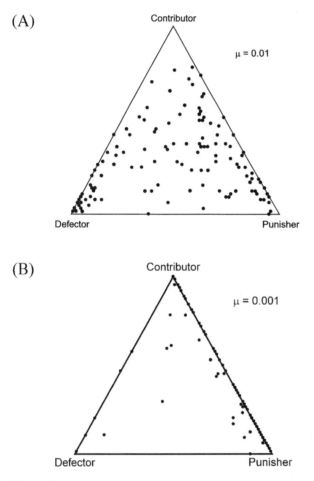

Figure 7.5
Decreasing the mutation rate reduces the number of groups in which defectors are common. Each point represents the frequencies of each of the three strategies in 1 of 128 groups during a single, representative time period ($t = 1500$) from the interval in time ($t = 1000$–2000) over which we calculated the average steady state frequencies. There are not 128 points because many groups have the same frequencies. In (A) $\mu = 0.01$ while (B), $\mu = 0.001$, n $= 64$, and other parameters are as in the base case. If punishment and group selection are eliminated ($p = k = e = 0$), these mutation rates maintain "cooperation" (now just an individually disadvantageous trait) approximately at frequencies 0.1 and 0.01 respectively. When defectors are less common, punishing is less costly, and therefore group selection is more effective at maintaining punishment at high frequency. Note, however, even when there are many groups in which defectors are common as in (A) group selection can still maintain punishment and therefore sustain cooperation in fairly sizable groups.

payoff advantage of second order free-riders compared to altruistic punishers.

Additional sensitivity analyses suggest that these results are robust. In addition to the results described in the last several paragraphs, we have studied the sensitivity of the model to variations in the remaining parameter values. Increasing e, the error rate, reduces the steady state amount of cooperation. Reducing N adds random noise to the results.

We also tested the sensitivity of the model to three structural changes. We modified the payoffs so that each cooperative act produces a per capita benefit of b/n for each other group member and also modified the extinction model so that the probability of group extinction is proportional to the difference between warring groups in average payoffs including the costs of punishment (rather than simply the difference in frequency of cooperators). The dynamics of this model are more complicated because group selection now acts against altruistic punishers as punishment reduces mean group payoffs. However, the correlated effect of group selection on cooperation still tends to increase punishment as in the original model. The relative magnitude of these two effects depends on the magnitude of the per capita benefit to group members of each cooperative act, b/n. For reasonable values of b, ($2c, 4c$, and $8c$), the results of this model are qualitatively similar to those shown above.

We also investigated a model in which the amount of cooperation and punishment vary continuously. An individual with cooperation value x behaves like a cooperator with probability x and a defector with probability $1 - x$. Similarly, an individual with a punishment value y behaves like an altruistic punisher with probability y and a nonpunisher with probability $1 - y$. New mutants are uniformly distributed. The steady state mean levels of cooperation in this model are similar to the base model.

Finally, we studied a model without extinction analogous to a recent model of selection among stable equilibria due to biased imitation (Boyd and Richerson 2002). In this model, populations are arranged in a ring, and individuals imitate only other individuals drawn from the neighboring two groups. Cooperative acts produce a per capita benefit b/n so that groups with more cooperators have higher average payoff, and thus cooperation will, all other things being equal, tend to spread because individuals are prone to imitate successful neighbors. We could find no reasonable parameter combination that led to significant steady state levels of cooperation in this last model.

7.4 Discussion

We have shown that while the logic underlying altruistic cooperation and altruistic punishment is similar, their evolutionary dynamics are not. In the absence of punishment, within-group adaptation acts to decrease the frequency of altruistic cooperation, and as a consequence, weak drift-like forces are insufficient to maintain substantial variation between groups. In groups where altruistic punishers are common, defectors are excluded, and this maintains variation in the amount of cooperation between groups. Moreover, in such groups, punishers bear few costs, and altruistic punishers decrease only very slowly in competition with contributors. As a result, group selection is more effective at maintaining altruistic punishment than maintaining altruistic cooperation.

These results suggest that group selection can play an important role in human cultural evolution, because rapid cultural adaptation preserves cultural variation among groups. The importance of group selection is always a quantitative issue. There is no doubt that selection among groups favors individually costly, group-beneficial behaviors. The question is always: Does group selection play an important role under plausible conditions? Our results suggest that group selection acting on genetic variation will not be important even when punishment is possible, because natural selection will rarely be strong enough to overcome homogenizing effects of migration between groups, and, as a result, there will be insufficient genetic variation among groups. In contrast, rates of cultural adaptation are often greater than rates of mixing—as is reflected by the parameter values used in our simulations. With these parameter values, cooperation is sustained in groups on the order of 100 individuals. If the "individuals" in the model represent family groups (on the grounds that they migrate together and adopt common practices), altruistic punishment could be sustained in groups of 600 people—a size much larger than typical foraging bands and approximately the size of many ethno-linguistic units in nonagricultural societies.

References

Aoki, Kenichi. "A Condition for Group Selection to Prevail over Counteracting Individual Selection," *Evolution* 36 (1982): 832–842.

Axelrod, Robert, and William D. Hamilton. "The Evolution of Cooperation," *Science* 211 (1981): 1390–1396.

Boehm, Christopher. "Egalitarian Behavior and Reverse Dominance Hierarchy," *Current Anthropology* 34, 3 (June 1993): 227–254.

Bowles, Samuel. "Individual Interactions, Group Conflicts, and the Evolution of Preferences," in Steven N. Durlauf and H. Peyton Young (eds.), *Social Dynamics*. Cambridge, MA: MIT Press, 2001, pp. 155–190.

Boyd, Robert, and Peter J. Richerson. "The Evolution of Cooperation," *Journal of Theoretical Biology* 132 (1988): 337–356.

——— and Peter J. Richerson. "Group Beneficial Norms Can Spread Rapidly in a Structured Population," *Journal of Theoretical Biology* 215 (2002): 287–296.

Clutton-Brock, T. H., and G. A. Parker. "Punishment in Animal Societies," *Nature* 373 (1995): 58–60.

Crow, James F., and Motoo Kimura. *An Introduction to Population Genetic Theory*. New York: Harper & Row, 1970.

Eshel, Ilan. "On the Neighbor Effect and the Evolution of Altruistic Traits," *Theoretical Population Biology* 3 (1972): 258–277.

Gintis, Herbert. "The Hitchhiker's Guide to Altruism: Genes, Culture, and the Internalization of Norms," *Journal of Theoretical Biology* 220, 4 (2003): 407–418.

Hauert, Christoph, Silvia DeMonte, Josef Hofbauer, and Karl Sigmund. "Volunteering as Red Queen Mechanism for Cooperation in Public Goods Game," *Science* 296 (May 2002): 1129–1132.

Henrich, Joseph. "Cultural Transmission and the Diffusion of Innovations," *American Anthropologist* 103 (2001): 992–1013.

——— and Robert Boyd. "Why People Punish Defectors: Weak Conformist Transmission Can Stabilize Costly Enforcement of Norms in Cooperative Dilemmas," *Journal of Theoretical Biology* 208 (2001): 79–89.

Rogers, Alan R. "Group Selection by Selective Emigration: The Effects of Migration and Kin Structure," *American Naturalist* 135, 3 (March 1990): 398–413.

Rogers, E. M. *Diffusion of Innovations*. New York: Free Press, 1983.

Sethi, Rajiv, and E. Somanathan. "The Evolution of Social Norms in Common Property Resource Use," *American Economic Review* 86, 4 (September 1996): 766–788.

Sober, Elliot, and David Sloan Wilson. *Unto Others: The Evolution and Psychology of Unselfish Behavior*. Cambridge, MA: Harvard University Press, 1998.

Soltis, Joseph, Robert Boyd, and Peter Richerson. "Can Group-functional Behaviors Evolve by Cultural Group Selection: An Empirical Test," *Current Anthropology* 36, 3 (June 1995): 473–483.

Trivers, R. L. "The Evolution of Reciprocal Altruism," *Quarterly Review of Biology* 46 (1971): 35–57.

8   Norm Compliance and Strong Reciprocity

Rajiv Sethi and E. Somanathan

8.1   Introduction

A central feature of strong reciprocity is the propensity to punish others for opportunistic actions and to reward them for acts of uncommon generosity, where such rewards and punishments are not motivated by the prospect of future gain. The social norms that serve as the benchmark for evaluating behavior may vary from one culture to another, but given some such set of broadly shared norms, strong reciprocity provides a decentralized mechanism for their enforcement. The extent and persistence of strong reciprocity poses something of a theoretical puzzle because monitoring and sanctioning activities, while potentially beneficial to the group, place a net material burden on the reciprocator. Since opportunistic individuals choose to comply with or violate norms based on the likelihood and severity of sanctioning they anticipate, such individuals will always outperform reciprocators within any group. Even under complete compliance, reciprocators incur costs that opportunists are able to avoid. One would expect this payoff differential to exert evolutionary pressure on the population composition until reciprocators are entirely displaced from the group. This suggests that any population composed of immutable groups with no intergroup mobility will not sustain strong reciprocity in the long run.

The situation can be quite different if groups can dissolve and new groups are formed periodically. Strong reciprocity differs from pure altruism in one important respect: The presence of reciprocators in a group can, under very general conditions, alter the behavior of opportunists in such a manner as to benefit all members of the group (including reciprocators).[1] This creates the possibility that in groups containing reciprocators, *all* group members including reciprocators obtain greater payoffs than are obtained in homogeneous groups of self-regarding individuals. We argue below that under these circumstances, reciprocators can invade a population of opportunists when groups are dissolving and new groups are forming according to a process of purely random (non-assortative) matching. Furthermore, we show that even when these conditions are not satisfied (so that an opportunistic population is stable), there may exist additional stable population states in which reciprocators are present.

The conditions under which strong reciprocity can survive and spread in evolutionary competition with opportunism within the context of a common pool resource environment are explored in this chapter. Such environments consist of economically valuable resources to which multiple unrelated users have access. Common pool resources have been the dominant form of property through all of human prehistory and history until the advent of agriculture and remain economically significant to this day. Coastal fisheries, grazing lands, forests, groundwater basins, and irrigation systems are all examples of resources that have traditionally been held as common property. A well-known problem that arises in the management of such resources is that when all appropriators independently attempt to maximize their own private gains from resource extraction, the result is a "tragedy of the commons"—with overextraction resulting in excessive resource depletion. The tragedy is that all appropriators may end up with smaller net gains than would be obtained under a system of resource management in which restraints on extraction were enforced. In the absence of a government, such enforcement can only come from the appropriators themselves through a decentralized system of monitoring and enforcement.

Strong reciprocity can motivate individuals to undertake such monitoring and enforcement. Field studies of local commons, of which there are several thousand, show that in many cases resource extraction is regulated and restrained by a complex network of social norms held in place by credible threats of sanction.[2] Such systems coerce ordinarily self-interested individuals to behave in ways that reflect prosocial concerns. Overextraction is therefore limited, and it is possible for all individuals (including reciprocators) to obtain higher material rewards than the tragedy of the commons model would predict. In this chapter, we argue that this effect helps us understand not only how local commons have been able to survive conditions of extreme scarcity, but also how strong reciprocity itself has been able to survive under evolutionary pressure.

The evolutionary theory of strong reciprocity advanced in sections 8.2 and 8.3 relies on the ability of reciprocators to make a credible commitment to monitor and sanction norm violators even when it is not in their interest to do so. Alternative evolutionary accounts of strong reciprocity that differ in significant ways from this one have been proposed, and these are reviewed in section 8.4. Aside from the power of commitment, two additional themes—which we identify as assortation and parochialism—appear repeatedly in this literature. Our survey of this sometimes technical and specialized literature is neither exhaustive nor mathematical and should be accessible to a broad range of researchers across disciplinary boundaries.

8.2 Common Property

The following simple model of common pool resource extraction provides an analytical framework within which the question of preference evolution can be explored.[3] Consider a group of individuals with shared access to a resource that is valuable but costly to appropriate. Each appropriator makes an independent choice regarding her level of resource extraction. The aggregate amount of resource extraction is simply the sum of all individual extraction levels. The total cost of extraction incurred by the group as a whole rises with aggregate extraction in accordance with the following hypothesis: The higher the level of aggregate extraction, the more it costs to extract an *additional* unit of the resource. The share of the total cost of extraction that is paid by any given appropriator is equal to the share of that appropriator's extraction in the total extraction by the group. These are standard assumptions in the analysis of common pool resource environments and imply that an increase in extraction by one appropriator raises the cost of extraction for *all* appropriators.

Figure 8.1 depicts the manner in which aggregate benefits and costs vary with the level of aggregate extraction. The straight line corresponds to aggregate extraction and the curve to the aggregate costs of extraction. The costs rise gradually at first and then rapidly, so that there is a unique level of aggregate extraction X at which *net benefits* are maximized. If each appropriator were to extract an equal share of this amount, the resulting outcome would be optimal from the perspective of the group. However, if all appropriators were to chose this

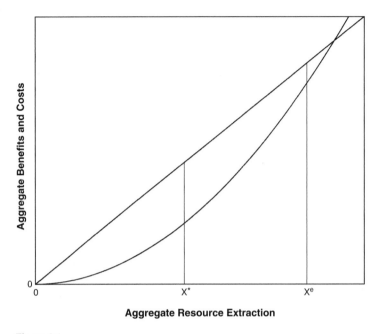

Figure 8.1
Aggregate costs and benefits of extraction.

level of extraction, self-interested individuals would prefer to extract more, since this would increase their own private payoffs. The fact that this increase would come at the cost of lowering the combined payoff to the group as a whole would not deter a self-interested appropriator. If all appropriators were self-interested, and made independent choices regarding their extraction levels, the resulting level of aggregate extraction would *not* be optimal from the perspective of the group. It is possible to show that in an equilibrium of the game played by a group of self-interested appropriators, each appropriator would choose the same extraction level and that the resulting aggregate extraction X^e would exceed X (as shown in figure 8.1). The level of extraction under decentralized, self-interested choice is *inefficient*. Each member of the group could obtain higher payoffs if all were forced to limit their extraction. This is the tragedy of the commons, in which the optimal pursuit of one's own interest by each appropriator leads to lower payoffs for all than could be realized under a system of "mutual coercion, mutually agreed upon" (Hardin 1968).

Coordinated mutual coercion, however, requires a central authority capable of imposing sanctions on violators. Can groups avoid the tragedy of the commons even in the absence of centralized enforcement? Consider the possibility that individuals may monitor each other (at a cost) and impose decentralized sanctions on those who choose extraction levels that are above some threshold. Specifically, suppose that individuals are of two types, whom we call reciprocators and opportunists. Reciprocators comply with and enforce a norm that prescribes, for each individual, an equal share of the efficient extraction level X^*.[4] Reciprocators monitor others at a cost and are able to detect and sanction all violators. Violators incur a cost as a result of each sanction. Opportunists simply choose extraction levels that maximize their private net benefits from extraction. In doing so, they face a choice between norm compliance, which allows them to escape punishment, and norm violation, which enables them to choose optimal extraction levels. Which of these two options is more profitable for a given opportunist depends on the population composition of the community and the choices made by other opportunists.

Consider a group in which both reciprocators and opportunists are present. The opportunists are involved in a strategic interaction in which each must determine her level of extraction. In equilibrium, opportunists fall into one of two groups: those who violate the norm and incur the cost of being punished and those who comply with the norm and escape punishment. It can be shown that this game has a unique equilibrium in which all opportunists who violate the norm will choose the same extraction level. For reasons discussed earlier in this chapter the extraction level of violators will exceed that of those individuals (some of whom may be opportunists) who are in compliance with the norm.

The equilibrium number of violators will depend, among other things, on the severity of the sanction that reciprocators impose, and it can be shown that the equilibrium number of violators is nonincreasing in the severity of the sanction. This is illustrated in figure 8.2 for a particular specification of the model (with one reciprocator in a group of thirty individuals). The relationship between the number of violators and the severity of the sanction is nonlinear. A relatively small sanction can achieve some compliance, and the extent of compliance rises rapidly with the severity of the sanction at first. However, achieving complete or almost complete compliance requires very substantial increases in sanction severity. The reason is because increased compliance by others reduces the incremental cost of extraction and therefore raises the incentives to violate the norm. To counteract this phenomenon, the penalty from violation must rise commensurately.

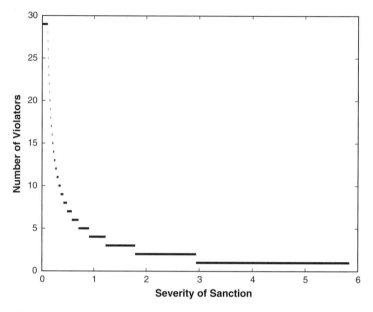

Figure 8.2
Severity of sanctions and the incidence of compliance.

Not all opportunists need to receive the same payoff, since the pay-offs from compliance and norm violation are not necessarily equal in equilibrium. All opportunists earn more than reciprocators, however. This is the case because compliance is an option that opportunists may choose to exercise, and since they do not engage in monitoring or enforcement, compliance always yields opportunists a greater payoff than reciprocators can ever attain. Hence if opportunists choose to violate the norm, they do so in the expectation that this will be at least as profitable as compliance, and hence strictly more profitable than the behavior of reciprocators. This raises the question of how reciprocators can survive under evolutionary pressure.

8.3 Evolution

Suppose that groups are formed by randomly sampling individuals from a large global population, a certain proportion of which are reciprocators. Groups formed in this manner will show some variation in composition as a direct result of randomness in the sampling process. If the global population share of reciprocators is close to zero, there will be a very high probability that most communities consist entirely of opportunists, and most reciprocators will find themselves in communities in which no other reciprocators are present. Similarly, if the global population share of reciprocators is close to one, most groups will consist exclusively of reciprocators and most opportunists will find themselves in groups without other opportunists. For intermediate values of the global population composition, there will be greater variety across groups and most groups will consist of a mixture of reciprocators and opportunists.

The average payoff obtained by opportunists in any given group is fully determined by the composition of the group. Hence, the average payoff to opportunists in the population as a whole is obtained by taking a weighted average of opportunist payoffs, with the weight applied to each type of group proportional to the probability with which this type of group will form. The same procedure applied to reciprocator payoffs yields the average payoff to reciprocators in the population as a whole. When these average payoffs differ, the population composition itself will change. We assume that the dynamics of the population composition are such that the type with the higher payoff grows relative to the type with the lower payoff (a special case of this is the replicator dynamics). We are interested in identifying stable rest points in this dynamic process with a view toward identifying whether or not reciprocators can be present at such states.

Consider first a population consisting only of opportunists. Can reciprocators invade such a population under evolutionary dynamics? Note that when the global reciprocator share is small, almost all reciprocators find themselves in groups with exactly one reciprocator, while almost all opportunists find themselves in groups with *no* reciprocators. In groups of the former type, reciprocators necessarily obtain lower payoffs than do opportunists (regardless of the extent of compliance). However, this does not imply that a population of opportunists must be stable. Such a population will be *unstable* as long as reciprocators obtain greater payoffs in groups consisting of a single reciprocator than do opportunists in groups consisting of no reciprocators. This is clearly possible only if the presence of a single reciprocator induces at least some opportunists to choose compliance, and this in turn depends on the severity of the sanction.

It can be shown that if the severity of the sanction falls below some threshold (which depends on group size and the cost parameter), then an opportunist population is necessarily stable. On the other hand, if

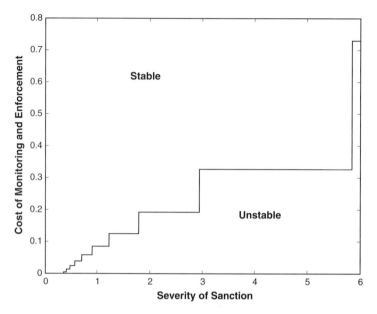

Figure 8.3
Conditions for the instability of an opportunist population.

the severity of the sanction exceeds this threshold, then an opportunist population will be invadable if the cost to reciprocators of imposing sanctions is sufficiently small. In particular, raising the severity of sanctions increases or leaves unchanged the range of costs that are consistent with the instability of the opportunist population. However, there is a boundary that the enforcement cost cannot exceed if an opportunist population is to be invadable, no matter how great the severity of sanctions happens to be. Figure 8.3 illustrates this phenomenon for a particular specification of the model.

While an opportunist population may or may not be stable, a population consisting of reciprocators alone is unstable for all parameter values. As the global reciprocator population share approaches one, reciprocators almost certainly find themselves in homogeneous groups in which each person complies with the norm and pays the cost of monitoring, while opportunists almost certainly find themselves in groups in which they are the only opportunist. Since they have the option of complying with the norm and escaping both the monitoring cost and the sanction, they can guarantee for themselves a payoff strictly greater than that which reciprocators get in all-reciprocator

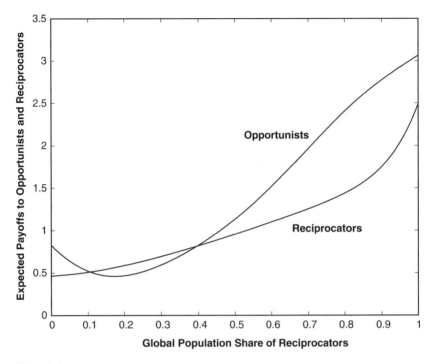

Figure 8.4
Multiple stable steady states.

groups. Since this is feasible, their optimal choice must yield them
at least this amount. Opportunists therefore have a greater expected
payoff than reciprocators when they are sufficiently rare in the global
population.

For those parameter values that render an opportunist population
unstable, the only stable states will be polymorphic (that is, they will
consist of a mixture of the two types). Polymorphic states can also arise
when an opportunist population is *stable*, and it is not difficult to find
parameter ranges consistent with two or even three stable states. Figure 8.4 shows how the average payoffs obtained by opportunists and
reciprocators vary with the population share of the latter in the case of
one such example. Aside from the stable state in which only opportunists are present, there is a second stable state in which about 40 percent
of the population is composed of reciprocators. In fact, it is easy to find
specifications in which three stable states exist—one of which consists
almost exclusively of reciprocators.

The reason why a mixture of reciprocators and opportunists can be stable—even when a population consisting only of opportunists is itself stable—is subtle. If the severity of sanctions is insufficiently great, a single reciprocator in a group of opportunists will induce little or no compliance, and opportunists will outperform reciprocators when the population share of the latter is small. However, when the population share of reciprocators is not too small, most groups in which reciprocators find themselves will also contain other reciprocators, and in such groups there may be significant compliance. Opportunists will do even better than reciprocators in any such group, but even with random group formation, the probability with which an opportunist finds herself in a group with significant compliance will be somewhat lower than the probability with which reciprocators find themselves in such groups. This effect can outweigh the effect of greater opportunist payoffs in each group and permit a mixed population to be stable.

This evolutionary theory of reciprocity is based on the power of *commitment*. Reciprocators are able to influence the behavior of opportunists in their group because they can credibly commit to punishing them if they violate the norm of limited resource extraction. Their commitment to do so is credible because they are strong reciprocators who prefer to punish violators even at some material cost to themselves. As a result, the disadvantage faced by reciprocators within their group can be outweighed by the fact that groups in which they are present can be significantly more successful than those in which they are absent. In the next section, we review other approaches to the evolution of strong reciprocity that do not rely on commitment but rather on assortative interaction or parochialism.[5]

8.4 Assortation, Parochialism, and Identifiability

The preceding analysis was based on the hypothesis of random (non-assortative) group formation. If, instead, group formation is sufficiently assortative, stable norm compliance can occur even in the absence of a sanctioning mechanism. To take an extreme case, suppose that there were perfect assortation so that all groups were homogeneous. In this case, each opportunist would be in a group in which all appropriators extract opportunistically, while each reciprocator would be in a group in which all appropriators extract efficiently. Reciprocators would obtain greater net benefits and opportunists would be displaced under evolutionary selection. It is easily seen that the same outcome arises if there is a sufficiently high degree of assortative interaction.[6]

How might assortative interaction among unrelated individuals arise? One possibility is that group formation results from a process of conscious choice in which reciprocators seek out those of their own type. Even if individuals of all types prefer to be in groups consisting largely of reciprocators, this will result in assortative interaction as long as reciprocators avoid interaction with opportunists. Endogenous group formation along these lines requires some degree of type identifiability—for instance, through a signal by which reciprocators can be identified. When the signal is informative but imperfect, some opportunists will appear to be reciprocators and vice versa. The resulting sorting process leads to partial assortation: Reciprocators are more likely to be matched with other reciprocators than with opportunists.

Opportunists who happen to be matched with reciprocators do extremely well because they violate the norm while others in their group are in compliance. However, as long as the degree of assortation is sufficiently great, this advantage can be swamped by the disadvantage that opportunists face in being more likely to be matched with other opportunists. If, in addition, the process of sorting on the basis of signal observation is costly, then the long-run population will consist of a mixture of types. The intuition for this is that when most members of the population are reciprocators, then investment in sorting not worthwhile and individuals forego the opportunity to seek out reciprocators and avoid opportunists. This allows the share of opportunists to grow until a point is reached when reciprocators find investment in sorting to be worthwhile.[7]

A less direct route to assortative interaction occurs when individuals may be *ostracized* from groups for noncompliance with social norms. In this case, opportunists must take into account not simply the direct payoff consequences of norm compliance and violation, but also the payoff implications of possible detection and expulsion. Since opportunists violate norms with greater frequency than do reciprocators, they will be expelled with greater likelihood. The result is assortative interaction: Reciprocators are more likely than opportunists to be in a group with a large proportion of reciprocators. This compensates for the losses incurred by costly sanctioning of noncooperative behavior, and both types can coexist in the long run.[8]

Even in the absence of assortative interaction, reciprocity can survive if individuals condition their *behavior* on the distribution of types in their group. We refer to this dependence of actions on the group composition as parochialism. The basic idea can be illustrated by considering the extreme case in which reciprocators comply with the norm and engage in monitoring and enforcement only if they are present in sufficiently large numbers to ensure complete compliance on the part of opportunists. In this case, the behavior (and hence the payoffs) of opportunists and reciprocators are identical in groups containing an insufficient number of reciprocators. The remaining groups achieve norm compliance and significantly higher payoffs, although opportunists in such groups escape the cost of monitoring and hence have a payoff advantage over reciprocators. If the cost of monitoring is sufficiently small, this advantage to opportunists will be outweighed by the fact that reciprocators are more likely to find themselves in groups that achieve norm compliance and efficiency, even under non-assortative group formation. In this case, reciprocators will survive and spread in a population consisting largely of opportunists, just as they would under assortative interaction. Suppose further that the monitoring costs incurred by reciprocators in groups in which they predominate decrease their payoffs below those of opportunists in these groups. If opportunists are rare, most groups containing both types will be of this kind, and opportunists will therefore invade a population of reciprocators. In this case, the model predicts the evolution of a mixed population.[9]

The preceding discussion has been based on the assumption that individuals know the composition of their group, as would be the case if reciprocators and opportunists could be distinguished by some observable trait. In this situation, an opportunist who carried the trait identifying reciprocators would outperform identifiable opportunists and would gradually displace the latter in the population. As this happened, however, it would generate selection pressure favoring reciprocators who could distinguish themselves from the disguised opportunists. Reciprocators who evolved a signal that achieved this objective would reap the gains from efficient norm compliance in the presence of their own type. Hence, rather than assuming that reciprocators and opportunists are either perfectly distinguishable or perfectly indistinguishable, it is more realistic to assume that they are neither.

As in the earlier discussion of assortative interaction, this assumption can be made by supposing that prior to choosing actions, each individual emits a signal with some fixed probability that depends on the individual's type. Specifically, suppose that reciprocators are more likely to emit the signal than are opportunists. After the signaling phase, each member of the group updates her assessment of the probability distribution describing the composition of the group. When the global population consists almost exclusively of opportunists, it is extremely likely that even a person who emits the reciprocator signal is an opportunist. This follows from the fact that the fraction of the population who are opportunists with reciprocator signals will be much larger than the fraction of the population who are reciprocators with reciprocator signals. The signal then conveys almost no information, and opportunists will not be deterred from overextraction by the prospect of punishment even when they are matched with a person with a signal. Recognizing this, reciprocators will behave exactly like opportunists when the opportunist population share is large. Thus, both types ignore the signal, choose the same inefficient extraction level, and get the same payoff.

Now consider the other extreme case of a population consisting almost exclusively of reciprocators. Again, the reciprocator signal will convey virtually no information since it is extremely likely, regardless of whether or not the signal is observed, that each player in one's group is a reciprocator. In this situation, if reciprocators were to engage in monitoring, then opportunists would always comply with the norm and get higher payoffs than reciprocators by escaping the monitoring cost. If, on the other hand, reciprocators did not monitor, then opportunists would extract more than the norm, thus getting higher payoffs than reciprocators. In either case, we see that opportunists will always be able to invade a reciprocator population. (Reciprocators will always comply with the norm since they expect with near-certainty that the other group members are fellow reciprocators.)

However, there will exist an intermediate range for the global population composition such that the reciprocator signal does convey useful information. This case is complicated and we illustrate it under the simplifying assumption that the group size is two. Suppose that reciprocators who emit a reciprocator signal comply with the norm and engage in monitoring, and that reciprocators who do not emit reciprocator signals never monitor and comply if and only if they are matched with someone who emits the reciprocator signal. Given this behavior of reciprocators, opportunists' best response, provided the damage from punishment is high enough, is to comply when their partner emits a reciprocator signal and to extract more than the norm when their partner emits none. In this case, players emitting reciprocator signals do much better than those emitting none. Within this group, opportunists obtain greater payoffs than reciprocators since they never monitor and comply only when they observe a reciprocator signal from their partner. Nevertheless, this advantage can be outweighed by the fact that reciprocators are more likely to emit reciprocator signals in the first place.[10]

Can reciprocity be evolutionarily stable even in the absence of commitment, assortation, or parochialism? If the costs of monitoring and sanctioning are negligible when there is complete norm compliance, there can be stable groups consisting of a mixture of reciprocators and pure cooperators (who comply with, but do not enforce, the norm). This stability is of a rather tenuous nature since it can be disrupted by the periodic appearance of individuals who violate the norm and are punished by reciprocators for doing so. If, however, behavior is transmitted across generations through a cultural process that is partly *conformist* (in the sense that widespread behaviors are replicated at greater rates than less common but equally rewarding behaviors), then such groups can be stable in a more robust sense. Conformist transmission, however, can result in the stabilization of virtually any behavioral norms, including those that are antisocial and inefficient. One way to reduce the multiplicity of potential outcomes is to allow for cultural selection to operate in *structured populations*. In this model, groups are located in accordance with a spatial pattern in which each group has well-defined neighbors. Members of groups that exhibit efficient norms will enjoy higher material payoffs than members of groups that do not, and such norms may therefore spread through the population by the imitation of successful practices found in neighboring groups. The study of structured populations holds considerable promise in helping identify additional mechanisms for the survival and spread of strong reciprocity.[11]

One further direction in which work on the evolution of reciprocity can profitably proceed is the following. Several researchers have recently provided parsimonious representations of preferences that can be used to account simultaneously for data from a variety of strategic environments. These specifications are free of any particular experimental context and reflect concerns for distribution, efficiency, and reciprocity.[12] Evolutionary models can build on this literature by shifting focus from the analysis of behavioral norms in particular environments to the emergence and stability of general purpose rules that are equipped to deal with multiple and novel situations.

8.5 Conclusions

Social norms that have evolved in a particular economic environment often continue to govern behavior in other contexts. Even as the relative economic importance of traditional local commons has diminished with the expansion of state and private property, norms of restraint and enforcement that arose as a substitute for governments and markets in earlier environments continue to make their presence felt in more modern institutions such as firms, unions, and bureaucracies. Compliance with such norms often results in greater economic efficiency than does opportunistic behavior. Viewed in this light, norms of reciprocity are an important component of social capital, and an understanding of their origins and persistence may help to prevent their erosion. The literature on the evolution of strong reciprocity is a patchwork of models, each of which emphasizes a different mechanism under which reciprocators can survive in competition with purely opportunistic individuals. We have identified three broad themes—commitment, parochialism, and assortation—that appear repeatedly in the literature. These effects, separately or in combination, are largely responsible for the departures from narrow self-interest that humans display in the experimental laboratory and in daily life.

Appendix

The claims made in sections 8.2–8.3 in the text are proved formally below. The common pool resource game involves n players with appropriator i choosing extraction x_i at a cost $(aX)x_i$ where $X = \sum_{i=1}^{n} x_i$ denotes aggregate extraction. The payoffs of individual i are:

$$\pi_i = x_i(1 - aX). \tag{1}$$

The efficient level of aggregate extraction maximizes aggregate payoffs $\sum_{i=1}^{n} \pi_i = X(1 - aX)$ and is given by:

$$X^* = \frac{1}{2a}. \tag{2}$$

Reciprocators comply with and enforce a norm that prescribes, for each individual, the extraction level:

$$x^r = \frac{1}{n}X^* = \frac{1}{2an}. \tag{3}$$

Reciprocators monitor others at a cost $\gamma > 0$ and are able to detect and sanction all violators. Violators incur a cost δ as a result of each sanction. Opportunists simply choose extraction levels that maximize their payoffs (1). Let r denote the number of reciprocators in the community. A opportunist i who has chosen to extract optimally (and hence violate the norm) must choose a level of extraction:

$$x_i = \frac{1 - aX}{a}.$$

Since X is common to all individuals, all opportunists who violate the norm will choose the same extraction level. Let x^v denote this level, and let $v \le n - r$ represent the number of opportunists who choose it. Then:

$$X = (n - v)x^r + vx^v.$$

Using the two previous equations we obtain:

$$ax^v = 1 - a((n - v)x^r + vx^v)$$

which, using (3), simplifies to yield:

$$x^v = \frac{1}{2an}\left(\frac{n + v}{1 + v}\right) \tag{4}$$

Aggregate extraction is

$$X = (n - v)\frac{1}{2an} + v\frac{1}{2an}\left(\frac{n + v}{1 + v}\right) = \frac{1}{2an}\left(\frac{n + v(2n - 1)}{1 + v}\right) \tag{5}$$

Using (1), (4), and (5) and taking into account the sanctions imposed on violators, we get:

$$\pi^v = x^v(1 - aX) - \delta r = \frac{1}{4a}\frac{(n + v)^2}{n^2(1 + v)^2} - \delta r \tag{6}$$

where π^v is the payoff from violation. The payoff from compliance is:

$$\pi^c = x^r(1 - aX) = \frac{1}{4a}\left(\frac{n + v}{n^2(1 + v)}\right). \tag{7}$$

In equilibrium, a unilateral deviation should not benefit any opportunist. If $v \in [1, n - r - 1]$, this implies the following conditions:

$$\frac{1}{4a}\left(\frac{n + v}{n^2(1 + v)}\right) \ge \frac{1}{4a}\frac{(n + v + 1)^2}{n^2(2 + v)^2} - \delta r \tag{8}$$

$$\frac{1}{4a} \frac{(n+v)^2}{n^2(1+v)^2} - \delta r \geq \frac{1}{4a} \left(\frac{n+v-1}{n^2 v} \right) \tag{9}$$

The first states that an opportunist in compliance cannot profit by switching to noncompliance; the second that an opportunist in violation cannot profit by switching to compliance. If $v = 0$ in equilibrium, only the former condition need be satisfied, and if $v = 1$, only the latter.

The parameters $n, a,$ and δ and the number of reciprocators r define a game played by the $n - r$ opportunists who choose their extraction levels strategically, with the number of violators v being determined in equilibrium. Let this game be denoted $\Gamma(n, a, \delta, r)$. We then have:

Proposition 1 Every game $\Gamma(n, a, \delta, r)$ has a unique equilibrium. The equilibrium number of violators v is nonincreasing in δ.

From (8–9), the number of violators v at any asymmetric equilibrium must satisfy:

$$F(v) \leq \delta \leq G(v) \tag{10}$$

where:

$$F(v) = \frac{1}{4ar} \frac{(n+v+1)^2}{n^2(2+v)^2} - \frac{1}{4ar} \left(\frac{n+v}{n^2(1+v)} \right)$$

$$G(v) = \frac{1}{4ar} \frac{(n+v)^2}{n^2(1+v)^2} - \frac{1}{4ar} \left(\frac{n+v-1}{n^2 v} \right)$$

Note that $F(v - 1) = G(v)$. Hence, (10) defines a sequence of intervals $\{[F(v), F(v - 1)]\}_{v=1}^{n-r-1}$ such that there is an asymmetric equilibrium with v violators if and only if $\delta \in [F(v), F(v - 1)]$. If δ does not fall within any of these intervals, then equilibrium is symmetric. If $\delta > F(0)$, there is no violation in equilibrium, while if $\delta < F(n - r)$ there is no compliance in equilibrium. Note that raising δ lowers or leaves unchanged the equilibrium value of v.

Proposition 1 allows us to write the number of violators as a function of the number of reciprocators $v = v(r)$. This in turn defines aggregate extraction and the payoffs from compliance and violation as functions of r. The payoff obtained by reciprocators is therefore

$$\pi^r(r) = \pi^c(r) - \gamma. \tag{11}$$

and the mean payoff received by opportunists is:

$$\pi^m(r) = \frac{v(r)\pi^v(r) + (n - r - v(r))\pi^c(r)}{n - r}. \tag{12}$$

Suppose that the share of reciprocators in the population as a whole is given by ρ, and that this population is randomly distributed across communities. The probability that a community formed in this manner will contain precisely r reciprocators is given by:

$$p(r, \rho) = \frac{n!}{(n - r)!r!}\rho^r(1 - \rho)^{n-r}.$$

The expected payoffs of reciprocators and opportunists in the population as a whole is given by:

$$\bar{\pi}^r(\rho) = \frac{\sum_{r=1}^n p(r, \rho)\pi^r(r)}{\sum_{r=1}^n p(r, \rho)}$$

$$\bar{\pi}^m(\rho) = \frac{\sum_{r=0}^{n-1} p(r, \rho)\pi^m(r)}{\sum_{r=1}^n p(r, \rho)}$$

The mean payoff in the population as a whole is simply:

$$\bar{\pi}(\rho) = \rho\bar{\pi}^r(\rho) + (1 - \rho)\bar{\pi}^m(\rho).$$

Suppose that the evolution of the population share ρ is governed by the replicator dynamics:

$$\dot{\rho} = (\bar{\pi}^r(\rho) - \bar{\pi}(\rho))\rho.$$

Then we have:

Proposition 2 Suppose n and a are given. Then there exists $\bar{\delta} > 0$ such that an opportunist population is stable if $\delta \leq \bar{\delta}$. If $\delta > \bar{\delta}$, then there exists a nondecreasing and bounded function $\bar{\gamma}(\delta)$ such that an opportunist population is stable if and only if $\gamma > \bar{\gamma}(\delta)$.

The stability of $\rho = 0$ depends on whether or not $\pi^m(0)$ is greater than $\bar{\pi}^r(1)$. This is because:

$$\lim_{\rho \to 0} \bar{\pi}^m(\rho) = \pi^m(0)$$

$$\lim_{\rho \to 0} \bar{\pi}^r(\rho) = \pi^r(1)$$

All opportunists violate the norm when $r = 0$, so in this case $v = n$ and:

$$\pi^m(0) = \pi^v(0) = \frac{1}{4a} \frac{(n+n)^2}{n^2(1+n)^2} = \frac{1}{a(1+n)^2}.$$

From (11) and (7), we have:

$$\pi^r(1) = \frac{1}{4a} \left(\frac{n+v}{n^2(1+v)} \right) - \gamma$$

Hence:

$$\pi^r(1) - \pi^m(0) = \frac{1}{4a} \left(\frac{n+v}{n^2(1+v)} \right) - \frac{1}{a(1+n)^2} - \gamma$$

$$= \frac{1}{4} \frac{(n-1)(n^2 - n - 3vn - v)}{an^2(1+v)(1+n)^2} - \gamma$$

The first term is positive if and only if $n^2 - n - 3vn - v > 0$. This requires:

$$v < \left(\frac{n-1}{3n+1} \right) n$$

There exists $\bar{\delta} > 0$ such that the above will not be satisfied for any $\delta < \bar{\delta}$, in which case the opportunist population must be stable. If $\delta > \bar{\delta}$, then stability holds if and only if $\gamma < \bar{\gamma}$ where:

$$\bar{\gamma} = \frac{1}{4} \frac{(n-1)(n^2 - n - 3vn - v)}{an^2(1+v)(1+n)^2}.$$

The right-hand side of the above expression is decreasing in v. Since v is nonincreasing in δ, $\bar{\gamma}$ is nondecreasing in δ. Finally we have:

Proposition 3   A reciprocator population is unstable for all parameter values.

The stability of $\rho = 1$ requires $\pi^r(n)$ to be greater than $\pi^m(n-1)$. When $r = n - 1$, the single opportunist can comply with the norm and obtain a payoff $\pi^r(n) + \gamma$. Since this payoff is feasible, under optimal choice we must have $\pi^m(n-1) \geq \pi^r(n) + \gamma > \pi^r(n)$. Hence $\rho = 1$ is unstable.

Notes

1. Altruism may also have this effect, but does so in a narrower range of environments which exclude those considered in this chapter (Bester and Güth 1998).

2. For an overview of the evidence from field studies, see Bromley (1992) and Ostrom (1990). Laboratory experiments designed to replicate common pool resource environments reveal extensive sanctioning behavior that is broadly consistent with the findings from field studies (Ostrom, Walker, and Gardner 1992); see also Fehr and Fischbacher (this volume, chapter 6).

3. A mathematical analysis of this model with proofs of all claims made in the text may be found in the appendix.

4. It is not essential to the argument that the norm prescribe behavior that is optimal in this sense, only that it result in greater payoffs for the group than would be observed under opportunistic extraction.

5. The section to follow draws on our considerably more extensive survey (Sethi and Somanathan 2003). Other evolutionary models of reciprocity that rely on the power of commitment include Güth and Yaari (1992), Güth (1995), Sethi (1996), Huck and Oechssler (1999), and Friedman and Singh (1999). Gintis (2000) and Sethi and Somanathan (2001) analyze models in which both commitment (the power to influence the actions of others) and parochialism (the conditioning of one's behavior on the composition of one's group) play a role.

6. This is, of course, analogous to Hamilton's argument that an altruistic gene will spread in a population if individuals share a sufficiently high proportion of their genes on average with those with whom they interact (Hamilton 1964).

7. This model of partial assortation on the basis of signaling is due to Frank (1987, 1988); see also Guttman (2002). For a model in which prior cooperative acts are themselves used as signals, see Nowak and Sigmund (1998).

8. See Bowles and Gintis (2004) for a model along these lines.

9. Gintis (2000) models this effect in an empirically motivated model of public goods provision.

10. See Frank (1987), Robson (1990), Guttman (2002) and Smith and Bliege Bird (this volume, chapter 4) for further discussion and variations on the theme of signaling.

11. Models in which stable mixtures of reciprocators and pure cooperators can arise include Axelrod (1986) and Sethi and Somanathan (1996); see Gale, Binmore, and Samuelson (1995) for similar findings in a different context. A discussion of conformist transmission and its implications may be found in Boyd and Richerson (1995). The model of structured populations mentioned here is due to Boyd and Richerson (2000); see also Boyd et al. (this volume, chapter 7).

12. Important contributions include Rabin (1993), Levine (1998), Fehr and Schmidt (1999), Bolton and Ockenfels (2000), Falk and Fischbacher (1998), Dufwenberg and Kirchsteiger (1998), and Charness and Rabin (2002); see also Falk and Fischbacher (this volume, chapter 6).

References

Axelrod, R. 1986. "An Evolutionary Approach to Norms." *American Political Science Review* 80:1095–1111.

Bester, H., and W. Güth. 1998. "Is Altruism Evolutionarily Stable?" *Journal of Economic Behavior and Organization* 34:193–209.

Bolton, G. E., and A. Ockenfels. 2000. "ERC: A Theory of Equity, Reciprocity and Competition." *American Economic Review* 90:166–193.

Bromley, D., ed. 1992. *Making the Commons Work*. San Francisco: ICS Press.

Bowles, S. and H. Gintis. 2004. "The Evolution of Strong Reciprocity," *Theoretical Population Biology* 65:17–28.

Boyd, R., H. Gintis, S. Bowles, and P. J. Richerson. 2004. Chapter 7, this volume.

Boyd, R., and P. J. Richerson. 1985. *Culture and the Evolutionary Process*. Chicago: University of Chicago Press.

Boyd, R., and P. J. Richerson. 2000. "Group Beneficial Norms Can Spread Rapidly in a Structured Population." Mimeo. University of California at Los Angeles.

Charness, G., and M. Rabin. 2002. "Understanding Social Preferences with Simple Tests." *Quarterly Journal of Economics* 117:817–869.

Dufwenberg, M., and G. Kirchsteiger. 1998. "A Theory of Sequential Reciprocity." Center Discussion Paper 9837. Tilburg University.

Falk, A., and U. Fischbacher. 1998. "A Theory of Reciprocity." Mimeo. University of Zürich.

Falk, A., and U. Fischbacher. 2004. Chapter 5, this volume.

Fehr, E., and U. Fischbacher. 2004. Chapter 6, this volume.

Fehr, E., and K. M. Schmidt. 1999. "A Theory of Fairness, Competition, and Cooperation." *Quarterly Journal of Economics* 114:817–868.

Frank, R. H. 1987. "If *Homo economicus* Could Choose His Own Utility Function, Would He Want One with a Conscience?" *American Economic Review* 77:593–604.

Frank, R. H. 1988. *Passions within Reason: The Strategic Role of the Emotions*. New York: W. W. Norton.

Friedman, D., and N. Singh. 1999. "On the Viability of Vengeance." Mimeo. University of California at Santa Cruz.

Gale, J., K. Binmore, and L. Samuelson. 1995. "Learning to be Imperfect: The Ultimatum Game." *Games and Economic Behavior* 8:56–90.

Gintis, H. 2000. "Strong Reciprocity and Human Sociality." *Journal of Theoretical Biology* 206:169–179.

Güth, W. 1995. "An Evolutionary Approach to Explaining Cooperative Behavior by Reciprocal Incentives." *International Journal of Game Theory* 24:323–344.

Güth, W., and M. Yaari. 1992. "Explaining Reciprocal Behavior in Simple Strategic Games: An Evolutionary Approach." In U. Witt (ed.) *Explaining Forces and Change: Approaches to Evolutionary Economics*. Ann Arbor: University of Michigan Press.

Guttman, J. M. 2003. "Repeated Interaction and the Evolution of Preferences for Reciprocity." *Economic Journal* 113:631–656.

Hamilton, W. D. 1964. "The Genetical Evolution of Social Behavior." *Journal of Theoretical Biology* 7:1–16.

Hardin, G. 1968. "The Tragedy of the Commons." *Science* 162:1243–1248.

Huck, S., and J. Oechssler. 1999. "The Indirect Evolutionary Approach to Explaining Fair Allocations." *Games and Economic Behavior* 28:13–24.

Levine, D. K. 1998. "Modeling Altruism and Spitefulness in Experiments." *Review of Economic Dynamics* 1:593–622.

Nowak, M. A., and K. Sigmund. 1998. "Evolution of Indirect Reciprocity by Image Scoring." *Nature* 393:573–577.

Ostrom, E. 1990. *Governing the Commons: The Evolution of Institutions for Collective Action.* Cambridge: Cambridge University Press.

Ostrom, E., J. Walker, and R. Gardner. 1992. "Covenants with and without a Sword: Self-Governance Is Possible." *American Political Science Review* 86:404–417.

Rabin, M. 1993. "Incorporating Fairness into Game Theory and Economics" *American Economic Review* 83:1281–1302.

Robson, A. 1990. "Efficiency in Evolutionary Games: Darwin, Nash, and the Secret Handshake." *Journal of Theoretical Biology* 144:379–396.

Sethi, R. 1996. "Evolutionary Stability and Social Norms." *Journal of Economic Behavior and Organization* 29:113–140.

Sethi, R., and E. Somanathan. 1996. "The Evolution of Social Norms in Common Property Resource Use." *American Economic Review* 86:766–788.

Sethi, R., and E. Somanathan. 2001. "Preference Evolution and Reciprocity." *Journal of Economic Theory* 97:273–297.

Sethi, R., and E. Somanathan. 2003. "Understanding Reciprocity." *Journal of Economic Behavior and Organization* 50:1–27.

Smith, E. A., and R. B. Bird. 2004. Chapter 4, this volume.

IV

Reciprocity and Social Policy

9 Policies That Crowd out Reciprocity and Collective Action

Elinor Ostrom

9.1 Introduction

The extensive empirical research presented in this volume and elsewhere (see reviews by Bowles 1998; Frey and Jegen 2001; E. Ostrom 1998, 2000) challenges the assumption that human behavior is driven in all settings entirely by external material inducements and sanctions. Instead of assuming the existence of a single type of "profit maximizing" or "utility maximizing" individual, a better foundation for explaining human behavior is the assumption that multiple types of individuals exist in most settings. Among the types of individuals likely to be present in any situation are "rational egoists," who focus entirely on their own expected material payoffs. Neoclassical economics and non-cooperative game theory have usually assumed that rational egoists are the *only* type of player that scholars need to assume in order to generate useful and validated predictions about behavior. Substantial research in nonmarket experimental settings now provides strong evidence that in addition to rational egoists, many settings also involve "strong reciprocators," who are motivated by both intrinsic preferences and material payoffs. As discussed in this volume, strong reciprocators will frequently adopt strategies of conditional cooperation and conditional punishment in settings where individuals can observe each other's behavior.

Laboratory experiments of social dilemmas, trust games, dictator games, and ultimatum games repeatedly find higher-than-predicted cooperative behavior that cannot be explained by theories assuming the existence of only rational egoists. "It is a well known fact in the experimental literature that in games like the trust game, there is always a 30–40 percentage of individuals who act in a purely egoistic way" (Frey and Benz 2001, 9). This leaves 60 to 70 percent of the other individuals who tend to follow more complex strategies involving some levels of trust and reciprocity. Furthermore, the proportion of different types of individuals is likely to change over time due to the self-selection of individuals into diverse types of situations and due to endogenous changes in preferences and expectations over time as a result of the patterns of interactions and outcomes achieved (see E. Ostrom and Walker 2003).

A considerable body of contemporary policy analysis is, however, based on the earlier widely accepted presumption that all individuals are strictly rational egoists motivated entirely by external payoffs. When rational egoists find themselves in a wide diversity of collective-action situations, the predicted result is a deficient equilibrium of zero or very low contributions to joint outcomes. Consequently, centrally designed and externally implemented material incentives—both positive and negative—are seen as universally needed to overcome these Pareto-deficient equilibria. Leviathan is alive and well in our policy textbooks. The state is viewed as a substitute for the shortcomings of individual behavior and the presumed failure of community. Somehow, the agents of the state are assumed to pay little attention to their own material self-interest when making official decisions and to know and seek "the public interest."

For contemporary policy analysis to have a firm empirical foundation, it is necessary to adopt a broader theory of human behavior that posits multiple types of individuals—including rational egoists as well as strong reciprocators—and examines how the contexts of collective action affect the mix of individuals involved.

In section 9.3, I will briefly review the evidence regarding intrinsic motivations. The evidence shows that in some settings (particularly those where individuals lose a sense of control over their own fate), providing external inducements to contribute to collective benefits may actually produce counterintentional consequences. External incentives may "crowd out" behaviors that are based on intrinsic preferences so that lower levels of contributions are achieved with the incentives than would be achieved without them (Frey 1994, 1997). External incentives may also "crowd in" behaviors based on intrinsic preferences and enhance what could have been achieved without these incentives.

In section 9.4, I will then discuss the delicate problem of designing institutions that enhance cooperation rather than crowding it out. Instead of relying on the state as the central, top-down substitute for all public problem solving, it is necessary to design complex, polycentric orders that involve both public governance mechanisms and private market and community institutions that complement each other (see McGinnis 1999a, 1999b, 2000). Reliance primarily on national governments crowds out public and private problem solving at regional and local levels (and radical decentralization would crowd out public problem solving at regional and national levels). Effective institutional designs create complex, multi-tiered systems with some levels of duplication, overlap, and contestation. The policy analyst's penchant for neat, orderly hierarchical systems needs to be replaced with a recognition that complex polycentric systems are needed to cope effectively with complex problems of modern life.

9.2 Testing the Predictions of the Standard Model of Rational Choice

One of the great advantages of contemporary game theory and formal models of collective-action theory is that they generate clear predictions of expected behavior in specific types of situations. Given precise models of collective-action situations and clear predictions of expected behavior, it is possible to set up experimental laboratory designs that enable one to test the empirical veracity of the predictions. With the substantial methodological advances in conducting experimental laboratory research (Smith 1982; Plott 1979), this method has become a useful tool for social scientists in the testing of theories and the replication of findings by multiple scholars in diverse cultures. Experimental research related to the theory of collective action has generated very clear predictions that have repeatedly been challenged in the lab. Let us briefly discuss two related sets of predictions and results.

9.2.1 Predictions and Empirical Results from Linear Public Good Games

When individuals are in a one-shot linear public good situation, each individual can choose between contributing nothing to the provision of a benefit that all will share or contributing some portion of a given endowment of assets. Each individual is predicted to contribute zero assets. When the game is repeated a finite number of times, each individual would contribute zero assets in the last round, and because of backward induction, each individual is predicted to contribute zero assets in each and every round leading up to the final round.

Not only do we have evidence from many field settings that individuals do contribute to the provision of public goods (see, for example, Loveman 1998; Kaboolian and Nelson 1998), there is similar evidence from a large number of carefully controlled laboratory experiments. Between 40 to 60 percent of subjects in a one-shot linear public good situation contribute assets to the provision of a public good (Dawes, McTavish, and Shaklee 1977; Isaac, Walker, and Thomas 1984; Davis and Holt 1993; Ledyard 1995; Offerman 1997). About the same percentage of subjects contribute tokens in the first round of a finitely repeated public good experiment. The rate of contribution, however, decays over time, approaching but never reaching the predicted zero level (Isaac and Walker 1988). Because of the decay toward zero contributions in the experiment's last ten rounds, an initial reaction by theorists was that it took subjects ten rounds to learn the rational way to play the game. Subsequent experiments extended the pre-announced time horizon to 20, 40, and 60 repetitions. These showed that subjects tended to keep cooperation levels varying in the 30 to 50 percent range for long sequences of time and that the decay toward zero contributions did not occur a few rounds prior to the announced final round (Isaac, Walker, and Williams 1994).

9.2.2 Predictions and Empirical Evidence Related to Second- and Third-Level Social Dilemmas

Not only is there a clear prediction concerning the lack of provision in public good situations, participants are viewed as helpless in getting out of such situations. An effort to arrive at an agreement for determining how much of a public good should be provided and how the costs of provision should be shared would take time and effort to achieve. Once achieved, everyone would benefit whether or not they had contributed to the design of such an agreement. Thus, the prediction is that no one would participate in the effort to extract themselves from the initial dilemma. Furthermore, monitoring compliance to such an agreement and sanctioning those who did not give their agreed-upon share would be costly for those who might think about undertaking such an activity. Again, everyone would benefit from such activities whether or not they had contributed. Thus, no one is expected to invest any of their own resources in monitoring and sanctioning activities. But this is not what is found in many settings.

For example, in experiments where subjects are offered an opportunity to pay a fee in order to assess a fine against someone else, subjects are willing to expend their own resources to punish non-cooperators (E. Ostrom, Walker, and Gardner 1992; Fehr and Gächter 1998; Yamagishi 1986). Similar to field settings, subjects in a lab are rather indignant and angry at others who do not do their share in protecting a common-pool resource or providing a public good. These subjects give up costly resources to sanction noncooperators. And, when individuals agree upon their own sanctioning system, they do not need to use it extensively—as the compliance rate with a self-imposed harvesting limit and sanctioning system is extremely high (E. Ostrom, Gardner, and Walker 1994).

Cardenas, Stranlund, and Willis (2000) report on a common-pool resource experiment conducted in the Colombian countryside with *campesinos* who frequently have to deal with resource problems in their everyday life. In one of the experimental conditions, the *campesino* subjects were given a choice of withdrawal levels from the resource that would be monitored by an external observer. The externally imposed rule was that the subjects should harvest at an optimal level for group returns, or face a realistic but low level of monitoring and a sanction imposed by the outside observer. The subjects in this experimental condition actually increased their withdrawal levels. This is in marked contrast to their own behavior in those experiments where the subjects could talk on a face-to-face basis and no rule was imposed. What was remarkable about this experiment was that subjects, who were simply allowed to communicate with one another on a face-to-face basis, were able to achieve a higher joint return than the subjects who had an optimal but imperfectly enforced rule imposed on them. As the authors conclude:

We have presented evidence that indicates that local environmental policies that are modestly enforced, but nevertheless are predicted by standard theory to be welfare-improving, may be ineffective. In fact, such a policy can do more harm than good, especially in comparison to allowing individuals collectively to confront local environmental dilemmas without intervention. We have also ... presented evidence that the fundamental reason for the poor performance of external control is that it crowded out group-regarding behavior in favor of greater self-interest. (Cardenas, Stranlund, and Willis 2000, 1731)

It has also been found that individuals in both experimental and field settings are willing to invest substantial time and energy in designing and adapting rules so that they can achieve collective outcomes. In field settings, the time and effort may be substantial (Lam

1998; Tang 1992; Gibson, McKean, and Ostrom 2000; Varughese and Ostrom 2001). When local users feel a sense of ownership and dependence on a local resource, many of them invest intensively in designing and implementing ingenious local institutions—some of which are sustained for centuries (E. Ostrom 1990).

Being involved in a face-to-face discussion about solving their own overharvesting problem may generate unexpected capabilities and learning. Frohlich and Oppenheimer (2003) designed an experiment in which one set of five subjects first faced an "incentive compatible device" (ICD) in dealing with a repeated Prisoner's Dilemma (PD) game that randomized who was to receive the payoffs from their decisions. While using this device, players were indeed able to achieve high levels of joint benefits, but about the same level as a control group that was allowed to communicate on a face-to-face basis during the initial phase of the experiment. Frohlich and Oppenheimer had hypothesized that the experience of playing within an incentive compatible device should carry over to a second phase when the same subjects played seven rounds of a PD game without the device. They expected that subjects who had experienced this device in the first phase would contribute more after the removal of the device. Frohlich and Oppenheimer ultimately had to reject their own hypothesis, however. "Without discussion, there was no carryover effect. With discussion, the ICD, possibly due to the decoupling of ethical concern and behavior, led to significantly lowered levels of contributions than were found in the regular PD" (Frohlich and Oppenheimer 2003, 289). They found that face-to-face communication had a higher level of positive carryover than the ICD.

Frohlich and Oppenheimer concluded that the use of an incentive compatible device—at least the one that they used in the experiment—could be "a two-edged sword, and ought to be studied further before being advocated widely" (Frohlich and Oppenheimer 2003, 289). In reasoning about their unexpected finding, they considered how the institution affected the problem-solving process of those involved. When making a decision within the ICD, subjects "confront a situation in which their self-interest and the interests of all others coincide exactly. What is best for them is, by explicit design, best for the group as a whole" (Frohlich and Oppenheimer 2003, 290). Thus, these individuals could make a decision without facing any tension between the self-interested and the ethically best strategy. Subjects did not need to take the impact of their decisions on others into account as contrasted with their own best interest. "They don't have to flex their ethical muscles" (Frohlich and Oppenheimer 2003, 290).

9.3   Multiple Types of Players and Intrinsic Preferences

These (and closely related) empirical findings consistently challenge predictions based on a presumption that all individuals can be characterized by a single model of rational behavior when they interact outside a highly competitive market setting. Furthermore, preferences have not only been considered to be entirely self-interested, but also fixed and unchanged by the experience of being within a particular institutional arrangement. It is thus necessary to reconstruct our basic theories of collective action and to assume that at least some participants are not rational egoists (Sen 1977). At least some individuals in social dilemma situations follow or can learn norms of behavior—such as those of reciprocity, fairness, and trustworthiness—that lead them to take actions that are directly contrary to those predicted by contemporary rational choice theory.

In other words, the behavior of many individuals is based on intrinsic preferences related to how they prefer to behave (and would like others to behave) in situations requiring collective action to achieve joint benefits or avoid joint harm. Intrinsic preferences lead some individuals to be conditional cooperators—willing to contribute to collective action so long as others also contribute—as well as conditional punishers—willing to sanction others who do not behave as agreed upon or as accepted norms or rules prescribe so long as they believe others are also conditional sanctioners. Intrinsic preferences transform some dilemmas into assurance games where there are two equilibria and not just one (Chong 1991; Sen 1974). On the other hand, some individuals do behave in a manner that closely approximates the prediction for how rational egoists will behave. Thus, one needs to assume multiple types of actors rather than only rational egoists.

In many ongoing field situations, humans obtain considerable information about each other and are able to engage in collective action with those that they estimate share similar norms. In such situations, some rational egoists will survive along with strong reciprocators so that it is not possible to rely exclusively on the intrinsic motivation of all participants to cooperate—especially if cooperation must be sustained over time. Thus, in many cases, intrinsic motivation must be backed up by institutions that enable those individuals motivated to solve collective-action problems while protecting them from free-riders and untrustworthy partners.

The rules crafted in many common-property regimes tend to increase the probability of long-term interactions among participants. Further, appropriation rights tend to be designed so that actions can be monitored at a relatively low cost by other participants. When individuals can monitor each other, they increase the probability that those who break rules will become known to others in the community. Thus, the rules crafted by robust self-organized, common-property regimes increase the probability that reciprocity will be widely practiced (Lam 1998; Tang 1992; Gibson, McKean, and Ostrom 2000; E. Ostrom 2000).

Evidence that institutions can crowd out intrinsic motivations (as well as crowding them in) has been mounting over the past three decades since Titmuss (1970) first raised this possibility. Psychological research provides evidence that intrinsic motivation is diminished when individuals feel that their own self-determination or self-esteem is adversely affected (Deci and Ryan 1985; Deci, Koestner, and Ryan 1999). In a recent review of this theory, Frey and Jegen (2001, 594–595) identify the psychological conditions when crowding out or crowding in is likely to occur:

1. External interventions *crowd out* intrinsic motivation if the individuals affected perceive them to be *controlling*. In this case, both self-determination and self-esteem suffer, and the individuals react by reducing their intrinsic motivation in the activity controlled.

2. External interventions *crowd in* intrinsic motivation if the individuals concerned perceive it as *supportive*. In this case, self-esteem is fostered, and individuals feel that they are given more freedom to act, thus enlarging self-determination.

A recent meta-analysis of 128 laboratory studies that have explored the effect of extrinsic rewards on intrinsic motivation found that tangible rewards tend to have a substantially negative effect on intrinsic motivation (Deci, Koestner, and Ryan 1999). As the authors conclude:

Although rewards can control people's behavior—indeed, that is presumably why they are so widely advocated—the primary negative effect of rewards is that they tend to forestall self-regulation. In other words, reward contingencies undermine people's taking responsibility for motivating or regulating themselves. When institutions—families, schools, businesses, and athletic teams, for example—focus on the short-term and opt for controlling people's behavior, they may be having a substantially negative long-term effect. (Deci, Koestner, and Ryan 1999, 659)

There are obviously many interactions where "controlling people's behavior" is what is desirable. Individuals, in their role as citizens, are not, however, someone else's employees or agents. Intrinsic values are important sources of citizens' motivation to participate in political life by volunteering to do community service, finding solutions to community problems, and paying taxes.

Paying taxes is obviously one of the most important acts that citizens in a contemporary democratic system make. In a survey of prior studies of taxpayer behavior, Snaveley (1990, 70) concluded that studies repeatedly show "compliance policies which emphasize increasing risk for tax evasion will not in themselves be sufficient to curb cheating." He urges that policymakers adopt a more comprehensive approach to increasing the rate of taxpayer compliance by encouraging the development of "taxpaying values" through education programs that stress service. "Taxpayer decisions are influenced by a combination of economic self-interest factors and noneconomic criteria, therefore, both the coercive and service/values policy approaches are necessary. The choice to be made is one of balancing the two types of policies" (Snaveley 1990, 70).

Paying taxes is obviously one of the methods used by governments at all levels for solving collective-action problems by requiring funds from beneficiaries to provide public goods and protect common-pool resources. When there is a clear relationship between the taxes that an individual pays and the goods and services obtained, taxes also represent an important link between citizens and their officials. In some cases, relatively long-lived local institutions have been seriously challenged by a lack of understanding by officials and by policy analysts of how the institutions operated and why an effective and clear linkage between resource users and their officials is so important. An intriguing example is from Taiwan, where a weakening of this linkage between resource users and their officials has led to a weakening of the links between officials and investment in resources, and in the amount of time that resource users spend monitoring each other's behavior and the condition of the resource.

In Taiwan, a set of seventeen irrigation associations has been responsible for the operation and maintenance of a large number of Taiwan's

irrigation systems. The irrigation associations were corporations organized by farmers, who have paid fees to their local irrigation association for many years. The irrigation association, in turn, took
substantial responsibility for the day-to-day maintenance and operation of local canals, while the Government of Taiwan has undertaken
responsibility for the construction and operation of the larger irrigation
works. The irrigation associations have repeatedly been acclaimed as
major contributors to efficient irrigation in the country and thus to substantial agricultural development (Levine 1977; Moore 1989; Lam
1996).

Taiwan, like other countries whose economies are less and less dependent on agriculture and more dependent on industrial and service
industries, has been trying to find ways of adjusting a variety of economic policies. Furthermore, the rural population still has a significant vote and national politicians have been vying for support in
rural areas. In the early 1990s, politicians argued that farmers faced
hard times and could not make a decent living. As Wai Fung Lam
described, "The government, argued these politicians, should not burden the farmers with irrigation fees. In 1993, after much political negotiation, the government agreed to pay the irrigation fees on behalf of
the farmers" (Lam forthcoming, 7–8). As it turned out, both major national parties supported the cancellation of irrigation fees as no one
wanted to be seen as against the farmer, even though many of the officials familiar with irrigation expressed substantial concern about the
long-term consequences.

The cancellation of the fee has had substantially adverse consequences. Farmers are much less likely to volunteer work activities,
pay voluntary group fees, or pay much attention to what is happening on the canals and in the ecological environment around them as
they had done before (Wade 1995). As one irrigation association official expressed it: "The problem facing irrigation management at the
field level is not simply a matter of finding one or two farmers to serve
as [local group] leaders, the more serious challenge is that nowadays
fewer and fewer farmers have good knowledge of their own systems
and understand how to engage with one another in organizing collective action" (quoted in Lam forthcoming, 12). Maintenance of the systems has been declining precipitously, and the cost of water supply
has been increasing rather than decreasing. Thus, systems that have
been robust for a long period of time have largely been destroyed by
an effort "to help" farmers by reducing the burden on them—a "bur-

den" that they had earlier placed on themselves. Thus, understanding the difference between an internally constituted rule and method for financing services and an externally imposed inducement or sanction is crucial in efforts to enhance the capabilities of citizens to engage in collective action.

In a fascinating study of citizens' willingness to accept a nuclear waste repository in their community—an example of a classic NIMBY (not in my back yard) problem—Frey and Oberholzer-Gee (1997) conducted a survey of citizens in a region of Switzerland where officials were attempting to find a location for such a facility. Respondents were initially asked if they were willing to accept a facility in their community. About half (50.8 percent) of the respondents indicated a willingness to have a nuclear waste facility in their community. When the *same* respondents were asked their willingness to accept such a facility if the Swiss parliament offered substantial compensation to all residents of a community that accepted the facility, the level of willingness dropped dramatically to 24.6 percent. Being offered a financial reward to accept a NIMBY-type project thus led one-quarter of the respondents to change their minds and oppose the placement of the facility in their community.

Some scholars have accepted the possibility that material incentives may crowd out intrinsic motivations in some settings, but are skeptical that the overall effect is negative (Lazear 2000). In other words, if external incentives generate sufficient effort, this may be a more efficient way to motivate citizens and employees than relying as much on intrinsic motivation.

Frey and Benz (2001) report on a recent experiment conducted at the University of Zürich that directly addresses this question. They designed an experiment based on the trust game in which a first player (the principal) may send part of an endowment to a second player (the agent) that is then tripled in value. In the second stage, after being informed of the amount sent by the principal, the agent selects a costly but complementary combination of variables referred to as work quantity and work quality that will return funds to the principal if positive values are chosen. In the base experiment, a profit-maximizing subject should choose the minimal level of work quantity and work quality, since there is no opportunity for the principal to punish the agent for choosing the minimal level. Knowing that a rational egoist will keep all of the funds sent by the principal, the principal should offer the minimum feasible contract in the first place. Prior experiments, however, had already shown that a substantial proportion of subjects in both roles contributed substantially higher-than-minimum levels to the other player (see, for example, Berg, Dickhaut, and McCabe 1995; Kirchler, Fehr, and Evans 1996; E. Ostrom and Walker 2003).

In this experimental design, Frey and Benz added an experimental condition whereby the principal has a possibility to punish the agent for shirking. They found that this material incentive had a dramatic effect on the agent's contribution to the quantity dimension (which could be monitored and punished), but also in regard to the second dimension that could not be monitored and punished. The agents who showed at least a potential propensity to cooperate voluntarily responded to the threatened monitoring and sanctioning of their contribution by strongly reducing their effort in the work dimension that could not be monitored, while modestly increasing the work dimension that could be monitored. Further, the introduction of "performance incentives" led the intrinsically motivated agents to exert significantly lower overall efforts when both dimensions were considered. As Frey and Benz (2001, 19–20) conclude:

The economic incentive in itself changes the frame of the exchange relationship across treatments. Over and above the relative price effect they produce, incentives undermine part of the underlying intrinsic motivation by transforming a relational contract into a purely transactional contract.... Individuals lower their intrinsic efforts in the dimensions where they have the leeway to do so, i.e., in those areas where they do not face the countervailing relative price effect provided by the incentive mechanism.

Ernst Fehr and Bettina Rockenbach (2003) have also conducted a fascinating and relevant experiment using a one-shot trust game. In their experiment, there were three conditions under which a principal could allocate an amount (up to the ten monetary units) to a trustee:

(1) the principal could simply record a "desired back-transfer" that the principal would like to receive back from the trustee,

(2) the principal could indicate that he or she planned to impose a fine of four monetary units if the trustee did not return the desired level, or

(3) the principal could indicate a plan not to waive the imposition of a fine.

Fehr and Rockenbach found that trustees paid back substantial funds under all conditions and used reciprocity in determining the amount they paid back—the more the principal transferred, the more the trustee paid back. Across all investment levels by a principal, however, the trustees sent back more funds when the principal refrained from imposing the fine and returned the lowest amount when the principal imposed the fine. Fehr and Rockenbach conclude that "strong reciprocity" can help explain this paradoxical behavior.

First, refraining from the threat of fining, although the threat is available, could itself be perceived as a fair act, which induces the trustees to increase their cooperation. Second, attempts to use the sanction to enforce an unfair distribution of income may be perceived as hostile acts, inducing the trustees to reduce cooperation. (Fehr and Rockenbach 2003, 139–140)

Prior research in regard to the performance of police officers in field settings has found similar patterns without being able to precisely measure the relative investment. In regard to policing, researchers have argued that performance rewards based on crime fighting primarily reduce the contribution that officers are willing to make in regard to noncrime service to citizens. In light of his extensive research on police, Herman Goldstein concluded that the "traditional methods for measuring the rewarding of efficiency of both individual officers and organizational units place no positive value on the quality of the police response in other than crime-related situations" (cited in Brown 1977, 91). In other words, if an officer is "only rewarded for 'crook catching,' and given no recognition for treating people decently, he simply does not have any incentive to be a public servant" (Brown 1977, 91).

Three important lessons can be derived from these research efforts and other recent theoretical and empirical research based on an assumption of multiple types of players including rational egoists and conditional cooperators who have adopted norms of fairness, reciprocity, and trust. The first lesson is that many individuals are motivated by social norms that affect intrinsic motivation or are at least capable of learning social norms and using them to guide some of these decisions. Second, it is possible for individuals who adopt these norms to survive in repeated situations where they face rational egoists as well as others who share similar norms. So long as they can identify one another, trustworthy fair reciprocators actually achieve higher material rewards over time than rational egoists! In other words, they can flourish. The third lesson is that achieving some reliable information about the trustworthiness of others is crucial to this accomplishment. Consequently, institutions that enhance the level of information that participants obtain about one another is essential to increase the capacity of individuals to solve collective-action problems. Information rules are as important (or more important) in solving collective-action problems than payoff rules, but payoff rules have been the primary focus of a considerable percentage of public policy initiatives. This is not the only problem, however, with the types of public policies that have been recommended—and in some cases implemented—based on currently accepted theory.

9.4   Public Policies Based on the Extant Theory of Collective *In*action

The theory of collective *in*action articulated in 1965 by Mancur Olson was reinforced by the powerful metaphor of the "tragedy of the commons" articulated by Garrett Hardin in 1968 and by considerable work in non-cooperative game theory examining various collective-action problems related both to public goods and to common-pool resource problems. The 1960s and 1970s were an era in which considerable faith existed in the capacity of strong national governments to solve both social and environmental problems through the application of rational planning and the design of incentives to induce positive and deter negative behavior. Many national policies—especially in developing countries—were adopted on the presumption that local users of natural resources were unable to cope effectively with the governance and management of local forests, water resources, wildlife, and fisheries (Gibson 1999; Arnold 1998). In many countries, control over natural resources was turned over to a national bureaucracy charged with the responsibility of devising efficient and effective ways of utilizing these resources and sustaining their long-term productivity (Bromley et al. 1992; Agrawal 1999).

In many settings where individuals have managed small- to medium-sized resources for centuries by drawing on local knowledge and locally crafted institutions, their disempowerment led to a worsening of environmental problems rather than to their betterment (Finlayson and McCay 1998; Wunsch and Olowu 1995; Shivakoti and Ostrom 2002). Weak and frequently corrupt bureaucratic agencies were not able to monitor use of these resources effectively, let alone devise effective plans for their long-term sustainability (Repetto 1986). What had been *de facto* community property became *de jure* government property. In reality, it then became *de facto* open access and unregulated property (Bromley et al. 1992).

Furthermore, citizens are effectively told two rather devastating messages in regard to the long-term development and sustenance of a democratic society. First, public pronouncements stress that only short-term selfish actions are expected from "the common people." When this is the case, solving collective-action problems requires public policies that are based on externally designed and monitored inducements. What we know from social psychological research, however, is that external inducements tend to "crowd out" intrinsic motivations when individuals feel like they have lost control. Or, as Bruno Frey (1997, 44) has stressed, "a constitution designed for knaves tends to drive out civic virtues." When intrinsic motivations are crowded out, substantially more material resources are required to induce effort than when incentives support a sense of control and reliance on intrinsic as well as material incentives. When citizens feel a moral obligation to pay their taxes, it is possible to design a tax collection service that keeps collection costs at a low level. An effective tax system, however, requires that most citizens accept the norm that they should pay taxes. To achieve this objective over the long run, the tax system must function in a fair manner and citizens must be able to trust that others are also contributing their fair share (Rothstein 1998).

The second message contained in the policy literature is that citizens do not have the knowledge or skills needed to design appropriate institutions to overcome collective-action problems. Professional planners are, on the other hand, assumed to have the skills to analyze complex problems, design optimal policies, and implement these policies. Citizens are effectively told that they should be passive observers in the process of design and implementation of effective public policy. The role of citizenship is reduced to voting every few years between competing teams of political leaders. Then, citizens are supposed to sit back and leave the "driving" of the political system to the experts hired by these political leaders. Let us briefly examine whether the assumption that national officials can actually select optimal policies for the regulation of natural resources is realistic.

Over the last fifteen years, colleagues associated with the Workshop in Political Theory and Policy Analysis have collected thousands of written cases of resources managed by local users of inshore fisheries, irrigation systems, and grazing lands (Schlager 1994; Schlager and Ostrom 1992; Blomquist 1992; Agrawal 1994; E. Ostrom, Gardner, and

Walker 1994; Tang 1992; Lam 1998; Hess 1999). In Nepal, for example, we have now collected data about the rules and general management strategies used to govern and manage over 200 irrigation systems including systems that are managed by government agencies (agency managed irrigation systems, or AMIS) as well as those managed by the farmers themselves (farmer managed irrigation systems, or FMIS). We have consistently found that FMIS are able to achieve a higher agricultural yield than AMIS, that water is distributed more equitably in FMIS than AMIS, and that the irrigation systems are better maintained by FMIS than by AMIS (see Lam 1998; Joshi et al. 2000; Shivakoti and Ostrom 2002).

What is striking, moreover, is the difference in how rules are enforced by the farmers themselves on their own systems versus government officials on the government systems. On 23 percent of the AMIS systems, farmers report that government officials are likely to record official infractions. In contrast, farmers on 58 percent of the FMIS report that their own farmer-monitors record infractions observed (Joshi et al. 2000, 76). In addition, fines are more likely to actually be imposed within FMIS than within AMIS. Furthermore, farmers also report that rules are highly likely to be followed 65 percent of the time in FMIS and only 35 percent of the time in AMIS (Joshi et al. 2000, 76). Thus, rules and sanctions devised by the farmers themselves—and monitored by individuals who are responsible to the farmers—are more likely to be enforced and lead to higher levels of rule compliance than rules and sanctions imposed by an external agency. Rules enforced by FMIS crowd in cooperation levels rather than crowding out cooperation.

We are now engaged in a massive ten-country comparative, over-time study of diverse forest institutions (Gibson, McKean, and Ostrom 2000; Poteete and Ostrom 2004). We have again found that resource systems where local users have considerable authority to make their own rules and enforce them are able to increase the level of cooperation achieved as contrasted to systems where rules are imposed from the outside. We are also paying particular attention to the specific rules that individuals use to regulate entry and allocate uses of local resources.

What one learns from this research is the huge variety of rules that are used in practice—many combinations of which are successful. For example, we have identified twenty-seven different types of boundary rules used by self-organized resource regimes (for specifics, see E.

Ostrom 1999). Many of these rules enhance the likelihood that individuals know each other and will be engaged over the long-term with one another. In other words, the endogenously designed rules enhance the conditions needed to solve collective-action problems. We have also identified over 100 authority rules used to allocate resource users' rights to the flow from a resource system (E. Ostrom 1999). Many of these rules focus on time, space, and technology rather than on the quantity of resource flow allocated. Consequently, these rules increase the information that individuals obtain about the actions taken by others at a low cost. Compliance rates increase when individuals feel that others are also following the rules.

The policy of assigning all authority to a central agency to design rules is based on a false conception that there are only a few rules that need to be considered and that only experts know these options and can design optimal policies. Our empirical research strongly challenges this assumption. There are thousands of individual rules that can be used to manage resources. *No one, including a scientifically trained professional staff, can do a complete analysis of any particular situation.*

All policies need to be viewed as experiments (Campbell 1969). The possibility of errors is always present given human limitations. Thus, creating some redundancy in the design of rules for well-bounded local resources (or communities) encourages considerable experimentation essential to discover some of the more successful combinations of rule systems (Low et al. 2001). Further, ecological systems vary from one place to another and from one mix of species to another. The combination of rules that works well for lobster fisheries may be a disaster for deep-sea fisheries (and vice versa) (Wilson et al. 2001). A good combination of rules for a river system that has multiple regulatory devices, such as dams, may be a disaster for a run-of-the-river system, and vice versa.

Thus, instead of proposing highly centralized governance systems, the best empirical evidence we can bring to bear on the question of building sustainable democratic systems for sustainable resource use is to design polycentric systems (V. Ostrom 1987, 1997). A polycentric system has multiple semiautonomous units of governance located at small, regional, national, and now international scales of organization (Keohane and Ostrom 1995). Some of these governance units may be organized in the private sector while others are organized in the public sector. Government is not the only form of governance that humans have devised over the centuries. The essential elements of dynamic polycentric systems are mechanisms for generating information about patterns of interactions and outcomes and mechanisms for oversight and self-correction. A completely decentralized system of small local units without overlap is as incapable of learning and self-correction as a fully centralized system. Large-scale, overlapping units are an essential part of a modern democratic system. However, smaller- to medium-scale units are also a necessary part of an overall polycentric system.

Modern policy analysis needs to catch up with contemporary empirical and theoretical research. The two implicit messages contained in much of contemporary public policy analysis are not only inefficient and ineffective, they are dangerous for the long-term sustainability of democratic systems of governance. The first message undermines the normative foundations of a free society. It basically says that it is okay to be narrowly self-interested and to wait for externally imposed inducements or sanctions before voluntarily contributing to collective action. The second message undermines the positive foundations of a free society by destroying the capacity of citizens to experiment with diverse ways of coping with multiple problems and to learn from this experimentation over time. This message basically says that there is one best way of solving all collective-action problems and it is only knowable to experts. Citizens are viewed as having little to contribute to the design of public policies.

Thus, much of contemporary policy analysis and the policies adopted in many modern democracies crowd out citizenship and voluntary levels of cooperation. They do this by crowding out norms of trust and reciprocity, by crowding out the knowledge of local circumstances, by crowding out the discussion of ethical issues with others who are affected, and by crowding out the experimentation needed to design effective institutions. Crowding out reciprocity, cooperation, and citizenship is a waste of human and material resources and presents a serious challenge to the sustainability of democratic institutions over time.

Notes

An earlier version of this paper was presented at a conference on "Intrinsic Motivation in Law and Business" in Gerzensee, Switzerland, June 18–22, 2001. The author thanks the MacArthur Foundation and the Ford Foundation for financial support; Bruno Frey, Herbert Gintis, and two anonymous reviewers for very useful comments; and Patty Lezotte for her excellent editing of multiple versions of this paper.

References

Agrawal, Arun. 1994. "Rules, Rule Making, and Rule Breaking: Examining the Fit between Rule Systems and Resource Use." In *Rules, Games, and Common-Pool Resources.* Eds. Elinor Ostrom, Roy Gardner, and James M. Walker. Ann Arbor: University of Michigan Press, 267–282.

———. 1999. *Greener Pastures: Politics, Markets, and Community among a Migrant Pastoral People.* Durham, NC: Duke University Press.

Arnold, J. E. M. 1998. *Managing Forests as Common Property.* FAO Forestry Paper #136. Rome, Italy: Food and Agriculture Organization of the United Nations.

Berg, Joyce, John W. Dickhaut, and Kevin McCabe. 1995. "Trust, Reciprocity, and Social History." *Games and Economic Behavior* 10(1):122–142.

Blomquist, William. 1992. *Dividing the Waters: Governing Groundwater in Southern California.* Oakland, CA: ICS Press.

Bowles, Samuel. 1998. "Endogenous Preferences: The Cultural Consequences of Markets and Other Economic Institutions." *Journal of Economic Literature* 36:76–111.

Bromley, Daniel W., David Feeny, Margaret McKean, Pauline Peters, Jere Gilles, Ronald Oakerson, C. Ford Runge, and James Thomson, eds. 1992. *Making the Commons Work: Theory, Practice, and Policy.* Oakland, CA: ICS Press.

Brown, Lee P. 1977. "Bridges over Troubled Waters: A Perspective on Policing in the Black Community." In *Black Perspectives on Crime and the Criminal Justice System: A Symposium.* Ed. Robert L. Woodson. Boston, MA: G. K. Hall, 79–105.

Campbell, Donald T. 1969. "Reforms as Experiments." *American Psychologist* 24:409–429.

Cardenas, Juan-Camilo, John K. Stranlund, and Cleve E. Willis. 2000. "Local Environmental Control and Institutional Crowding-out." *World Development* 28(10):1719–1733.

Chong, D. 1991. *Collective Action and the Civil Rights Movement.* Chicago: University of Chicago Press.

Davis, Douglas D., and Charles A. Holt. 1993. *Experimental Economics.* Princeton, NJ: Princeton University Press.

Dawes, Robyn M., Jeanne McTavish, and Harriet Shaklee. 1977. "Behavior, Communication, and Assumptions about Other People's Behavior in a Commons Dilemma Situation." *Journal of Personality and Social Psychology* 35:1–11.

Deci, E. L., R. Koestner, and R. M. Ryan. 1999. "A Meta-analytic Review of Experiments Examining the Effects of Extrinsic Rewards on Intrinsic Motivation." *Psychological Bulletin* 125.

Deci, E. L., and R. M. Ryan. 1985. *Intrinsic Motivation and Self-Determination in Human Behavior.* New York: Plenum Press.

Fehr, Ernst, and S. Gächter. 1998. "Cooperation and Punishment." Working paper. Zürich, Switzerland: University of Zürich.

Fehr, Ernst, and Bettina Rockenbach. 2003. "Detrimental Effects of Sanctions on Human Altruism." *Nature* 442 (March 13): 137–140.

Finlayson, A. C., and Bonnie J. McCay. 1998. "Crossing the Threshold of Ecosystem Resilience: The Commercial Extinction of Northern Cod." In *Linking Social and Ecological Systems: Management Practices and Social Mechanisms for Building Resilience*. Eds. Fikret Berkes and Carl Folke. Cambridge: Cambridge University Press.

Frey, Bruno S. 1994. "How Intrinsic Motivation Is Crowded Out and In." *Rationality and Society* 6:334–352.

———. 1997. *Not Just for the Money: An Economic Theory of Personal Motivation*. Cheltenham, England: Edward Elgar.

Frey, Bruno S., and Matthias Benz. 2001. "Motivation Transfer Effect." Working paper. Zürich: University of Zürich, Institute for Empirical Research in Economics.

Frey, Bruno S., and Reto Jegen. 2001. "Motivation Crowding Theory: A Survey of Empirical Evidence." *Journal of Economic Surveys* 15:589–611.

Frey, Bruno S., and F. Oberholzer-Gee. 1997. "The Cost of Price Incentives: An Empirical Analysis of Motivation Crowding Out." *American Economic Review* 87:746–755.

Frohlich, Norman, and Joe A. Oppenheimer. 2003. "Optimal Policies and Socially Oriented Behavior: Some Problematic Effects of an Incentive Compatible Device." *Public Choice* 117:273–293.

Gibson, Clark C. 1999. *Politicians and Poachers: The Political Economy of Wildlife Policy in Africa*. New York: Cambridge University Press.

Gibson, Clark C., Margaret McKean, and Elinor Ostrom, eds. 2000. *People and Forests: Communities, Institutions, and Governance*. Cambridge, MA: MIT Press.

Hardin, Garrett. 1968. "The Tragedy of the Commons." *Science* 162:1243–1248.

Hess, Charlotte. 1999. *A Comprehensive Bibliography of Common Pool Resources*. (CD-ROM) Bloomington: Indiana University, Workshop in Political Theory and Policy Analysis.

Isaac, R. Mark, and James M. Walker. 1988. "Group Size Effects in Public Goods Provision: The Voluntary Contributions Mechanism." *Quarterly Journal of Economics* 103:179–199.

Isaac, R. Mark, James M. Walker, and Susan Thomas. 1984. "Divergent Evidence on Free Riding: An Experimental Examination of Some Possible Explanations." *Public Choice* 43:113–149.

Isaac, R. Mark, James M. Walker, and Arlington Williams. 1994. "Group Size and the Voluntary Provision of Public Goods: Experimental Evidence Utilizing Large Groups." *Journal of Public Economics* 54:1–36.

Joshi, Neeraj N., Elinor Ostrom, Ganesh P. Shivakoti, and Wai Fung Lam. 2000. "Institutional Opportunities and Constraints in the Performance of Farmer-Managed Irrigation Systems in Nepal." *Asia-Pacific Journal of Rural Development (APJORD)* 10:67–92.

Kaboolian, L., and B. J. Nelson. 1998. "Creating Organizations of Concord: Lessons for Collective Goods Theory." Working paper. Berkeley: University of California, School of Public Policy and Social Research.

Keohane, Robert O., and Elinor Ostrom, eds. 1995. *Local Commons and Global Interdependence: Heterogeneity and Cooperation in Two Domains*. London: Sage.

Kirchler, E., Ernst Fehr, and R. Evans. 1996. "Social Exchange in the Labor Market: Reciprocity and Trust versus Egoistic Money Maximization." *Journal of Economic Psychology* 17:313–341.

Lam, Wai Fung. 1996. "Institutional Design of Public Agencies and Coproduction: A Study of Irrigation Associations in Taiwan." *World Development* 24(6):1039–1054.

———. 1998. *Governing Irrigation Systems in Nepal: Institutions, Infrastructures, and Collective Action*. Oakland, CA: ICS Press.

———. Forthcoming. "Reforming Taiwan's Irrigation Associations: Getting the Nesting of Institutions Right." In *Asian Irrigation in Transition: Responding to Challenges*. Eds. Ganesh Shivakoti, Douglas Vermillion, Wai Fung Lam, Elinor Ostrom, Ujjwal Pradhan, and Robert Yoder. New Delhi: Sage Publications India.

Lazear, Edward P. 2000. "Performance Pay and Productivity." *American Economic Review* 90(5):1346–1361.

Ledyard, John O. 1995. "Is There a Problem with Public Goods Provision?" In *The Handbook of Experimental Economics*. Eds. John Kagel and Alvin Roth. Princeton, NJ: Princeton University Press, 111–194.

Levine, Gilbert. 1977. "Management Components in Irrigation System Design and Operation." *Agricultural Administration* 4:37–48.

Loveman, M. 1998. "High-Risk Collective Action: Defending Human Rights in Chile, Uruguay, and Argentina." *American Journal of Sociology* 104:477–525.

Low, Bobbi S., Elinor Ostrom, Robert Costanza, and James Wilson. 2001. "Human-Ecosystems Interactions: A Basic Dynamic Integrated Model." In *Institutions, Ecosystems, and Sustainability*. Eds. Robert Costanza, Bobbi S. Low, Elinor Ostrom, and James Wilson. New York: Lewis Publishers, 33–57.

McGinnis, Michael, ed. 1999a. *Polycentric Governance and Development: Readings from the Workshop in Political Theory and Policy Analysis*. Ann Arbor: University of Michigan Press.

———, ed. 1999b. *Polycentricity and Local Public Economies: Readings from the Workshop in Political Theory and Policy Analysis*. Ann Arbor: University of Michigan Press.

———, ed. 2000. *Polycentric Games and Institutions: Readings from the Workshop in Political Theory and Policy Analysis*. Ann Arbor: University of Michigan Press.

Moore, Mike. 1989. "The Fruits and Fallacies of Neoliberalism: The Case of Irrigation Policy." *World Politics* 17(1):733–750.

Offerman, T. 1997. *Beliefs and Decision Rules in Public Goods Games: Theory and Experiments*. Dordrecht, the Netherlands: Kluwer.

Olson, Mancur. 1965. *The Logic of Collective Action: Public Goods and the Theory of Groups*. Cambridge, MA: Harvard University Press.

Ostrom, Elinor. 1990. *Governing the Commons: The Evolution of Institutions for Collective Action*. New York: Cambridge University Press.

———. 1998. "Self-Governance of Common-Pool Resources." In *The New Palgrave Dictionary of Economics and the Law*, vol. 3. Ed. Peter Newman. London: Macmillan Press, 424–433.

———. 1999. "Coping with Tragedies of the Commons." *Annual Review of Political Science* 2:493–535.

———. 2000. "Collective Action and the Evolution of Social Norms." *Journal of Economic Perspectives* 14(3):137–158.

Ostrom, Elinor, and James Walker, eds. 2003. *Trust and Reciprocity: Interdisciplinary Lessons from Experimental Research*. New York: Russell Sage Foundation.

Ostrom, Elinor, Roy Gardner, and James M. Walker. 1994. *Rules, Games, and Common-Pool Resources*. Ann Arbor: University of Michigan Press.

Ostrom, Elinor, James M. Walker, and Roy Gardner. 1992. "Covenants with and without a Sword: Self-Governance is Possible." *American Political Science Review* 86:404–417.

Ostrom, Vincent. 1987. *The Political Theory of a Compound Republic: Designing the American Experiment*. 2d rev. ed. Oakland, CA: ICS Press.

———. 1997. *The Meaning of Democracy and the Vulnerability of Democracies: A Response to Tocqueville's Challenge*. Ann Arbor: University of Michigan Press.

Plott, Charles R. 1979. "The Application of Laboratory Experimental Methods to Public Choice." In *Collective Decision Making: Applications from Public Choice Theory*. Ed. Clifford S. Russell. Baltimore, MD: Johns Hopkins University Press, 137–160.

Poteete, Amy, and Elinor Ostrom. 2004. "Heterogeneity, Group Size, and Collective Action: The Role of Institutions in Forest Management." *Development and Change* 35:435–461.

Repetto, Robert. 1986. *Skimming the Water: Rent-seeking and the Performance of Public Irrigation Systems*. Research report no. 4. Washington, DC: World Resources Institute.

Rothstein, B. 1998. *Just Institutions Matter: The Moral and Political Logic of the Universal Welfare State*. Cambridge: Cambridge University Press.

Schlager, Edella. 1994. "Fishers' Institutional Responses to Common-Pool Resource Dilemmas." In *Rules, Games, and Common-Pool Resources*. Eds. Elinor Ostrom, Roy Gardner, and James M. Walker. Ann Arbor: University of Michigan Press, 247–265.

Schlager, Edella, and Elinor Ostrom. 1992. "Property-Rights Regimes and Natural Resources: A Conceptual Analysis." *Land Economics* 68:249–262.

Sen, Amartya K. 1974. "Choice, Orderings and Morality." In *Practical Reason: Papers and Discussions*. Ed. S. Körner. Oxford: Blackwell.

———. 1977. "Rational Fools: A Critique of the Behavioral Foundations of Economic Theory." *Philosophy and Public Affairs* 6:317–344.

Shivakoti, Ganesh P., and Elinor Ostrom, eds. 2002. *Improving Irrigation Governance and Management in Nepal*. Oakland, CA: ICS Press.

Smith, Vernon L. 1982. "Microeconomic Systems as an Experimental Science." *American Economic Review* 72:923–955.

Snaveley, Keith. 1990. "Governmental Policies to Reduce Tax Evasion: Coerced Behavior versus Services and Values Development." *Policy Sciences* 23:57–72.

Tang, Shui Yan. 1992. *Institutions and Collective Action: Self Governance in Irrigation*. Oakland, CA: ICS Press.

Titmuss, R. M. 1970. *The Gift Relationship*. London: Allen and Unwin.

Varughese, George, and Elinor Ostrom. 2001. "The Contested Role of Heterogeneity in Collective Action: Some Evidence from Community Forestry in Nepal." *World Development* 29(5):747–765.

Wade, Robert. 1995. "The Ecological Basis of Irrigation Institutions: East and South Asia." *World Development* 23(12):2041–2049.

Wilson, James, Robert Costanza, Bobbi S. Low, and Elinor Ostrom. 2001. "Scale Misperceptions and the Spatial Dynamics of a Social-Ecological System." In *Institutions, Ecosystems, and Sustainability*. Eds. Robert Costanza, Bobbi S. Low, Elinor Ostrom, and James Wilson. New York: Lewis Publishers, 59–75.

Wunsch, James S., and Dele Olowu, eds. 1995. *The Failure of the Centralized State: Institutions and Self-Governance in Africa*. 2d ed. Oakland, CA: ICS Press.

Yamagishi, Toshio. 1986. "The Provision of a Sanctioning System as a Public Good." *Journal of Personality and Social Psychology* 51:110–116.

10   Reciprocity and the Welfare State

Christina M. Fong, Samuel Bowles, and Herbert Gintis

A man ought to be a friend to his friend and repay gift with gift. People should meet smiles with smiles and lies with treachery.

From the *Edda*, a thirteenth-century collection of Norse epic verse

10.1   Introduction

The modern welfare state is a remarkable human achievement. In the world's advanced economies, a substantial fraction of total income is regularly transferred from the better off to the less well off, and the governments that preside over these transfers are regularly endorsed by publics (Atkinson 1999). The modern welfare state is thus the most significant case in human history of a voluntary egalitarian redistribution of income among total strangers. What accounts for its popular support?

  We suggest below that a compelling case can be made that people support the modern welfare state because it conforms to deeply held norms of reciprocity and conditional obligations to others. Economists have for the most part offered an alternative (empirically implausible) theory of self-regarding human motivation to explain who votes for redistribution. The most widely accepted model of the demand for redistribution in economics is the *median voter model*, which holds that each voter desires a personal wealth-maximizing level of redistribution. Under appropriate assumptions, it follows that the redistribution implemented by a government elected under a majority rule system is that preferred by the median-income voter. Because the distribution of income is generally skewed to the right (there are a few very rich individuals), the median voter is poorer than the mean voter and will therefore demand a positive level of redistribution.

An important implication of this model is that demand for redistribution decreases as personal income increases (Roberts 1977). But personal income is a surprisingly poor predictor of support for redistribution (Gilens 1999; Fong 2001). A large fraction of the poor oppose income redistribution and a large fraction of the rich support it. Among respondents of a nationally representative American survey (Gallup Organization 1998) who have annual household incomes of at least $150,000 and expect their lives to improve in the next five years, 24 percent responded that the government should "redistribute wealth by heavy taxes on the rich," and 67 percent respond that the "government in Washington, DC, should make every possible effort to improve the social and economic position of the poor." Equally striking is the fact that among the respondents with annual family incomes of less than $10,000 who did not expect to be better off in five years, 32 percent report that the government should *not* redistribute wealth by heavy taxes on the rich, and 23 percent say that the poor should help themselves rather than having the government "make every possible effort to improve the ... position of the poor."[1]

Thus, while self-interest is an important human motive, and income does explain some of the variance in redistributive attitudes, other motives appear to be at work. Abundant evidence from across the social sciences—much of it focusing on the United States with similar findings in smaller quantities from other countries around the world—has shown that when people blame the poor for their poverty, they support less redistribution than when they believe that the poor are poor through no fault of their own. That is, generosity toward the poor is conditional on the belief that the poor work hard (Williamson 1974; Heclo 1986; Farkas and Robinson 1996; Gilens 1999; Miller 1999). For instance, in a 1972 sample of white women in Boston, the perceived work ethic of the poor was a far better predictor of support for aid to the poor than one's family income, religion, education, and a host of other demographic and social background variables (Williamson 1974). Indeed in predicting support for such aid, the addition of a single variable measuring beliefs about work motivation tripled the explanatory power of all the above background variables together. Moffitt, Ribar, and Wilhelm (1998) were among the first economists to report findings on this relationship. They used the General Social Survey, a large nationally representative data set with observations in nearly every year since 1972 to show that those who believe that people get ahead by "lucky breaks or help from others" rather than hard work prefer more spending on welfare. Fong (2001) used nationally representative data from a 1998 Gallup Social Audit to show that the effects of beliefs about the causes of income on demands for redistribution are surprisingly large and cannot be explained by missing measures of self-interest. Alesina, Glaeser, and Sacerdote (2001) have reported related findings from the World Values Survey. Americans have much stronger beliefs that poverty is caused by laziness than Europeans: 60 percent of Americans say the poor are lazy compared to just 27 percent of Europeans. The authors argue that this could be an important explanation for the small size of the American welfare state compared to the average European welfare state.

Our interpretation of these findings is that people are willing to help the poor, but they withdraw support when they perceive that the poor cheat or fail to cooperate by not trying hard enough to be self-sufficient and morally upstanding. Within economics, our view is most similar to the taxpayer resentment view of the demand for redistribution modeled by Besley and Coate (1992) and the effect of reciprocity sentiments on redistributive public finance by Serge Kolm (1984).[2] Our view is also consistent with interpretations by Heclo (1986) and Gilens (1999), who cite evidence that Americans support a wide array of benefits for the poor and are primarily opposed to "welfare," presumably because "welfare" refers to means-tested cash assistance, which may be perceived as a program that benefits able-bodied adults who choose to have children out of wedlock and prefer not to work. Our interpretation is also compatible with equity theory and attribution theory. According to equity theory, people should receive resources from a system that are proportional to their contributions (Walster, Walster, and Bersheid 1978; Deutsch 1985; Miller 1999). Attribution theorists argue that people are less likely to help someone if they determine that the person is individually responsible for his or her outcome (Weiner 1995; Skitka and Tetlock 1993).

Economists have been skeptical of non-selfish models for several reasons. First, there could be unmeasured self-interest variables that explain the support for redistribution. In particular, those with low-mean, high-variance incomes may be more likely to think that poverty is due to bad luck and also more likely to demand redistribution out of self-interest for insurance against a low income. We soundly reject this hypothesis in section 10.4.

Second, people who think that effort plays a major role in income generation may be concerned about the incentive effects of taxation or transfers rather than the "worthiness" of recipients (Piketty 1995). We do have two pieces of evidence, however, that incentive costs cannot fully explain attitudes towards redistribution. One is that were incentive costs of taxation the problem, those who believe that effort is important should support less government spending in general. Yet, as we show in section 10.4, the belief that effort is important to getting ahead in life is negatively correlated with support for redistribution and positively correlated with support for military spending. Another is that, as described in section 10.3, subjects in a behavioral experiment on charitable giving to welfare recipients gave significantly more money when they were randomly paired with a welfare recipient who said she would like to work than when randomly paired with a welfare recipient who said she would not like to work. There were no disincentive costs in this experiment, so some other interpretation is necessary.

This experimental result also addresses a third concern that economists have raised: People who do not want to give to the poor may say that the poor are lazy to justify their selfishness. This cannot explain why randomly assigned treatment conditions in the charity experiment just described had significant effects on giving to welfare recipients.

Concern about the "undeserving poor" is pronounced in the United States, but is far from absent in Europe. In figure 10.1 we show that in twelve European countries, those who say that poverty is the result of laziness support less government redistribution and are less concerned about unemployment, poverty, and inequality than those who do not. The data are from a Eurobarometer survey conducted in 1989 (Reif and Melich 1993), representative of the population aged fifteen and over in the twelve European Union countries of that time. Of the data set's 11,819 respondents, we use the 8,239 who answered all of the questions included in our analysis. Our dependent variable is the sum of responses to four questions about

(1) the importance of fighting unemployment;

(2) the importance of fighting poverty;

(3) the importance of reducing differences between regions within the country by helping regions that are less developed or in difficulties; and

(4) whether the public authorities in the country do all that they should for poor people.

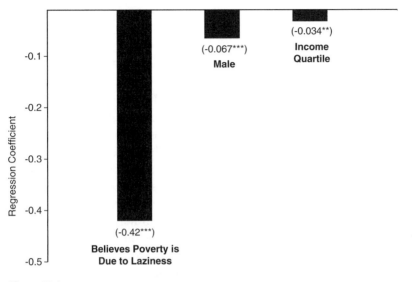

Figure 10.1
Explaining concern about poverty using data from twelve European countries.
Note: Bars represent ordinary least squares coefficients (value of the estimated coefficient
is in parentheses) predicting concern about poverty. The dependent variable is standardized so that the estimated coefficient represents the effect of the variable indicated on
concern about poverty measured in standard deviation units. The equation also includes
age and country dummy variables. Significance levels are based on robust standard
errors that allow for clustered errors within countries. This regression uses sample
weights, although the results are not sensitive to them. There are 8239 observations,
$R^2 = .161$. ***Significant at the 1 percent level. **Significant at the 5 percent level.

The measure increases in concern about poverty, unemployment, inequality, and the belief that the public authorities do not "do enough
for poor people." For simplicity, we refer to this composite measure as
"concern about poverty."

Our independent variable of primary interest is the belief that poverty is caused by laziness rather than being caused by bad luck, injustice, or no reason at all, or that poverty is inevitable.[3] The other
variables included in the regression are family income quartiles, sex,
and age. Note that item 4 in our dependent variable is explicitly country specific. Cross-country comparisons of a question like this are of little value because people in a country with a generous redistribution
system may care very much about poverty but believe that their own
government is doing a good job of addressing it. The other three items
used to construct our dependent measure are subject to the same concern, albeit to a lesser extent. To account for the effects of unmeasured

differences between countries, we use fixed effects to allow for country differences in mean responses.

The results, presented in figure 10.1, show that those who say that poverty is caused by laziness are less concerned about poverty than the rest of the respondents by a 0.42 standard deviation. In contrast, family income has a very modest effect.[4] The difference in concern about poverty between the richest and poorest quartiles is less than a quarter as great as the difference between those who think that poverty is due to laziness and those who do not. The respondent's sex has a significant effect on concern about poverty (independent of income and the other regressors), with men being less concerned than women.

We do not doubt that self-regarding motives often underpin apparently generous actions. Rather, we suggest that they do not always do so. Understanding egalitarian politics today requires a reconsideration of *Homo economicus*, the unremittingly self-regarding actor of economic theory. We do not wish to replace the textbook self-regarding actor, however, with an equally one-dimensional altruistic actor willing to make unconditional and personally costly contributions to the less well off. Rather, we believe that *strong reciprocity* better explains the motivations behind support for the welfare state. By "strong reciprocity," we mean a propensity to cooperate and share with others similarly disposed, even at personal cost, and a willingness to punish those who violate cooperative and other social norms, even when punishing is personally costly and cannot be expected to entail net personal gains in the future (see chapter 1).

Strong reciprocity goes considerably beyond self-interested forms of cooperation, which we term "weak reciprocity" and which include market exchange and tit-for-tat behavior—what biologists call "reciprocal altruism."

As we will see, all three of our *personae—Homo economicus*, the strong reciprocator, and even the pure altruist—are represented in most groups of any size. For this reason, egalitarian policymaking, no less than the grand projects of constitutional design, risks irrelevance if it ignores the irreducible heterogeneity of human motivations. The problem of institutional design is not, as the classical economists thought, that uniformly self-regarding individuals be induced to interact in ways producing desirable aggregate outcomes. Instead, it is that a mix of motives—self-regarding, reciprocal, and altruistic—interact in ways that prevent self-regarding individuals from exploiting generous individuals and unraveling cooperation when it is beneficial.

10.2   The Origins of Reciprocity

Earlier chapters of this book presented the experimental evidence for strong reciprocity. Historical evidence also supports the notion that support for redistribution is often based on strong reciprocity motives. In his *Injustice: The Social Bases of Obedience and Revolt*, Barrington Moore Jr. (1978, 21) sought the common motivational bases—"general conceptions of unfair and unjust behavior"—for the moral outrage fueling struggles for justice that have recurred throughout human history. "There are grounds," he concludes from his wide-ranging investigation

For suspecting that the welter of moral codes may conceal a certain unity of original form ... a general ground plan, a conception of what social relationships ought to be. It is a conception that by no means excludes hierarchy and authority, where exceptional qualities and defects can be the source of enormous admiration and awe. At the same time, it is one where services and favors, trust and affection, in the course of mutual exchanges, are ideally expected to find some rough balancing out. (Moore 1978, 4–5, 509)

Moore termed the general ground plan he uncovered "the concept of reciprocity—or better, mutual obligation, a term that does not imply equality of burdens or obligations ..." (Moore 1978, 506) In similar manner, James Scott (1976) analyzed agrarian revolts, identifying violations of the "norm of reciprocity" as one the essential triggers of insurrectionary motivations.

Casual observation of everyday life, ethnographic and paleoanthropological accounts of hunter-gatherer foraging bands from the late Pleistocene to the present, and historical narratives of collective struggles have combined to convince us that strong reciprocity is a powerful and ubiquitous motive.

10.3   Experimental Evidence on Unilateral Income Transfers

Behavioral experiments with human subjects provide overwhelming evidence against *Homo economicus*. Many of these experiments have been described in chapters 1 and 5 of this book, and will not be repeated here. However, there is additional evidence dealing more directly with charitable redistribution. Consider, for instance, the *dictator game*. In this game, one of two mutually anonymous players, the "proposer," is given a sum of money (typically $10), asked to choose any part of the sum to give to the second player, and permitted to keep the rest. *Homo economicus* gives nothing in this situation, whereas in actual experimental situations, a majority of proposers give positive amounts, typically ranging from 20 percent to 60 percent of the total (Forsythe et al. 1994).

Using dictator games, researchers have shown that people are more generous to individuals they perceive to be worthy recipients and bargaining partners. For example, Eckel and Grossman (1996) found that subjects in dictator games gave roughly three times as much when the recipient was the American Red Cross than when it was an anonymous subject. More recently, Fong (2004) conducted charity games (*n*-donor dictator games) in which several dictators were paired with a single real-life welfare recipient. The treatment conditions were randomly assigned and differed according to whether the welfare recipient expressed strong or weak work preferences on a survey that she completed. Dictators read the welfare recipients' surveys just prior to making their offers. Dictators who were randomly assigned to welfare recipients who expressed strong work preferences gave significantly more than dictators who were assigned to recipients that expressed weak work preferences. These experiments provide evidence for our view that strong reciprocity is a common motivation.

Another result that is consistent with reciprocity is that cooperating and punishing behavior are very sensitive to the situation framing the interaction. In early research on what is known as *inequality aversion*, Loewenstein, Thompson, and Bazerman (1989) found that distributional preferences are sensitive to social context. They asked subjects to imagine themselves in various hypothetical situations. In one, the subject and another college student share the gains and losses from a jointly produced product. In another, the subject and a neighbor split the profit from selling a vacant lot between their homes. In a third, the subject is a customer dividing the proceeds from an expired rebate or the cost of repairs with a salesperson.

These scholars found that subjects care about relative payoffs even more than they care about their absolute payoffs. They also found that, controlling for the subjects' own payoffs, earning less than the other person had a strong negative effect on utility in all situations and relationship types. However, an effect on utility of earning *more* than the other person (referred to as advantageous inequality) was also present and depended on the relationship and the situation. Subjects disliked advantageous inequality if the relationship was friendly. However, if the relationship was unfriendly, advantageous inequality had little effect on their satisfaction level. Interestingly, these researchers found that subjects preferred advantageous inequality in the customer/salesperson scenario, but disliked it in the other two scenarios (producing a product and splitting the proceeds from an empty lot).

Although there may be many additional factors contributing to the context dependence of behavior, the finding that subjects are more averse to advantageous inequality (or, equivalently, desire higher relative payoffs for the other subject) in friendly relationships than in unfriendly relationships is fully consistent with our interpretation of reciprocity. In another example, fraternity brothers at the University of California–Los Angeles (UCLA) were asked to rank outcomes in a Prisoner's Dilemma situation under five different scenarios: interacting with a fellow fraternity brother, a member of another (unnamed) fraternity, a non-fraternity student at UCLA, a student from the nearby rival University of Southern California, and an officer from the UCLA Police Department. They showed a strong preference for mutual cooperation over defection against one's partner when playing with fraternity brothers, with the rankings reversing with increasing social distance—they were as willing to exploit the University of Southern California students as the UCLA police (Kollock 1997)!

10.4   Survey Evidence

These results support our interpretation of attitudinal survey results, which show that people support more government redistribution to the poor if they think that poverty is caused by bad luck rather than laziness. Our interpretation of this is that because of strong reciprocity, people wish to help those who try to make it on their own, but for reasons beyond their own control cannot. People wish to punish—or withhold assistance from—those who are able but unwilling to work hard. However, there are several alternative explanations for the effect of beliefs about the worthiness of the poor that are consistent with pure self-interest. In this section, we test these alternative explanations and find that self-interest alone cannot explain the relationship between beliefs about the worthiness of the poor and support for redistribution. These results are based on Fong (2001).

We use the 1998 Gallup Poll Social Audit Survey, "Haves and Have-Nots: Perceptions of Fairness and Opportunity," a randomly selected national sample of 5,001 respondents. In each test, we use the set of all individuals who responded to all of the questions used in the regression, unless noted otherwise.[5]

Relative to other commonly used surveys, the Gallup survey has a large sample size for a large number of questions on inequality and distribution. The sample size permits running regressions with full controls on narrow segments of the sample—namely, high income and low income sub-samples. There are several self-interest measures that include not only the usual objective socioeconomic variables, but also subjective measures of economic well-being and future expectations. These may widen the net intended to capture self-interest.

To construct our dependent variable, we added the responses to the five questions below, signing the responses so that the measure increases in support for redistribution.

1. People feel differently about how far a government should go. Here is a phrase which some people believe in and some don't. Do you think our government should or should not redistribute wealth by heavy taxes on the rich? (response categories: should, should not)

2. Some people feel that the government in Washington, DC, should make every possible effort to improve the social and economic position of the poor. Others feel that the government should not make any special effort to help the poor, because they should help themselves. How do you feel about this? (response categories: government should help the poor, the poor should help themselves)

3. Which one of the following groups do you think has the greatest responsibility for helping the poor: churches, private charities, the government, the families and relatives of poor people, the poor themselves, or someone else? (response categories: groups other than the poor, the poor themselves)

4. Do you feel that the distribution of money and wealth in this country today is fair, or do you feel that the money and wealth in this country should be more evenly distributed among a larger percentage of the people? (response categories: distribution is fair, should be more evenly distributed)

5. Do you think that the fact that some people in the United States are rich and others are poor (1) represents a problem that needs to be fixed, or (2) is an acceptable part of our economic system? (response categories: problem, acceptable)

Two sets of measures of the causes of income are used in this study. The first contains two questions concerning the importance of effort and luck in causing wealth and poverty and one question on whether or not there is plenty of opportunity to work hard and get ahead in America today. The second set is a series of questions about the importance of various factors, including race and sex, for getting ahead in life.

Self-interest is measured by income and other variables likely to predict current and future tax obligations and current and future reliance on social insurance or redistribution programs. In figures 10.2 and 10.3, we control for self-interest by including income, race, sex,

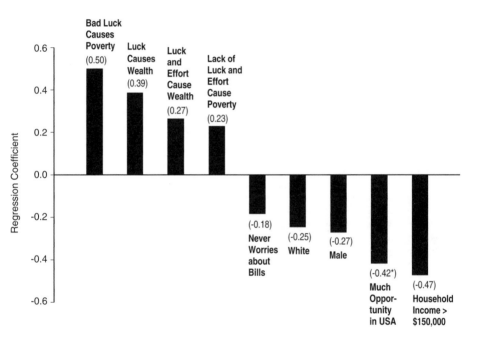

Figure 10.2

Determinants of the support for redistribution.

Note: Bars represent ordinary least squares coefficients (value of the estimated coefficient is in parentheses) predicting support for redistribution. The dependent variable is standardized so that the estimated coefficient represents the effect of the variable indicated on concern about poverty measured in standard deviation units. The equation also includes: seven additional income dummies, age, a dummy for attended college, and dummies for "worries about bills most of the time," and "worries about bills some of the time." The omitted category for household income is less than $10,000 per year. The omitted categories for causes of poverty and wealth are "lack of effort" and "strong effort" respectively. To simplify the presentation of race effects, we use the sample of white and black respondents only. Omitted category for "worries about bills" is "all of the time." There are 3417 observations. $R^2 = .260$. This regression uses sample weights, although the results are not sensitive to them. We use robust standard errors. All coefficients are significant at the 1 percent level.

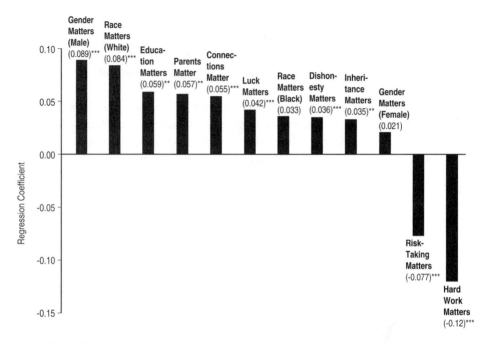

Figure 10.3
Effects on the support for redistribution of beliefs about the importance of various factors in getting ahead in life.
Notes: Bars represent ordinary least squares coefficients (value of the estimated coefficient is in parentheses) predicting support for redistribution. The dependent variable is standardized. Independent variables are the respondent's belief in the importance of the factor shown to getting ahead in life. The coefficients are the estimated effects of a one-point increase in the response scale for a given belief on standard deviations of support for redistribution. Regressions also include all of the self-interest measures included in figure 10.2. The number of observations was 3,437. This regression uses sample weights, although the results were not sensitive to them. $R^2 = .184$. ***Significant at the 1 percent level. **Significant at the 5 percent level.

education, age, and the frequency with which respondents worry about meeting family expenses in the regressions.[6]

In figure 10.2, we present results from an ordinary least squares regression that predicts support for redistribution using two sets of variables: (1) beliefs about the causes of wealth and poverty, and (2) the measures of self-interest. To facilitate interpreting the coefficients, we have standardized the dependent variable to have a mean of zero and a standard deviation of one. The interpretation is as follows: those who say that bad luck alone causes poverty are a 0.50 standard deviation higher in their support for redistribution than those who think lack of effort alone causes poverty. Those who think that good luck alone causes wealth are a 0.39 standard deviation higher on the support for redistribution scale than those who think effort alone causes wealth, and people who respond that there is plenty of opportunity in the United States to get ahead scored a 0.42 standard deviation lower in support for redistribution than people who do not think there is plenty of opportunity.

Measures of self-interest also have significant effects in the expected direction on support for redistribution. Those who are in the highest income category (annual household income greater than $150,000) scored a 0.47 standard deviation lower on support for redistribution than those in the lowest income category (income less than $10,000). Those who almost never worry about bills are significantly less supportive of redistribution than those who worry all of the time. The self-interest variables are jointly significant at the 1 percent level.

The effect of being white is large and highly significant, and the effect of being male is even larger. At first glance, this may appear to contradict an empirical regularity that among the socioeconomic variables, race has one of the largest and most reliable effects while sex does not. However, if we omit the beliefs variables, the magnitude of the effects of race and sex increase and become roughly equivalent in size. This is consistent with the argument, put forth by Gilens (1999), that the effect of race is mediated by beliefs about the characteristics of the poor, especially poor blacks.

If we take the view that all of the socioeconomic variables together capture self-interest, then the effect of self-interest appears considerably larger than if we simply consider the size of the coefficient on income. Using ordered probit to estimate similar equations, Fong (2001) has estimated the sizes of the effects of the independent variables on the probabilities of scoring in each of the six categories of the support for redistribution scale. In an equation that controls for both beliefs about the causes of wealth and poverty and a large number of objective and subjective measures of and proxies for self-interest, the effects of being in the least privileged category (non-white, female, single, union member, part-time worker, no college education, in lowest income category, household size greater than four, and almost always worries about bills) as opposed to the most privileged are similar in size to the effects of believing that luck alone causes wealth and poverty, as opposed to believing that effort alone causes wealth and poverty.

Could our results be driven by missing self-interest variables? People who believe that poverty is caused by bad luck or circumstances beyond individual control may be those who have low-mean, high-variance incomes. Such individuals may have higher expectations of needing government assistance in the future, and therefore demand more redistribution purely out of self-interest. For similar reasons, those who believe that the poor are lazy may simply be people who have higher-mean, lower-variance incomes and therefore less self-interest in redistribution. If this is true, then the effect of these beliefs on redistributive policy preferences may have nothing to do with the psychology of holding the poor accountable and blaming them for their outcomes. It would simply be the case that beliefs about the causes of income are correlated with a person's financial position, which in turn determines his or her demand for redistribution.

If the beliefs about the causes of poverty and wealth operate through self-interest, then they should have no effect among people at the top and bottom of the distribution of income who expect to remain there. Those who do not expect to benefit should demand no redistribution at all, regardless of their beliefs about the causes of income, while those who expect to benefit should register the highest degree of support for redistribution regardless of their beliefs about the causes of income. To test whether this is the case, we use sub-samples of (1) individuals with incomes over $75,000 per year who expect to be better off in five years than they are today and who worry about bills less often than "all of the time"; (2) individuals with incomes under $10,000 per year; and (3) individuals with incomes under $30,000 per year who do not expect to be better off in five years than they are today and who worry about bills more often than "almost never."

In all of these sub-samples, a quite inclusive set of measures capturing self-interest is jointly insignificant. That is, we cannot reject the hypothesis that every single socioeconomic variable has a coefficient of zero. Yet, beliefs about roles of luck, effort, and opportunity in generating life outcomes were jointly significant for all three sub-samples and in most cases were individually significant in the expected directions as well.[7] Therefore, among those individuals who are poor and do not expect their lives to improve and those individuals who believe that lack of effort causes poverty oppose redistribution. Analogously, support for redistribution is high among those securely well off respondents who believe that poverty is the result of bad luck.

In another test of self-interest, we use questions on the respondents' views on the importance of various factors, including a person's race and sex, to getting ahead in life. Figure 10.3 presents an ordinary least squares regression of support for redistribution on the importance of various determinants of success, controlling for the same socioeconomic variables included in the regression presented in figure 10.2. Beliefs that "willingness to take risks" and "hard work and initiative" explain "why some people get ahead and succeed in life and others do not" have highly significant negative effects on support for redistribution. Beliefs that education, people's parents, connections, good luck, dishonesty, and inherited money explain why some people get ahead have significant positive effects on support for redistribution. In addition, beliefs that a person's sex is important to getting ahead have significant positive effects on support for redistribution for men, while the effect of this belief for women is also positive but smaller and statistically insignificant. Beliefs that a person's race is important to getting ahead in life have significant positive effects for whites, while the effect of these beliefs for blacks is positive but smaller and statistically insignificant.

If people think that a person's race and sex are important to getting ahead in life, then the effects of these beliefs on self-interested demand for redistribution should operate in opposite directions for those who expect to benefit and those who expect to lose from racial or gender discrimination.[8] In other words, whites who think race is important to getting ahead will expect to be economically advantaged and would have fewer self-interested reasons to support redistribution than whites who think that race does not matter. Similar reasoning holds for men who think a person's sex is important to getting ahead in life.

However, using an alternative form of the same regression presented in figure 10.3, we find that the effect of believing that a person's sex is important to getting ahead in life is significantly more positive for men than it is for women. This interaction effect is significant at the 1 percent level (unreported). As we have seen, this is inconsistent with self-interest, because men and whites with these beliefs would expect to benefit from discrimination and hence have less likelihood of benefiting from redistributive programs.

Concerns about the incentive effects of taxation are a final mechanism through which self-interest might cause beliefs that the poor are lazy and the rich industrious to decrease the demand for redistribution.

When earned income is more sensitive to work effort, taxation may cause greater effort disincentives and reduce aggregate income. If so, then beliefs about the roles of effort, luck, and opportunity in generating income may affect the level of support for redistribution through concerns about incentive costs of redistribution (Piketty 1995). This type of incentive concern should not apply only to redistribution, but to any tax-funded expenditure, including expenditures such as national defense.

According to this tax-cost hypothesis, if beliefs that income is caused by factors under individual control decrease demand for redistribution, then they should decrease demand for other kinds of tax-funded expenditures (including defense spending) as well. But there is no evidence that tax cost concerns adversely affect the demand for public expenditures. Using the 1990 General Social Survey, we estimate ordered probit regressions predicting support for spending on welfare, national defense, halting the rising crime rate, and dealing with drug addiction, respectively.[9] The independent variables are beliefs that the poor are poor because of lack of effort, and five demographic variables (income, education, race, sex, and age). In the samples reported above, the belief that the lack of effort causes poverty has a highly significant negative effect on support for redistribution. However, these same beliefs have no effect on support for spending on crime or drug addiction, and they have a significant positive effect on support for spending on defense. If these beliefs simply measure tax cost concerns, then their effect on support for all of these expenditure items should have been negative.

However, even more convincing evidence on this point comes from the experiment including actual welfare recipients described earlier in this section. There were no disincentive costs in this experiment, yet student subjects gave more to the welfare recipients with the stronger work commitments. These results lend support to previously made hypotheses about well-known patterns in survey data. Heclo (1986) reports that 81 percent of survey respondents favor public funding for child care if the mother is a widow who is trying to support three children, while only 15 percent favor such funding when the mother has never married and is not interested in working. Heclo also reports the results of a survey in which the wording of a question about support for public redistribution was manipulated so that some subjects were asked about spending on "welfare" while others were asked about spending on "assistance for the poor," or "caring for the poor." In that experiment, 41 percent of respondents stated that there is too much spending on welfare and 25 percent stated that there is too little. By contrast, only 11 percent and 7 percent of the respondents said that there is too much spending on assistance for and caring for the poor, respectively, and 64 percent and 69 percent said that there is too little spending on assistance for and caring for the poor, respectively. In a similar vein, Page and Shapiro (1992) report that support for social security spending has been very high and stable over time, while support for spending on welfare has been consistently low. The interpretation commonly given for findings such as these is that people are less generous to recipients who they think are not working when they could and should be, or who are otherwise considered to be in questionable moral standing (Heclo 1986; Gilens 1999). We have shown that these findings cannot be explained away by a fuller and more rigorous account of self-interest.

10.5   Strong Reciprocity and the Welfare State: Unhappy Marriage?

The following generalizations sum up the relevance of the experimental, survey, and other data to the problem of designing and sustaining programs to promote economic security and eliminate poverty. First, people exhibit significant levels of generosity, even towards strangers. Second, beliefs about the causes of high and low incomes matter. Third, people contribute to public goods and cooperate to collective endeavors and consider it unfair to free-ride on the contributions and efforts of others. Fourth, people punish free riders at substantial costs to themselves, even when they cannot reasonably expect future personal gain from these actions of punishment (chapters 1, 5–8, this volume).

It would not be difficult to design a system of income security and economic opportunity that would tap rather than offend the motivations expressed in these four generalizations. Such a system would be generous towards the poor, rewarding those individuals who perform socially valued work and who seek to improve their chances of engaging in such work, as well as to those individuals who are poor through accidents not of their own making, such as illness and job displacement.

While strong reciprocity may support egalitarianism, it may also help explain opposition to welfare state policies in some of the advanced market economies during the past few decades. Specifically, in light of the empirical regularities outlined above, we suspect the following to be true as well: Egalitarian policies that reward people independent of whether and how much they contribute to society are considered unfair and are not supported, even if the intended recipients are otherwise worthy of support and even if the incidence of noncontribution in the target population is rather low. This would explain the opposition to many welfare measures for the poor, particularly since such measures are thought to have promoted various social pathologies. At the same time it explains the continuing support for Social Security and Medicare in the United States, since the public perception is that the recipients are "deserving" and the policies are thought not to support what are considered antisocial behaviors. The public goods experiments reported in chapter 5 of this volume are also consistent with the notion that tax resistance by the nonwealthy may stem from their perception that the well-to-do are not paying their fair share.

A striking fact about the decline in the support for the former Aid to Families with Dependent Children, food stamps, and other means-tested social support programs in the United States, however, is that overwhelming majorities oppose the *status quo*, whatever their income, race, or personal history with such programs. This pattern of public sentiment, we think, can be accounted for in terms of the principle of strong reciprocity.

We rely mainly on two studies. The first study, Farkas and Robinson (1996), analyze data collected in late 1995 by Public Agenda, a nonprofit, nonpartisan research organization. The authors conducted eight focus groups around the country, then did a national survey involving half-hour interviews of 1,000 randomly selected Americans plus a national oversample of 200 African-Americans. The second study, political scientist Martin Gilens' *Why Americans Hate Welfare*, is an analysis and review of several polls executed during the 1990s and earlier by various news organizations.[10]

In the Public Agenda survey, 63 percent of respondents thought the welfare system should be eliminated or "fundamentally overhauled" while another 34 percent thought it should be "adjusted somewhat." Only 3 percent approved of the system as is (Farkas and Robinson 1996, 9). Even among respondents from households receiving welfare, only 9 percent expressed basic approval of the system, while 42 percent wanted a fundamental overhaul and an additional 46 percent wanted some adjustments.

The cost of welfare programs cannot explain this opposition. While people generally overstate the share of the Federal budget devoted to welfare (Farkas and Robinson 1996, 9), this cannot account for the observed opposition.[11] Farkas and Robinson note that

By more than four to one (65 percent to 14 percent), Americans say the most upsetting thing about welfare is that "it encourages people to adopt the wrong lifestyle and values," not that "it costs too much tax money." ... Of nine possible reforms presented to respondents—ranging from requiring job training to paying surprise visits to make sure recipients deserve benefits—reducing benefits ranked last in popularity.

The cost, apparently, is not the problem. In focus groups:

Participants invariably dismissed arguments about the limited financial costs of welfare in almost derisive terms as irrelevant and beside the point. (Farkas and Robinson 1996, 9–10)

Nor can the perception of fraud account for this opposition. It is true that 64 percent of respondents (and 66 percent of respondents on welfare) believe welfare fraud is a serious problem. However most do not consider it more serious than in other government programs, and only 35 percent of survey respondents would be more "comfortable with welfare" if fraud were eliminated (Farkas and Robinson 1996, 11–12).

In commenting on this fact Martin Gilens (1999, 1, 2) observes that "Politics is often viewed, by élites at least, as a process centered on the question 'who gets what.' For ordinary Americans, however, politics is more often about 'who *deserves* what' and the welfare state is no exception." In the Public Agenda study, respondents overwhelmingly consider welfare to be unfair to working people and addictive to recipients. By a more than five-to-one margin (69 percent to 13 percent overall, and 64 percent to 11 percent for people receiving welfare), respondents say that recipients abuse the system (for instance, by not looking for work) rather than actually cheating the system (for example, by collecting multiple benefits) (Farkas and Robinson 1999, 12). Moreover, 68 percent of respondents and (59 percent of welfare-receiving respondents) think that welfare is "passed on from generation to generation, creating a permanent underclass." In the same vein, 70 percent of respondents (and 71 percent of welfare-receiving respondents) say welfare makes it "financially better for people to stay on welfare than to get a job," 57 percent (62 percent of welfare recipients) think welfare encourages "people to be lazy" and 60 percent (64 percent of welfare recipients) say the welfare system "encourages people to have kids out of wedlock." (Farkas and Robinson 1999, 14–15) Note that the welfare recipients and other citizens hold similar views in this respect.

That the respondents are correct in thinking that the welfare state cause these behaviors is beside the point. Whether or not welfare *causes* (for example) out of wedlock births or fosters an unwillingness to work, citizens object that the system provides financial support for those who undertake these socially disapproved behaviors. Their desire is to bear witness against the behavior and to disassociate themselves from it, whether or not their actions can change it.

Racial stereotyping and opposition to welfare are closely associated. The public agenda survey shows that whites are much more likely than African-Americans to attribute negative attributes to welfare recipients and much more likely to blame an individual's poverty on lack of effort. Gilens (1999) writes that the survey data show,

> For most white Americans, race-based opposition to welfare is not fed by ill-will toward blacks, nor is it based on whites' desire to maintain their economic advantages over African Americans. Instead race-based opposition to welfare stems from the specific perception that, as a group, African Americans are not committed to the work ethic.

There is some evidence that people are more tolerant of redistributions to their own ethnic and racial categories than they are of redistribution to other ethnic or racial categories. Erzo Luttmer (2001) found for a U.S. sample that individuals are more opposed to welfare if they live in neighborhoods where a higher percentage of welfare recipients are of a different race. Luttmer's findings are consistent with our reciprocity interpretation of redistributive politics, in light of the evidence that when people identify with a social group, they are more likely to blame outgroup members (holding these members individually responsible) for their bad outcomes and behaviors and to give outgroup members little credit (holding factors other than the outgroup member's voluntary control responsible) for their good outcomes and behaviors (Brewer and Miller 1996). However, the salience of race in Luttmer's U.S. data may not be as pronounced in other cultural contexts, since the characteristics that determine who are "insiders" and who are "outsiders" is culturally specific. Taking account of the *fact* that many Americans see the current welfare system as a violation of deeply held reciprocity norms does not require that policy makers adopt punitive measures and stingy budgets for the poor. Indeed, the public strongly supports income support measures when asked in ways that make the deserving nature of the poor clear: a 1995 New York Times/CBS poll, for instance, found that twice as many agreed as disagreed that "it is the responsibility of the government to take care of people who can't take care of themselves."

10.6   Conclusion

Like Petr Kropotkin (1989[1903]) a century ago, we find compelling evidence for the force of human behavioral predispositions to act both generously and reciprocally rather than self-interestedly in many social situations. While many economists have failed to appreciate the practical importance of these predispositions in policy matters, their salience was not missed by Frederick Hayek (1978, 18, 20):

> [The] demand for a just distribution ... is ... an atavism, based on primordial emotions. And it is these widely prevalent feelings to which prophets (and) moral philosophers ... appeal by their plans for the deliberate creation of a new type of society.

If we are right, economists have misunderstood both the support for the welfare state and the revolt against welfare (where it has occurred), attributing the latter to selfishness by the electorate rather than the failure of many programs to tap powerful commitments to fairness and generosity and the fact that some programs appear to violate deeply held reciprocity norms. Egalitarians have been successful in appealing to the more elevated human motives precisely when they have shown that dominant institutions violate norms of reciprocity and may be replaced by institutions more consistent with these norms.

To mobilize rather than offend reciprocal values, public policies should recognize that there is substantial support for generosity towards the less well off as long as they have tried to make an effort to improve their situation and are in good moral standing. The task of politically viable egalitarian policy design might thus begin by identifying those behaviors that entitle an individual to reciprocation. Among these behaviors in the United States today would be saving when one's income allows, working hard, and taking risks in both productive endeavors and schooling. Persistent poverty is often the result of low returns to socially admired behaviors: low wages for hard work, a low rate of return on savings, costly access to credit for those wishing to engage in uncertain entrepreneurial activities, and educational environments so adverse as to frustrate even the most diligent student. Policies designed to raise the returns of these activities when undertaken by the less well off would garner widespread support. A second principle of reciprocity-based policy design should be to insure individuals against the vagaries of bad luck without insuring them against the consequences of their own actions, particularly when these actions violate widely held social norms against such things as illicit drug use or child bearing in the absence of reasonable guarantees of adequate parenting.

Many traditional egalitarian projects, such as land reform and employee ownership, are strongly consistent with reciprocity norms, since they make people the owners not only of the fruits of their labors, but more broadly of the consequences of their actions (Bowles and Gintis [1998] and Bowles and Gintis [1999] provide overviews based on contemporary principal-agent models). The same may be said of more conventional initiatives such as improved educational opportunities and policies to support home ownership. There is good evidence, for example, that home ownership promotes active participation in local politics and a willingness to discipline personally those engaging in antisocial behaviors in the neighborhood (Sampson, Raudenbush, and Earls 1997). An expansion of subsidies designed to promote employment and increase earnings among the poor, suggested by Edmund Phelps (1997), would tap powerful reciprocity motives. Similarly, social insurance programs might be reformulated along lines suggested by John Roemer (1993) to protect individuals from risks over which they have no control, while not indemnifying people against the results of their own choices (other than providing a minimal floor to living standards). In this manner, for example, families could be protected against regional fluctuations in home values—the main form of wealth for most people—as Robert Shiller (1993) has shown. Other forms of insurance could partially protect workers from shifts in demand for their services induced by global economic changes.

An egalitarian society can be built on the basis of these and other policies consistent with strong reciprocity, along with a guarantee of an acceptable minimal living standard consistent with the widely documented motives of basic needs generosity. But if we are correct, economic analysis will be an inadequate guide to policymaking in the area unless it revises its foundational assumptions concerning human motivation.

Notes

1. The numbers of observations for these questions were 78 and 79 for the poor group and 294 and 281 for the rich group. Gilens (1999) makes similar observations using earlier data.

2. See Moffitt (1983) for an early model of welfare stigma. See also Lindbeck, Nyberg, and Weibull (1995) for related work that addresses the role of work norms in redistributive politics and treats such norms as endogenous to the provision of government transfers.

3. The exact wording of this questions is: "Why, in your opinion, are there people who live in need? Here are four opinions; which is the closest to yours? 1. Because they have been unlucky; 2. Because of laziness and lack of willpower; 3. Because there is much injustice in our society; 4. It is an inevitable part of modern progress; 5. None of these." Our dummy variable is one for respondents who answered "Because of laziness and lack of willpower," and zero for respondents who gave one of the other four responses.

4. These results do not depend on the particular sample and specification that we present. In all specifications, the effect of moving up to the next income quartile is an order of magnitude smaller than the effect of believing that poverty exists because the poor are lazy. When the question about whether or not the public authorities are doing enough for the poor was omitted from our composite measure of concern about poverty, the effect of income was not even significant, regardless of whether other demographic variables were included in the regression, while the effect of beliefs that the poor are lazy remained large and highly significant.

5. We drop non-responses and "don't know" responses. Another option would be to include "don't know" as a valid response. However, how and why people develop well-defined preferences and beliefs is beyond the scope of this chapter. We focus on why people oppose or support income redistribution given that their beliefs and preferences are well-defined.

6. There are several additional questions that might capture self-interest that are excluded from the model presented here. See Fong (2001) for a discussion and analysis of these variables.

7. Space limitations prevent us from presenting these results here. However, the finding using ordered probit are presented in Fong (2001).

8. We assume that people agree on which group benefits and which loses when they believe that a person's race or sex is important to getting ahead.

9. The sample size in these regressions ranges from 584 to 594.

10. A third study by Weaver, Shapiro, and Jacobs (1995), drawing in addition on National Opinion Research Council and General Social Survey data, comes to broadly similar conclusions.

11. As a general rule, non-experts vastly overstate the share of the tax revenues devoted to things of which they disapprove, whether it be foreign aid, welfare, AIDS research, or military expenditure—the opposition is generally the cause of the exaggeration, not *vice versa*.

References

Alesina, Alberto, Edward Glaeser, and Bruce Sacerdote. "Why Doesn't the United States Have a European-Style Welfare State?" *Brookings Papers on Economic Activity* 2 (2001): 187–278.

Atkinson, A. B. *The Economic Consequences of Rolling Back the Welfare State.* Cambridge, MA: MIT Press, 1999.

Besley, Timothy, and Stephen Coate. "Understanding Taxpayer Resentment and Statistical Discrimination," *Journal of Public Economics* 48 (1992): 165–183.

Bowles, Samuel, and Herbert Gintis. "Schooling, Skills and Earnings: A Principal-Agent Approach," in Kenneth Arrow, Samuel Bowles, and Steven Durlauf (eds.), *Meritocracy and Economic Inequality.* Princeton, NJ: Princeton University Press, 1998.

———. *Recasting Egalitarianism: New Rules for Markets, States, and Communities.* Erik Olin Wright (ed.). London: Verso, 1999.

Brewer, Marilynn B., and Norman Miller. *Intergroup Relations.* Pacific Grove, CA: Brooks/Cole Publishing Company, 1996.

Deutsch, Morton. *Distributive Justice.* New Haven: Yale University Press, 1985.

Eckel, Catherine, and Philip Grossman. "Altruism in Anonymous Dictator Games," *Games and Economic Behavior* 16 (1996): 181–191.

Edda. "Havamal." In D. E. Martin Clarke (ed.), *The Havamal, with Selections from Other Poems in the Edda.* 1923.

Farkas, Steve, and Jean Robinson. *The Values We Live By: What Americans Want from Welfare Reform.* New York: Public Agenda, 1996.

Fong, Christina M. "Social Preferences, Self-Interest, and the Demand for Redistribution," *Journal of Public Economics* 82,2 (2001): 225–246.

———. "Empathic Responsiveness: Evidence from a Randomized Experiment on Giving to Welfare Recipients." Carnegie-Mellon University, 2004.

Forsythe, Robert, Joel Horowitz, N. E. Savin, and Martin Sefton. "Replicability, Fairness and Pay in Experiments with Simple Bargaining Games," *Games and Economic Behavior* 6,3 (May 1994): 347–369.

Gallup Organization, *Haves and Have-Nots: Perceptions of Fairness and Opportunity.* Gallup Press, 1998.

Gilens, Martin. *Why Americans Hate Welfare.* University of Chicago Press, 1999.

Hayek, Frederick. *The Three Sources of Human Values.* London: London School of Economics, 1978.

Heclo, Hugh. "The Political Foundations of Antipoverty Policy." In Sheldon H. Danziger and Daniel H. Weinberg (eds.), *Fighting Poverty: What Works and What Doesn't.* Cambridge: Harvard University Press, 1986, 312–341.

Kollock, Peter. "Transforming Social Dilemmas: Group Identity and Cooperation." In Peter Danielson (ed.), *Modeling Rational and Moral Agents.* Oxford: Oxford University Press, 1997.

Kolm, Serge-Christope. *La Bonne Economie: La Réciprocité Générale*. Presses Universitaires de France: Paris, 1984.

Kropotkin, Petr. *Mutual Aid: A Factor in Evolution*. New York: Black Rose Books, 1989(1903).

Lindbeck, Assar, Sten Nyberg, and Jörgen Weibull. "Social Norms and Incentives in the Welfare State," *Quarterly Journal of Economics* 114 (1995): 1–35.

Loewenstein, George F., Leigh Thompson, and Max H. Bazerman. "Social Utility and Decision Making in Interpersonal Contexts," *Journal of Personality and Social Psychology* 57, 3 (1989): 426–441.

Luttmer, Erzo F. P. "Group Loyalty and the Taste for Redistribution," *Journal of Political Economy* 109, 3 (June 2001): 500–528.

Miller, David. *Principles of Social Justice*. Cambridge, MA: Harvard University Press, 1999.

Moffitt, Robert. "An Economic Model of Welfare Stigma," *American Economic Review* 73 (1983): 1023–1035.

―――, David Ribar, and Mark Wilhelm. "Decline of Welfare Benefits in the U.S.: The Role of Wage Inequality," *Journal of Public Economics* 68, 3 (June 1998): 421–452.

Moore, Barrington Jr. *Injustice: The Social Bases of Obedience and Revolt*. White Plains: M. E. Sharpe, 1978.

Page, Benjamin, and Robert Shapiro. *The Rational Public: Fifty Years of Trends in American's Policy Preferences*. Chicago: University of Chicago Press, 1992.

Phelps, Edmund S. *Rewarding Work: How to Restore Participation and Self-Support to Free Enterprise*. Cambridge, MA: Harvard University Press, 1997.

Piketty, Thomas. "Social Mobility and Redistributive Politics," *Quarterly Journal of Economics* 110, 3 (August 1995): 551–584.

Reif, Karlheinz, and Anna Melich. *Euro-Barometer 31A: European Elections, 1989: Post-Election Survey, June–July 1989 [Computer File]*. Conducted by Faits et Opinions, Paris. ICPSR ed. Ann Arbor, MI: Inter-university Consortium for Political and Social Research, 1993.

Roberts, Kevin. "Voting over Income Tax Schedules," *Journal of Public Economics* 8 (December 1977): 329–340.

Roemer, John. "A Pragmatic Theory of Responsibility for the Egalitarian Planner," *Philosophy and Public Affairs* 22 (1993): 146–166.

Sampson, Robert J., Stephen W. Raudenbush, and Felton Earls. "Neighborhoods and Violent Crime: A Multilevel Study of Collective Efficacy," *Science* 277 (August 15, 1997): 918–924.

Scott, James C. *The Moral Economy of the Peasant: Rebellion and Subsistence in Southeast Asia*. New Haven, CT: Yale University Press, 1976.

Shiller, Robert J. *Macro Markets: Creating Institutions for Managing Society's Largest Economic Risks*. Oxford: Clarendon Press, 1993.

Skitka, Linda, and Philip Tetlock. "Providing Public Assistance: Cognitive and Motivational Processes Underlying Liberal and Conservative Policy Preferences," *Journal of Personality and Social Psychology* 65, 6 (1993): 1205–1223.

Walster, Elaine, G. William Walster, and Ellen Berscheid. *Equity, Theory and Research*. Boston: Allyn and Bacon, 1978.

Weaver, R. Kent, Robert Y. Shapiro, and Lawrence R. Jacobs. "Poll Trends: Welfare," *Public Opinion Quarterly* 39 (1995): 606–627.

Weiner, Bernard. *Judgments of Responsibility: A Foundation for a Theory of Social Conduct*. New York: The Guilford Press, 1995.

Williamson, John B. "Beliefs about the Motivation of the Poor and Attitudes toward Poverty Policy," *Social Problems* 21, 5 (June 1974): 734–747.

11   Fairness, Reciprocity, and Wage Rigidity

Truman Bewley

11.1   Introduction

Most empirical tests of the many competing theories of wage rigidity use publicly available data on pay rates and employment that reveal little about the institutions and motivations that explain wage behavior. In order to learn more, some economists have analyzed unusual sources of data or have conducted surveys and experiments. Management scientists and organizational psychologists have for years been collecting data relevant to wage rigidity. I here report on what I know of these sources of information about the origins of wage rigidity.

11.2   Are Wages and Salaries Downwardly Rigid?

It is sensible to check whether wages really are downwardly rigid before considering why they are. This question is surprisingly hard to answer, because appropriate data are lacking. It is not even clear what the appropriate definition of the wage should be. A firm's marginal costs depend on the average hourly nominal labor cost per job. Employee welfare depends on total nominal compensation per worker. A third possibility is nominal compensation for an employee with a given job tenure and continuing in the same position with the same employer under fixed working conditions. If the employee is paid by the hour, it is the hourly rate and the benefits that count. Total compensation is the relevant pay rate for salaried employees. This third definition is the one most closely associated with employees' and managers' notions of fairness and hence is most pertinent to the managerial concerns that explain downward wage rigidity.

In order to adhere even more closely to the sense of fairness prevailing in business, it might be advisable to include only base pay and exclude variable components, such as bonuses. The three pay rates can change independently. For instance, the average hourly labor costs of a job can increase with no change in any worker's pay, if the seniority of workers assigned to the job increases. Similarly, changes in hours worked or in job assignments can change an individual's total pay without changing hourly pay rates or labor costs per job. There are conceptual ambiguities associated with benefits. For instance, if an increase in the costs of a given medical insurance policy were shared between the firm and its work force, the firm's nominal labor cost per job would increase, but workers would probably feel that the total value of their medical benefits had decreased.

A wage cut should be defined as a reduction in the wage of the third definition of wage—the pay of an employee continuing to work under unchanged conditions. Unfortunately, this pay rate is the most difficult to measure, because it requires knowledge of much more than just total pay.

Lebow, Saks, and Wilson (1999) is the only study I know of that measures the first definition of wage—the firm's average labor costs. The authors use U.S. Bureau of Labor Statistics data and find that wage costs are somewhat rigid downward, although there is a considerable amount of wage reduction.

There is a large literature that uses surveys of the pay of individual workers to study variation in the third kind of wage. The studies include McLaughlin (1994, 1999), Lebow, Stockton, and Wascher (1995), Card and Hyslop (1997), Kahn (1997), Fehr and Goette (1999), and Smith (2000, 2002). Some of these authors had to struggle with possible errors in the reporting of wage rates. All of the studies suffer from ignorance of changes in hours worked, job assignments, bonuses, or working conditions, so that it is not clear that the data reveal the wage of the third definition. All the studies report large amounts of wage reduction.

Surveys of firms on wage rigidity reach conflicting conclusions. Roger Kaufman (1984), Alan Blinder and Don Choi (1990), Jonas Agell and Per Lundborg (1999), and myself, Bewley (1999), simply asked employers whether they had reduced pay. The responses probably apply to the third definition of wage, but there is no way to be sure. None of the firms in Kaufman's sample of 26 British firms had considered nominal wage cuts during the recession occurring at the time of his study. Blinder and Choi found a high incidence of pay reduction, in 5 of the 19 American firms they studied. Agell and Lundborg, on the other hand, found almost no wage cutting; two out of 153 responding Swedish firms had experienced nominal wage cuts during the previous seven years, a period of high unemployment and low inflation. The wage cuts that did occur were for just a few employees. The near absence of wage cutting may be explained by institutional factors specific to Sweden. Although I conducted my survey during a recession and actively sought out firms that had cut pay, I found a low incidence of pay cuts; of 235 businesses studied, 24 had reduced the base pay of some or all employees during the recession of the early 1990s.

Similarly conflicting results appear in surveys of union wage agreements. In *Current Wage Developments* and the *Monthly Labor Review*, the Bureau of Labor Statistics reports on general wage changes for both union and nonunion manufacturing production workers for the years 1959 through 1978. These data show a negligible number or wage reductions; cuts for less than a half a percent of the workers in every year.[1] (The corresponding percentage for my sample was 0.14 percent.) Conflicting evidence has been found by Mitchell (1985), who uses Bureau of Labor Statistics data to calculate that 13 percent of all workers covered by major new contracts suffered wage cuts in 1983. Similarly, Fortin (1996) finds that 6 percent of 1,149 large non–cost-of-living-adjusted union wage settlements in Canada from 1992 to 1994 involved wage cuts.

Much less ambiguous evidence of downward rigidity in the third kind of wage is contained in the few studies that use company records to learn the histories of job assignments, hours worked, and pay of individual employees. The studies include Baker, Gibbs, and Holmstrom (1994); Wilson (1996); and Altonji and Devereux (2000). Unfortunately, these authors study only three firms; Baker, Gibbs, and Holmstrom study one firm, Wilson studies two, one of which is the firm studied by Baker, Gibbs, and Holmstrom, and Altonji and Devereux study the third. Only Altonji and Devereux report data on hourly workers. The other two studies have information only on salaried employees.

All three studies find a negligible number of pay reductions. Altonji and Devereux find that 2.5 percent of hourly workers experienced wage cuts, but almost all of these were "associated with changes between full and part time status, or with changes in whether performance incentives are part of compensation." These findings are reinforced by a telephone survey Akerlof, Dickens, and Perry (1996) made of 596 people in the Washington, DC, area. The key question was "Excluding overtime, commissions, and bonuses, has your base rate of pay changed since a year ago today?" A negligible number reported pay reductions. Given the form of the question, this evidence probably pertains to the third definition of wages. Contradicting this evidence are two similar surveys conducted in New Zealand in 1992 and 1993, where 8 percent and 5 percent, respectively, of the respondents reported hourly wage reductions (Chapple, 1996, tables 11.2 and 11.3). More work should be done. No one has yet conducted a large survey that accurately measures the incidence of cuts in pay according to the third definition of wages.

11.3   Evidence from Surveys by Economists

There are six surveys by economists of business managers responsible for compensation policy. The goal of five of these was to learn the reasons for downward wage rigidity—the studies of Roger Kaufman (1984), Alan Blinder and Don Choi (1990), Jonas Agell and Per Lundborg (1995, 1999), Carl Campbell and Kunal Kamlani (1997), and Bewley (1999). The sixth study, that of David Levine (1993), also contains relevant information. Although the findings of the studies differ to some extent, they give a consistent picture of the sources of wage rigidity. I also discuss a paper by Jennifer Smith (2002), who analyzes a survey of British workers.

I first summarize my own findings, based on interviews with 246 company managers and 19 labor leaders in the northeastern United States during the early 1990s when unemployment was high because of a recession. I present my findings as reflecting the views of managers, although labor leaders had almost exactly the same opinions on the matters discussed. The primary resistance to wage reduction comes from upper management, not from employees. The main reason for avoiding pay cuts is that they damage morale. Morale has three components. One is identification with the firm and an internalization of its objectives. Another is trust in an implicit exchange with the firm and with other employees; employees know that aid given to the firm or to co-workers will eventually be reciprocated, even if it goes unnoticed. The third component is a mood that is conducive to good work. The mood need not be a happy one, though happiness is important for the performance of some jobs, such as those that involve dealing with customers. The mood could be dislike of an unpleasant job combined with grim focus on achievement or pride in accomplishment. Good morale is not equivalent to happiness or job satisfaction. Workers may be content simply because they do nothing. Good morale has to do with a willingness voluntarily to make sacrifices for the company and for coworkers.

A general sense of fairness is conducive to good morale; it contributes to an atmosphere of mutual trust. The sense of fairness is created by having supervisors treat workers decently, by having impartial rules for settling disputes and determining promotions and job assignments, and by using reasonable standards for setting the relative pay of different employees. These standards are often elaborate systems and are termed "internal pay structures." They clearly determine pay differentials on the basis of such factors as training, experience, tenure at the firm, and productivity. The structures are extremely important, because any perceived pay inequity within a firm may cause indignation and disrupt work. The standards of internal equity are somewhat arbitrary, can depend strongly on company tradition, and may not specify that pay be proportional to productivity. Many employers believe that productivity of the work force as a whole is maximized when pay increases less than productivity, although some individuals might produce more if given stronger financial incentives.

There is a division of opinion within business about how sensitive pay should be to productivity. Big income differentials due to differences in productivity can cause resentment, especially if productivity is difficult to measure (which it often is). Nevertheless many firms use piece rates when productivity can be measured unambiguously, and even when piece rates are impractical ordinary notions of equity require that differences in people's contributions be rewarded financially to some extent. The sensitivity of pay to productivity may be blunted by the influence of other factors on pay, such as longevity with the firm. No matter how sensitive the pay of individuals is to their productivity, firms automatically keep the average pay of broad categories of workers roughly equal to the value of their average marginal product by adjusting the number of workers in each category to the profit maximizing level.

Managers are concerned about morale because of its impact on labor turnover, recruitment of new employees, and productivity. Disgruntled employees are likely to quit as soon as they find another job. A company's best recruiters are its employees, so it is important not to have them go around complaining about their company. Morale has little impact on productivity in the sense of speed in carrying out routine tasks. Habit and working conditions largely determine this sort of productivity. Managers have in mind the impact of morale on workers' willingness to do the extra thing, to encourage and help each other, to make suggestions, and to work well even when not supervised. Also, workers with bad morale waste time complaining to each other. In considering the impact of morale on productivity, it is important to realize that supervision is so expensive that many employees are not closely supervised and have a significant amount of freedom on the job. Except in some low-level jobs, employers rely on workers' voluntary cooperation and do not simply give orders.

When considering why wage cuts hurt morale, it is necessary to distinguish new from existing employees. The morale of existing employees is hurt by pay cuts because of an insult effect and a standard of living effect. Workers are used to receiving regular pay increases as a reward for good work and loyalty and so interpret a pay cut as an affront and a breach of implicit reciprocity, even if the pay of all employees is reduced. Individual workers may take a pay cut less personally if everyone's pay falls, but when everyone in a company suffers, they all complain to each other and stimulate each other's discontent. The standard of living effect is the resentment caused by the fall in income. Workers blame their employer when they find their lifestyles curtailed. This effect is closely related to what experimental economists call "loss aversion."

The arguments just given do not apply to newly hired workers. They probably would hardly care if their firm had a general pay cut just before they were hired. It is possible, however, to reduce the pay of newly hired workers while continuing to give normal pay increases to existing employees; new workers hired after a certain date would simply be paid according to a reduced pay scale. Some firms have experimented with such two-tier pay structures. Managers say that new workers hired in the lower tier might be glad at first to have their jobs, but that their attitude would change after they learned that their pay violated the traditional internal pay structure. They would believe they were being treated unfairly, their resentment would hurt their morale, and their discontent could spread to others.

Resistance to wage reduction and the need for internal pay equity stem from ideas of fairness that usually refer to some reference wage. The reference wage for pay cuts is the previous wage. The reference wage for internal equity is that of other workers within the firm with similar qualifications and similar jobs. The fairness of wages has little to do with profits or productivity, although both workers and managers find it appropriate that employees share to some extent in the success of their company. While managers attempt to use reasonable criteria when establishing an internal pay structure, once a structure is established, tradition by itself makes it a standard of fairness.

The explanation of downward pay rigidity just given is closely related to the morale theory proposed by Solow (1979), Akerlof (1982), and Akerlof and Yellen (1988, 1990). They assert that morale and hence productivity increase with the wage and that the trade-off between labor costs and productivity determines a wage that is independent of the unemployment rate. Akerlof (1982) uses his gift exchange model to explain the link between the wage and morale. According to this model, workers offer more effort than is demanded by the employer in exchange for pay rates in excess of market clearing levels, so that effort increases with the wage level.

I do not believe that this theory is fully accurate, however, because employers say they do not see much connection between effort or morale and wage levels; productivity and morale do not increase with pay levels, although they can be hurt by pay reductions or disappointingly small raises. Even generous pay increases do not increase morale or productivity, because workers quickly get used to increases and grow to believe they have a right to them. They soon lose track of any idea that they should offer extra effort in exchange for higher pay. Employers do not think about a trade-off between labor costs and the productivity of existing employees when determining pay levels, though managers do consider the trade-off between labor costs and the quality of labor that a firm can attract and retain.

In the theory of Akerlof, Solow, and Yellen, morale depends on the level of the wage, whereas in the explanation I have described, wages affect morale only when reduced. What is accurate in the Akerlof-Solow-Yellen theory is the idea that employers avoid cutting pay because doing so would hurt morale. What the theory misses is that employees usually have little notion of a fair or market value for their services and quickly come to believe they are entitled to their existing pay, no matter how high it may be. Workers do not use pay rates at other firms as reference wages because they know too little about them. Exceptions to this statement may occur when workers are represented by an active labor union that keeps them informed about what other firms are paying.

Although pay cuts are unusual, they do occur and usually do not have the harmful effects described by managers when arguing that pay should not be cut. The explanation for this inconsistency is that pay cuts are accepted by the work force if they prevent a firm from closing or if they save a large number of jobs. Managers are confident that they can convince employees that a pay cut is necessary, if it is in fact the case.

One of the puzzles discussed in the literature on wage rigidity has been why firms lay off workers rather than reduce their pay. I found that most managers believe that the elasticity of their company's demand for labor is so low that pay cuts would not reduce an excess supply of labor within the firm. The elasticity is small, because direct labor is a small fraction of marginal costs and the price elasticity of product demand is far from infinite. Only in firms with a high elasticity of product demand, such as construction companies, is it believed that pay cuts can significantly increase the demand for labor. Many of the pay cuts that occurred in the companies I researched were made in these types of firms or in ones that were in danger of closing. Other firms where pay reduction was an alternative to layoffs were those that laid off workers simply to save money, not to get rid of excess labor (and there were many such companies). The main argument for preferring layoffs to pay cuts is that layoffs do less damage to morale. Laid off workers suffer, but they are no longer in the firm. In the words of one manager, "Layoffs get the misery out the door." Good management practice is to delay potential layoffs until the employer can make a large number all at once, and then to assure those who remain that there will be no more layoffs for some time.

Any damage to morale from layoffs is temporary, whereas that of a pay reduction is long-term. Other arguments are that layoffs increase productivity (whereas pay cuts hurt it) and that layoffs give management some control over who leaves (whereas the best workers are likely to quit when pay is reduced). The tendency for the best workers to quit is a concern in many firms, because the leveling effects of internal equity on pay mean that pay for workers within a given job category increases less than their contribution to profits as this contribution increases. Another consideration is that feasible layoffs often save much more money than feasible pay cuts, which usually cannot be more than about 20 percent of base pay. Layoffs save the fixed costs of employment, which are substantial, whereas cuts reduce only the variable part of pay.

Another puzzle appearing in economics literature is why unemployed workers do not try to take jobs away from employed people by offering to replace them at lower pay. Robert M. Solow (1990) has proposed that the unemployed do not engage in such undercutting because of a social convention against it. I found that explicit undercutting is impossible for most people, because they do not know exactly what job they are applying for or what its pay is. However, it is not uncommon during periods of high unemployment for job applicants to offer to work for extremely low pay. These offers are not frowned upon but are almost never accepted, except to reduce pay during the initial probationary period of employment, because accepting the offers would violate the internal pay structure and could demoralize the new hire.

A similar puzzle is why firms do not replace employees during recessions with cheaper unemployed workers. In reply to this question, Assar Lindbeck and Dennis J. Snower (1988) proposed, with their insider-outsider theory—that firms seldom replace workers because old employees who remained would harass and refuse to cooperate with and train the replacements, thereby reducing their productivity. I found that the main reasons employers do not replace employees are that the new ones would lack the skills of the existing ones and replacement would demoralize the work force. The skills would be lost in part because many of them are specific to the firm. Managers agreed that after replacement, the unreplaced workers would probably boycott the new ones, but asserted that other factors took precedence as an explanation of why employees were not replaced during recessions.

John Maynard Keynes (1936) proposed that downward wage rigidity is explained by employees' preoccupation with pay differentials among workers in similar jobs at different firms. I found, however, that such external pay differentials are not an issue, except in highly unionized industries. In most companies, employees know so little about pay rates at other firms that they do not know whether or not they are underpaid. Although labor unions do try to keep their members informed of pay rates at other companies, unions are weak in the United States.

A popular explanation of wage rigidity is the "No Shirking Theory" of Shapiro and Stiglitz (1984). According to their model, managers induce workers to perform well by firing them if their productivity falls below a prescribed level. Being fired is more costly to the worker the higher is the wage, so that higher wages make it possible to insist on greater productivity. According to Shapiro and Stiglitz's theory, managers set wages so as to optimize the trade-off between wage costs and productivity. This theory does not really explain downward wage rigidity, because it implies that wages should decline when unemployment increases. As unemployment rises, however, it becomes harder to find a new job, so that losing a job is more costly to the worker. The theory also implies that firms can then obtain the same productivity at lower wages, which is not necessarily the case.

Despite these drawbacks, the No Shirking Theory is popular among economists. However, when I asked managers and labor leaders about it, they almost always told me that it did not apply. As was explained in connection with the Akerlof's gift exchange model, employers do not see much connection between pay and morale. Nor do employers obtain cooperation by threatening to fire shirkers. To do so would create a negative atmosphere that could damage morale and encourage rebelliousness. Workers may malinger on the job, but are seldom dismissed for doing so, except during the short probationary period after hiring. Shirking is usually dealt with through discussions and reprimands, and workers are normally fired only because of a pattern of egregious behavior. Managers elicit effort by clearly explaining to employees what is expected of them, identifying their shortcomings in a constructive manner, pointing out the importance of the tasks they perform, showing interest in and appreciation of their work, and making them feel they are valued members of the organization. Most employees like to work, and cooperate, and please their boss.

Despite the inapplicability of the no shirking theory, the incentive mechanism it posits can be effective. For instance, employees do work harder during economic slowdowns when new jobs are difficult to find and layoffs are imminent, especially if layoffs are done on the basis of performance—that is, if the least productive workers in a job category are laid off first. The increase in effort occurs both because job loss becomes more dangerous during an economic slowdown and because workers try to avoid layoffs by being cooperative and productive. Because layoffs stem from circumstances not controlled by management, they do not generate the hostility that might be generated by systematically firing slackers.

Although firing is not used to stimulate work effort, financial incentives are thought to be very effective in doing so and are believed not to impair morale. Incentives can even improve morale, because workers find it fair that they be rewarded for their contributions to the company. Provided incentives are not exaggerated, they contribute to internal equity. Discipline and even firing can contribute to internal equity as well, because workers who make the effort to do their job well and obey company rules can be outraged if they see others get away with flagrant misbehavior. The main purposes of firing are to protect the company from malefactors and incompetents and to maintain internal equity. Dismissals that are managed correctly earn managers respect. What needs to be avoided is an atmosphere of retribution that menaces everyone. This assertion appears not to apply, however, to low-level jobs. There was evidence that employers do sometimes use coercion to motivate workers in low-paying jobs that require little training and where employees are easily supervised.

Another popular explanation of wage rigidity is the adverse selection model of Andrew Weiss (1980, 1990). There are two versions of this model, dealing with quits and hiring, respectively. In the quits version, managers prefer layoffs to pay cuts because the best workers leave if pay is reduced, whereas if managers lay off workers, they can select those who leave. According to the hiring version, managers believe that the higher is the level of pay that a job applicant is willing to accept, the higher his or her unobservable quality will be, and pay offers to new hires are determined by the trade-off between worker quality and pay. Weiss asserts that the relation between pay and job candidate quality is determined by alternative employment in the secondary sector, where quality is perfectly observable. The secondary sector consists of home production or jobs that have high turnover and are usually part-time. The hiring version of Weiss's adverse selection theory applies to the primary sector, where jobs are long-term and usually full-time. He assumes that real wages in the secondary sector are downwardly rigid because of constant returns to labor in production in this sector. According to the theory, this downward rigidity is then transferred to the primary sector through the impact of adverse selection on hiring pay.

I found strong support for Weiss's theory as it applies to quits, but none as it applies to hiring. Although managers believe that a pay cut would cause their best employees to quit, I found no evidence that recruiters use pay aspirations as an indicator of job candidate quality. Job recruiters treated the trade-off between pay and worker quality as a basic fact of life, but they did not learn more about candidate quality from pay demands. Recruiters used the trade-off as a reason for not reducing pay only for skills that were in short supply despite the economic slowdown. For most skills, they believed they could hire all the workers they needed during the recession at lower rates of pay. The secondary sector does not sustain candidates' reservation wages. Hiring pay is more flexible in the secondary than the primary sector—the opposite of the effect predicted by Weiss's theory. Two-tier or multiple-tier wage structures are commonplace in the secondary sector, because the part-time and casual nature of the jobs keeps workers from getting to know each other well and so reduces the need to avoid internal pay inequities.

Kaufman's (1984) results support my main findings. He conducted interviews in twenty-six British firms in 1982 during a period of high unemployment. He too found that employers "believed they could find qualified workers at lower wages." He found that employers avoid replacing workers with cheaper ones because of the value of skills and of long-term employment relationships. Employers avoid pay cuts because of concerns about productivity. Because supervision is costly, employers rely "heavily on the goodwill of their employees." Workers view wages as "a reward for performing competently" and would regard a wage cut as an "affront." Employers avoid hiring new employees at lower pay rates than existing ones because doing so would create "intolerable frictions," especially with "the newer workers who would eventually become disgruntled about the two tier wage structure." Managers feel they can cut nominal pay if "severe cutbacks or closure will be necessary unless the nominal wage cuts are enacted."

Blinder and Choi (1990) interviewed managers at nineteen firms, and their findings largely agree with my own. They found little evidence to support Andrew Weiss's idea that job candidates' wage demands are useful indicators of productivity. Few of Blinder and Choi's nineteen respondents thought that a higher wage would induce greater work effort, although a majority thought that a wage cut would diminish effort. The majority said that effort would decrease after a wage cut because of reduced morale. None mentioned the decreased penalty for being fired. A majority of their respondents believed that higher unemployment would bring greater work effort.

All respondents answering the question felt that a wage cut would increase labor turnover, although only one of the five firms that had recently reduced pay had experienced a significant increase in quits. "The reason for the wage cut seemed to matter.... Generally, wage reductions made to save the firm from failure or to align wages with those of competitors are viewed as justifiable and fair while those made just to raise profits are not." Managers felt strongly that having a wage policy that was viewed as unfair "would affect work effort, quits, and the quality of future applicants.... Attitudes like this must be strong deterrents to implementing an 'unfair' wage policy though ... that does not necessarily rule out wage reductions under the right circumstances" (Blinder and Choi 1990, 1008–1009). Blinder and Choi found strong support for the idea that worker concern about relative wages is a reason for downward wage rigidity. The question they asked, however, did not distinguish between internal and external pay comparisons, so the support their findings give to Keynes' relative wage theory is ambiguous.

Campbell and Kamlani (1997) surveyed 184 firms, sending questionnaires to managers who were asked to rate the importance of various statements on a scale from one to four. Most of Campbell and Kamlani's findings agree with my own and those of the other surveys. Their respondents attached the greatest importance to the idea that wage cuts would induce the best workers to quit, which is Weiss's adverse selection idea as it applies to quits (Weiss 1990). Campbell and Kamlani found that the best workers are valued because pay does not increase in proportion to productivity and employees' skills are often firm-specific. Other important management concerns were that a wage cut would increase turnover (and hence hiring and training costs) and would generate bad feeling that would lead to less work effort. Campbell and Kamlani found less support for the idea that pay cuts would make recruitment more difficult and found no support for the no shirking model. Managers did not agree that cutting pay would decrease effort because of a reduced fear of job loss, but did agree that effort would decline because of decreased gratitude and loyalty.

Furthermore, good management-worker relations were thought to have a much greater impact on effort than high wages, close supervision, or high unemployment. There was also no support for the insider-outsider theory. Most managers did not believe that if the firm discharged some of its current workers and replaced them with new ones at a lower wage that the old workers who remained would harass and refuse to cooperate with the newly hired ones. The reasons for a pay cut matter—its negative impact on effort would be greater if the firm were profitable than if it were losing money. There is an asymmetry between the impact of wage increases and decreases; the deleterious effect a wage decrease would have on effort would greatly exceed the positive effect of a wage increase. Similarly, a wage decrease would have a worse impact on effort and morale than having paid the lower wage for a long time.

Agell and Lundborg (1995, 1999, 2003) did questionnaire surveys of managers in Swedish manufacturing firms, obtaining responses from 179 firms in 1991 and from 157 of those firms in a follow-up survey in 1998. A strong majority of the respondents felt that a nominal wage cut would be strongly resisted by employees and that at least 50 percent of the firm's jobs would have to be threatened to make a cut acceptable. This finding may be influenced by the fact that Swedish laws make it difficult to reduce pay. The respondents gave strong support to Keynes's theory that the desire to preserve external wage relativities explains downward wage rigidity. The inconsistency between this finding and my own is probably explained by the much greater importance of labor unions in Sweden than in the United States. Agell and Lundborg found little or no support for the no shirking model. Managers did not regard shirking as very common, and "employees who were repeatedly caught shirking were punished by a simple verbal rebuke" (Agell and Lundborg 1999, 11). Like Campbell and Kamlani, Agell and Lundborg found that good management-worker relations were much more important to work effort than high wages, supervision, or unemployment. When managers were asked to list the factors most important to worker motivation, "they answered that their employees ought to be given stimulating work assignments, and to feel involved in decision-making. Some stressed that it was important that all employees felt noticed and trusted, and provided with continuous feedback and appreciation" (Agell and Lundborg 2003, 25, 16). As the authors note, these answers were very similar to the ones I heard from U.S. managers.

Managers reported that higher unemployment increased worker effort, and workers seemed to be providing more effort in 1998 (when there was high unemployment) than in 1991 (when there was little). These findings on the effect of unemployment confirm those of myself and of Kaufman. Like Blinder and Choi, Agell and Lundborg found little support for Weiss's idea that job candidates' reservation wages are a useful signal of productivity (Agell and Lundborg 1999, table 11.6). Agell and Lundborg also found little support for Solow's theory about undercutting. They found (as I also found in my research) that offers to work for little pay were not uncommon, although fewer such offers occurred in 1998 than in 1991, perhaps because the much higher unemployment rate in 1998 discouraged job searching. Managers usually rejected low offers, because accepting them would create pay inequities within the firm and low bidders were thought to have poor skills (Agell and Lundborg 1995, 299). In my survey, I often heard the first explanation, but seldom the second.

Levine (1993) obtained responses to questionnaires on pay policy from 139 compensation managers of large American corporations. The questions focused on the determinants of wages and salaries rather than on the reasons for downward wage rigidity. Nevertheless, he found that the unemployment rate and other measures of excess demand for labor had almost no impact on pay. Also, internal equity considerations took precedence over changes in market pay rates in the determination of relative pay rates for closely related jobs and skills.

In summary, the six surveys—Kaufman (1984), Blinder and Choi (1990), Campbell and Kamlani (1997), Agell and Lundborg (1995, 1999, 2003), and Levine (1993)—are largely consistent and point to an explanation of wage rigidity based on morale rather than on the kind of incentives that play a role in the no shirking model or in Weiss's model of adverse selection in hiring. Adverse selection in quits does seem to be part of the explanation of wage rigidity, however.

I turn next to the analysis by Jennifer Smith (2002) of nine years of data from the British Household Panel Study of 6,000 employed workers from 1991 to 1999. She used data on the 70 percent of workers who did not change employers or job grades over the nine-year period. The data include monthly income and responses to questions about job and pay satisfaction. She found that in a typical month, about 28 percent of workers suffered nominal pay cuts (in the sense that their monthly income declined) and the pay of about 6 percent of workers was frozen (in that their monthly nominal income did not change). Smith studied the association between changes in satisfaction and monthly income and found that workers who suffered cuts were on average less satisfied than those who enjoyed pay increases, although the difference in satisfaction was not striking. Of those workers whose income fell, nearly 40 percent were satisfied with their pay and nearly 60 percent were satisfied with their job.

Smith also found that those workers whose pay was frozen were just as satisfied as those whose income declined. She interpreted this finding as evidence against the morale theory of wage rigidity outlined earlier in this chapter, because according to that theory pay cuts should cause greater unhappiness than do pay freezes. The theory, of course, may be wrong, but it is not clear what conclusions should be drawn from Smith's analysis, because she probably does not have data on pay cuts and freezes in the sense of the third definition given in the previous section, and this is the definition that is relevant to downward wage rigidity. Monthly incomes can fluctuate for a great many reasons—such as changes in overtime, shifts, job assignments, bonuses, or hours, and Smith has information on none of these variables except for hours, and she is not sure the data on hours are accurate. Pay raises, freezes, and cuts have to do with the rules by which pay is calculated.

A great deal more information is required than total monthly income in order to detect changes in these rules. I find it extremely unlikely that an average of 28 percent of the work force suffered pay cuts from one month to the next according to the proper definition of pay cut. Another issue is that actual pay cuts often turn out to do little harm to morale, because they are done for a good reason and are accepted by workers as fair. When managers say that pay cuts would hurt morale, they refer to unjustified cuts. Also, job and pay satisfaction are probably not good measures of morale. I imagine, nevertheless, that workers who suffered true pay cuts would be a great deal less satisfied than workers who had received raises.

11.4   Evidence from Experimental Economics

Experimental evidence is accumulating that primarily agrees with what managers say about their own choices and about worker motivation. The most important finding is the prevalence of reciprocity. Many people, when placed experimentally in the role of worker or employer, give extra effort when offered extra pay or offer extra pay after receiving extra effort, even when no *quid pro quo* is required. People also reciprocate bad for bad. In experiments, subjects incur a cost in order to harm others who have hurt them. The general willingness to reciprocate good for good is the essence of good morale. Negative reciprocity is what underlies the insult effect of pay cuts, which is resentment caused by the firm's perceived breach of positive reciprocity; workers expect employers to offer pay increases, not cuts, in exchange for loyalty and effort. The pervasiveness of negative reciprocity probably explains managers' belief that the systematic use of firing would not motivate employees to work well. Another finding is that financial incentives do inspire effort, provided they are framed in a way that avoids any impression of menace. Surveys of the experimental literature are Fehr and Gächter (1998b, 2000), Fehr and Falk (2002), and chapter 5 of this volume.

A series of laboratory experiments demonstrate the importance of reciprocity in mock employment relationships (Fehr, Kirchsteiger, and Riedl [1993, 1998]; Kirchler, Fehr, and Evans [1996]; Fehr et al. [1998]; and Gächter and Falk [2002]). In these experiments, there are two types of subjects (employers and workers) and two stages of interaction. During the first stage, each employer makes a wage offer, which is either accepted or rejected by some worker. Acceptance leads to employment and to the second stage, where either the worker or the experimenter chooses an effort level. An employer can employ only one worker, and a worker can work for only one employer. An employed worker's payoff is the wage minus a cost, which is increasing in the effort level. The employer's payoff increases in the effort level and, of course, decreases with the wage.

Notice that the employer has no way to enforce the worker's effort choice. The two stages are repeated, usually 10 to 15 times. In some experiments, one worker and one employer are paired for all the repetitions. In others, the experimenter changes the pairings after every repetition. In still another version, the pairings are established at each repetition by competitive bidding for workers and jobs. In such market interactions, there are more workers than employers, so that market-clearing wages should be little more than the workers' reservation level, which equals their cost of effort.

Experimenters consistently find that if workers choose the effort level, the average wage is considerably higher than the reservation level, even when competitive bidding should force wages down to it. Furthermore, the workers' average effort is higher than the minimum allowed and increases with the wage offered. In addition, the wage is little more than the reservation level if the experimenter chooses the effort level and there is competitive bidding with an excess supply of labor. These results hold even when the employer and worker interact only once. That is, workers offer extra effort in exchange for a higher than minimal wage, even though wages are agreed on before workers choose effort levels and employers never have another opportunity to reward or punish workers. Employers anticipate and exploit workers' reciprocity by offering generous wages.

This series of experiments show that only some people reciprocate. Others behave selfishly and offer the minimum amount of effort. Some employers who would otherwise behave selfishly are probably induced to offer generous wages by the expectation that some workers will react to them by offering liberal amounts of effort. Because wages fall to minimal levels when the experimenter fixes the effort level, we may tentatively conclude that employers' behavior is driven mainly by the expectation of reciprocation, not by a sense of fairness—that is, by a desire to divide evenly the economic surplus generated by the worker-employer interaction.

The tendency to reciprocate may be built into the human psyche. Rilling et al. (2002) used magnetic resonance imaging to study the reactions of the brain during repeated play of the prisoner's dilemma game and found that experiencing cooperative responses and deciding to cooperate were both accompanied by patterns of brain activity normally associated with pleasure.[2]

All these findings support the explanation of wage rigidity proposed by Akerlof (1982) in his gift exchange model. I pointed out earlier that this theory does not seem to apply in a business context because workers quickly grow to believe that they deserve whatever pay they receive. Experiments do not continue for long enough to capture this habituation effect.

What is important about the experiments is that they reveal that a significant fraction of the population reciprocates. In addition, the experimental findings do reflect some of the practices that managers explained to me. When setting the pay of new hires, recruiters sometimes offer a little more than applicants expect in order to get the relationship with them started off on the right footing and to create excitement about the new job. One of the many reasons recruiters dislike hiring overqualified applicants is that they are likely to be disgruntled because their pay disappoints their expectations.

Fehr and Falk (1999) performed interesting modifications of the experiments of Fehr, Kirchsteiger, and Riedl (1993) and others described earlier in this chapter. Fehr and Falk make the bidding for jobs and workers two-sided rather than one-sided in the situation with competitive bidding and an excess supply of workers—that is, workers as well as employers can make wage offers. The authors found that when the experimenter determines the effort, level employers accept only the lowest offers, and wages are forced down almost to the reservation level. When the workers choose the effort level, however, the wage is higher, just as in experiments where only employers make offers. Workers make many low offers to try to obtain a job, but these are refused, apparently because the employers hope to incite high effort by paying good wages. The experimental employers' behavior corresponds to that of actual firms that usually refuse workers' offers to work for very little.

Burda et al. (1998) have performed experiments involving wage cuts. In their work, an employer and worker are matched for two periods, and in each of them the employer makes a wage offer, which the worker may accept or reject. If the worker rejects the offer, the employer may (after paying a fixed training cost) hire a fictitious worker at a market wage, which the actual worker also receives (as if hired by some other fictitious firm). The market wage is predetermined by the experimenters and declines from the first to the second period. In the experiments, there is little wage rigidity; the wages that employers and employees agree on tend to decline along with the market wage. The employer and worker in effect play two successive ultimatum games, the bargaining position of the worker weakens from the first to the second game, and as a result the wage declines. There is no reciprocation of effort for income that could give rise to an insult effect, and the standard of living effect does not apply, since the workers do not live from their earnings. The experiments, therefore, provide evidence that without these two effects wages would be downwardly flexible.

Experimental evidence supports the view of businesspeople that financial incentives are effective, even when negative, provided they are not presented in a hostile manner. For instance, Nagin et al. (1998) report on a field experiment performed by a telemarketing firm. In this firm, the telemarketers' pay increased with the number of successful solicitations they claimed, and the company monitored these claims by calling back a fraction of the people declared to be successes. The company secretly varied the fraction of bad calls reported to employees while increasing the true call back rate. By analyzing the company's data, the authors found that cheating increased as the fraction of bad calls reported declined, so that workers did respond to variation in the negative incentive.

Laboratory experimental work by Fehr and Gächter (1998a) and Brown, Falk, and Fehr (2002) shows that the possibility of negative rewards does not keep reciprocation from being a powerful incentive. Fehr and Gächter (1998a) performed the two stage experiments of Fehr, Kirchsteiger, and Riedl (1993) with the modification that at stage one, the employer requested an effort level. The authors compared the results with experiments where in a third stage the employer could reward or punish the worker. The amount of the reward or punishment was chosen by the employer and was not announced in advance. The employer incurred a cost that increased with the absolute magnitude of the reward or punishment. Despite the cost, many employers did reward high effort and punish low effort, and workers on average offered more effort and earned lower wages in the three stage than in the two stage experiments.

Brown, Falk, and Fehr (2002) repeated the two stage experiments of Fehr, Kirchsteiger, and Riedl (1993) 15 times under two conditions. Under one, employers and workers could identify each other by a number, and employers could make offers to a particular worker. This arrangement made it possible for an employer and worker to form a long-term relationship. In the other condition, the identifying numbers were reassigned in every period, so that long-term relationships were impossible. When identity numbers remained stable, individual workers and employers did form relationships that were valuable to both, because they could establish a pattern of exchanging high effort for high wages. Employers could and many did punish workers for low effort by dismissing them—that is, by ceasing to make them offers. Average wages and effort were considerably higher when identity numbers were stable than when they were reassigned, so workers were not discouraged from reciprocating by the threat of dismissal. The fact that the negative incentives were not made explicit may have diminished any bad impression they made in the experiments of Fehr and Gächter (1998a) and Brown, Falk, and Fehr (2002). Another explanation for the effectiveness of the negative incentives may have to do with the presence of both selfish and reciprocating workers. Although the reciprocating workers might have been offended by the possibility of punishment, selfish ones might have been induced to offer more effort by the prospect of reward and risk of punishment.

Other experiments that imitate the no shirking model provide additional evidence that punishments do not crush reciprocation and discourage effort. These experiments are described in Fehr, Kirchsteiger, and Riedl (1996); Fehr, Gächter, and Kirchsteiger (1997); Fehr, Klein, and Schmidt (2001); and Fehr and Gächter (2002). The experiments have the form of the two-stage experiments described in Fehr, Kirchsteiger, and Riedl (1993), except that the employer requests a certain effort level and a worker is fined with a fixed probability if the effort level offered falls short of that demanded by the employer—that is, if the worker shirks. In its offer, the employer specifies a wage, the fine, and the effort level demanded. The no shirking model of Shapiro and Stiglitz (1984) also includes a probability of a worker's being caught shirking, and the fine in the experiment corresponds to being fired. One finding is that the threat of being fined elicits more than the minimum possible level of effort. Also, some reciprocation exists, in that employers obtain effort above the level they demand when they offer generous wages. Probably because employers hope for reciprocation, they often request effort levels that are too high to be enforced by the fine. The average level of actual effort is reduced by a considerable amount of shirking that may reflect reciprocation of the hostility perceived in the possibility of being fined.

The evidence is mixed on the degree to which the specification of fines discourages reciprocity. Fehr, Klein, and Schmidt (2001) and Fehr and Gächter (2002) compare experimental labor relations models imitating the no shirking model (as in Fehr, Kirchsteiger, and Riedl [1996]) with labor relations models that depend solely on reciprocity or trust (as in Fehr, Kirchsteiger, and Riedl [1993]). In the trust model, the employer offers a wage and makes a nonbinding effort request, and the worker then offers an effort level. The no shirking model is as described in the previous paragraph. The two papers report opposite results. In Fehr and Gächter (2002), the trust model achieves higher actual effort than the no shirking model.[3] In Fehr, Klein, and Schmidt (2001), the no shirking model achieves higher effort. I see no way of explaining the discrepancy, as the payoffs are nearly the same in the two experiments and the differences between them do not seem relevant.[4] Fehr and Gächter (2002) go on to make another comparison that shows that the fine may vex workers to some extent. Fehr and Gächter compare the no shirking model with a mathematically equivalent bonus model, in which the punishment is deprivation of a bonus rather than a fine. The bonus model gives rise to greater effort than the no shirking model, but less than the trust model.

Further experimental evidence of the harmful effects of negative incentives is contained in Fehr and Rockenbach (2002). In their experiments, subjects play a game, in which an investor chooses a quantity of money to give to a respondent and specifies the amount he or she would like the respondent to return. The amount given is tripled by the experimenter, so if the investor gives x the respondent receives 3x. The respondent then chooses how much to return to the investor. In another version of the game, the investor, when making the gift to the respondent, may commit to imposing a fine of a fixed magnitude on the respondent if he or she returns less than the amount requested by the investor. On average, respondents were least generous when the fine was imposed, more generous when there was no possibility of a fine, and most generous when the investor could impose a fine but chose not to do so.

Two papers by Falk, Fehr, and Fischbacher (2000, 2003) provide experimental evidence that perceived intentions as well as the desire for a fair division affect reciprocation. Falk, Fehr, and Fischbacher (2000) report on experiments with a variant of the game (just described) of Fehr and Rockenbach (2002). On the first move, the investor may take money away from or give money to the respondent, and the respondent may then in turn give or take money away from the investor. In another version of the game, the experimenter determines the investor's move according to a random distribution. In both versions, respondents on average react by taking money back if it is taken from them and give money back when it has been given to them. Their responses are, however, of a larger magnitude when the first move is chosen by the investor rather than by the experimenter.

This behavior shows that the respondents' behavior was driven to some extent by a desire to even the winnings from the game, but above all by an urge to reciprocate the good or bad intentions of the investor. Falk, Fehr, and Fischbacher (2003) reach the same conclusion from experiments with various ultimatum games. Player A can propose one of two possible splits of 10 monetary units to a respondent. One possibility is always an $(8, 2)$ split—8 for the proposer and 2 for the respondent. Alternatives are $(5, 5)$, an even split, or $(2, 8)$, $(10, 0)$, or even $(8, 2)$, the last of which means that there is really no alternative. Respondents reject the $(8, 2)$ split more frequently the less fair it seems in comparison with the alternative. For instance, $(8, 2)$ is rejected most often if $(5, 5)$ is the alternative and least often if $(10, 0)$ is the alternative.

These results provide some—but not strong—support for managers' assertions that using firing systematically to stimulate effort would dampen morale and depress productivity. I suspect that the effects managers refer to are difficult to capture experimentally, because firing is a much more severe punishment than can be imposed in the laboratory, and it is hard to reproduce in a laboratory the menacing atmosphere that could be created in a workplace by frequent firings or by the threat of firing.

11.5 Evidence from Organizational Psychology and Managerial Science

Although early investigations by managerial scientists and organizational psychologists of the relations between pay, morale, and productivity contradicted some of what managers say about these matters, the subject has since evolved and now much of what managers say is being corroborated by research. Recall that managers assert that pay levels have little impact on motivation or performance, but that financial incentives linked to performance can increase productivity considerably. These conclusions have been supported by a large amount of research by management scientists and psychologists, which I do not describe. The relevant literature is reviewed in Vroom (1964, 252) and Lawler (1971, 133).

The management intuitions that did not receive much support in early research had to do with the link between morale and productivity. Morale was measured from questionnaire evidence on job satisfaction, organizational commitment, and loyalty. Performance was measured through direct observation or by supervisors' evaluations. There are many valuable reviews of the large amount of literature on these management topics (Brayfield and Crockett 1955; Herzberg et al. 1957, chapter 4; Vroom 1964, 181–186; Locke 1976, 1330–1334; Iaffaldano and Muchinsky 1985; and Mathieu and Zajac 1990). The general conclusion is that the correlations between the measures of morale and performance are positive, but small. The measures of performance include those of both individuals and groups. In a way, these findings confirm what managers say, because most of them assert that good morale is not the same as happiness. There is a considerable amount of evidence that job satisfaction is negatively related to quitting and absences. The literature on this subject is reviewed in Brayfield and Crockett (1955), Herzberg et al. (1957, 106–107), Vroom (1964, 175–180), Locke (1976, 1331–1332), Price (1977, 79), Steers and Rhodes (1978), Mobley (1982, 95–105), Staw (1984, 638–645), and Mathieu and Zajac (1990).

There was interesting research in the 1950s that did support management feelings about the importance of morale. The investigators made experimental changes in management practices to determine the relation between work groups' attitudes and performance (Viteles 1953, chapter 8; Seashore 1954; Whyte et al. 1955 and 1961; and Likert 1961,

chapter 3). A main conclusion was that performance is positively associated with pride in the work group or firm, but is not related to other
attitudes.

In response to the failure to find a significant relation between job
satisfaction and performance, researchers studied the link between job
attitudes and workers' doing things for employers that are outside of
their normal duties. Contact with business may have led scholars to
look for such a connection, because managers claim that the impact of
good morale on productivity is felt mainly through employees' willingness to do more than the minimum required of them. Doing more
than the minimum has been given various names, such as *spontaneous
behavior* (Katz 1964), *prosocial behavior* (O'Reilly and Chatman 1986;
Brief and Motowidlo 1986), *extra-role behavior* (O'Reilly and Chatman
1986), and most commonly *organizational citizenship behavior* (Organ
1988). These concepts differ to some extent. Dennis Organ defines
five categories of organization citizenship behaviors: altruism (helping
other workers), conscientiousness (obeying company rules), sports-
manship (good humored toleration of inconveniences), courtesy (con-
siderate treatment of fellow workers), and civic virtue (participation in
the internal political life of the organization).

A first question is whether good morale increases organizational citizenship behavior. Organizational psychologists have done most of the
research on this topic. They typically start with a number of loosely
defined concepts, such as job satisfaction, perceptions of fairness in the
work place, and organizational citizenship behavior, and then try to
determine how these are related by analyzing responses to questionnaires from a sample of several hundred people. Each concept is usually broken into several components, such as Organ's five categories of
organizational citizenship behavior, and a list of questions is associated
with each. Employees answer questions on job satisfaction and perceptions of fairness, and employees or their supervisors answer questions
on organizational citizenship behavior. Factor analysis is used to check
whether responses to the questions are such that those corresponding
to one conceptual component are highly correlated with each other
and have less correlation with responses to other questions. The relations among the concepts and their components are then estimated using regression analysis, which is used in nearly the same way that it is
in economics. The advantage of such surveys over laboratory experiments is that they can investigate real-life situations where there are
long-term associations between workers and employers, whereas the

subjects in laboratory experiments are usually college students. The disadvantage of surveys is that it is much harder to establish causation than it is with experiments.

The findings of organizational psychologists do not all agree, but their work supports the conclusion that typical measures of morale, such as job satisfaction and organizational commitment, do have a positive relation with organizational citizenship behavior. What is more important is that a perception of fairness within a business organization has a positive relation with both job satisfaction and organizational citizenship behavior and may be the dominant factor affecting both. Furthermore, procedural justice—especially the interactional aspect of procedural justice—is more closely related to job satisfaction and organizational citizenship behavior than is distributive justice. Distributive justice has to do with the actual allocation of rewards to employees, whereas procedural justice has to do with the system used to arrive at the allocation. Interactional justice has to do with the consideration, politeness, and respect with which superiors treat their subordinates.

Another conclusion is that organizational citizenship behavior depends less on employees' mood than on their conscious perceptions about their jobs. The impact of fairness on organizational citizenship behavior is discussed in Organ and Konovsky (1989); Moorman (1991, 1993); Folger (1993); Moorman, Niehoff, and Organ (1993); Niehoff and Moorman (1993); Podsakoff and MacKenzie (1993); Organ and Ryan (1995); Konovsky and Organ (1996); Netemeyer et al. (1997). Moorman (1991) discusses the relative impact of the various forms of justice. The impact of mood is discussed in Organ and Konovsky (1989), George (1991), and Moorman (1993). The relative impacts of mood and cognitive job satisfaction are discussed in Organ and Konovsky (1989) and Moorman (1993). The impact of job satisfaction and commitment on organizational citizenship behavior is discussed in O'Reilly and Chatman (1986); Puffer (1987); Farh, Podsakoff, and Organ (1990); Moorman (1991); Organ and Lingl (1995); Organ and Ryan (1995); Konovsky and Organ (1996); Netemeyer et al. (1997); and MacKenzie, Podsakoff, and Ahearne (1998). Good reviews of the impact of Fairness, on organizational citizenship behavior are Organ (1988, 1990), Schnake (1991), Greenberg (1993), and Organ and Moorman (1993).

Another connection between morale and organizational citizenship behavior is made through studies of the impact of leadership style on subordinates' organizational citizenship behavior. A distinction is made between transactional and transformational leadership. The transactional style asserts itself by means of praise and admonishment, whereas the transformational style inspires people to go beyond their personal interests and think of the interests of the company or task. The transformational style attempts to entice people to identify with the company, and the transactional style focuses on people's self-interest. The transformational style is intended to create the kind of good morale that business people usually have in mind. Investigators have found that transformational leadership has a strong positive impact on both in-role job performance and on organizational citizenship behavior, that its impact exceeds that of transactional leadership, and that its impact is due in part to workers' increased trust in the leadership. The relevant studies are Podsakoff et al. (1990); Podsakoff, MacKenzie, and Bommer (1996); and MacKenzie, Podsakoff, and Rich (2001).

An obvious question is whether organizational citizenship behavior increases a company's profitability. Managers apparently think that it does, because there is evidence that supervisors' performance evaluations of subordinates are strongly and positively influenced by organizational citizenship behavior. Papers that establish this connection are MacKenzie, Podsakoff, and Fetter (1991, 1993) and Podsakoff, MacKenzie, and Hui (1993). A few studies have measured the impact of organizational citizenship behavior on the performance of work groups in various settings and have found the effects to be positive. These studies include George and Bettenhausen (1990), Podsakoff and MacKenzie (1994, 1997), Walz and Niehoff (1996), and Podsakoff, Ahearne, and MacKenzie (1997). The observed correlations may be spurious, however, because there is evidence from laboratory experiments that the high performance of a work group may have a positive influence on perceptions within the group of organizational citizenship behavior (Bachrach, Bendoly, and Podsakoff, 2001). The subject is reviewed in Podsakoff et al. (2000).

Some interesting recent work has explored the connection between identification with an organization on the one hand and quits and performance (especially extra-role performance) on the other hand. Tom Tyler has participated in much of this work. He thinks of identification with a company as internalization of its goals and asserts that identification occurs as a result of judgments about organizational status (which he calls pride), and about status within the organization (which he calls respect). Pride has to do with a favorable view of the organization as a whole, and respect has to do with being treated well within it. Status judgments can be comparative or autonomous, where a comparative judgment relates an organization or person to others and an autonomous judgment is an absolute one about the overall organization. Tyler believes that if people identify with an organization, they will want it to succeed, because its success will strengthen their own self-image. Identification with an organization is, in my opinion, a much better interpretation of what managers mean by "good morale" than are job satisfaction and even organizational commitment. Tyler and his co-authors find that identification is a dominant explanation of voluntary cooperation with organizations. In the context of business organizations, identification with the company is a much more important explanatory factor than the financial rewards received from it. These investigators find that identification has a greater impact on organizational citizenship, extra-role, or discretionary behavior, as opposed to in-role or mandatory behavior (that is, behavior required by a job description). The primary impact of pride is on rule following or conscientiousness, whereas the primary impact of respect is on helping behavior (that is, assisting coworkers). Autonomous judgments of status have a much bigger effect than comparative ones.

Tyler and his coauthors assert that perceptions of fairness and especially procedural justice have an important impact on judgments about the status of an organization and hence on willingness to identify with it. Recall that management scientists cited earlier (Morris Viteles [1953], Stanley Seashore [1954], William Whyte et al. [1955, 1961], and Rensis Likert [1961]), also found a connection between pride in an organization and performance. The work of Tyler and his colleagues is reported in Tyler (1999) and Tyler and Blader (2000, 2001). Abrams, Ando, and Hinkle (1998) observe a close association between identification with an organization and intentions to quit. Much of the work of Tyler and his co-authors on identification and cooperation with organizations has been done in the context of political, social, and educational institutions, but the recent studies just cited have to do with businesses. This interesting work raises the question of why people identify with organizations. Status is an incomplete explanation, since the term status has little independent content and includes all possible reasons for liking an organization. It is interesting that fairness has a strong influence on status and that people are proud of organizations that treat them and others fairly, but researchers have given no explanation of why this is so.

An obvious question is what evidence has been collected on the impact of actual pay cuts or pay freezes on morale. The only works I have found on the subject are Greenberg (1989, 1990) and Schaubroeck, May, and Brown (1994). In the first paper, Greenberg finds from a survey that workers did feel underpaid after a 6 percent pay cut, but job satisfaction did not decline and employees instead paid more attention to the nonfinancial advantages of their jobs. In the second paper, Greenberg (1990) reports that theft of company property increased after a 15 percent pay cut. In this paper, he conducted an experiment in which he gave employees a good explanation of the pay cut in one plant where the pay cut occurred but not in another where it also occurred. In the plant where the explanation was made, feelings of pay inequity and pilferage were less than in the other plant. This evidence supports the assertions managers make that employees tolerate pay cuts more easily if they feel they are justified and that it is possible to persuade workers that cuts are necessary.

These conclusions are further reinforced by the work of Schaubroeck, May, and Brown (1994), who studied the reactions of salaried employees to a pay freeze. These investigators also conducted an experiment, giving a good explanation to some of the employees who were affected by the pay freeze and not to others. The explanations of the freeze diminished resentment. For those who did not receive the explanation, job dissatisfaction increased with self-reported economic hardship resulting from the freeze, and there was no such relation for those who did receive the explanation.

11.6   Conclusion

Perhaps the outstanding conclusion to be drawn from the works discussed in this chapter is the importance of fairness to labor performance. It is not easy to judge what fairness means. Fairness certainly does not mean an equal distribution of the benefits from a company's operations; pay levels within firms are far from egalitarian. Even workers doing the same job may receive very different pay because of many factors, such as longevity with the company, skills acquired, and productivity. Fairness is recognized in business as being inherently ambiguous. For instance, judgments about the fairness of internal pay structures are said to depend strongly on company tradition. Other evidence that fairness does not mean equality of gains is evidence from organizational psychology that procedural and interactive justice are more important to an impression of fairness than is distributive justice. A very significant finding is that of Tyler and Blader (2000, 2001) that perceptions of procedural justice contribute to pride in an organization.

We do not know why people so urgently desire fairness. Is it because it contributes to an atmosphere of positive reciprocation where people like to exchange favors? Does fairness make people feel more secure? Do people feel that fairness is right and want their surroundings to accord with their moral precepts? Do people simply want to have a level playing field on which to compete? It is to be hoped that further empirical work will give more insight into these questions.

An understanding of the need for fairness would contribute a great deal to understanding how organizations obtain cooperation and to the explanation of wage rigidity. A sense of fairness is probably the most important determinant of good company morale. Other important factors are close ties among coworkers and the significance attached to the firm's output. One reason pay cuts can be resented is that they can dissolve the sense of fairness. Workers accept a pay cut if they feel it is fair and they see it as fair when it saves a significant number of jobs.

Another important conclusion is that firms try to gain the cooperation of employees by getting them to identify with the company and to internalize its objectives. As Tyler and Blader (2000, 2001) have emphasized, an atmosphere of fairness makes workers more willing to do these things. It would be useful to know why fairness promotes identification with a company and why people identify with organizations at all. That they do is clear.

Notes

I am grateful to Professor Jennifer Smith of the University of Warwick for her comments.

1. These data are cited in Akerlof, Dickens, and Perry (1996, 8).

2. I owe this reference to Angier (2002), who makes the connection with the experimental work of Ernst Fehr.

3. See figure 6 in Fehr and Fischbacher (2002).

4. In Fehr, Klein, and Schmidt (2001), the employer chooses the type of model used, there is no excess supply of labor, and the experimenter matches one worker to one employer in each period. In Fehr and Gächter (2002), the experimenter chooses the model, there is an excess supply of labor, and the matching of workers to employers is determined by market bidding.

References

Abrams, Dominic, Kaori Ando, and Steve Hinkle. (1998), "Psychological Attachment to the Group: Cross-Cultural Differences in Organizational Identification and Subjective Norms as Predictors of Workers' Turnover Intentions," *Personality and Social Psychology Bulletin* 24, 1027–1039.

Agell, Jonas, and Per Lundborg. (1995), "Theories of Pay and Unemployment: Survey Evidence from Swedish Manufacturing Firms," *Scandinavian Journal of Economics* 97, 295–307.

———. (1999), "Survey Evidence on Wage Rigidity and Unemployment: Sweden in the 1990s," Office of Labour Market Policy Evaluation, Uppsala, Sweden, Discussion Paper 1999, 2.

———. (2003), "Survey Evidence on Wage Rigidity and Unemployment: Sweden in the 1990s," *Scandinavian Journal of Economics* 105, 15–29.

Akerlof, George A. (1982), "Labor Contracts as Partial Gift Exchange," *Quarterly Journal of Economics* 97, 543–569.

Akerlof, George A., William T. Dickens, and George Perry. (1996), "The Macroeconomics of Low Inflation," *Brookings Papers on Economic Activity* 1–76.

Akerlof, George A., and Janet Yellen. (1988), "Fairness and Unemployment," *American Economic Association, Papers and Proceedings* 78, 44–49.

———. (1990), "The Fair Wage-Effort Hypothesis and Unemployment," *The Quarterly Journal of Economics* 105, 255–283.

Altonji, Joseph G., and Paul J. Devereux. (2000), "The Extent and Consequences of Downward Nominal Wage Rigidity," in Solomon W. Polachek (ed.), *Worker Well-Being*, vol. 19 of *Research in Labor Economics* 383–431.

Angier, Natalie. (2002), "Why We're so Nice: We're Wired to Cooperate," *New York Times*, Science Section, July 23, 2002.

Bachrach, Daniel G., Elliot Bendoly, and Philip M. Podsakoff. (2001), "Attributions of the 'Causes' of Group Performance as an Alternative Explanation of the Relationship between Organizational Citizenship Behavior and Organizational Performance," *Journal of Applied Psychology* 86(6), 1285–1293.

Baker, George, Michael Gibbs, and Bengt Holmstrom. (1994), "The Wage Policy of the Firm," *Quarterly Journal of Economics* 109, 921–955.

Bewley, Truman F. (1999), *Why Wages Don't Fall During a Recession*. Cambridge, MA: Harvard University Press.

Blinder, Alan S., and Don H. Choi. (1990), "A Shred of Evidence on Theories of Wage Stickiness," *Quarterly Journal of Economics* 105, 1003–1015.

Brayfield, A. H., and W. H. Crockett. (1955), "Employee Attitudes and Employee Performance," *Psychological Bulletin* 52, 396–424.

Brief, Arthur P., and Stephan J. Motowidlo. (1986), "Prosocial Organizational Behaviors," *Academy of Management Review* 11(4), 710–725.

Brown, Martin, Armin Falk, and Ernst Fehr. (2002), "Contractual Incompleteness and the Nature of Market Interactions," Institute for Empirical Research in Economics, University of Zurich, Working Paper No. 38.

Burda, Michael, Werner Güth, Georg Kirchsteiger, and Harald Uhlig. (1998), "Employment Duration and Resistance to Wage Reductions: Experimental Evidence," Tilburg University, Center for Economic Research Discussion Paper No. 9873.

Campbell, Carl, and Kunal Kamlani. (1997), "The Reasons for Wage Rigidity: Evidence from Survey of Firms," *Quarterly Journal of Economics* 112, 759–789.

Card, David, and Dean Hyslop. (1997), "Does Inflation 'Grease the Wheels of the Labor Market'?" in Christina D. Romer and David H. Romer (eds.), *Reducing Inflation, Motivation and Strategy*. Chicago: University of Chicago Press.

Chapple, Simon. (1996), "Money Wage Rigidity in New Zealand," *Labour Market Bulletin: A Journal of New Zealand Labour Market Research* 23–50.

Falk, Armin, Ernst Fehr, and Urs Fischbacher. (2000), "Testing Theories of Fairness—Intentions Matter," Institute for Empirical Research in Economics, University of Zurich, Working Paper No. 63.

———. (2003), "On the Nature of Fair Behavior," *Economic Inquiry* 41, 20–26.

Farh, Jiing-Lih, Philip M. Podsakoff, and Dennis Organ. (1990), "Accounting for Organizational Citizenship Behavior: Leader Fairness and Task Scope Versus Satisfaction," *Journal of Management* 16(4), 705–721.

Fehr, Ernst, and Armin Falk. (1999), "Wage Rigidity in a Competitive Incomplete Contract Market," *Journal of Political Economy* 107, 106–134.

———. (2002), "Psychological Foundations of Incentives," *European Economic Review* 46, 687–724.

Fehr, Ernst, and Urs Fischbacher. (2002), "Why Social Preferences Matter—The Impact of Non-Selfish Motives on Competition, Cooperation and Incentives," *The Economic Journal* 112, C1–C33.

Fehr, Ernst, and Simon Gächter. (1998a), "How Effective Are Trust- and Reciprocity-Based Incentives?" In A. Ben-Ner and L. Putterman (eds.), *Economics, Values and Organizations*. Cambridge: Cambridge University Press.

———. (1998b), "Reciprocity and Economics: The Economic Implications of *Homo Reciprocans*," *European Economic Review* 42, 845–859.

———. (2000), "Fairness and Retaliation: The Economics of Reciprocity," *Journal of Economic Perspectives* 14(3), 159–181.

———. (2002), "Do Incentive Contracts Undermine Voluntary Cooperation?" Institute for Empirical Research in Economics, University of Zurich, Working Paper No. 34.

Fehr, Ernst, Simon Gächter, and Georg Kirchsteiger. (1997), "Reciprocity as a Contract Enforcement Device—Experimental Evidence," *Econometrica* 65, 833–860.

Fehr, Ernst, and Lorenz Goette. (1999), "How Robust Are Nominal Wage Rigidities?" Discussion Paper, University of Zurich.

Fehr, Ernst, Erich Kirchler, Andreas Weichbold, and Simon Gächter. (1998), "When Social Norms Overpower Competition—Gift Exchange in Experimental Labor Markets," *Journal of Labor Economics* 16, 324–351.

Fehr, Ernst, Georg Kirchsteiger, and Arno Riedl. (1993), "Does Fairness Prevent market Clearing? An Experimental Investigation," *Quarterly Journal of Economics* 108, 437–459.

———. (1996), "Involuntary Unemployment and Non-Compensating Wage Differentials in An Experimental Labour Market," *Economic Journal* 106, 106–121.

———. (1998), "Gift Exchange and Reciprocity in Competitive Experimental Markets," *European Economic Review* 42, 1–34.

Fehr, Ernst, Alexander Klein, and Klaus M. Schmidt. (2001), "Fairness, Incentives and Contractual Incompleteness," Institute for Empirical Research in Economics, University of Zurich, Working Paper No. 72.

Fehr, Ernst, and Bettina Rockenbach. (2002), "Detrimental Effects of Incentives on Human Altruism," Working Paper, University of Zurich.

Folger, Robert. (1993), "Justice, Motivation, and Performance: Beyond Role Requirements," *Employee Responsibilities and Rights Journal* 6(3), 239–248.

Fortin, Pierre. (1996), "The Great Canadian Slump," *Canadian Journal of Economics* 29, 761–787.

Gächter, Simon and Armin Falk. (2002), "Reputation and Reciprocity: Consequences for the Labour Relation," *Scandinavian Journal of Economics* 104, 1–26.

George, Jennifer M. (1991), "State or Trait: Effects of Positive Mood on Prosocial Behaviors at Work," *Journal of Applied Psychology* 76(2), 299–307.

George, Jennifer M., and Kenneth Bettenhausen. (1990), "Understanding Prosocial Behavior, Sales Performance, and Turnover: A Group-Level Analysis in a Service Context," *Journal of Applied Psychology* 75(6), 698–709.

Greenberg, Jerald. (1989), "Injustice and Cognitive Reevaluation of the Work Environment," *Academy of Management Journal* 32, 174–184.

———. (1990), "Employee Theft as a Reaction to Underpayment Inequity: The Hidden Cost of Pay Cuts," *Journal of Applied Psychology* 75(5), 561–568.

———. (1993), "Justice and Organizational Citizenship: A Commentary on the State of the Science," *Employee Responsibilities and Rights Journal* 6(3), 249–256.

Herzberg, Frederick, Bernard Mausner, Richard O. Peterson, and Dora Capwell. (1957), *Job Attitudes: Review of Research and Opinion*. Pittsburgh: Psychological Service of Pittsburgh.

Iaffaldano, Michelle T., and Paul M. Muchinsky. (1985), "Job Satisfaction and Job Performance: A Meta-Analysis," *Psychological Bulletin* 97(2), 251–273.

Kahn, Shulamit. (1997), "Evidence of Nominal Wage Stickiness from Microdata," *American Economic Review* 87(5), 993–1008.

Katz, Daniel. (1964), "The Motivational Basis of Organizational Behavior," *Behavioral Science* 9, 131–146.

Kaufman, Roger. (1984), "On Wage Stickiness in Britain's Competitive Sector," *British Journal of Industrial Relations* 22, 101–112.

Keynes, John Maynard. (1936), *The General Theory of Employment, Interest, and Money.* London: Macmillan.

Kirchler, Erich, Ernst Fehr, and Robert Evans. (1996), "Social Exchange in the Labor Market: Reciprocity and Trust Versus Egoistic Money Maximization," *Journal of Economic Psychology* 17, 313–341.

Konovsky, Mary A., and Dennis W. Organ. (1996), "Dispositional and Contextual Determinants of Organizational Citizenship Behavior," *Journal of Organizational Behavior* 17, 253–266.

Lawler, Edward E. III. (1971), *Pay and Organizational Effectiveness: A Psychological View.* New York: McGraw-Hill.

Lebow, David E., Saks, Raven E., and Wilson, Beth Anne. (1999), "Downward Nominal Wage Rigidity: Evidence from the Employment Cost Index," Finance and Economics Discussion Series, Divisions of Research and Statistics and Monetary Affairs, Federal Reserve Board, Washington, DC, Paper No. 1999-31.

Lebow, David E., David J. Stockton, and William L. Wascher. (1995), "Inflation, Nominal Wage Rigidity, and the Efficiency of Labor Markets," Board of Governors of the Federal Reserve System, Finance and Economic Discussion Series, 94-45.

Levine, David I. (1993), "Fairness, Markets, and Ability to Pay: Evidence from Compensation Executives," *American Economic Review* 83, 1241–1259.

Likert, Rensis. (1961), *New Patterns of Management.* New York: McGraw-Hill.

Lindbeck, Assar, and Dennis J. Snower. (1988), "Cooperation, Harassment, and Involuntary Unemployment: An Insider-Outsider Approach," *American Economic Review* 78, 167–188.

Locke, Edwin A. (1976), "The Nature and Causes of Job Satisfaction," in M. D. Dunnette (ed.), *Handbook of Industrial and Organizational Psychology.* Chicago: Rand McNally, 1297–1356.

MacKenzie, Scott B., Philip M. Podsakoff, and Michael Ahearne. (1998), "Some Possible Antecedents and Consequences of In-Role and Extra-Role Salesperson Performance," *Journal of Marketing* 62 (July), 87–98.

MacKenzie, Scott B., Philip M. Podsakoff, and Richard Fetter. (1991), "Organizational Citizenship Behavior and Objective Productivity as Determinants of Managerial Evaluations of Salespersons' Performance," *Organizational Behavior and Human Decision Processes* 50, 123–150.

———. (1993), "The Impact of Organizational Citizenship Behavior on Evaluations of Salesperson Performance," *Journal of Marketing* 57, 70–80.

MacKenzie, Scott B., Philip M. Podsakoff, and Gregory A. Rich. (2001), "Transformational and Transactional Leadership and Salesperson Performance," *Journal of the Academy of Marketing Science* 29(2), 115–134.

Mathieu, John E., and Dennis M. Zajac. (1990), "A Review and Meta-Analysis of the Antecedents, Correlates, and Consequences of Organizational Commitment," *Psychological Bulletin* 108, 171–194.

McLaughlin, Kenneth J. (1994), "Rigid Wages?" *Journal of Monetary Economics* 34, 383–414.

———. (1999), "Are Nominal Wage Changes Skewed Away from Wage Cuts?" *Federal Reserve Bank of St. Louis Review* 81(3), 117–132.

Mitchell, Daniel J. B. (1985), "Shifting Norms in Wage Determination," *Brookings Papers on Economic Activity*, 575–599.

Mobley, William H. (1982), *Employee Turnover: Causes, Consequences, and Control*. Reading, MA: Addison-Wesley.

Moorman, Robert H. (1991), "Relationship between Organizational Justice and Organizational Citizenship Behaviors: Do Fairness and Perceptions Influence Employee Citizenship?" *Journal of Applied Psychology* 76(6), 845–855.

———. (1993), "The Influence of Cognitive and Affective Based Job Satisfaction Measures on the Relationship between Satisfaction and Organizational Citizenship Behavior," *Human Relations* 46(6), 759–776.

Moorman, Robert H., Brian P. Niehoff, and Dennis W. Organ. (1993), "Treating Employees Fairly and Organizational Citizenship Behavior: sorting the Effects of Jobs Satisfaction, Organizational Commitment, and Procedural Justice," *Employee Responsibilities and Rights Journal* 6(3), 209–225.

Nagin, Daniel, James Rebitzer, Seth Sanders, and Lowell Taylor. (1998), "Monitoring and Motivation in an Employment Relationship: An Analysis of a Field Experiment," Discussion Paper, Carnegie-Mellon University.

Netemeyer, Richard G., James S. Boles, Daryle O. McKee, and Robert McMurrian. (1997), "An Investigation into Antecedents of Organizational Citizenship Behaviors in a Personal Selling Context," *Journal of Marketing* 61, (July), 85–98.

Niehoff, Brian P., and Robert H. Moorman. (1993), "Justice as a Mediator of the Relationship between Methods of Monitoring and Organizational Citizenship Behavior," *Academy of Management Journal* 36(3), 527–556.

O'Reilly, Charles III, and Jennifer Chatman. (1986), "Organizational Commitment and Psychological Attachment: The Effects of Compliance, Identification, and Internalization on Prosocial Behavior," *Journal of Applied Psychology* 71(3), 492–499.

Organ, Dennis W. (1988), *Organizational Citizenship Behavior*. Lexington, MA: Lexington Books.

———. (1990), "The Motivational Basis of Organizational Citizenship Behavior," in Barry M. Staw and L. L. Cummings (eds.), *Research in Organizational Behavior* 12, 43–72.

Organ, Dennis W., and Mary Konovsky. (1989), "Cognitive Versus Affective Determinants of Organizational Citizenship Behavior," *Journal of Applied Psychology* 74(1), 157–164.

Organ, Dennis W., and Andreas Lingl. (1995), "Personality, Satisfaction, and Organizational Citizenship Behavior," *The Journal of Social Psychology* 135(3), 339–350.

Organ, Dennis W., and Robert H. Moorman. (1993), "Fairness and Organizational Citizenship Behavior: What Are the Connections?" *Social Justice Research* 6(1), 5–18.

Organ, Dennis W., and Katherine Ryan. (1995), "A Meta-analytic Review of Attitudinal and Dispositional Predictors of Organizational Citizenship Behavior," *Personnel Psychology* 48, 775–802.

Podsakoff, Philip M., Michael Ahearne, and Scott B. MacKenzie. (1997), "Organizational Citizenship Behavior and the Quantity and Quality of Work Group Performance," *Journal of Applied Psychology* 82(2), 262–270.

Podsakoff, Philip M., and Scott B. MacKenzie. (1993), "Citizenship Behavior and Fairness in Organizations: Issues and Directions for Future Research," *Employee Responsibilities and Rights Journal* 6(3), 257–269.

———. (1994), "Organizational Citizenship Behaviors and Sales Unit Effectiveness," *Journal of Marketing Research* 31, (August), 351–363.

———. (1997), "Impact of Organizational Citizenship Behavior on Organizational Performance: A Review and Suggestions for Future Research," *Human Performance* 10(2), 133–151.

Podsakoff, Philip M., Scott B. MacKenzie, and William H. Bommer. (1996), "Transformational Leader Behaviors and Substitutes for Leadership as Determinants of Employee Satisfaction, Commitment, Trust, and Organizational Citizenship Behaviors," *Journal of Management* 22(2), 259–298.

Podsakoff, Philip M., Scott B. MacKenzie, and Chun Hui. (1993), "Organizational Citizenship Behaviors and Managerial Evaluations of Employee Performance: A Review and Suggestions for Future Research," in Ferris, Gerald R. (ed.), *Research in Personnel and Human Resources Management* 11, 1–40.

Podsakoff, Philip M., Scott B. MacKenzie, Robert H. Moorman, and Richard Fetter. (1990), "Transformational Leader Behaviors and Their Effects on Followers' Trust in Leader, Satisfaction, and Organizational Citizenship Behaviors," *Leadership Quarterly* 1(2), 107–142.

Podsakoff, Philip M., Scott B. MacKenzie, Julie Beth Paine, and Daniel G. Bachrach. (2000), "Organizational Citizenship Behaviors: A Critical Review of the Theoretical and Empirical Literature and Suggestions for Future Research," *Journal of Management* 26(3), 513–563.

Price, James L. (1977), *The Study of Turnover*. Ames, IA: Iowa State University Press.

Puffer, Sheila M. (1987), "Prosocial Behavior, Noncompliant Behavior, and Work Performance Among Commission Salespeople," *Journal of Applied Psychology* 72(4), 615–621.

Rilling, James K., David A. Gutman, Thorsten R. Zeh, Giuseppe Pagnoni, Gregory S. Berns, and Clinton D. Kits. (2002), "A Neural Basis for Social Cooperation," *Neuron* 35(2), 395–405.

Schaubroeck, John, Douglas R. May, and R. William Brown. (1994), "Procedural Justice Explanations and Employee Reactions to Economic Hardship: A Field Experiment," *Journal of Applied Psychology* 79(3), 455–460.

Schnake, Mel. (1991), "Organizational Citizenship: A Review, Proposed Model, and Research Agenda," *Human Relations* 44(7), 735–759.

Seashore, Stanley. (1954), *Group Cohesiveness in the Industrial Work Group*. Ann Arbor: University of Michigan Press.

Shapiro, Carl, and Joseph E. Stiglitz. (1984), "Equilibrium Unemployment as a Worker Discipline Device," *American Economic Review* 74, 433–444.

Smith, Jennifer C. (2000), "Nominal Wage Rigidity in the United Kingdom," *The Economic Journal* 110, C176–C195.

———. (2002), "Pay Cuts and Morale: A Test of Downward Nominal Rigidity," Warwick Economic Research Paper No. 649, Department of Economics, University of Warwick.

Solow, Robert M. (1979), "Another Possible Source of Wage Stickiness," *Journal of Macroeconomics* 1, 79–82.

———. (1990), *The Labor Market as a Social Institution*. Cambridge, MA: Basil Blackwell.

Staw, Barry M. (1984), "Organizational Behavior: A Review and Reformulation of the Field's Outcome Variables," *Annual Review of Psychology* 35, 627–666.

Steers, Richard M., and Susan R. Rhodes. (1978), "Major Influences on Employee Attendance: A Process Model," *Journal of Applied Psychology* 63, 391–407.

Tyler, Tom R. (1999), "Why People Cooperate with Organizations: An Identity-Based Perspective," *Research in Organizational Behavior* 21, 201–246.

Tyler, Tom R., and Steven L. Blader. (2000), *Cooperation in Groups: Procedural Justice, Social Identity, and Behavioral Engagement*. Philadelphia, PA: Psychology Press.

———. (2001), "Identity and Cooperative Behavior in Groups," *Group Processes and Intergroup Relations* 4(3), 207–226.

Viteles, Morris S. (1953), *Motivation and Morale in Industry*. New York: W. W. Norton.

Vroom, Victor H. (1964), *Work and Motivation*. New York: John Wiley.

Walz, Sandra M., and Brian P. Niehoff. (1996), "Organizational Citizenship Behaviors and Their Relationship with Indicators of Organizational Effectiveness in Limited Menu Restaurants," in J. B. Keys and L. N. Dosier (eds.), *Academy of Management Best Papers Proceedings*. Statesboro, GA: George Southern University, 307–311.

Weiss, Andrew. (1980), "Job Queues and Layoffs in Labor Markets with Flexible Wages," *Journal of Political Economy* 88, 526–538.

———. (1990), *Efficiency Wages, Models of Unemployment, Layoffs, and Wage Dispersion*. Princeton, NJ: Princeton University Press.

Whyte, William Foote, et al. (1955), *Money and Motivation: An Analysis of Incentives in Industry*. New York: Harper and Brothers.

———. (1961), *Men at Work*. Homewood, IL: Corsey Press, Inc.

Wilson, Beth Ann. (1996), "Movement of Wages over the Business Cycle: an Intra-Firm View," Federal Reserve Board, Discussion Paper.

12   The Logic of Reciprocity: Trust, Collective Action, and Law

Dan M. Kahan

12.1   Introduction

The *Logic of Collective Action* has for decades supplied the logic of public policy analysis.[1] In this pioneering application of public choice theory, Mancur Olson elegantly punctured the premise—shared by a diverse variety of political theories—that individuals can be expected to act consistently with the interest of the groups to which they belong. Absent externally imposed incentives, wealth-maximizing individuals, he argued, will rarely find it in their interest to contribute to goods that benefit the group as a whole, but rather will "free ride" on the contributions that other group members make. As a result, too few individuals will contribute sufficiently, and the well-being of the group will suffer.[2] These are the assumptions that currently dominate public policy analysis and ultimately public policy across a host of regulatory domains—from tax collection to environmental conservation, from street-level policing to policing of the internet.

But as a wealth of social science evidence (much of it appearing elsewhere in this volume) now makes clear, Olson's *Logic* is false. In collective action settings, individuals adopt not a materially calculating posture, but rather a richer, more emotionally nuanced *reciprocal* one. When they perceive that others are behaving cooperatively, individuals are moved by honor, altruism, and like dispositions to contribute to public goods even without the inducement of material incentives. When, in contrast, they perceive that others are shirking or otherwise taking advantage of them, individuals are moved by resentment and pride to retaliate. In that circumstance, they will withhold beneficial forms of cooperation even if doing so exposes them to significant material disadvantage.[3]

This behaviorally realistic picture of human motivation suggests not only an alternative account of when collective action problems will arise, but also an alternative program for solving (or simply avoiding) them through law. Whereas the conventional logic of collective action counsels the creation of appropriate external incentives, the new logic of reciprocity suggests the importance of promoting *trust*. Individuals who have faith in the willingness of others to contribute their fair share will voluntarily respond in kind. Spontaneous cooperation of this sort, moreover, breeds even more of the same, as individuals observe others contributing to public goods and are moved to reciprocate. In this self-sustaining atmosphere of trust, reliance on costly incentive schemes becomes less necessary. By the same token, individuals who lack faith in others can be expected to resist contributing to public goods, inducing still more persons to withhold their cooperation as a means of retaliating. In this self-sustaining atmosphere of distrust, even strong (and costly) regulatory incentives are likely to be ineffective in promoting desirable behavior.

Indeed, such incentives may well undermine the conditions of trust necessary to hold collective action problems in check. Conspicuous rewards and punishments can imply that others *aren't* inclined to cooperate voluntarily, a message that predictably weakens individuals' commitment to contributing to public goods. In addition, incentive schemes tend to mask the extent to which individuals are inclined to contribute to public goods voluntarily, thereby weakening the tendency of observable cooperation to generate reciprocal cooperation by others. In short, manipulating material incentives may not only be an inefficient regulatory strategy for solving collective action problems; it may often be a self-defeating one.

This chapter will elaborate upon and apply these claims. It begins by distilling from the reciprocity literature a set of behavioral dynamics pertinent societal collective action problems. It then shows how these dynamics can be used to analyze and improve policymaking in various regulatory fields, with a particular emphasis on tax compliance, the siting of noxious facilities, and the policing of street crime.

12.2 The Logic of Reciprocity

Accepted for decades on a combination of faith and anecdote, the premises of the conventional theory of collective action have only recently been subjected to sustained and rigorous empirical examina-

	Conventional Theory	Reciprocity Theory
Agents	Wealth Maximizers	Emotional/Moral Reciprocators
Collective Behavior	Unique Equlibrium	Multiple Equilibria
Promoting Cooperation	Incentive	Trust
Variability of Preferences	Homogeneous	Heterogeneous

Figure 12.1
Agents: Wealth maximizers vs. Emotional/Moral reciprocators.

tion. This research suggests an alternative "strong reciprocity theory" that differs from conventional collective action theory in four important respects, as reflected in figure 12.1. Each of the contrasts between the conventional theory and the strong reciprocity theory merits specific attention.

12.2.1   Agents: Wealth Maximizers versus Reciprocators

The first pair of contrasting elements relates to the nature of individuals' utility functions. The conventional theory assumes that individuals in collective action settings—ones that take the form of a standard Prisoners' Dilemma—behave like wealth maximizers. That is, they refuse to contribute to collective goods and instead free-ride on the contributions made by others, who, as wealth maximizers, also contribute nothing. The strong reciprocity model, in contrast, sees individuals as moral and emotional reciprocators. Most persons think of themselves and want to be understood by others as cooperative and trustworthy and are thus perfectly willing to contribute their fair share to securing collective goods. By the same token, however, most individuals hate being taken advantage of. Accordingly, if they perceive that most other individuals are shirking, they hold back too to avoid feeling exploited.

Individuals who care only about maximizing their wealth are at best *weak reciprocators*. If a rational wealth maximizer anticipates that she will be engaged in recurring transactions with another identifiable agent over a sufficiently long period of time under circumstances where both can observe and keep track of one another's actions, then her best strategy is to reward cooperation with cooperation and defection with defection in a "tit-for-tat" pattern.[4] Emotional and moral reciprocators, in contrast, are *strong reciprocators*. They will condition their contributions to collective goods on the contributions of others even in fleeting transactions with multiple actors whose behavior they cannot keep track of and whose identities they can't even discern.

The prevalence of this sort of strong reciprocity is supported by a vast body of evidence. Much of it is experimental in nature. So-called "public goods" experiments—laboratory constructs designed to simulate collective action problems—have consistently shown that the willingness of individuals to make costly contributions to collective goods is highly conditional on their perception that others are willing to do so.[5] Empirical studies of real-world behavior corroborate this finding. Individuals have been shown, for example, to reciprocate the disposition of others to give (or not) to charity,[6] to refrain (or not) from littering,[7] and to wait their turn (or not) in lines.[8] Indeed, individuals behave like reciprocators even in *market*s: econometric and other forms of field research, for example, suggest that when firms compensate their workers more generously, workers reciprocate by voluntarily working harder.[9]

12.2.2   Collective Behavior: Unique versus Multiple Equilibria

The strong reciprocity theory also takes issue with the conventional theory's view of collective behavior. In typical collective action settings, the conventional theory treats defection or free-riding as the dominant strategy for every individual. Accordingly, the theory predicts a single collective behavioral equilibrium: universal noncooperation.

Under the strong reciprocity theory, in contrast, there is no "dominant" individual strategy. Individuals prefer to contribute if they believe others are inclined to contribute, but to free-ride if they believe that others are inclined to free-ride.

Such interdependencies tend to generate patterns of collective behavior characterized by *multiple equilibria* punctuated by *tipping points*.[10] If, for whatever reason, some individuals conclude that those around them are inclined to contribute, they'll respond by contributing in kind, prompting still others to contribute, and so forth and so on until a highly cooperative state of affairs takes root. But if some individuals conclude that others are free-riding, then they will respond by free-riding, too, spurring others to do the same, and so forth and so on until a condition of mass noncooperation becomes the norm.

This dynamic has also been empirically documented. In multi-round public goods experiments, for example, contribution levels tend to migrate steadily toward or away from the social optimum depending on whether subjects behaved relatively cooperatively or noncooperatively early on.[11] Scholars have also documented that the incidence of littering, recycling, smoking in public, safe sex, and other types of behavior that affect collective welfare are likewise subject to feedback effects and multiple equilibria—generating dramatic variations in their incidence across space and over time.[12]

12.2.3   Promoting Cooperation: Incentives versus Trust
The strong reciprocity theory and the conventional theory also disagree about policy prescriptions. The conventional theory sees incentives as the solution to collective action problems: Because wealth maximizers cannot be counted on to contribute to public goods, they must be prodded to do so with either rewards or punishments that bring their individual interests into alignment with their collective ones.

The strong reciprocity theory suggests an alternative policy—the promotion of trust. If individuals can be made to believe that others are inclined to contribute to public goods, they can be induced to contribute in turn, even without recourse to incentives. When permitted to communicate during in multi-round public goods experiments, for example, subjects tend to assure one another that they will contribute rather than free-ride. Although unenforceable, such assurances do in fact prompt larger contributions, which subjects quickly increase toward the social optimum as they observe others doing the same.[13] Face-to-face assurance-giving, in sum, promotes trust, which in turn generates reciprocal cooperation.

Indeed, field and laboratory research suggests that incentives, far from solving collective action problems, can sometimes actually magnify them by dissipating trust. The simple existence of an incentive scheme can be seen as a *cue* that other individuals are not inclined to cooperate voluntarily: if they were, incentives would be unnecessary. This inference can in turn trigger a reciprocal disposition to withhold voluntary cooperation, thereby undercutting—if not wholly displacing—the force of the incentive. In addition, the existence of incentives can *mask* voluntary contributions to public goods, thereby

diluting the power of such contributions to trigger reciprocal cooperation. Relatedly, incentives can *crowd out* dispositions such as altruism
by extinguishing the opportunity of individuals to demonstrate (to
themselves and to others) that they are willing to sacrifice material
gain for the public good. If for any of these reasons, the advent of a
material incentive induces even a few individuals to contribute less to
a public good, moreover, reciprocity dynamics will induce still others
to contribute less, thereby inducing others to do the same. This new
noncooperative equilibrium that results is likely to be impervious to
the subsequent removal of material incentives.[14]

It would be a mistake, however, to conclude that material incentives
invariably diminish trust. They are most likely to have that effect,
research suggests, when individuals start out with the belief that
most other individuals are inclined to contribute to some public good
voluntarily—when the advent of material incentives creates the greatest risk of adverse cueing, masking, and crowding out. But things are
likely to be different if individuals start out with the belief that most
other individuals are inclined to shirk or free-ride. In that case, the advent of a credible reward or penalty can work—not just by changing
individuals material incentives, but by changing (in a positive way)
their impression of the willingness of other individuals to behave cooperatively rather than noncooperatively in a collective action setting.

An example is the power of higher-than-average wages to elicit
higher-than-average productivity in the workplace. Workers naturally
suspect their firms of being unwilling to share a fair portion of the surplus generated by the workers' labor. But when a firm offers workers
a wage that exceeds the industry average, workers are likely to infer
that that particular firm *is* willing to divide the surplus fairly. They
therefore respond by voluntarily working more productively, which
inclines the firm to maintain or even raise their wages. The result is a
self-sustaining form of reciprocal cooperation that obviates the need
for costly performance monitoring regimes.

12.2.4 Variability of Preferences: Homogeneous versus Heterogeneous

Finally, the conventional theory and the strong reciprocity theory differ
on the variability of preferences across individuals. The conventional
theory imagines that the disposition to free-ride in collective action
settings is relatively uniform. In contrast, the evidence on which the
strong reciprocity theory rests suggests that the disposition to cooper-

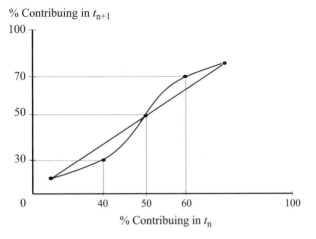

Figure 12.2
Heterogeneity of collective action dispositions.

ate varies. In public goods experiments that generate multiple equilibria, for example, neither universal cooperation nor universal defection is the final resting point.

It makes more sense, then, to envision a distribution of cooperative dispositions across the population.

A relatively small fraction of the population (consisting, perhaps, of those who've been trained in neoclassical economics) consists of committed free-riders, who shirk no matter what anyone else does, and another small fraction (consisting maybe those who've read too much Kantian moral philosophy) of dedicated cooperators, who contribute no matter what. But most individuals are reciprocators who cooperate conditionally on the willingness of others to contribute. Moreover, some reciprocators are relatively intolerant: they bolt as soon as they observe anyone else free-riding. Others are relatively tolerant, continuing to contribute even in the face of what they see as a relatively modest degree of defection. And a great many more—call them neutral reciprocators—fall somewhere in between.

Under these circumstances, individuals are unlikely fully to overcome collective action problems through reciprocity dynamics alone. No matter how cooperative the behavior of others, the committed free-riders will always free-ride if they can get away with it. Indeed, their shirking could easily provoke noncooperative behavior by the less tolerant reciprocators, whose defection in turn risks inducing the neutral reciprocators to abandon ship, thereby prompting even the tolerant reciprocators to throw in the towel, and so forth and so on. If this unfortunate chain reaction takes place, a state of affairs once characterized by a reasonably high degree of cooperation could tip decisively toward a noncooperative equilibrium in which only the angelic unconditional cooperators are left contributing (probably futilely) to the relevant public good.

Maximum cooperation, then, probably requires that reciprocity dynamics be supplemented with *appropriately tailored* incentives—most likely in the form of penalties aimed specifically at persistent free-riders. Although trust and reciprocity elicit cooperation from most players, some coercive mechanism remains necessary for the small population of dedicated free-riders, who continue to hold out in the face of widespread spontaneous cooperation, thereby depressing the contributions made by relatively intolerant reciprocators. In the face of a credible penalty, however, the committed free-riders fall into line. The existence of such penalties in turn assures the less tolerant reciprocators that their cooperation won't make them chumps; they thus continue to cooperate, less out of material interest than out of positive reciprocal motivations. And because the less tolerant reciprocators contribute, so do the neutral and tolerant reciprocators, generating an equilibrium of near-universal cooperation. Again, these dynamics are borne out by empirical evidence, particularly from public goods experiments where subjects can retaliate against defectors.[15]

The uneven effect of penalties in promoting and dissipating trust calls attention to the *expressive* dimension of incentives. Incentives do more than affect individuals' calculations of the costs and benefits of particular forms of conduct; they also shape their impressions of the attitudes and intentions of those around them.[16] Laboratory and real-world schemes that use *generally applicable incentives* convey the message that noncooperation is the norm, and thus stifle the reciprocal motivations of even neutral reciprocators, whose defection predictably spills over onto even the most forgiving ones. Targeted retaliation, in contrast, conveys a very different message. Because all individuals are aware from social experience that there are some committed free-riders out there, no one is surprised or disappointed to see penalties aimed at *those types*. Accordingly, such penalties don't create the cueing, masking, or crowding out effects associated with more generalized incentive regimes. On the contrary, penalties understood to be necessitated only by the existence of committed free-riders have a trust-enhancing effect, for they imply that *most* individuals are *not* inclined to shirk. Targeted retaliation works, in sum, because it simultaneously coerces dedicated free-riders, calms unforgiving reciprocators, and *avoids* confusing or demoralizing neutral and forgiving reciprocators.

12.3   Tax Compliance

Tax compliance is the consummate collective action problem from a public policy point of view. Society collects taxes to finance a variety of goods—from education to highways to national defense—that benefit its members collectively. Nevertheless, it is in the individual material interest of every citizen to free-ride on her fellow citizens' contributions to these goods while withholding any contribution of her own. Accordingly, the conventional theory predicts that individuals, as wealth maximizers, will evade their taxes unless furnished with incentives—in the form of threatened penalties—that make the expected return from evasion smaller than the expected return from compliance.[17]

This account of tax evasion is embarrassingly ill-supported by empirical evidence. Econometric studies have concluded that the expected penalty for evasion explains little if any of the variation in compliance across space or over time.[18] Survey measures also find only very modest correlation between reported compliance and individuals' subjective perception of the expected penalty for evasion.[19] Finally, laboratory experiments that simulate the decision to evade taxes suggest that probability and severity of detection can influence individual decisions to evade, but only when they are set at levels far in excess of those associated with actual policies.[20]

Substantially more important, empirical research suggests, is a complex of factual beliefs and emotional dispositions. Thus, an individual's perception of the extent of evasion is a powerful predictor of compliance behavior: the higher an individual believes the rate of tax-cheating to be, the more likely he or she is to cheat as well.[21] The prospect of shame (or potential stigma) and guilt have a similar effect. The more likely an individual believes it is that she will be condemned by others should she be caught, the more likely she is to refrain from evading. By the same token, the more regret or remorse that an individual believes she'd experience for engaging in evasion, the less likely she is to engage in that crime.[22]

These are exactly the factors one would expect to influence tax compliance if individuals behave like moral and emotional reciprocators. A strong reciprocator wants to understand herself and be understood by others as fair, but she loathes being taken advantage of. With tax collection as with other collective action settings, the extent to which others appear to be contributing to the good in question determines which of these sensibilities comes into play. *If* most other individuals seem to be paying their taxes, then evasion will provoke either guilt, shame, or both in the reciprocator who covets the respect of others and of herself. If, in contrast, most individuals appear to be evading taxes, then complying will not make her feel guilty or ashamed at all; it will make her feel like a sucker.

This interpretation of the data is confirmed by an experiment that tested how the 1986 Tax Reform Act affected compliance levels.[23] One hypothesis, suggested by the conventional theory, was that individuals would become more or less willing to evade depending on whether the Act had increased or decreased their relative tax burden. The study found no such correlation. What *did* shift patterns of compliance, the researchers found, were the types of interactions that individuals had with other taxpayers in the months leading up to the reform: those who encountered others who expressed a positive attitude toward, and commitment to complying with, the Tax Reform Act displayed greater commitment to complying with it themselves, whereas those who encountered others who expressed *negative* attitudes displayed less commitment.[24] This effect, moreover, was explained completely by variation in the shame and guilt that the two groups of taxpayers anticipated for failing to pay their taxes.[25] In other words, as moral and emotional reciprocators, these individuals naturally felt guilt and shame for failing to contribute to the public good of tax compliance in proportion to their perception that others were or were not contributing.

The conventional theory of collective action is just as weak at explaining variance in tax compliance across nations as it is in explaining compliance across individuals. Tax compliance rates vary dramatically across nations. Essentially none of this variance, however, can be explained by differences in the expected penalty for evasion. More important, researchers have concluded, are differences in public attitudes toward tax laws. In some nations (including the United States), individuals tend to view paying their taxes as an important civic obligation and are highly motivated to pay for that reason. In other nations (including many in Western Europe), individuals regard tax obligations much more casually (akin, say, to traffic regulations in the United

States) and display no particular moral aversion to evading them if they feel they can safely do so.[26]

Varying national "tax cultures" of this sort are perfectly understandable under the strong reciprocity theory. Because individuals are reciprocators, their decisions in a collective action setting feed on each other, generating multiple high- and low-cooperation equilibria independent of the material payoffs associated with cooperating or defecting. If individuals believe that those around them are inclined to pay their taxes, they will (as a result of guilt, shame, pride and the like) be more likely to comply, thereby strengthening the perception that individuals are generally inclined to pay. If, in contrast, individuals believe that those around them are inclined to evade, resentment will inhibit them from complying, strengthening the perception that most individuals are inclined to cheat. In other words, what we should expect to see under the strong reciprocity theory is exactly what we do see—competing and relatively durable norms toward tax compliance.[27]

The empirical evidence also bears out the strong reciprocity theory's anxiety about the effect of self-defeating material incentives. Experimental evidence suggests that when taxpayers are exposed to information highlighting the penalties for evasion, they respond in much the same way that subjects in public goods experiments do when furnished with generalized material incentives to contribute—namely, by contributing *less*.[28] Researchers have also found that highly politicized auditing campaigns tend to provoke a *higher* incidence of tax cheating rather than a lower one.[29]

The mechanism for these effects appears to be social cueing. When government engages in dramatic gestures to make individuals aware that the penalties for tax evasion are being increased, it also causes individuals to infer that more taxpayers than they thought are choosing to cheat. This *distrust* of one's neighbors triggers a reciprocal motive to evade, which dominates the greater material incentive to comply associated with the higher than expected penalty.[30]

Is there a way for tax enforcers to *bolster* taxpayers' trust in one another? One policy that seems to do that is simply to advise citizens that the vast majority of taxpayers *are* in fact complying. In a study sponsored by the Minnesota Department of Revenue, researchers sent letters to a group of individuals stating that tax compliance rates were in fact much higher than what public opinion polls suggested citizens believed them to be. The individuals who received these letters subsequently reported more income and claimed fewer deductions than did individuals in a control group. This is exactly what the phenomenon of strong reciprocity would predict: when they learn that others are in fact disposed to contribute their fair share, individual taxpayers, just like individuals in public good experiments, cooperatively respond in kind. Likewise, consistent with the strong reciprocity theory—and at odds with the conventional economic one—the Minnesota study found that individuals advised of high compliance rates paid more taxes than did individuals who received letters advising them that their returns would be subject to a greater rate of auditing![31]

Another policy that appears to promote trust and hence bolster reciprocal cooperation is the enactment of popular reforms. As the study of the 1986 Tax Reform Act demonstrates, such reforms promote the expression of positive views toward the law. When exposed to these views, individuals infer that others are inclined to comply. This conclusion in turn triggers the disposition to reciprocate. In effect, the enactment of popular reforms generates an environment of face-to-face assurance giving that builds trust and a resulting disposition to cooperate, in much the same way that discussion promotes cooperation in public goods experiments.

The contribution that strong reciprocity makes to tax compliance doesn't imply that the Internal Revenue Service (IRS) should disavow punishments for evasion altogether. That would be foolhardy because of the variability of individual dispositions to cooperate in collective action settings. With no risk of punishment, evasion would become commonplace among dedicated cheaters, whose defections would in turn unleash a contagious form of demoralization among the vast run of reciprocity-minded taxpayers.

The difference between effective incentives and ineffective ones, experimental and other empirical data suggest, lies in the social meanings that they express. Enforcers should therefore carefully select cases to nourish the perception that tax evaders are deviants, not normal citizens.[32] It is already commonly believed that a certain number of individuals of exceptional venality will evade taxes even when nearly all the rest of us are complying. The existence of coercive incentives understood to be aimed at *those* persons, then, doesn't dispel trust; on the contrary, it helps to assure the honest multitudes that they are not being exploited when they choose to pay their taxes. A model case, in this sense, was the tax-fraud prosecution of hotel magnate Leona

Helmsley, who expressed open contempt for income taxes as something that "only the little people pay."[33]

In addition, officials should always juxtapose trust-enhancing information with penalties. Auditing crackdowns and other high-profile modes of enforcement may backfire, the evidence suggests, because they function as a *cue* that evasion is widespread. To counteract this inference, enforcers should be sure that the *good news* that the vast majority of citizens voluntarily comply always gets at least equal billing with the bad news that a small minority don't. They should take advantage of the attention that high-profile prosecutions naturally attract to publicize positive information akin to that shown to generate even higher rates of compliance in the Minnesota Tax Experiment.

Unfortunately, tax authorities often do just the opposite. Competing with other agencies and programs for appropriations, the IRS routinely exaggerates the inadequacy of its own enforcement powers and the resulting extent of evasion.[34] Usually timed to be reported by the media the week before personal income taxes are due, IRS-generated stories of the agency's own inefficacy in enforcing the law predictably generates resentment in those who routinely obey it.[35] "Are You a Chump?" a *Forbes* magazine cover story asked its tax-paying readers as the magazine reported on the supposed decimation of the IRS' enforcement capacity.[36]

The United States, in truth, enjoys a relatively high tax compliance rate. But that hardly means that things can't be made worse. Like other high-cooperation equilibria sustained by reciprocity dynamics, the disposition of Americans voluntarily to pay their taxes can be "tipped." If by rattling its saber one day and pleading poverty the next, the IRS succeeds in inducing enough taxpayers to believe that cheating is indeed widespread, the result could be a self-reinforcing wave of evasion. This could create a new, low-cooperation equilibrium that, as the durability of Europe's disobedient tax culture attests, can be very difficult to reverse. Ironically, by embracing the conventional-theory strategy of "incentives, incentives, and more incentives," the IRS risks making tax compliance into exactly the type of intractable collective action problem that the conventional theory envisions it to be.

12.4   "Not in My Backyard"

Various types of public facilities—including highways, airports, prisons, hazardous waste dumps, and the like—impose disproportionate burdens (noise, perceived physical danger, health risks) on persons who live near them. Accordingly, even when individuals recognize the benefits of these facilities for society at large, they often resist efforts to locate them within their own communities—a phenomenon that political scientists refer to as the "not in my backyard" phenomenon or "NIMBY."[37]

The conventional theory of collective action sees NIMBY as another expression of individuals' propensity to withhold costly contributions to public goods and instead to free ride on the contributions of others. Accordingly, the standard model proposes an incentives-based solution: that the communities best-situated to host a particular facility be compensated for the burden associated with it, presumably out of the proceeds of a tax imposed on the individuals who benefit from the facility but who reside elsewhere.[38]

This strategy, however, has an unimpressive track record. In the twenty years since Massachusetts enacted a widely lauded compensation scheme, not a single community has accepted—or been forced to accept—a hazardous-waste facility siting.[39] The results have been the same in numerous other states and Canadian provinces that have tried to induce communities to accept potentially hazardous facilities with compensation.[40]

Indeed, there is evidence that compensation schemes at least sometimes make the NIMBY problem *worse*. According to some studies, residents often bridle at "compensation offers ... as attempts to buy them off or bribe them."[41] The potential of incentives to backfire in this way has been confirmed experimentally by Swiss economists Bruno Frey and Felix Oberholzer-Gee, who showed that a compensation offer dramatically reduced (from just over 50 percent to less than 25 percent) the number of laboratory subjects willing to assent to a nuclear waste storage facility in their community.[42]

It would be a mistake, however, to conclude that compensation schemes *never* work. At least some opinion studies have shown that offers of compensation can significantly increase willingness to accept the siting of a noxious facility.[43] Moreover, compensation in one form or another has nearly always been a part of the successful waste-facility *siting* efforts in the United States and Canada in recent decades.[44]

While failures predominate, it's fair to conclude that "studies show a high degree of variability in the ability of compensation to change public opinion" toward *siting*.[45] But precisely because they are *not* uniformly positive, these results furnish little support for the conventional theory's account of NIMBY. Clearly, something more than the weighing of material costs and benefits is going on when communities decide whether to resist or to accept noxious facilities.

That something more, opinion analyses suggest, is the moral and emotional reaction of residents to siting proposals. Individuals who interpret the decision to impose a site on their community as signifying the low social status of its residents—who believe that they are being "dumped on," symbolically as well as literally—are more likely to resist.[46] Those who distrust government institutions generally also are less likely to tolerate the siting of a noxious facility in their vicinity,[47] as are those who believe that societal benefits and burdens in general, and the burdens associated with a particular facility, are being distributed inequitably.[48] The perception that the racial composition of the community is playing a role in this process can create intense opposition in minority communities, which historically have been least able to muster the political resources necessary to resist forced sitings.[49]

These are the sorts of factors that one would expect to influence the reactions of individuals who behave like moral and emotional reciprocators with respect to civic obligations. When called upon to accept risks or inconveniences in the interest of the public good, individuals who believe that societal benefits and burdens are being inequitably distributed by fundamentally unjust political institutions unsurprisingly answer, "No."

Reciprocal motivations also explain another factor relevant to the acceptance of toxic waste facilities: the *origin* of the wastes. A wealth-maximization model suggests that waste source should be irrelevant: home-grown wastes are every bit as hazardous as out-of-town ones. But in fact, individuals are much more likely to accept disposal facilities for wastes produced locally.[50] This makes sense insofar as individuals are likely to accept a waste disposal facility in a spirit of positive reciprocation when they understand that the waste was generated by beneficial local activities.

The uneven effect of compensation schemes also conforms to the logic of reciprocity, which implies that the effect of incentives in dissipating or promoting trust depends critically on citizens' moral and emotional priors. Imagine a society whose citizens begin with the belief that societal burdens *are* being equitably distributed through a *just* political process. We might expect those individuals, as reciprocators, to be relatively accepting of noxious facilities in their community. If authorities try to purchase acceptance with incentives, however, these same individuals might revise their views, inferring that other communities must in fact be *unwilling* to accept such impositions voluntarily. As a result of this perverse cueing effect, the NIMBY phenomenon will *grow* in strength, as individuals reciprocate the perceived resistance to such facilities by strengthening their own resistance to them.

This reaction plausibly explains the results the experiment conducted by Frey and Oberholzer-Gee. Homogeneous, democratic, and small, Switzerland has an admirable history of resolving disputes over the allocation of societal benefits and burdens through a fair process of deliberative give-and-take. The Swiss subjects in this experiment therefore interpreted the offer of a cash payment as evidence that the norm of mutual accommodation had broken down in the case of nuclear waste and became predictably indignant at attempts to buy their assent to a risk that others refused to endure.

But now imagine the perhaps more typical U.S. or Canadian case of a community whose residents start off with the belief that society's resources are being *inequitably* distributed as a result of a fundamentally *unjust* political system. As reciprocators, they are likely to resist the nearby *siting* of a noxious facility. Yet in this kind of political climate, there is at least some potential for compensation to work. Not only does compensation help to offset the material inconveniences or risks associated with the facility, the very offering of it conveys a degree of respect that previously had been denied them by powerful institutions and interests.

Case studies suggest that compensation is most likely to have this positive effect when incentives are part of a negotiated, "bottom-up" siting process rather than a centrally administered "top-down" one.[51] Even with compensation, the imposition of a site by a centralized bureaucracy is likely to provoke negative reciprocal motivations. The authority of administrators to dictate the site location suggests that others are unwilling to accept the facility voluntarily, a signal that is reinforced by the need to offer compensation. When voluntary acceptance is solicited, however, communities that historically have been disadvantaged are likely to feel respected and empowered; compensation is no longer seen as degrading. In addition, the process of negotiation is likely to create a climate akin to the face-to-face discussions in public goods games: When they are able to discuss the situation with remote political authorities, and are granted veto power, local communities are likely to be assured that others are willing to contribute their fair share to dealing with the problem. Accordingly, they reciprocate positively by showing greater receptivity to placement of the facility.

These effects, case studies suggest, feed on each other, generating multiple behavioral equilibria. Again, in Massachusetts, which enacted a top-down, dictate-plus-compensation regime in the 1980s, one community after another fought off attempts to locate hazardous waste facilities within their borders, whereas in Wisconsin, which has a bottom-up, negotiated-compensation scheme, a succession of communities have come forward to accept such facilities.[52] Provinces in western Canada have had similar strings of successes with the negotiated-compensation strategy.[53]

The key to solving NIMBY, in short, is trust. Various sources of evidence suggest that individuals *can* be made receptive to the siting of noxious facilities in their communities *if* they can be made to believe that society is committed to treating their interests with respect. Appropriately structured bottom-up, negotiated-compensation schemes—ones framed to emphasize respect for the interests and autonomy of prospective host communities—are one way to reverse deep-seated resentments and thus excite a reciprocal openness to siting decisions. If individuals *can't* be made to believe that the burden of accepting a noxious facility is being fairly reciprocated either in kind or by like sacrifices, the current of resentment that fuels NIMBY will be difficult to reverse, even with financial incentives.

12.5 Street Crime

The conventional theory sees crime prevention as just another collective action problem. As a society, we are all better off when we universally refrain from theft and like forms of predation. But as individuals, each one of us is better off free-riding on whatever restraint our neighbors display while engaging in as much looting and pillaging as possible. Public order is, in short, a public good, one that will always be in short supply if individuals are left to their own devices. If this is how one thinks of the problem of crime, then the obvious solution is to create incentives that bring individual interests into alignment with collective ones. Hence, the threat of punishments for those who break the law.

The conventional theory of collective action thus naturally gives rise to the law enforcement strategy of deterrence, which can be neatly formalized in terms first proposed by Bentham[54] and later refined by Becker.[55] As wealth maximizers, individuals, according to this theory, commit crime when the *gain, G,* is greater than the *expected punishment,* which is equal to product of the specified penalty, *P,* and the certainty, *C,* that it will be imposed. Thus, crime is deterred when $P \times C > G$.[56]

Of course, it is efficient or collectively wealth-maximizing to deter crime only if the social cost of $P \times C$ is less than the social losses associated with the crimes that $P \times C$ deters. Accordingly, society must be attentive to the cost of various $P \times C$ pairings. This attentiveness generally favors severity over certainty, since maintaining a high likelihood of detection and conviction (*C*) requires a continuing investment in police officers, judges, prosecutors, public defenders, and so forth, whereas a high level of punishment (*P*)—assuming it deters and thus doesn't have to be imposed all that often—won't cost much to implement and will allow society to economize on the various components of law enforcement.[57]

This turns out to be a fair summary of the guiding philosophy of American criminal law enforcement in the last twenty-five years—the results of which do little to vindicate the wisdom of the conventional theory. Variance in the severity of punishment has consistently been shown to explain little, if any, of the variance in incidences of robbery, burglary, homicide, drug dealing, and other street crimes across place and time. Certainty of conviction makes a difference, although a relatively small one.[58]

What matters much more are a diverse collection of social conditions and public attitudes. Thus, communities characterized by low "social organization"—as measured by the quality and vitality of voluntary civic associations—tend to have more crime.[59] So do ones where institutions lack "legitimacy," as measured by the willingness of individuals to view the decisions of lawmakers and -enforcers as intrinsically entitled to deference.[60] "Social influence"—the tendency of individuals to conform their behavior to those around them—also contributes to the incidence of crime, generating multiple crime-rate equilibria independent of the expected penalty for law-breaking.[61]

Where these factors are conducive to criminality, many individuals will break the law *notwithstanding* very severe penalties. Indeed, there is reason to believe that severe penalties can deleteriously affect the attitudes and social conditions that lead to crime: massive incarceration, particularly when concentrated in minority, inner-city communities, disrupts social organization and taxes institutional legitimacy.[62]

Because it thus results in a great number of citizens being sent to jail for a long periods of time, the conventional deterrence strategy turns out not to be particularly cost-effective after all—not to mention morally problematic on a host of nonutilitarian grounds.

The contribution that social conditions of this sort make to street criminality—and the potentially perverse effect of the classical deterrence strategy on these conditions—can be systematized and refined by the strong reciprocity theory. The diverse psychological and social factors that predict crime suggest that reciprocity dynamics are at work within not just one but rather *three* interlocking collective action dynamics. The first consists in whatever mismatch exists between the interests of society in law-abiding behavior and the interests of individuals in committing crime. This is the *public order* collective action problem that occupies the attention of the conventional theory. The contribution that social influence makes to crime suggests that in this collective action setting as in others, many individuals behave like reciprocators—they tend to respect the security of others in their persons and property in proportion to their perception that others are doing the same.[63]

The second collective action problem focuses on the collective good of *community self-policing*. Neighborhoods can do a lot to protect themselves from crime. Individuals can watch over one another's residences. People can take an interest in the activities of one another's children, alerting parents when they see neighborhood kids veering into trouble or even taking the effort to steer them out of trouble themselves.[64] Individuals can make their communities safer just by maintaining a conspicuous presence on its sidewalks and streets, especially at night.[65] It collectively benefits the community when everyone engages in these activities. Yet it remains in the interest of each individual to free ride on the willingness of others to monitor and mentor, and simply hang out while attending exclusively to his or her own private business, especially where such activities can expose those who engage in them to risk or inconvenience.

The impact of social organization on crime suggests that reciprocity dynamics play a large role in determining how citizens respond to the community self-policing dilemma as well. Where they regularly encounter each other in voluntary associations—from churches to school groups, from neighborhood improvement organizations to local chambers of commerce—citizens are much more likely to observe other individuals contributing to common endeavors and to reciprocate by doing the same. In atomized communities, in contrast, individuals are necessarily thrown back on their own devices; they are much less likely to see examples of public-spirited behavior and thus much less likely to sustain self-reinforcing patterns of common regard and concern.[66]

The third collective action problem hinges on the public good of *citizen-police cooperation*. The police obviously benefit when citizens cooperate with them by supplying them with information about crime.[67] Citizens benefit, too, when the police diligently attend to their needs and treat them with respect in daily encounters. Yet it will often be in the individual interest of citizens and police officers not to behave in these ways. When individuals report crimes, they expose themselves at a minimum to inconvenience, but also to the risk of violent retaliation at the hands of those they are reporting.[68] Where the law is perceived to be illegitimate, or enforcers arbitrary or biased, individuals who cooperate with the police are likely to experience personal guilt or to be stigmatized by other members of the community.[69] For their part, the police might perceive that forgoing aggressive treatment of private citizens sometimes makes it harder for them to ferret out information necessary to solve crimes, or even exposes *them* to physical risk.[70] They might also prefer to avoid the risks and inconveniences associated with safeguarding private citizens from crime.

Reciprocity dynamics figure significantly in a community's capacity to negotiate this collective action problem as well. Citizens are most disposed to cooperate with police when institutions enjoy a high level of legitimacy. Whether institutions are perceived as legitimate, it has been shown, is determined largely by whether citizens believe they are being treated in a fair and respectful way by police and other decisionmakers.[71] In effect, citizens reciprocate respectful treatment with cooperation and obedience, and disrespectful treatment with resistance—not only to the directives of individual decisonmakers, but to the commands of the law more generally.[72] How compliant or resistant, deferential or defiant citizens are perceived to be no doubt influences the willingness of the police in turn to interact with them in a civil rather than a coercive fashion and otherwise respond attentively to their needs.[73]

The inefficacy of the conventional deterrence strategy is a consequence of the effects it has in inhibiting reciprocal cooperation within these three collective action settings. Considered in isolation, the effect of the conventional deterrence strategy on the public-order collective action problem is ambiguous. It's implausible to think that the threat of punishment has no restraining influence, particularly on individuals who for whatever reason are not restrained by the socially inculcated dispositions such as shame and guilt.[74] At the same time, as the effect of high-profile tax auditing campaigns suggests, it seems reasonable to infer that conspicuously severe penalties for street crimes might sometimes operate as a *cue* that criminality is in fact widespread, an inference that, through reciprocity dynamics, would dilute the motivation of some individuals to respect the rights of others.

But even assuming that its effect on the public order dilemma is positive on the whole, the classical deterrence strategy clearly has a negative effect on the community–self-policing and the citizen–police-cooperation dilemmas. Public law enforcement and community self-policing are, economically speaking, substitutes for one another—the more a community has of one, the less it needs of the other in order to hold crime in check. Accordingly, as the state purports to assume a larger share of the deterrence burden through adoption of severe penalties, it actually undermines (at least to some extent) the incentive that individuals have to collaborate with each other to safeguard their communities from crime.[75] As public enforcement suppresses community self-policing in this way, citizens have less occasion to observe one another making conspicuous contributions to the safeguarding of their own communities from crime. Having less exposure to monitoring, mentoring, and creating a street presence individuals (as reciprocators) become even less inclined to engage in such behavior themselves.[76] In effect, severe penalties crowd out and mask the disposition of individuals to contribute to community self-policing, making it all the more necessary to employ severe penalties.

Severe penalties also discourage individuals from cooperating with the police. Such penalties increase the likelihood that the targets of reporting will retaliate. Indeed, if severe penalties are used to compensate for a low certainty of detection and conviction, most individuals will perceive that the likelihood of obtaining any benefit from reporting is largely futile anyway. In addition, particularly in minority communities, severe penalties help to construct the perception that the system is unjust. Accordingly, it is when the state penalizes criminal wrongdoing severely that individuals are most likely to be inhibited from cooperating out of guilt or fear of being branded a collaborator. Confronted with an uncooperative citizenry, the police are likely to respond by engaging in heavy-handed enforcement—to compensate for the dearth of private tips, protect their own security, or simply to vent their frustration. This behavior by the police will in turn provoke citizens to be even less cooperative. Deprived of the benefits associated with community support—which turns out to be the most potent weapon for combating gangs[77]—the state will be forced to resort to even more severe penalties, thereby aggravating the citizen-police cooperation problem all the more.[78]

Ultimately, the negative effect of the classical deterrence strategy on the community–self-policing and citizen–police-cooperation dilemmas vitiates whatever positive effect the strategy might have had on the public-order dilemma. Convinced that those in the community will not do anything to stop crime, and resentful of a heavy-handed state, individuals are likely to respond by engaging in more law breaking, which then feeds on itself as the spectacle of rampant criminality induces others to abandon whatever compunction they might have felt not to prey on their neighbors. The result is a self-sustaining high crime-rate equilibrium, fueled by distrust and various forms of negative reciprocity.

Is there a strategy for combating street crime that we should expert to work better from a reciprocity point of view? There is—namely, the selective delegation of law enforcement and punishment functions to networks of private anti-crime associations.

Chicago has implemented a model form of this type of community policing. Under CAPS—the Chicago Alternative Policing Strategy— the Chicago Police Department divided the city's most crime-ridden neighborhoods into a collection of "advisory councils," which usually were comprised of no more than two or three city blocks. Each council was assigned a "beat officer," who was under strict instructions (at a time when the white mayor desperately feared a successful challenge from a minority candidate) to translate the council's grievances into an agenda of problems to be solved by policing strategies acceptable to community residents.[79]

The strategies that turned out to be the most acceptable involved the selective privatization of a variety of law-enforcement tasks. One of these was order-maintenance policing. In events dubbed "Operation Beat Feet," "March for Peace," and "Good Guys Loitering," the advisory councils organized large numbers of law-abiding citizens to occupy the streets of disorderly neighborhoods. By establishing a "positive people presence," these citizens transformed those neighborhoods into law-abiding ones during hours when they otherwise might have been expected to be a center of criminal activity.[80]

CAPS also privatized criminal investigations. At advisory council "beat meetings," citizens frequently complained about sources of disorder that the police lacked the resources to investigate. When this happened, the citizens themselves were encouraged to gather the evidence necessary to obtain legal relief. On one occasion, citizens facilitated the closure of a noisy tavern, that attracted disorderly patrons by furnishing evidence of chronic health code violations. On another occasion, citizens contributed to the jailing of a slumlord, whose rundown tenement had become the site of drug-dealing and gang activity, by collecting evidence of "reckless disregard" for public safety.[81]

Finally, CAPS facilitated instances of private shaming. One involved a two-year picketing campaign, in which homeowners demonstrated outside the home of a slumlord who had allowed his properties to become the sites of deadly gang activity. The demonstrators "were fed up with the noise, crime, violence, and general unrest that stemmed from the problem buildings.... They hoped they could make the building owner as uncomfortable in his home as he was making them in theirs."[82]

This form of highly participatory and decentralized law enforcement proved to be as successful as it was unorthodox. Examining crime and opinion data, criminologists Wesley Skogan and Susan Hartnett have concluded that in the neighborhoods in which CAPS operated, trust in the police grew significantly, as did trust among neighbors. All forms of street crime—from drug distribution to robbery to homicide—dropped.[83]

The behavioral mechanisms at work in CAPS can again be explained in reciprocity terms. In effect, CAPS promoted trust, and hence reciprocal cooperation, within each of the three collective action settings that construct the problem of street crime. First of all, CAPS had a positive effect on the community–self-policing dilemma. Whereas traditional policing strategies risk displacing community self-policing, CAPS assigned certain highly conspicuous elements of law enforcement to community residents themselves. As they observed their neighbors attending and speaking up at council meetings—and thereafter participating in order-maintenance demonstrations, public shamings, and the like, citizens learned that their neighbors *were* in fact willing to take an active role in safeguarding their community from crime. Those who formed this impression could thereafter have been expected to reciprocate, either by participating in CAPS initiatives or by entering into less formal arrangements to watch out for one another's interests.

The CAPS approach to community policing also helped to promote positive reciprocity within citizen–police-cooperation setting. Citizens long accustomed to seeing the police as simultaneously indifferent to their needs and disrespectful of their rights were now exposed to highly responsive and solicitous officers. Unsurprisingly, citizens grew more trustful and thus more willing to cooperate with the police. In addition, CAPS made it easier to cooperate with the police by negating social meanings that can make such behavior an occasion for guilt or ostracism. Those who took part in CAPS were not likely to view themselves or to be viewed by others as turning their fellow citizens over to an alien or occupying force; rather they were participating in forms of self-governance visibly supported by other members of the community. The police, too, no doubt reciprocated the greater willingness of citizens to cooperate with them by treating citizens more respectfully in return, thereby generating an even greater willingness among citizens to cooperate with the police.

Because it had these effects on the community–self-policing and citizen–police-cooperation problems, CAPS likely had a positive effect on the public-order dilemma as well. In a climate in which they trust each other and the state more, individuals are more likely to obey the law. Through reciprocity dynamics, moreover, such obedience feeds on itself.

The strong reciprocity theory explains why we should expect selective privatization to result in a self-sustaining, high-cooperation, low-crime equilibrium. And it implies that this equilibrium is likely to be a stable and lasting one.

12.6   Other Applications

The strong reciprocity theory has implications for a broad range of policy problems in addition to tax collection and the siting of noxious facilities. It's possible to sketch several in broad outline.

12.6.1   Fraud and Corruption

Like the disposition of individuals to engage in tax evasion, the disposition of individuals to engage in fraud or corruption appears to depend on whether they think other individuals are engaged in such behavior.[84] This implies that high-profile campaigns to crackdown on such behavior, like high-profile crackdowns on tax evasion, can backfire.[85] Indeed, when government invests more to deter fraud, individuals have less incentive to invest in credibly signaling to others that they are trustworthy and honest, and hence reliable as trade partners. Because individuals reciprocate honesty with honesty, the suppression of individuals' efforts to display honesty to others will predictably reduce the disposition of individuals to behave honestly, thus making penalties for dishonesty less effective. A better policy, again, is to make citizens aware that those around them are basically honest.

Or at least that is the best policy where individuals are in fact generally honest. In a condition of pervasive distrust—such as that which exists in many former Eastern bloc nations—strong penalties for fraud and dishonesty may be the only thing that works. Moreover, in such a climate, penalties for dishonesty may in fact promote rather than undermine trust. Individuals who resent fraud and corruption are likely to interpret the advent of credible penalties as evidence that others around them now feel the same way they do and are prepared to do something about it. Some of those individuals will be moved to reciprocate by behaving more honestly themselves, inducing still others to do the same, until a new condition of self-reinforcing cooperation is reached—at which point maintenance of high penalties may be less necessary.[86]

12.6.2   Information and Technology

Ideas are understood to be a classic public good. We all benefit from useful inventions, engaging works of literature, effective medicines, and the like. But why should any *one* of us endure the cost associated with producing them when we can freely avail ourselves of the inventive labors borne by others? The conventional theory again resorts to incentives, here in the form of intellectual property rights that permit inventors to exclude others from use of their ideas absent the payment of a fee.[87]

But strong reciprocity complicates the picture once again. A growing body of work has documented that within certain fields—including basic scientific research and many types of computer software development—individuals will reciprocate spontaneous contributions to a collaborative inventive enterprise with like contributions of their own, generating innovations that rival and often surpass the quality of those achieved through proprietary modes of production.[88] When this happens, the deadweight losses and administrative costs inevitably associated with intellectual property rights needn't be endured to secure the public benefits of invention. Indeed, university scientists, computer hackers, and other reciprocal producers tend to suspend the free exchange of ideas once they come to suspect that those with whom they are collaborating are intent on appropriating the commercial value of those innovations for themselves.[89] An intellectual property regime that is insensitive to the contribution that reciprocity norms make to invention can thus stifle rather than stimulate innovation.

12.6.3 Democracy

The application of the conventional model of collective action to democratic politics yields public choice theory. According to this theory, citizens, because they are self-interested wealth maximizers, will forego public spirited deliberation and instead organize themselves into interest groups for the purpose of extracting rents.[90] To combat this dynamic, policy analysts have proposed a wide variety of structural devices—from campaign finance laws[91] to term limits[92] to line item vetoes[93] to budget process reforms[94]—all of which seek to raise the cost or reduce the benefits of organizing into special-interest pressure groups.

The strong reciprocity model suggests a different analysis. As a positive matter, it points to a substantial body of empirical research suggesting that the behavior of elected representatives is limited by informal norms that discourage unconstrained efforts to redirect public resources toward one's own constituencies.[95] Thus, reciprocity dynamics already make at least some contribution to containing special-interest politics.

As a prescriptive matter, the strong reciprocity model warns us not to assume that structural reforms will invariably reinforce reciprocity norms in this setting. Policies designed to counteract public choice pressures do more than change political actors' incentives to engage in rent-seeking; they also broadcast to citizens and their representatives that rent-seeking is the behavior we *expect* political actors to engage in whenever it is in their interest to do so. Because individuals are reciprocators, they are likely to respond to this message by displaying even *less* restraint in the pursuit of their material interests in democratic political life. Thus, reforms aimed at reducing incentives to behave in a self-interested fashion might well dissipate reciprocity-based norms that now hold such behavior at least partially in check, and thereby increase special-interest rent-seeking on net. The strong reciprocity model thus underscores the anxiety that too readily accepting the public choice picture can make it the reality of our political life.[96]

At the same time, however, the strong reciprocity model under-scores how reforms that reflect different assumptions might stimulate public spiritedness. For example, scholars have proposed that the state award citizens two types of monetary grants: "stakes" that they can use as they see fit upon adulthood and "patriot dollars" that they can contribute to the political campaigns of their choice.[97] The first of these proposals expresses a societal commitment to assuring individuals a fair chance to realize their life plans, the second society's commitment to assuring individuals a fair chance to influence the political process irrespective of their personal wealth. It's plausible to believe that many citizens will reciprocate the goodwill embodied in these schemes by contributing more readily to the well-being of society and by refrain-ing from purely self-seeking political behavior. And when citizens ob-serve public-spirited behavior of this sort, still more citizens will be moved to behave in the same way. These proposals, then, are another example of how appropriately expressive law—even in the form of cash subsidies—can be expected to accentuate reciprocal cooperation.

12.6.4 Good Samaritanism

Breaking with the traditional Anglo-American position, several U.S. states have in recent years enacted laws that oblige individuals to assist strangers in need when they can do so without risk to themselves. Such laws are intended to counter the supposed growing indifference of Americans—particularly urban-dwelling ones—toward the well-being of strangers.[98]

The strong reciprocity theory, however, warns that such laws may do more to construct than to remedy such indifference. Some individu-als will see the apparent necessity of a penalty for nonassistance as confirmation that most citizens don't genuinely care about strangers' well-being. Those individuals, the strong reciprocity model predicts, will respond by showing less concern themselves. Financial incentives to assist others are also likely to obscure *morally* motivated acts of assistance, thereby diluting a signal of good intentions that would otherwise have moved individuals to reciprocate in kind.

Substantial experimental evidence suggests that it simply is not the case that Americans are disinclined to render assistance to strangers in need.[99] The way to strengthen citizens' resolve to render such assis-tance, the strong reciprocity theory implies, is to correct the mispercep-tion that others lack such resolve—a goal that can be achieved through public commendations of individuals who engage in heroic behavior.

12.7   Conclusion

The main—indeed only—selling point of the conventional theory of collective action is its asserted behavioral realism. Individuals, it tells us, are inherently self-seeking. Accordingly, we can't count on them voluntarily to subordinate their material interests to the good of society; rather we must alternately bribe and threaten them through a costly regulatory apparatus, the maintenance of which not only depletes our common resources but itself creates myriad opportunities for advantage-seeking by self-interested individuals and groups. It is hard to imagine a less inspiring account of our motives and our prospects. But if the ugly picture the conventional theory paints is *right*, then we'd be fools to avert our eyes from it.

It turns out, however, that the conventional theory *isn't* right. Individuals in collective action settings might not behave like saints, but they don't behave like fiends either. They *can* be counted on to contribute to collective goods, the emerging literature on strong reciprocity shows, *so long as they perceive that others are inclined to do the same*. Bribes and threats are not nearly so necessary as the conventional theory would have us believe; the law can instead enlist our cooperation by furnishing us with grounds to *trust* one another to contribute our fair share to society's needs. Indeed, when the law relies only on bribes and threats, it breeds the impression that citizens can't trust one another to contribute to collective goods voluntarily, thereby undermining their motivation to reciprocate one another's public spiritedness. Whatever truth there is in the conventional theory is an artifact of the common acceptance of that theory's bleak assumptions.

So we should now reject them. To replace the conventional theory of collective action, we should construct a new and more appealing one founded on our nature as reciprocators. The logic of reciprocity not only reflects a more realistic understanding of individual emotional and moral commitments. It makes the hope that citizens will be morally and emotionally committed to contribute to the common good more realistic.

Notes

1. See Mancur Olson, The Logic of Collective Action (1965).

2. See id. at 1–2.

3. See Herbert Gintis, Samuel Bowles, Robert Boyd, and Ernst Fehr, Moral Sentiments and Material Interests: Origins, Evidence, and Consequences, chapter 1 of this volume; Ernst Fehr and Simon Gächter, Reciprocity and Economics: The Economic Implications of Homo Reciprocans, 42 *Euro. Econ. Rev.* 845 (1998); Ernst Fehr and Urs Fischbacher, The Economics of Strong Reciprocity, in chapter 5 of this volume.

4. This conclusion is elegantly demonstrated by a variety of different means by Robert Axelrod in *The Evolution of Cooperation* (1984).

5. See Fehr and Gächter, supra note 3.

6. See Peter H. Reingen, Test of a List Procedure for Inducing Compliance with a Request to Donate Money, 67 *J. Applied Psy.* 110 (1982); see also Robert B. Cialdini, *Influence: Science and Practice* 96–97 (describing techniques used to create impressions of widespread charitable giving) (3d ed. 1993).

7. See Elliot Aronson, *The Social Animal* 29–30 (7th ed. 1995); Robert B. Cialdini, Raymond R. Reno, and Carl A. Kallgren, "A Focus Theory of Normative Conduct: Recycling the Concept of Norms to Reduce Littering in Public Places, 58 *J. Personality & Social Psy.* 1015 (1990).

8. See Stanley Milgram, Hilary James Liberty, Raymond Toldeo, and Joyce Wackenhut, Response to Intrusion into Waiting Lines, 51 *J. Personality & Social Psych.* 683 (1986); Bernd Schmitt, Laurette Dubé, and France Leclerc, Intrusions into Waiting Lines: Does the Queue Constitute a Social System? 63 *J. Personality & Social Psych.* 806 (1992).

9. See Truman Bewley, Fairness, Reciprocity, and Wage Rigidity, chapter 11 of this volume; George A. Akerlof, Labor Contracts as Partial Gift Exchange, 47 *Q.J. Econ.* 543 (1982); William Dickens and Lawrence Katz, Inter-Industry Wage Differences and Theories of Wage Determination, NBER Working Paper No. 2271, at 25–26 (1987); Lawrence Katz and Lawrence Summers, Industry Rents: Evidence and Implications, in Brookings Papers on Economic Activity, Microeconomics 209 (1989). See generally *Efficiency Wage Models of the Labor Market* (George A. Akerlof and Janet Yellen, eds., 1986).

10. These patterns are illustrated graphically in figure 12.3.

In this particular representation, there are three equilibria. One (selected arbitrarily for illustration) is around 50 percent: if participants in a collective action setting perceive that about half of the other participants are contributing in the period t_n, then about half will choose to contribute in the period t_{n+1}, which means that about that many will contribute in the period t_{n+2}, and so forth and so on. But this middle equilibrium is relatively unstable. If as a result of some exogenous shock, more than 50 percent are induced to contribute in t_n (say, 60 percent), then an even higher percentage than that will be willing to contribute in t_{n+1} (70 percent), leading a still higher percentage in t_{n+2}, and so forth and so on until contribution levels top out at the high-cooperation equilibrium at the upper right hand corner. Similarly, if for some reason less than 50 percent contribute in t_n (say, 40 percent), then an even smaller percentage will contribute in t_{n+1} (30 percent), leading to an lower contribution level in t_{n+2}, and so forth and so on until contributions bottom out at the low-cooperation equilibrium on the lower left hand corner. The corner equilibria, moreover, are relatively stable: exogenous shocks may result in temporary boosts or drops in contributions but unless they are big enough to push the contribution level back across the 50 percent tipping point, collective behavior will quickly settle back into the corner equilibrium from which it started. See generally Thomas C. Schelling, *Micromotives and Macrobehavior* (1978) (developing formal model of tipping points and feedback

% of Population

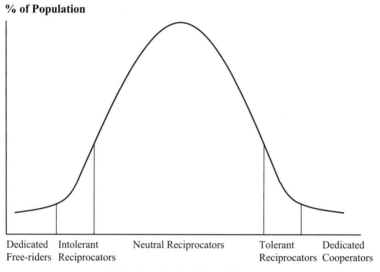

| Dedicated | Intolerant | Neutral Reciprocators | Tolerant | Dedicated |
| Free-riders | Reciprocators | | Reciprocators | Cooperators |

Collective Action Disposition

Figure 12.3
Multiple equilibria and tipping points.

effects); Randal C. Picker, Simple Games in a Complex World: A Generative Approach to the Adoption of Norms, 64 *U. Chi. L. Rev.* 1225 (1997) (same).

11. See generally Armin Falk and Urs Fischbacher, Modeling Strong Reciprocity, chapter 6 of this volume.

12. See, for example, Robert Cooter, Normative Failure Theory of Law, 82 *Cornell L. Rev.* 947, 976–977 (1997); Timur Kuran and Cass R. Sunstein, Availability Cascades and Risk Regulation, 51 *Stan. L. Rev.* 683, 688–689, 746 (1998); Cass R. Sunstein, On the Expressive Function of Law, 144 *U. Pa. L. Rev.* 2021, 2032–2036 (1996).

13. See John O. Ledyard, Public Goods: A Survey of Experimental Research, in *The Handbook of Experimental Economics* 111, 156–168 (John H. Kagel and Alvin E. Roth eds., Princeton University Press 1995); Elinor Ostrom, Collective Action and the Evolution of Social Norms, 14 *J. Econ. Perspectives* 137, 146 (2000).

14. See Elinor Ostrom, Policies that Crowd Out Reciprocity and Collective Action, chapter 9 of this volume. See generally Bruno S. Frey, *Not Just for the Money: An Economic Theory of Personal Motivation* (1997); Uri Gneezy and Aldo Rustichini, A Fine Is a Price, 29 *J. Legal Stud.* 1 (2000) (finding that fine increased rather than decreased abuse of day care center rules by parents); Uri Gneezy and Aldo Rustichini, Pay Enough or Don't Pay at All (unpublished manuscript, April 1999) (finding that incentives decreased rather than increased performance of individuals soliciting charitable donations); Richard M. Titmuss, *The Gift Relationship: From Human Blood to Social Policy* (1971) (finding incentives suppress donation of blood); Bruno S. Frey and Reto Jegen, Motivation Crowding Theory: A Survey of Empirical Evidence, *J. Econ. Surveys* (forthcoming).

15. See Gintis, et al., supra note 3; Fehr and Fischbacher, supra note 3; Ernst Fehr and Simon Gächter, Cooperation and Punishment in Public Goods Experiments, 90 *Am. Econ. Rev.* 980 (2000).

16. See generally Dan M. Kahan, Social Influence, Social Meaning, and Deterrence, 83 *Va. L. Rev.* 349 (1997).

17. See generally Micale G. Allingham and Agnar Sandomo, Income Tax Evasion: A Theoretical Analysis, 1 *J. Pub. Econ.* 323 (1972).

18. See id. at 842; Frank A. Cowell, *Cheating the Government: The Economics of Evasion* 74 (1990); Steven Klepper and Daniel Nagin, The Criminal Deterrence Literature: Implications for Research on Taxpayer Compliance, in 2 *Taxpayer Compliance* 126, 142 (J. Roth and J. T. Scholz ed., 1989).

19. See, for example, Harold G. Grasmick and Wilbur J. Scott, Tax Evasion and Mechanisms of Social Control: A Comparison with Grand and Petty Theft, 2 *J. Econ. Psych.* 213, 225, 226 table 2 (1982).

20. See James Andreoni, Brian Erard, and Jonathan Feinstein, Tax Compliance, 36 *J. Econ. Lit.* 818, 841 (1998).

21. See Robert B. Cialdini, Social Motivations to Comply: Norms, Values, and Principles, in 2 *Taxpayer Compliance* 215 (J. A. Roth and J. T. Scholz ed., 1989); James P. F. Gordon, Individual Morality and Reputations Costs as Deterrents to Tax Evasion, 33 *Euro. Econ. Rev.* 797 (1989); Klepper and Nagin, supra note 18, at 144; Steven M. Sheffrin and Robert K. Triest, Can Brute Deterrence Backfire? Perceptions and Attitudes in Taxpayer Compliance, in *Why People Pay Taxes* 193 (J. Slemrod ed., 1992).

22. See, for example, Grasmick and Scott, supra note 19, at 226 and table 4; Wilbur J. Scott and Harold G. Grasmick, Deterrence and Income Tax Cheating: Testing Interaction Hypotheses in Utilitarian Theories, 17 *J. Applied Behavioral Sci.* 395, 403 table 1 (1981).

23. Marco R. Steenbergen, Kathleen M. McGraw, and John T. Scholz, Taxpayer Adaptation to the 1986 Tax Reform Act: Do New Tax Laws Affect the Way Taxpayers Think About Taxes?, in *Why People Pay Taxes* 9 (Joel Slemrod ed. 1992).

24. See id. at 29–30.

25. See id.

26. See James Alm, Isabel Sanchez, and Ana De Juan, Economic and Noneconomic Factors in Tax Compliance, 48 *KYKLOS* 3 (1995); Cowell, supra note 18, at 102–103.

27. See Steven M. Sheffrin and Robert K. Triest, Can Brute Deterrence Backfire? Perceptions and Attitudes in Taxpayer Compliance, in *Why People Pay Taxes* 193, 194–195 (J. Slemrod ed., 1992) (suggesting interdependence of taxpayer decisionmaking should generate multiple behavioral equilibria); see also Cowell, supra note 18, 112–113 (developing theoretical model predicting multiple compliance equilibria based on interdependence of taxpayers' decisions to evade).

28. See Richard D. Schwartz and Soya Orleans, On Legal Sanctions, 34 *U. Chi. L. Rev.* 274, 298 (1967).

29. See Steven M. Sheffrin and Robert K. Triest, Can Brute Deterrence Backfire? Perceptions and Attitudes in Taxpayer Compliance, in *Why People Pay Taxes* 193, 211–213 (J. Slemrod ed., 1992).

30. See id.

31. See Stephen Coleman, *The Minnesota Income Tax Compliance Experiment: State Tax Results* (1996).

32. See Cialdini, supra note 21, at 215.

33. See the Wicked Witch Who Has Poisoned the Big Apple, *Times* (London), Sept. 3, 1989 ("'She deserves everything she gets, she's scum,' said one of hundreds of people who waited outside the federal courthouse in Manhattan on Wednesday to jeer at Leona.").

34. See, for example, David Cay Johnston, A Smaller I.R.S. Gives Up On Billions in Back Taxes, *N.Y. Times*, Apr. 13, 2001, at A1.

35. See, for example, Tom Brazaitis, Wimpy IRS Emboldens Cheats, *Plain Dealer* (Cleveland, OH), Apr. 18, 2001 at 11B; Amy Feldman and Joan Caplin, Should You Cheat on Your Taxes?, *Money*, Apr. 2001, at 108.

36. Janet Novack, Are You a Chump?, *Forbes*, Mar. 5, 2001, at 122.

37. See generally Don Munton, Introduction: The NIMBY Problem and Approaches to Facility Siting, in *Hazardous Waste Siting and Democratic Choice* 1 (D. Munton ed., 1996); Barry G. Rabe, *Beyond NIMBY: Hazardous Waste Siting in Canada and the United States* 1–2 (1994).

38. The classic statement of this analysis is Michael O'Hare, "Not on My Block You Don't": Facility Siting and the Strategic Importance of Compensation, 25 *Pub. Pol.* 407 (1977).

39. See Kent E. Portney, *Siting Hazardous Waste Treatment Facilities* 28 (1991); Rabe, supra note 37, at 36–37.

40. See id. at 39–44.

41. Munton, supra note 37, at 17.

42. See Frey, supra note 14, 69–75.

43. See Howard Kunreuther and Doug Easterling, The Role of Compensation in Siting Hazardous Facilities, 15 *J. Policy Analysis & Management* 601, 605–606 (1996); Howard Kunreuther, Douglas Easterling, William Desvousges, and Paul Slovic, Public Attitudes Toward Siting a High-Level Nuclear Waste Repository in Nevada, 10 *Risk Analysis* 469, 480 (1990).

44. See Munton, supra note 37, at 16; Douglas J. Lober, Beyond NIMBY: Public Attitudes and Behavior and Waste Facility Siting Policy 124–125 (Ph.D. Dissertation, Yale University, School of Forestry & Environ. Stud., 1993).

45. See at Kunreuther and Easterling, supra note 43, at 605.

46. Lober, supra note 44, at 120; see also Kunreuther et al., supra note 43, at 470; see also Paul Slovic, M. Layman, N. Kraus, James Flynn, J. Chalmers, and G. Gesell, Perceived Risk, Stigma, and Potential Economic Impacts of High-Level Nuclear Waste Repository in Nevada, in *Risk, Media, and Stigma* (James Flynn, Paul Slovic, and Howard Kunreuther eds., 2001).

47. See Robin Gregory, Howard Kunreuther, Doug Easterling, and Ken Richards, Incentive Policies to Site Hazardous Waste Facilities, 11 *Risk Analysis* 667, 672 (1991); Kunreuther et al., supra note 43, at 472; Lober, supra note 44, at 140–142.

48. See Kunreuther and Easterling, supra note 43, at 601–602; Lober, supra note 44, at 145.

49. See id. at 145; Rabe, supra note 37, at 21.

50. See Lober, supra note 44, at 126; Rabe, supra note 37, at 44.

51. See generally Kunreuther and Easterling, supra note 43, at 618; Munton, supra note 37, at 19–20; Rabe, supra note 37, at 59.

52. See Kunreuther and Easterling, supra note 43, at 618; Lober, supra note 44, at 222–223.

53. See Geoffrey Castle and Don Munton, Voluntary Siting of Hazardous Waste Facilities in Western Canada, in *Hazardous Waste Siting and Democratic Choice* 56–57 (D. Munton ed., 1996); Rabe, supra note 37, at 61–81.

54. See Jeremy Bentham, *An Introduction to the Principles of Morals and Legislation*, reprinted in *The Utilitarians* (1961).

55. See Gary Becker, Crime and Punishment: An Economic Approach, 76 *J. of Pol. Econ.* 169 (1968).

56. See id.

57. See id.; Richard Posner, An Economic Theory of Crime, 85 *Colum. L. Rev.* 1193 (1985).

58. See generally Daniel Nagin, Criminal Deterrence Research at the Outset of the Twenty-First Century, 23 *Crim. & J.* 1 (1998).

59. See Robert J. Sampson, Stephen W. Raudenbush, and Felton Earls, Neighborhoods and Violent Crime: A Multilevel Study of Collective Efficacy, 277 *Science* 918 (1997).

60. See Tom R. Tyler, *Why People Obey the Law* (1990).

61. See Kahan, supra note 16, at 359–360.

62. See Jeffrey Fagan and Tracey L. Meares, Punishment, Deterrence, and Social Control: The Paradox of Punishment in Minority Communities (Columbia Law School Public Law & Legal Theory Working Paper No. 10, Mar. 25, 2000).

63. See Kahan, supra note 61.

64. See generally Elijah Anderson, *Streetwise: Race, Class, and Change in an Urban Community* 3, 70–77 (1990) (discussing role of generalized youth supervision, and consequence of its deterioration, in containing crime in inner-city); Tracey L. Meares, Social Organization and Drug Law Enforcement, 35 *Am. Crim. L. Rev.* 191, 204, 207 (1998) (surveying empirical evidence).

65. See Jane Jacobs, *The Death and Life of Great American Cities* 29–35 (1961).

66. See Meares, supra note 64; Robert D. Putnam, *Bowling Alone: The Collapse and Revival of American Community* (2000).

67. See generally Martín Sánchez Jankowski, *Islands in the Street: Gangs and American Urban Society* 193, 202–203 (1991) (arguing that cooperation between community and police is both necessary and sufficient to destroy viability of criminal gangs).

68. See George Akerlof and Janet L. Yellen, Gang Behavior, Law Enforcement and Community Values, in *Values and Public Policy* 180 (Henry J. Aaron, Thomas E. Mann, and Timothy Taylor eds. 1994).

69. See id. at 181–182; Anderson, supra note 64, at 190, 195–196, 205.

70. See Tom R. Tyler, Trust and Law Abidingness: A Proactive Model of Social Regulation, 81 *B.U.L. Rev.* 361, 368–369 (2001).

71. See id. at 367–368, 376–378, 385–386.

72. See id. at 389.

73. See Anderson, supra note 64, at 202–203; cf. Tyler, supra note 70, at 369, 384 (noting potential for displays of aggression to feed on each other in encounters between police and citizens).

74. See generally Harold G. Grasmick and Donald E. Green, Legal Punishment, Social Disapproval and Internalization as Inhibitors of Illegal Behavior, 71 *Crim. L. & Criminology* 325 (1980).

75. See generally Tomas J. Philipson and Richard A. Posner, The Economic Epidemiology of Crime, 39 *J. L. & Econ.* 405 (1996); Keith Hylton, Optimal Law Enforcement and Victim Precaution, 27 *Rand J. Econ.* 197 (1996); Omri Ben-Shahar and Alon Harel, Blaming The Victim: Optimal Incentives for Private Precautions Against Crime, 11 *J. L. Econ. & Org.* 434 (1995).

76. See Anderson, supra note 64, at 57–58.

77. See Jankowski, supra note 67, at 202–203.

78. See Akerlof and Yellen, supra note 68, at 192–193, 195.

79. See generally Wesley G. Skogan and Susan M. Hartnett, *Community Policing Chicago Style* (1997).

80. See id. at 174–175, 225.

81. See id. at 166–167, 175–176.

82. Id. at 177–178.

83. See id.

84. See Jon Elster, *The Cement of Society: A Study of Social Order* 278–270 (1989); Peter H. Huang and Ho-Mou Wu, More Order without Law: A Theory of Social Norms and Organizational Cultures, 10 *J.L. Econ. Org.* 390 (1994).

85. Elster, supra note 84, at 270.

86. See generally Susan Rose-Ackerman, *Corruption and Government: Causes, Consequences, and Reform* (1999).

87. See generally Kenneth J. Arrow, Economic Welfare and the Allocation of Resources for Invention, in *The Rate and Direction of Inventive Activity: Economic and Social Factors*

609 (1962); Harold Demsetz, The Private Production of Public Goods, 13 *J.L. & Econ.* 293 (1970).

88. See, for example, Yochai Benkler, Coase's Penguin, or, Linux and the Nature of the Firm, *Yale L.J.* (2003); Arti Kaur Rai, Regulating Scientific Research: Intellectual Property Rights and the Norms of Science, 94 *Nw. U.L. Rev.* 77 (1999).

89. See Benkler, supra note 88; Rai, supra note 88.

90. Olson, note 1 above, is again the foundational work. See also James M. Buchanan and Gordon Tullock, *The Calculus of Consent: Logical Foundations of Constitutional Democracy* (1962).

91. See, for example, Ian Ayres and Jeremy Bulow, The Donation Booth: Mandating Donor Anonymity to Disrupt the Market for Political Influence, 50 *Stan. L. Rev.* 837 (1998).

92. See generally Elizabeth Garrett, Term Limitations and the Myth of the Citizen-Legislator, 81 *Cornell L. Rev.* 623 (1996) (critiquing use of term limits to counteract public choice dynamics).

93. See Elizabeth Garrett, Accountability and Restraint: The Federal Budget Process and the Line Item Veto Act, 20 *Cardozo L. Rev.* 871 (1999).

94. See Elizabeth Garrett, Rethinking the Structures of Decisionmaking in the Federal Budget Process, 35 *Harv. J. Leg.* 1113 (1998).

95. See generally Donald P. Green and Ian Shapiro, *Pathologies of Rational Choice Theory: A Critique of Applications in Political Science* (1994).

96. See Jerry Mashaw, *Greed, Chaos, and Governance: Using Public Choice to Improve Public Law* (1997).

97. Bruce Ackerman and Anne Alstott, *The Stakeholder Society* (1999); Bruce Ackerman and Ian Ayres, *Voting with Dollars* (Yale Univ. Press 2002).

98. See Daniel B. Yeager, A Radical Community Of Aid: A Rejoinder to Opponents of Affirmative Duties to Help Strangers, 71 *Wash. U.L.Q.* 1 (1993).

99. See Bibb Latene and John M. Darley, *The Unresponsive Bystander: Why Doesn't He Help?* (1970) (reporting experimental results showing that failure to intervene is attributable to errors in perception especially likely to occur in group settings).

References

Ackerman, Bruce, and Anne Alstott, *The Stakeholder Society* (1999).

Ackerman, Bruce, and Ian Ayres, *Voting with Dollars* (2002).

Akerlof, George, and Janet L. Yellen, Gang Behavior, Law Enforcement and Community Values, in *Values and Public Policy* 180 (Henry J. Aaron, Thomas E. Mann, and Timothy Taylor eds. 1994).

Akerlof, George A., and Janet Yellen, eds., *Efficiency Wage Models of the Labor Market* (1986).

Akerlof, George A., Labor Contracts as Partial Gift Exchange, 47 *Q.J. Econ.* 543 (1982).

Allingham, Micale G., and Agnar Sandomo, Income Tax Evasion: A Theoretical Analysis, 1 *J. Pub. Econ.* 323 (1972).

Alm, James, Isabel Sanchez, and Ana De Juan, Economic and Noneconomic Factors in Tax Compliance, 48 *KYKLOS* 3 (1995).

Anderson, Elijah, *Streetwise: Race, Class, and Change in an Urban Community* (1990).

Andreoni, James, Brian Erard, and Jonathan Feinstein, Tax Compliance, 36 *J. Econ. Lit.* 818 (1998).

Aronson, Elliot, *The Social Animal* (7th ed. 1995).

Arrow, Kenneth J., Economic Welfare and the Allocation of Resources for Invention, in *The Rate and Direction of Inventive Activity: Economic and Social Factors* 609 (1962).

Axelrod, Robert, *The Evolution of Cooperation* (1984).

Ayres, Ian, and Jeremy Bulow, The Donation Booth: Mandating Donor Anonymity to Disrupt the Market for Political Influence, 50 *Stan. L. Rev.* 837 (1998).

Becker, Gary, Crime and Punishment: An Economic Approach, 76 *J. of Pol. Econ.* 169 (1968).

Benkler, Yochai, Coase's Penguin, or, Linux and the Nature of the Firm, 112 *Yale L.J.* 369 (2002).

Ben-Shahar, Omri, and Alon Harel, Blaming the Victim: Optimal Incentives for Private Precautions Against Crime, 11 *J. L. Econ. & Org.* 434 (1995).

Bentham, Jeremy, *An Introduction to the Principles of Morals and Legislation*, reprinted in *The Utilitarians* (1961).

Bewley, Truman, Fairness, Reciprocity, and Wage Rigidity, chapter 11 of this volume.

Brazaitis, Tom, Wimpy IRS Emboldens Cheats, *Plain Dealer* (Cleveland, Ohio), Apr. 18, 2001 at 11B.

Buchanan, James M., and Gordon Tullock, *The Calculus of Consent: Logical Foundations of Constitutional Democracy* (1962).

Castle, Geoffrey, and Don Munton, Voluntary Siting of Hazardous Waste Facilities in Western Canada, in *Hazardous Waste SITING AND Democratic Choice* (D. Munton ed., 1996).

Cialdini, Robert B., *Influence: Science and Practice* (3d ed. 1993).

Cialdini, Robert B., Social Motivations to Comply: Norms, Values, and Principles, in 2 *Taxpayer Compliance* 215 (J. A. Roth and J. T. Scholz eds., 1989).

Cialdini, Robert B., Raymond R. Reno, and Carl A. Kallgren, A Focus Theory of Normative Conduct: Recycling the Concept of Norms to Reduce Littering in Public Places, 58 *J. Personality & Social Psy.* 1015 (1990).

Coleman, Stephen, *The Minnesota Income Tax Compliance Experiment: State Tax Results* (1996).

Cooter, Robert, Normative Failure Theory of Law, 82 *Cornell L. Rev.* 947 (1997).

Cowell, Frank A., *Cheating the Government: The Economics of Evasion* (1990).

Demsetz, Harold, The Private Production of Public Goods, 13 *J.L. & Econ.* 293 (1970).

Dickens, William, and Lawrence Katz, Inter-Industry Wage Differences and Theories of Wage Determination, NBER Working Paper No. 2271 (1987).

Elster, Jon, *The Cement of Society: A Study of Social Order* (1989).

Fagan, Jeffrey, and Tracey L. Meares, Punishment, Deterrence and Social Control: The Paradox of Punishment in Minority Communities (Columbia Law School Public Law & Legal Theory Working Paper No. 10, Mar. 25, 2000).

Falk, Armin, and Urs Fischbacher, Modeling Strong Reciprocity, chapter 6 of this volume.

Fehr, Ernst, and Urs Fischbacher, The Economics of Reciprocity, chapter 5 of this volume.

Fehr, Ernst, and Simon Gachter, Cooperation and Punishment in Public Goods Experiments, 90 *Am. Econ. Rev.* 980 (2000).

Fehr, Ernst, and Simon Gachter, Reciprocity and Economics: The Economic Implications of Homo Reciprocans, 42 *Euro. Econ. Rev.* 845 (1998).

Feldman, Amy, and Joan Caplin, Should You Cheat on Your Taxes? *Money*, Apr. 2001, at 108.

Frey, Bruno S., and Reto Jegen, Motivation Crowding Theory: A Survey of Empirical Evidence, 15 *J. Econ. Surveys* 589 (2001).

Frey, Bruno S., *Not Just for the Money: An Economic Theory of Personal Motivation* (1997).

Garrett, Elizabeth, Accountability and Restraint: The Federal Budget Process and the Line Item Veto Act, 20 *Cardozo L. Rev.* 871 (1999).

Garrett, Elizabeth, Rethinking the Structures of Decisionmaking in the Federal Budget Process, 35 *Harv. J. Leg.* 1113 (1998).

Garrett, Elizabeth, Term Limitations and the Myth of the Citizen & Legislator, 81 *Cornell L. Rev.* 623 (1996).

Gintis, Herbert, Samuel Bowles, Robert Boyd, and Ernst Fehr, Moral Sentiments and Material Interests: Origins, Evidence, and Consequences, chapter 1 of this volume.

Gneezy, Uri, and Aldo Rustichini, A Fine Is a Price, 29 *J. Legal Stud.* 1 (2000).

Gneezy, Uri, and Aldo Rustichini, Pay Enough or Don't Pay at All (unpublished manuscript, April 1999).

Gordon, James P. F., Individual Morality and Reputations Costs as Deterrents to Tax Evasion, 33 *Euro. Econ. Rev.* 797 (1989).

Grasmick, Harold G., and Wilbur J. Scott, Tax Evasion and Mechanisms of Social Control: A Comparison with Grand and Petty Theft, 2 *J. Econ. Psych.* 213 (1982).

Grasmick, Harold G., and Donald E. Green, Legal Punishment, Social Disapproval and Internalization as Inhibitors of Illegal Behavior, 71 *Crim. L. & Criminology* 325 (1980).

Green, Donald P., and Ian Shapiro, *Pathologies of Rational Choice Theory: A Critique of Applications in Political Science* (1994).

Gregory, Robin, Howard Kunreuther, Doug Easterling, and Ken Richards, Incentive Policies to Site Hazardous Waste Facilities, 11 *Risk Analysis* 667 (1991).

Huang, Peter H., and Ho-Mou Wu, More Order without Law: A Theory of SOCIAL Norms and Organizational Cultures, 10 *J.L. Econ. Org.* 390 (1994).

Hylton, Keith, Optimal Law Enforcement and Victim Precaution, 27 *Rand J. Econ.* 197 (1996).

Jacobs, Jane, *The Death and Life of Great American Cities* (1961).

Jankowski, Martin Sanche, *Islands in the Street: Gangs and American Urban Society* (1991).

Johnston, David Cay, A Smaller LR.S Gives Up On Billions in Back Taxes, *N.Y. Times*, Apr. 13, 2001, at Al.

Kahan, Dan M., Social Influence, Social Meaning, and Deterrence, 83 *Va. L. Rev.* 349 (1997).

Katz, Lawrence, and Lawrence Summers, Industry Rents: Evidence and Implications, in Brookings Papers on Economics Activity, Microeconomics 209 (1989).

Klepper, Steven, and Daniel Nagin, The Criminal Deterrence Literature: Implications for Research on Taxpayer Compliance, in 2 *Taxpayer Compliance* 126 (J. Roth and J. T. Scholz eds., 1989).

Kunreuther, Howard, and Doug Easterling, The Role of Compensation in Siting Hazardous Facilities, 15 *J. Policy Analysis & Management* 601 (1996).

Kunreuther, Howard, Douglas Easterling, William Desvousges, and Paul Slovic, Public Attitudes Toward Siting a High-Level Nuclear Waste Repository in Nevada, 10 *Risk Analysis* 469 (1990).

Kuran, Timur, and Cass R. Sunstein, Availability Cascades and Risk Regulation, 51 *Stan. L. Rev.* 683 (1998).

Latene, Bibb, and John M. Darley, *The Unresponsive Bystander: Why Doesn't He Help?* (1970).

Ledyard, John O., Public Goods: A Survey of Experimental Research, in *The Handbook of Experimental Economics* 111 (John H. Kagel and Alvin E. Roth eds., Princeton University Press 1995).

Lober, Douglas J., Beyond NIMBY: Public Attitudes and Behavior and Waste Facility Siting Policy 124–125 (Ph.D. Dissertation, Yale University, School of Forestry & Environ. Stud., 1993).

Mashaw, Jerry, *Greed, Chaos, and Governance: Using Public Choice to Improve Public Law* (1997).

Meares, Tracey L., Social Organization and Drug Law Enforcement, 35 *Am. Crim. L. Rev.* 191 (1998).

Milgram, Stanley, Hilary James Liberty, Raymond Toldeo, and Joyce Wackenphut, Response to Intrusion into Waiting Lines, 51 *J. Personality & Social Psych.* 683 (1986).

Munton, Don, Introduction: The NIMBY Problem and Approaches to Facility Siting, in *Hazardous Waste Siting and Democratic Choice* 1 (D. Munton ed., 1996).

Nagin, Daniel, Criminal Deterrence Research at the Outset of the Twenty-First Century, 23 *Crim. & J.* 1 (1998).

Novack, Janet, Are You a Chump?, *Forbes*, Mar. 5, 2001, at 122.

O'Hare, Michael, "Not on My Block You Don't": Facility Siting and the Strategic Importance of Compensation, 25 *Pub. Pol.* 407 (1977).

Olson, Mancur, *The Logic of Collective Action* (1965).

Ostrom, Elinor, Collective Action and the Evolution of Social Norms, 14 *J. Econ. Perspectives* 137 (2000).

Ostrom, Elinor, Policies that Crowd Out Reciprocity and Collective Action, chapter 9 of this volume.

Philipson, Tomas J., and Richard A. Posner, The Economic Epidemiology of Crime, 39 *J. L. & Econ.* 405 (1996).

Picker, Randal C., Simple Games in a Complex World: A Generative Approach to the Adoption of Norms, 64 *U. Chi. L. Rev.* 1225 (1997).

Portney, Kent E., *Siting Hazardous Waste Treatment Facilities* 28 (1991).

Posner, Richard, An Economic Theory of Crime, 85 *Colum. L. Rev.* 1193 (1985).

Putnam, Robert D., *Bowling Alone: The Collapse and Revival of American Community* (2000).

Rabe, Barry G., Beyond NIMBY: Hazardous Waste Siting in Canada and the United States (1994).

Rai, Arti Kaur, Regulating Scientific Research: Intellectual Property Rights and the Norms of Science, 94 *Nw. U.L. Rev.* 77 (1999).

Reingen, Peter H., Test of a List Procedure for Inducing Compliance with a Request to Donate Money, 67 *J. Applied Psy.* 110 (1982).

Rose-Ackerman, Susan, *Corruption and Government: Causes, Consequences, and Reform* (1999).

Sampson, Robert J., Stephen W. Raudenbush, and Felton Earls, Neighborhoods and Violent Crime: A Multilevel Study of Collective Efficacy, 277 *Science* 918 (1997).

Schelling, Thomas C., *Micromotives and Macrobehavior* (1978).

Schmitt, Bernd, Laurette Dube, and France Leclerc, Intrusions into Waiting Lines: Does the Queue Constitute a Social System? 63 *J. Personality & Social Psych.* 806 (1992).

Schwartz, Richard D., and Soya Orleans, On Legal Sanctions, 34 *U. Chi. L. Rev.* 274 (1967).

Scott, Wilbur J., and Harold G. Grasmick, Deterrence and Income Tax Cheating: Testing Interaction Hypotheses in Utilitarian Theories, 17 *J. Applied Behavioral Sci.* 395 (1981).

Sheffrin, Steven M., and Robert K. Triest, Can Brute Deterrence Backfire? Perceptions and Attitudes in Taxpayer Compliance, in *Why People Pay Taxes* 193 (J. Slemrod ed., 1992).

Skogan, Wesley G., and Susan M. Hartnett, *Community Policing Chicago Style* (1997).

Slovic, Paul, M. Layman, N. Kraus, James Flynn, J. Chalmers, and G. Gesell, Perceived Risk, Stigma, and Potential Economic Impacts of High-Level Nuclear Waste Repository in Nevada, in *Risk, Media, and Stigma* (James Flynn, Paul Slovic & Howard Kunreuther eds., 2001).

Steenbergen, Marco R., Kathleen M. McGraw, and John T. Scholz, Taxpayer Adaptation to the 1986 Tax Reform Act: Do New Tax Laws Affect the Way Taxpayers Think About Taxes? in *Why People Pay Taxes* 9 (Joel Slemrod ed. 1992).

Sunstein, Cass R., On the Expressive Function of Law, 144 *U. Pa. L. Rev.* 2021, 2032–2036 (1996).

Titmuss, Richard M., *The Gift Relationship: From Human Blood to Social Policy* (1971).

Tyler, Tom R., Trust and Law Abidingness: A Proactive Model of Social Regulation, 81 *B.U.L. Rev.* 361, 368–369 (2001).

Tyler, Tom R., *Why People Obey the Law* (1990).

The Wicked Witch Who Has Poisoned the Big Apple, *Times* (London), Sept. 3, 1989.

Yeager, Daniel B., A Radical Community of Aid: A Rejoinder to Opponents of Affirmative Duties to Help Strangers, 71 *Wash. U.L.Q.* 1 (1993).

13 Social Capital, Moral Sentiments, and Community Governance

Samuel Bowles and Herbert Gintis

13.1 Introduction

Social capital generally refers to trust, concern for one's associates, and a willingness to live by the norms of one's community and to punish those who do not. These behaviors were recognized as essential ingredients of good governance among thinkers from Aristotle to Thomas Aquinas and Edmund Burke. However, political theorists and constitutional thinkers since the late eighteenth century have taken *Homo economicus* as a starting point and partly for this reason have stressed other *desiderata*—notably, competitive markets, well-defined property rights, and efficient well-intentioned states. Good rules of the game thus came to displace good citizens as the *sine qua non* of good government.

The contending camps that emerged in the nineteenth and early twentieth centuries, advocating *laissez faire* on the one hand or comprehensive state intervention on the other as *the* ideal form of governance, defined the terms of institutional and policy for much of the twentieth century. Practically-minded people who (either by conscience or electoral constraint) had adopted less dogmatic stances in favor of seeking solutions to social problems never accepted the cramped intellectual quarters of this debate. But it flourished in academia, as a glance at mid or even late twentieth-century comparative economic systems texts will show. The shared implicit assumption of the otherwise polarized positions in this debate was that some appropriate mix of market and state could adequately govern the economic process. But the common currency of this debate—inflated claims on behalf of spontaneous order or social engineering—now seems archaic. Disenchanted with utopias of either the left or the right as the century drew to a close, and willing to settle for less heroic alternatives, many came to believe that market failures are the rule rather than the exception and that governments are neither sufficiently informed or sufficiently accountable to correct all market failures. Consequently, social capital was swept to prominence not on its merits, but on the defects of its alternatives.

Those to the left of center are attracted to the social capital idea because it affirms the importance of trust, generosity, and collective action in social problem solving, thus countering the idea that well-defined property rights and competitive markets could harness selfish motives to public ends to such an extent as to make civic virtue unnecessary. Proponents of *laissez faire* are enchanted with social capital because it holds the promise that where markets fail—in the provision of local public goods and many types of insurance for example—neighborhoods, parent-teacher associations, bowling leagues, indeed anything but the government, could step in to do the job.

American liberals, along with social democrats and market socialists, might not have joined in support of social capital had the limits of governmental capacity and accountability not been unmistakenly demonstrated in the bureaucratic arrogance and the dashed hopes of five-year plans around the world. Conservatives might have been less avid about social capital if their once-idealized institutions had fared better. But the Great Depression in the past century, as well as growing environmental concerns and rising inequalities at the century's close, tarnished the utopian capitalism of the textbooks. The demise of these liberal and conservative illusions of the past century thus cleared the intellectual stage for social capital's entry.

Thus, a decade ago, otherwise skeptical intellectuals and jaded policymakers surprised and impressed their friends by touting the remarkable correlation between choral societies and effective governance in Tuscany, warning of the perils of a nation that bowled alone, and quoting Alexis de Tocqueville on America as a nation of joiners. President George Bush the elder urged Americans to turn away from government to the "thousand points of light" of a vibrant civil society, and then-First Lady Hillary Clinton told us that "it takes a village to raise a child."

The social capital boom reflected a heightened awareness in policy and academic circles of real people's values (which are not the empirically implausible utility functions of *Homo economicus*)—researchers began to ask how people interact in their daily lives, in families, neighborhoods, and work groups, not just as buyers, sellers, and citizens.

All recognized the bankruptcy of the ideologically charged planning-versus-markets debate.

Perhaps social capital, like Voltaire's God, would have to have been invented had it not existed. It may even be a good idea. It is not a good *term*. Capital refers to a thing that can be owned—even a social isolate like Robinson Crusoe had an axe and a fishing net. By contrast, the attributes said to make up social capital describe relationships among people. "Community" better captures the aspects of good governance that explain social capital's popularity, as it focuses attention on what groups *do* rather than what people *own*. By a community, we mean a group of people who interact directly, frequently, and in multi-faceted ways. People who work together are usually communities in this sense, as are some neighborhoods, groups of friends, professional and business networks, gangs, and sports leagues. The list suggests that connection, not affection, is the defining characteristic of a community. Whether one is born into a community or one entered by choice, there are normally significant costs to moving from one to another.

In the next section we propose an alternative framework, which we term "community governance." We begin with some examples and describe some experimental evidence demonstrating the plausibility of the underlying behavioral assumptions. We doubt that the commonly used survey instruments are reliable predictors of actual behaviors. For example, Glaeser et al. (2000) found that the standard questions about trust, popularized by Fukuyama (1995) and others, are entirely uninformative about either the respondent's experimental behavior in a trust experiment for real money or the respondent's daily behavior (for instance, willingness to loan possessions to others). We then turn to some endemic problems with community governance and challenges to be addressed by those who share our conviction that policy design should recognize and enhance the complementarities among markets, states, and communities. Similar proposals are advanced by Ouchi (1980), Hayami (1989), Ostrom (1997; this volume, chapter 9) and Aoki and Hayami (2000). We close with some speculations about the future importance of community governance.

Our analysis is predicated on the fact, established in chapters 1 and 5 that the individual motivations supporting peer monitoring and other aspects of community governance are not captured by either the conventional self-interested preferences of *Homo economicus* or by unconditional altruism towards one's fellow community members. Rather, it is predicated on *strong reciprocity*, which is a predisposition to cooperate in a collective enterprise, and a predisposition to punish those who violate cooperative norms, both of which are individually costly but conducive to strong social capital.

We will attempt to show that

(i) community governance addresses market and state failures, although it typically relies on insider-outsider distinctions that may be morally repugnant;

(ii) well-designed institutions make communities, markets, and states mutual reinforcing rather than alternatives, although as described in chapter 9, poorly designed institutions can crowd out community governance;

(iii) some distributions of property rights are better than others at fostering community governance and assuring harmony among communities, states, and markets; and

(iv) the small scale local interactions that characterize communities are likely to increase in importance as the economic problems that community governance handles relatively well become more important.

13.2   Community Governance

Communities are part of good governance because they address certain problems that cannot be handled by individuals, by market exchange, or by state regulation. In some of Chicago's neighborhoods studied by Robert Sampson Steven Raudenbush, and Felton Earls (1997) for example, residents speak sternly to youngsters skipping school, creating a disturbance, or decorating walls with graffiti. Residents are also willing to intervene to maintain neighborhood amenities such as a local firehouse threatened with budget cuts. These are all examples of what the authors term "collective efficacy." In other neighborhoods residents adopt a more hands-off approach.

Sampson, Raudenbush and Earls found considerable variation in the neighborhood levels of collective efficacy—with examples of rich, poor, black, and white neighborhoods exhibiting both high and low levels. Remarkably, ethnic heterogeneity was considerably less important in predicting low collective efficacy than were measures of economic disadvantage, low rates of home ownership, and other indicators of residential instability. Where neighbors express a high level of collective efficacy, violent crime is markedly lower, controlling for a wide range of community and individual characteristics (including past crime rates). Chicago's neighborhoods illustrate the informal enforcement of community norms.

The Toyama Bay fishing cooperatives in Japan studied by Erika Seki and Jean-Philippe Platteau (Platteau and Seki [2001]) illustrate another aspect of community problem solving. Faced with variable catches, as well as the high level and changing nature of skills required, some fishermen have elected to share income, information, and training. One co-op which has been highly successful since its formation thirty-five years ago consists of the crews and skippers of seven shrimp boats. The boats share income and costs, repair damaged nets in common, and pool information about the changing location and availability of shrimp. Elder members pass on their skills, and the more educated younger members teach others the new high-tech methods using Loran and sonar. The co-op's income-pooling and cost-pooling activities allow its boats to fish in much riskier and higher yield locations, and the skill- and information-sharing raises profits and reduces productivity differences among the boats. Fishing, off-loading the catch, and marketing by individual boats are synchronized to increase the transparency of the sharing process and make opportunistic cheating on the agreement easy to detect.

The plywood workers who owned their firms in Oregon and Washington benefited from both the peer-monitoring of the Chicago neighbors and the risk-pooling of the fishermen (Craig and Pencavel 1995). They elected their managers and required of their members ownership of a share of the firm as a condition of employment, and employment in the firm as a condition of ownership. Before the industry moved to the southeastern United States, these co-ops had successfully competed with conventionally organized firms in the industry (both union and nonunion) for two generations. Their success was largely attributable to high levels of work commitment and savings on managerial monitoring of workers (when one firm converted to cooperative ownership, the supervisory staff was cut by three-quarters). The econometric analysis of Ben Craig and John Pencavel (1995) indicates that total factor productivity (output per unit of labor and capital combined) is significantly higher than in their conventional counterparts. When faced with cyclical downturns in the demand for plywood, the co-ops, unlike their competitors, do not fire or layoff workers, but rather elect to take cuts in either wages or hours, thus pooling the cyclical risk among all members rather than imposing it on a few (see also Pencavel [2001], and for other examples Hansen [1997], Ghemawat [1995], and Knez and Simester [2001]).

As these examples suggest, communities solve problems that might otherwise appear to be classic market failures or state failures: namely, insufficient provision of local public goods such as neighborhood amenities, the absence of insurance and other risk-sharing opportunities even when these would be mutually beneficial, exclusion of the poor from credit markets, and excessive and ineffective monitoring of work effort. Communities can sometimes do what governments and markets fail to do because their members, but not outsiders, have crucial information about other members' behaviors, capacities, and needs. Members use this information both to uphold norms (work norms among the plywood workers and the fishermen, community behavioral norms in Chicago) and to make use of efficient insurance arrangements that are not plagued by the usual problems of moral hazard and adverse selection (the fishermen and the plywood workers). This insider information is most frequently used in multilateral rather than centralized ways—taking the form of a raised eyebrow, a kind word, an admonishment, a bit of gossip, or ridicule—all of which may have particular salience when conveyed by a neighbor or a workmate whom one is accustomed to call one of "us" rather than "them."

Communities thus may make an important contribution to governance where market contracts and government fiats fail because the necessary information to design and enforce beneficial exchanges and directives cannot effectively be used by judges, government officials, and other outsiders. This is particularly the case where ongoing relationships among community members support trust, mutual concern, or sometimes simply effective multilateral enforcement of group norms. This idea, old hat in sociology, long predates recent interest in social capital even among economists. A generation ago, Kenneth Arrow and Gerard Debreu provided the first complete proof of Adam Smith's conjecture two centuries earlier on the efficiency of invisible hand allocations. But the axioms required by the Fundamental Theorem of Welfare Economics were so stringent that Arrow stressed the importance of what would now be called social capital in coping with its failure:

In the absence of trust ... opportunities for mutually beneficial cooperation would have to be foregone ... norms of social behavior, including ethical and moral codes [may be] … reactions of society to compensate for market failures. (Arrow 1971, 22)

Communities are one of the ways these norms are sustained (Bowles and Gintis 1998, 1999).

13.3   Communities and Incentives

The task of comparative institutional analysis today, having left behind the plan versus market debate, is to clarify what class of problems are handled well by differing combinations of institutions. Advances in contract theory, mechanism design, game theory, and related fields now allow economists to say quite a bit about this. Markets are attractive because of their ability to make use of private information. So where comprehensive contracts may be written and enforced at low cost, markets are often superior to other governance structures. Moreover, where residual claimancy and control rights can be closely aligned, market competition provides a decentralized and difficult to corrupt disciplining mechanism that punishes the inept and rewards high performers.

Like markets, the state is relatively well-suited for handling particular classes of problems. In particular, the state is attractive because it alone has the power to make and enforce the rules of the game that govern the interaction of private agents. Therefore, the state works well in cases where an economic process will be effective only if participating is mandatory (e.g., participating in a social insurance program or paying for national defense).

Communities, however, may solve problems that both states and markets are ill-equipped to address, especially where the nature of social interactions or of the goods and services being transacted makes contracting highly incomplete or costly. Community governance relies on dispersed private information often unavailable to states, employers, banks, and other large formal organizations to apply rewards and punishments to members according to their conformity with or deviation from social norms. An effective community monitors the behavior of its members, rendering them accountable for their actions. The presence of a significant fraction of strong reciprocators heightens the value of such dispersed information and opportunities for intrinsically motivated cooperation and punishment of antisocial behavior. In contrast with states and markets, communities more effectively foster and utilize the incentives that people have traditionally deployed to regulate their common activity: trust, solidarity, reciprocity, reputation, personal pride, respect, vengeance, and retribution, among others.

Several aspects of communities account for their unique capacities as governance structures. First, the probability that members of a community who interact today will interact in the future is high, and thus there is a strong incentive to act in socially beneficial ways in the present to avoid retaliation in the future. Second, the frequency of interaction among community members lowers the cost and raises the benefits associated with discovering more about the characteristics, recent behavior, and likely future actions of other members. The more easily acquired and widely dispersed this information, the more community members will have an incentive to act in ways that result in collectively beneficial outcomes. Third, communities overcome free-rider problems by its members directly punishing "antisocial" actions of others. Monitoring and punishment by peers in work teams, credit associations, partnerships, local commons situations, and residential neighborhoods is often an effective means of attenuating incentive problems that arise where individual actions affecting the well-being of others are not subject to enforceable contracts (Whyte 1955; Homans 1961; Ostrom 1990; Tilly 1981; Hossain 1988; Dong and Dow 1993; Sampson, Raudenbush, and Earls 1997).

To the extent that economists have sought to understand how communities work, they have treated individuals as self-interested and considered models in which self-interested agents would cooperate—even in interactions that at first glance appear to have defection as a dominant strategy. We have explained elsewhere why we find these explanations inadequate (Gintis 2000; Bowles 2004). By contrast, many behavioral scientists outside of economics have sought to explain communities by relations of altruism, affection, and other non–self-regarding motives. Many of these approaches, however, have treated the community organically without investigating whether or not its structural characteristics are consistent with conventional notions of equilibrium based on intentional action. We stress non–self-interested motives because we believe explaining how communities enforce norms through mutual monitoring requires going beyond this traditional model of the individual actor. The treatment of social penalties by Besley and Coate (1995) and of peer pressure by Kandel and Lazear (1992) reflect a similar dissatisfaction with the conventional behavioral model. Communities are often capable of enforcing norms, we suggest, because a considerable fraction of members are *strong reciprocators* who are willing to engage in the costly punishment of shirkers without a reasonable expectation of being personally repaid for their efforts (see chapter 1 and part II).

13.4   Community Failures

Like markets and governments, communities also fail. The personal and durable contacts that characterize communities require them to be of relatively small scale, and a preference for dealing with fellow members often limits their capacity to exploit gains from trade on a wider basis. Moreover, the tendency for communities to be relatively homogeneous may make it impossible to reap the benefits of economic diversity associated with strong complementarities among differing skills and other inputs. Neither of these limitations is insurmountable. By sharing information, equipment, and skills, for example, the Japanese co-op fishermen exploited economies of scale unattainable by less cooperative groups and reaped substantial benefits from the diversity of talents among the membership. Similarly cooperation in the local business networks in what is called "the third Italy" (along with their associated local governments) allows otherwise unviably small firms to benefit from economies of scale in marketing, research, and training—allowing their survival in competition with corporate giants. But compared to bureaucracies and markets, which specialize in dealing with strangers, the limited scope of communities often imposes inescapable costs.

A second "community failure" is less obvious. Where group membership is the result of individual choices rather than group decisions, the composition of groups is likely to be more culturally and demographically homogeneous than any of the members would like, thereby depriving people of valued forms of diversity. To envision this scenario, imagine that the populations of a large number of residential communities are made up of just two types of people easily identified by appearance or speech, and that everyone strongly prefers to be in an integrated group but not to be in a minority. If individuals sort themselves among the communities, there will be a strong tendency for all of the communities to end up perfectly segregated for reasons that Thomas Schelling (1978) pointed out in his analysis of neighborhood tipping. Integrated communities would make everyone better off, but they will prove unsustainable if individuals are free to move.

Young (1998) and Bowles (2003) provide models demonstrating this result.

Economists use the terms "market failures" and "state failures" to point to the allocative inefficiencies entailed by these governance structures, and so far our discussion of these along with community failures has conformed to the canon. But communities often fail in other, sometimes more egregious ways. Most individuals seek membership in a group of familiar associates and feel isolated without it. The baggage of belonging, however, often includes poor treatment of those who do not. The problem is exacerbated by the group homogeneity resulting from the neighborhood tipping community failure described in the previous paragraph. When insider-outsider distinctions are made on divisive and morally repugnant bases such as race, religion, nationality, or sex, community governance may contribute more to fostering parochial narrow-mindedness and ethnic hostility than to addressing the failures of markets and states. This downside of community becomes particularly troubling when insiders are wealthy and powerful and outsiders are exploited as a result.

The problem is endemic. Communities work because they are good at enforcing norms, and whether this is a good thing depends on what the norms are. The recent resistance to racial integration by the white residents of Ruyterwacht (near Cape Town) is as gripping an account of social capital in action as one can imagine (Jung 1998). Even more striking is Dov Cohen's (1998) study of differences in the relationship between violence and community stability indifferent U.S. regions. With Richard Nisbett (1996), Cohen has described a "culture of honor" that often turns public insults and arguments into deadly confrontations among white males in the South and West, but not in the North. Cohen's research confirms the finding that in the North, homicides stemming from arguments are less frequent in areas of higher residential stability, measured by the fractions of people living in the same house and people living in the same county over a five-year period. But this relationship is inverted in the South and West, as residential stability is positively and significantly related to the frequency of these homicides where the culture of honor is strong.

13.5 Enhancing Community Governance

Many adherents of the liberal philosophical tradition—whether conservative advocates of *laissez faire* or their social democratic and liberal socialist critics—have seen communities as anachronistic remnants of a less enlightened epoch that lacked the property rights, markets, and states adequate to the task of governance. In this view, communities are not part of the solution to the failures of markets and states, but part of the problem of parochial populism or traditional fundamentalism. Many holding this view have long since rejected any dogmatic adherence to either pole of the planning versus markets opposition. But these conceptual anchors still moor the ship of good government as firmly as ever, and debate now centers on finding the optimal location along the resulting continuum.

Those advocating social capital, or as we would prefer, community governance, as an important aspect of policymaking and institution-building have come to be dissatisfied with this view. They doubt (with Kenneth Arrow) that states or markets, in any combination, can be so perfected as to make norms redundant, and they believe that the substantial drawbacks of this third form of governance can be attenuated by adequate social policy. Many have also pointed to cases where efforts to perfect the market or assure the success of state interventions have destroyed imperfect but nonetheless valuable community-based systems of governance, suggesting that policy paradigms confined to states and markets may be counterproductive.

Unlike the utopian capitalism of textbook neoclassical economics and the utopian statism of its sub-branch called welfare economics (which during the 20th century imagined that governments have both the information and the inclination to offset market failures), there can be no blueprint for ideal community governance. As Elinor Ostrom (1990; volume, chapter 9), James Scott (1998), and other field researchers have stressed, communities solve problems in a bewildering variety of ways with hundreds of differing membership rules, *de facto* property rights, and decision-making procedures. But the cases described in this chapter may suggest some of the elements that are frequently found in well-governing communities and which might form part of a public policy aimed at enhancing the desirable aspects of community governance.

The first element, strongly supported by experimental evidence, is that members of the community should own the fruits of their success or failure in solving the collective problems they face. The Japanese fishermen, skippers and crew alike, own shares in the output of their co-op and hence directly benefit from its success in a way that employees on fixed wages would not. Among the Chicago residents, communities in which home ownership is common exhibit much higher levels of "collective efficacy," even after controlling for a large number of demographic and economic variables. The most likely explanation is that home owners benefit fully from their neighborhood improvement interventions—not only from the improved quality of life, but from the enhanced value of their homes as well. This interpretation is consistent with the fact that Sidney Verba and his collaborators (1995) found that controlling for a large number of demographic and other variables, U.S. home owners are more likely to participate in local but not national politics, and with Edward Glaeser and Denise Depasquale's (1999) findings in a sample of German individuals that changes in home ownership predict changes in levels of civic participation. Finally, the plywood worker-owners' success would be inexplicable were it not for the fact that as residual claimants on the income stream of the co-op, each individual owns the results of the others' efforts. As these examples suggest, in order to own the success of one's efforts, community members must generally own the assets with which they work or whose value is affected by what the community does.

Second, as we have seen in the public goods with punishment experiments, the unraveling of cooperation that often afflicts communities can be averted if opportunities for mutual monitoring and punishment of noncooperators are built into the structure of social interactions. Policies to increase the visibility of the actions of peers in communities, along with policies to enhance the effectiveness of forms of multilateral sanctioning of shirkers, may thus contribute to cooperative solutions to problems, even if a majority of members are self-interested. Huntergatherer bands that share food often practice the custom of eating in public, an effect of which is to make violations of the sharing rule evident to all. The Toyama Bay fishers' practice of offloading their catch at the same time likewise contributes to transparency in implementing their sharing rule.

An important feature of models in which cooperation in sizable groups is sustained by the punishment of shirkers is that multiple equilibria typically exist. When cooperation is common, the costs incurred by civic-minded punishers is small, and they can easily persist in a population. When cooperation is uncommon, those who punish shirkers will incur heavy costs and will likely be eliminated by any plausible evolutionary process (this volume, chapter 7). This suggests that a heterogeneous population with some civic-minded members (ready to punish those who violate norms) and some self-interested members may exhibit high or low levels of cooperation depending not on the distribution of types in the population, but rather on the recent history of the group.

There is a third desideratum for enhancing community governance. The cases described in this chapter and hundreds like them suggest that well-working communities require a legal and governmental environment favorable to their functioning. The Chicago residents' success in reducing crime could hardly have been realized had the police not been on call. The Japanese fishing co-ops numbering more than a thousand work within national and prefectural environmental and other regulations which they are free to complement by locally made rules, but not to override. A comparison of Taiwanese and South Indian farmer-managed irrigation organizations shows that the greater success of the former is due to the effective intervention of national governments in providing a favorable legal environment and handling cases in which the informal sanctions of the community would not be adequate (Lam 1996; Wade 1988) Similar community-governmental synergy is found in Tendler's study of the delivery of health care (1997) and Ostrom's account of urban infrastructure (1996), both of which focus on Brazil. The fact that governmental intervention has sometimes destroyed community governance capacities does not support a recommendation of *laissez faire*.

The face-to-face local interactions of community are thus not a substitute for effective government but rather a complement. Neglect of this point no doubt explains some of the popularity of the social capital concept. A Gallup Poll recently asked a large national sample of Americans "Which one of the following groups do you think has the greatest responsibility for helping the poor: churches, private charities, the government, the families and relatives of poor people, the poor themselves, or someone else?" The survey also asked if inequalities in income and wealth were "acceptable" or "a problem that needs to be fixed." While the sample was evenly split on the first question between the government on the one hand and all of the non-governmental responses on the other, those unconcerned about the level of inequality in the second question were almost three times as likely to support the private approach than the government solution (see this volume, chapter 10). Those favoring the social capital option in this case were seemingly more motivated by the fact that it would shrink government than by the hope that it would reduce inequality.

Thus, both a legal and governmental environment that complements the distinctive governance abilities of communities and a distribution of property rights that makes members the beneficiaries of community success are key aspects of policies to foster community problem-solving. Developing an institutional structure such that states, markets, and communities are mutually enhancing is a challenging task, however. For example, where property rights are ill-defined (and informal contractual enforcement is essential to mutually beneficial exchange), more precisely defined property rights may *reduce* the multifaceted and repeated nature of interpersonal contact on which community governance is based (Bowles and Gintis 1998). Similarly, there is considerable evidence that efforts to induce higher levels of work effort, compliance to norms, or environmental conservation by mobilizing self-interested motives through the use of fines and sanctions may undermine reciprocity and other social motives (see this volume, chapters 1 and 9; as well as sources cited in Bowles 1998 and Bowles 2004).

A fourth element in the community/good governance package: active advocacy of the conventional liberal ethics of equal treatment and enforcement of conventional anti-discrimination policies. That it is not unrealistic to hope that communities can govern effectively without repugnant behaviors favoring "us" against "them" is suggested by the many examples of well-working communities that do not exhibit the ugly parochial and divisive potential of this form of governance, including all of those above.

Other ways of empowering communities can be imagined, but some should be resisted on grounds that they heighten the difficult tradeoffs between good governance and parochialism mentioned in this chapter. For example, Alesina and La Ferrara (2000) found that among United States localities, participation in church, local service and political groups, as well as other community organizations is substantially higher where income is more equally distributed, even when a host of other possible influences are controlled. Their findings suggest that policies to increase income equality would enhance community governance. But they also found that racially and ethnically diverse localities, measured by the probability that two randomly selected members of the population would be of different racial or ethnic groups, had significantly lower levels of participation. One may hope that pro-community public policy would not seek to increase racial and ethnic homogeneity of groups for this reason.

But simply resisting government policies that homogenize is not sufficient. If Alesina and La Ferrara's results (and others like them) suggest that successful communities are likely to be relatively homogeneous, then a heavy reliance on community governance, in the absence of adequate counteracting policies, could promote higher levels of local homogeneity simply because the success of groups and their likely longevity will vary with how homogeneous they are. Thus, a competitive economy in which worker-owned cooperatives are common is likely to exhibit more homogeneous workplaces than one made up of conventional firms. The combination of within-group homogeneity and between-group competition, while effectively promoting some desirable forms of governance, seems a recipe for hostile "us versus them" sentiments. Dilemmas such as this one are not likely to disappear.

13.6   Economic Evolution and the Future of Community Governance

The age of commerce and the dawn of democracy were widely thought to mark the eclipse of community. Writers of all persuasions believed that markets, the state, or simply "modernization," would extinguish the values that throughout history had sustained forms of governance based on intimate and ascriptive relationships. According to the romanticist conservative Edmund Burke (1955[1790])

... The age of chivalry is gone. That of Sophisters, economists, and calculators has succeeded.... Nothing is left which engages the affection on the part of the commonwealth ... so as to create in us love, veneration, admiration or attachment.

The liberal Alexis de Tocqueville (1958[1832]) echoes Burke's fears in this comment on democratic culture in America during the 1830s:

Each [person] ... is a stranger to the fate of all the rest ... his children and his private friends constitute to him the whole of mankind; as for the rest of his fellow citizens, he is close to them but he sees them not ... he touches them but he feels them not; he exists but in himself and for himself alone ...

For the socialists Karl Marx and Friedrich Engels (1972[1848], 475)

The bourgeoisie ... has put an end to all feudal, patriarchal, idyllic relations. It has pitilessly torn asunder the motley feudal ties that bound man to his "natural superiors," and has left remaining no other nexus between man and man than naked self-interest ... [I]n place of the numberless indefeasible chartered freedoms, it has set up that single, unconscionable freedom—free trade.

Many who predicted the demise of community based their argument on the notion that communities owe their existence to a distinct set of pre-modern "values" that were bound to be extinguished by economic and political competition in markets and democratic states, or as Marx put it, by "the icy waters of egotistical calculation." Modern writers have also stressed that the parochialism on which communities thrive requires cultural commitments that are antithetical to modern social institutions. Talcott Parsons' sociological system, to mention one prominent example, consistently attributes "particularistic" values to more primitive levels of civilization, and "universalistic" values to the more advanced.

Fred Hirsch refered to the waning of precapitalist moral codes in similar vein:

This legacy has diminished with time and with the corrosive contact of the active capitalist values. As individual behavior has been increasingly directed to individual advantage, habits and instincts based on communal attitudes and objectives have lost out (Hirsch 1976, 117–118).

We do not doubt that markets and democratic states represent cultural environments in which some values flourish and others wither. Indeed, the dismay concerning their effects, expressed so long ago by Burke, Marx, and de Tocqueville, may have been prescient. But the basis for the rise, fall, and transformation of communities, if we are correct, is to be sought not in the survival of vestigial values of an earlier age, but in the capacity of communities, like that of markets and states, to provide successful solutions to assist in solving contemporary problems of social coordination.

Far from being an anachronism, community governance appears likely to assume more rather than less importance in the future. The reason is that the types of problems that communities solve, and which resist governmental and market solutions, arise when individuals interact in ways that cannot be regulated by complete contracts or by external *fiat* due to the complexity of the interactions or the private or unverifiable nature of the information concerning the relevant transactions. These interactions arise increasingly in modern economies, as information intensive team production replaces assembly lines and other technologies more readily handled by contract or *fiat* and as difficult to measure services usurp the preeminent role, as both outputs and inputs, once played by measurable quantities like kilowatts of power and tons of steel. In an economy increasingly based on qualities rather than quantities, the superior governance capabilities of communities are likely to be manifested in increasing reliance on the kinds of multilateral monitoring and risksharing exemplified in this chapter.

But the capacity of communities to solve problems may be impeded by hierarchical division and economic inequality among its members. Many observers believe, for example, that the limited inequality between managers and workers in the standard Japanese firm is a key contributor to information sharing between management and production workers (Aoki 1988). Dayton-Johnson and Bardhan (2002) have found that farmer members of irrigation organizations in Tamil Nadu, India and Guanajuato, Mexico are more likely to cooperate in making efficient use of water if status and class inequalities among them are limited. We survey other evidence as well as the theory underlying these comments in Baland, Bardhan, and Bowles (2002) and Bardhan, Bowles, and Gintis (2000). These results may reflect the same behavioral regularities underlying experimental results showing that cooperation in two-person non-repeated Prisoner's Dilemma games declines dramatically when the degree of conflict of interest implicit in the payoff matrix increases (Axelrod 1970; Rapoport and Chammah 1965).

If we are right that communities work well relative to markets and states where the tasks are qualitative and hard to capture in explicit contracts, and where the conflicts of interest among the members are limited, it seems likely that extremely unequal societies will be competitively disadvantaged in the future because their structures of privilege and material reward limit the capacity of community governance to facilitate the qualitative interactions that underpin the modern economy.

References

Alesina, Alberto, and Eliana La Ferrara, 2000. "Participation in heterogeneous communities." *Quarterly Journal of Economics* 115, 3: 847–904.

Aoki, Masahiko, *Information, Incentives, and Bargaining in the Japanese Economy*. Cambridge: Cambridge University Press, 1988.

————, and Yujiro Hayami, "Introduction," in Masahiko Aoki and Yujiro Hayami (eds.), *Communities and Markets in Economic Development*. Oxford: Oxford University Press, 2000.

Arrow, Kenneth J., "Political and Economic Evaluation of Social Effects and Externalities," in M. D. Intriligator (ed.), *Frontiers of Quantitative Economics*. Amsterdam: North Holland, 1971, 3–23.

Axelrod, Robert, *Conflict of Interest: A Theory of Divergent Goals with Applications to Politics*. Chicago: Markham, 1970.

Baland, Jean Marie, Pranab Bardhan, and Samuel Bowles, *Inequality, Cooperation and Environmental Sustainability*. New York: Russell Sage, 2005.

Bardhan, Pranab, Samuel Bowles, and Herbert Gintis, "Wealth Inequality, Credit Constraints, and Economic Performance," in Anthony Atkinson and François Bourguignon (eds.), *Handbook of Income Distribution*. Dortrecht: North-Holland, 2000.

Besley, Timothy, and Stephen Coate, "Group Lending, Repayment Incentives, and Social Collateral," *Journal of Development Economics* 46 (1995): 1–18.

Bowles, Samuel, "Endogenous Preferences: The Cultural Consequences of Markets and Other Economic Institutions," *Journal of Economic Literature* 36 (March 1998): 75–111.

———, *Microeconomics: Behavior, Institutions, and Evolution*. Princeton: Princeton University Press. 2004.

——— and Herbert Gintis, "The Moral Economy of Community: Structured Populations and the Evolution of Prosocial Norms," *Evolution & Human Behavior* 19,1 (January 1998): 3–25.

———, in Erik Olin Wright (ed.), *Recasting Egalitarianism: New Rules for Markets, States, and Communities*. London: Verso, 1999.

Burke, Edmund, *Reflections on the Civil War in France*. New York: Bobbs-Merrill, 1955(1790).

Cohen, Dov, "Culture, Social Organization, and Patterns of Violence," *Journal of Personality and Social Psychology* 75,2 (1998): 408–419.

Craig, Ben, and John Pencavel, "Participation and Productivity: A Comparison of Worker Cooperatives and Conventional Firms in the Plywood Industry," *Brookings Papers: Microeconomics* (1995): 121–160.

Dayton-Johnson, J., and Pranab Bardhan, "Inequality and the Governance of Water Resources in Mexico and South India," in Jean Marie Baland, Pranab Bardhan, and Samuel Bowles (eds.), *Inequality, Cooperation and Environmental Sustainability*. New York: Russell Sage, 2002.

de Tocqueville, Alexis, *Democracy in America, Volume II*. New York: Vintage, 1958(1832).

Dong, Xioa-yuan, and Gregory Dow, "Monitoring Costs in Chinese Agricultural Teams," *Journal of Political Economy* 101,3 (1993): 539–553.

Fukuyama, Francis, *The Social Virtues and the Creation of Prosperity*. New York: Free Press, 1995.

Ghemawat, Pankaj, "Competitive Advantage and Internal Organization: Nucor Revisited," *Journal of Economic and Management Strategy* 3,4 (winter 1995): 685–717.

Gintis, Herbert, *Game Theory Evolving*. Princeton, NJ: Princeton University Press, 2000.

Glaeser, Edward, David Laibson, Jose A. Scheinkman, and Christine L. Soutter, "Measuring Trust," *Quarterly Journal of Economics* 65 (2000): 622–846.

Glaeser, Edward L., and Denise DiPasquale, "Incentives and Social Capital: Are Homeowners Better Citizens?" *Journal of Urban Economics* 45,2 (1999): 354–384.

Hansen, Daniel G., "Individual Responses to a Group Incentive," *Industrial and Labor Relations Review* 51,1 (October 1997): 37–49.

Hayami, Yujiro, "Community, Market and State," in A. Maunder and A. Valdes (eds.), *Agriculture and Governments in an Independent World*. Amherst, MA: Gower, 1989, 3–14.

Hirsch, Fred, *Social Limits to Growth*. Cambridge, MA: Harvard University Press, 1976.

Homans, George, *Social Behavior: Its Elementary Forms*. New York: Harcourt Brace, 1961.

Hossain, M., "Credit for Alleviation of Rural Poverty: The Grameen Bank in Bangladesh," International Food Policy Research Institute Report 65. 1988.

Jung, Courtney, "Community is the Foundation of Democracy: But What If Your Community Looks Like This?" Working paper, Yale University. 1998.

Kandel, Eugene, and Edward P. Lazear, "Peer Pressure and Partnerships," *Journal of Political Economy* 100,4 (August 1992): 801–817.

Marc Knez and Duncan Simester, "Firm-Wide Incentives and Mutual Monitoring at Continental Airlines," *Journal of Labor Economics* 19,4 (2001): 743–772.

Lam, Wai Fung, "Institutional Design of Public Agencies and Coproduction: A Study of Irrigation Associations in Taiwan," *World Development* 24,6 (1996): 1039–1054.

Marx, Karl, and Friedrich Engels, "The Communist Manifesto," in Robert Tucker (ed.), *The Marx-Engels Reader, 2nd edition*. New York: W. W. Norton & Company, 1972(1848).

Nisbett, Richard E., and Dov Cohen, *Culture of Honor: The Psychology of Violence in the South*. Boulder, Westview Press, 1996.

Ostrom, Elinor, *Governing the Commons: The Evolution of Institutions for Collective Action*. Cambridge: Cambridge University Press, 1990.

———, "Crossing the Great Divide: Coproduction, Synergy, and Development," *World Development* 24,6 (1996): 1073–1087.

———, "The Comparative Study of Public Economies," Workshop in Political Theory and Policy Analysis: Center for the Study of Institutes, Population and Environmental Change, Indiana University. 1997.

Ouchi, William, "Markets Bureaucracies and Clans," *Administrative Sciences Quarterly* 25 (March 1980): 129–141.

John Pencavel, *Worker Participation: Lessons from the Worker co-ops of the Pacific North-West*. New York: Russell Sage Foundation, 2001.

Platteau, Jean-Philippe, and Erika Seki, "Community Arrangements to Overcome Market Failure: Pooling Groups in Japanese Fisheries," in M. Hayami and Y. Hayami (eds.), *Communities and Markets in Economic Development*. Oxford: Oxford University Press, 2001, 344–402.

Rapoport, Anatol, and Albert Chammah, *Prisoner's Dilemma*. Ann Arbor: University of Michigan Press, 1965.

Sampson, Robert J., Stephen W. Raudenbush, and Felton Earls, "Neighborhoods and Violent Crime: A Multilevel Study of Collective Efficacy," *Science* 277 (August 15, 1997): 918–924.

Schelling, Thomas C., *Micromotives and Macrobehavior*. New York: W. W. Norton & Co., 1978.

Scott, James, *Seeing Like A State: How Certain Schemes to Improve the Human Condition Have Failed*. New Haven: Yale University Press, 1998.

Tendler, Judith, *Good Government in the Tropics*. Baltimore: Johns Hopkins Press, 1997.

Tilly, Charles, "Charivaris, Repertoires and Urban Politics," in John M. Merriman (ed.), *French Cities in the Nineteenth Century*. New York: Holmes and Meier, 1981, 73–91.

Verba, Sidney, Kay Lehman Schlozman, and Henry Brady, *Voice and Equality: Civic Voluntarism in American Politics*. Cambridge, MA: Harvard University Press, 1995.

Wade, Robert, "Why Some Indian Villages Cooperate," *Economic and Political Weekly* 33 (April 16 1988): 773–776.

Whyte, William F., *Money and Motivation*. New York: Harper & Row, 1955.

Young, H. Peyton, *Individual Strategy and Social Structure: An Evolutionary Theory of Institutions*. Princeton, NJ: Princeton University Press, 1998.

Contributors

Truman Bewley, Professor of Economics, Yale University

Rebecca Bliege Bird, Assistant Professor, Department of Anthropological Sciences, Stanford University

Samuel Bowles, Research Professor and Director of the Behavioral Science Program, Santa Fe Institute and Professor of Economics, University of Siena

Robert Boyd, Professor of Anthropology, University of California–Los Angeles

Armin Falk, Institute for Empirical Research in Economics, University of Zürich

Ernst Fehr, head of the Institute for Empirical Research in Economics, University of Zürich

Urs Fischbacher, Institute for Empirical Research in Economics, University of Zürich

Christina M. Fong, Research Scientist, Department of Social and Decision Sciences, Carnegie-Mellon University

Herbert Gintis, Emeritus Professor of Economics, University of Massachusetts and External Faculty, Santa Fe Institute

Michael Gurven, Assistant Professor of Anthropology, University of California at Santa Barbara

Dan M. Kahan, Professor of Law, Yale Law School

Hillard Kaplan, Professor of Anthropology, University of New Mexico

Elinor Ostrom, Professor of Political Science, Indiana University

Peter J. Richerson, Professor of Environmental Science and Policy, University of California at Davis

Rajiv Sethi, Associate Professor of Economics, Barnard College, Columbia University

Joan Silk, Professor of Anthropology, University of California–Los Angeles

Eric A. Smith, Professor of Anthropology, University of Washington

E. Somanathan, Associate Professor of Economics, Indian Statistical Institute, Delhi

Index